ARTIFICIAL AND HUMAN INTELLIGENCE

ARTIFICIAL AND HUMAN INTELLIGENCE

Edited Review Papers presented at the International NATO
Symposium on Artificial and Human Intelligence
sponsored by the Special Programme Panel
held in Lyon, France
October, 1981

Edited by

Alick ELITHORN
and
Ranan BANERJI

1984

NORTH-HOLLAND – AMSTERDAM · NEW YORK · OXFORD
published in cooperation with NATO Scientific Affairs Division

© NATO – 1984

All rights reserved. No part of this publication may be reproduced, stored in a retrieval system or transmitted in any form or by any means, mechanical, photocopying, recording or otherwise, without the prior permission of the copyright owner.

ISBN 0 444 86545 4

Publishers:
ELSEVIER SCIENCE PUBLISHERS B.V.
P.O. Box 1991
1000 BZ Amsterdam
The Netherlands

Sole distributors for the U.S.A. and Canada:
ELSEVIER SCIENCE PUBLISHING COMPANY, INC.
52, Vanderbilt Avenue
New York, N.Y. 10017
U.S.A.

Library of Congress Cataloging in Publication Data

International NATO Symposium on Artificial and Human
   Intelligence (1981 : Lyon, France)
   Artificial and human intelligence.

   Bibliography: p.
   Includes index.
   1. Artificial intelligence--Congresses. 2. Intellect--
Congresses. I. Elithorn, Alick. II. Banerji, Ranan B.,
1928-   . III. North Atlantic Treaty Organization.
Scientific Affairs Division. IV. Title.
Q334.I575 1981   001.53'5   84-8154
ISBN 0-444-86545-4 (U.S.)

Printed in The Netherlands

ARTIFICIAL AND HUMAN INTELLIGENCE (A. Elithorn and R. Banerji, editors)
Elsevier Science Publishers, B.V.
© NATO, 1984

CONTENTS

Preface ix

Chapter 1
Expert behaviour and problem representations
Saul AMAREL   1

Chapter 2
Is complexity theory of use to AI?
Allen GOLDBERG and Ira POHL   43

Chapter 3
Knowledge-based self-organizing memory for events
Janet L. KOLODNER   57

Chapter 4
GPS and the psychology of the Rubik cubist
A study in reasoning about actions
Ranan B. BANERJI   67

Chapter 5
Toward combining empirical and analytical methods for inferring heuristics
Tom M. MITCHELL   81

Chapter 6
Search vs. knowledge: An analysis from the domain of games
Hans J. BERLINER   105

Chapter 7
Advice and planning in chess endgames
Ivan BRATKO   119

Chapter 8
ORBIT: A tool for building AI systems in an object-oriented style
Luc STEELS   131

Chapter 9
An integrated frame/rule architecture
Carl ENGELMAN and William M. STANTON   141

Chapter 10
Beliefs, points of view and multiple environments
Yorick WILKS and Janusz BIEN   147

Chapter 11
A framework of a mechanical translation between Japanese and English by analogy principle
Makoto NAGAO   173

Chapter 12
Tools for creating intelligent computer tutors
Tim O'SHEA, Richard BORNAT, Benedict DU BOULAY, Marc EISENSTADT and Ian PAGE   181

Chapter 13
Benchmark and yardstick problems: A systematic approach
A. ELITHORN, R. COOPER and A. TELFORD   201

Chapter 14
Approaches to human reasoning: An analytic framework
Robert J. STERNBERG and Maria I. LASAGA   213

Chapter 15
The distributed processing of knowledge and belief in the human brain
P.M. LAVOREL   229

Chapter 16
The bilateral cooperative model of reading: A human paradigm for artificial intelligence
M.M. TAYLOR   239

Chapter 17
Handling the unconscious
B. MELTZER   251

Chapter 18
An intrasystemic approach to belief
Gabriella AIRENTI, Bruno G. BARA and Marco COLOMBETTI   265

Chapter 19
An intelligent system can and must use declarative knowledge efficiently
Jacques PITRAT   271

Chapter 20
Common and uncommon issues in artificial intelligence and psychology
Robert J. STERNBERG   281

Chapter 21
A taxonomy for the social implications of computer technology
Ira POHL   289

Chapter 22
Reasoning in natural language for designing a data base
Marco COLOMBETTI, Giovanni GUIDA, Barbara PERNICI and Marco SOMALVICO   297

Chapter 23
A computerised structure for a generalized inference-engine
A.G. BURRING 305

Chapter 24
Expert evaluation in logic of environmental resources through natural language
Luiz MONIZ PEREIRA, Eugenio OLIVEIRA and Paul SABATIER 309

Chapter 25
A sketch on acquisition by higher cognitive concepts
Christopher U. HABEL and Claus-Rainer ROLLINGER 313

Chapter 26
Simulated computer systems for intelligence amplification
Gerard DE ZEEUW 315

Chapter 27
Non standard uses of **if**
D.S. BREE and R. SMIT 317

Chapter 28
Constraints and event sequences
Uwe HEIN 319

Chapter 29
Artificial psychology versus artificial intelligence
Jean-Claude PAGES 321

References 323

Subject index 335

Author index 341

PREFACE

The literature on Artificial Intelligence is already becoming unmanageable. As the proceedings of a conference organised at the behest of the NATO Scientific Committee held in somewhat spartan conditions this volume presents a distillation of stimulating and productive intellectual exchanges covering a wide range of disciplines. Consequently the contributions include several which will be compulsory reading for many years.

Artificial Intelligence is a relatively new field of scientific exploration which already has a chequered history. It is one of great promise but like nuclear research, genetic engineering and indeed like all scientific endeavour, it has potential for both good and evil and stirs deep feelings.

Electronic chips which comment on your driving may be a gimmick but effective intelligence systems which will listen to and respond to human speech are around a corner which is not very far away. Chess programs play at Master level. Medical programs diagnose disease and prescribe treatment. Techniques of Artificial Intelligence and expert systems are rapidly being introduced into human decision making systems. Indeed there are already a number of "Expert Systems" available on microcomputers which enable John Doe effectively to run his personal life in a more systematic way. There is a real danger not that true Artificial Intelligence is unobtainable but rather that market pressures will produce dime store systems. For some time Artificial Intelligence programs will be essentially bureaucratic and it is everyday experience that the smaller the bureaucratic mind the less flexible it is. Even at the highest level it can be a dangerous friend. Fortunately Research Workers in Artificial Intelligence however "expert" do not seem to ignore the social implications of their work and some of the very informed and concerned discussions which took place at this Symposium have been distilled and summarised in an evocative chapter in which Ira Pohl discusses the rights of machines.

Artificial Intelligence research is not the concern only of computer scientists and psychologists. The breadth of coverage and the quality of the contributions means that Artificial and Human Intelligence will for some time be a vade-mecum for research scientists, teachers and students from many disciplines.

Alick Elithorn

Chapter 1

EXPERT BEHAVIOUR AND PROBLEM REPRESENTATIONS

SAUL AMAREL

Department of Computer Science
Rutgers University, New Brunswick, NJ 08903, USA

Summary

Expert behaviour is characterized by high-performance problem solving behaviour in a specific domain. Commonly, this type of behaviour requires the conceptualization/formulation of a given problem within a highly "appropriate" representational framework, where "appropriateness" refers to computational efficiency, and it is task specific. The problem of how to choose an "appropriate" problem formulation, and how to change it to fit the characteristics of a task, is at the heart of the problem of problem representations in AI. In this paper, relationships between characteristics of "intelligent expert" systems and developmental processes of problem reformulation are discussed. The nature of problem reformulation sequences is explored in the context of expertise acquisition in the domain of Tower of Hanoi problems. Our work suggests that "intelligent expert" systems must have available large amounts of knowledge of various kinds – both domain independent and domain specific; they must have the ability to maintain several alternative formulations of a problem class and to move among them in a flexible manner as required by the specific problem on hand; and they must be able to perform a variety of theory formation and program synthesis tasks in order to improve their performance with experience.

1. Introduction. Relationship between expert behaviour and representations of problems

Expertise in a given domain is commonly characterized by skilful, *high performance*, problem solving activity in the domain. A human expert solves problems in his area of expertise more rapidly, more accurately, and with less conscious deliberation about his plan of attack than a novice does. Expert behaviour requires large amounts of *knowledge* of various types, and highly effective ways of *using* this knowledge in approaching the solution of new problems in a domain. The types of knowledge that an expert needs are about objects and processes in the domain; about general problem solving schemas

---

* This research was supported in part by the Division of Research Resources, National Institutes of Health, Public Health Service, Department of H.E.W., under Grant 5 P41 RROO643 to the Special research Resource: Computers in Biomedicine at Rutgers University, New Brunswick, NJ.

and methods; and about specific classes of problems in the domain together with methods that are well-tuned for solving them.

Essentially, expert problem solving requires the conceptualization/formulation of a given problem within the framework of one or more *problem solving schemas* in such a way that solutions can be attained with accuracy *and* with very little search. This means that available knowledge must be used in a very effective manner to instantiate parameters of the schemas in accordance with the needs of the task at hand. In other words, an expert problem solver works wihin a highly *approriate problem formulation* – where appropriateness refers mainly to computational efficiency and it is task specific.

The problem of how to choose an appropriate problem formulation, and how to change it to fit the characteristics of a task, is at the heart of the *problem of representation in problem solving*. This is a problem of fundamental importance in AI (Newell, 1969; Amarel, 1970, Korf, 1980): it has also proven to be a very difficult problem on which progress has been relatively slow in the last decade or so.

Recent studies of expert human behavior (Larkin et al., 1980), and the growing efforts within AI to develop expert systems in a variety of domains (Amarel et al., 1977; Feigenbaum, 1977), are now providing us with a new set of problems, concepts, and techniques that can be used to advantage in our basic studies of processes of problem formulation and re-formulation.

Experience with the development of expert systems is showing us that the processes of system specification and evolution are extremely demanding in time and computational resources, and they need to be better understood. The bulk of effort in expert system construction is directed to the task of *problem formulation* in a given domain. It involves the specification of relevant bodies of knowledge in forms that are appropriate for use in the solution of problems in a given class in accordance with a given method of reasoning (problem solving schema). Clearly, progress in basic studies of problem formulation is directly relevant to the task of expert system specification.

At present, expert systems acquire their expertise by "being told" how to behave as experts. Knowledge Engineering is providing the tools for fashioning expert systems in various domains. This involves mainly the acquiring, organizing and representing of knowledge in forms that produce expert behaviour. Also, since system building is evolutionary, these tools make it possible for a designer to easily change parts of the expert system in the course of its development. Improvements in performance are obtained mainly via changes in the bodies of knowledge that the system uses. The following types of concerns are encountered here: under what conditions is incremental growth of a body of knowledge sufficient for performance enhancement; at what point is knowledge to be restructured and used in a different way during reasoning. These are important questions in processes of *expertise acquisition*; and they are closely related to the problem of finding "appropriate" shifts in problem formulation. At present, problems of expertise acquisition in expert systems must be solved by the system designers. As the complexity of expert systems grows, it is becoming increasingly desirable to use AI methods for mechanizing (parts of) the expertise acquisition process. Recent psychological work on acquisition of problem solving skills in humans is providing valuable insights in this area (Anzai and Simon, 1979). Clearly, this work is also relevant to the basic problem of problem representation in problem solving.

There is considerable evidence that human experts have a set of powerful methods for handling in a highly efficient way problems in certain *restricted classes* of a domain (these are the expert's areas of special competence or expertise), and ways for recognizing that a given problem belongs to one of these classes and can be treated therefore by the appropriate special method. In addition, the human expert possesses a sufficient amount of basic knowledge in the domain to handle – by using weaker methods, and perhaps at a reduced level of efficiency – problems that fall outside the special classes. Thus, human expertise is characterized not only by *high preformance* in certain limited problem areas, but also by *robustness* in handling a spectrum of problems surrounding the areas of special competence. Furthermore, a human expert is able to *acquire problem solving skills* and to improve his expertise by learning from his problem solving experience. This includes the ability *to create* specialized methods for certain restricted problem classes. Thus, human expert behaviour is characterized by high performance, as well as by robustness and by skill acquisition/ developmental capabilities.

The emphasis of work on machine expert systems to date has been on building high-performance agents in specific classes of problems. Commonly, relevant knowledge is "hand-crafted" by designers in forms that are directly usable by the system. Characteristics of robustness and breadth are still difficult to mechanize. Work on processes of expertise acquisition and on mechanisms of performance improvement by learning is still in early stages of exploration. While much remains to be done in the area of "conventional" expert systems – i.e., on the development of methodologies and tools for building high-performance systems in relatively narrow domains – it is also important to start directing more attention to the problem of building "intelligent experts", i.e., expert systems that have characteristics of robustness and self-improvement of the type that human experts have – in addition to their ability to perform very well in a narrow domain. This has theoretical as well as pragmatic significance. The theoretical significance is clear. The pragmatic significance may be less clear; but it is based on the following considerations. For an expert system to be *useful* in a real life environment it needs *breadth*; it will be accepted by potential users if it can be relied upon to provide high performance in specific parts of a domain *and* also if it can provide (at least) some preliminary analysis and advice in parts of the domain that are outside the main areas of the system's expertise. To give a concrete example from our experience at Rutgers: we found that for a consultation system in the glaucomas to be clinically useful it must be highly expert in diagnosis and treatment of glaucomas * *and*, in addition, it must be able to recognize that certain "peripheral" cases must be referred to another related expert (in neuro-opthalmology, refraction, etc.). Also, a realistic expert system is likely to be very complex. To construct such a system within acceptable periods of time (years, not decades) it would be essential to provide it with (at least) some of the capabilities of expertise acquisition and self-improvement that are characteristic of human experts.

From the previous discussion it can be seen that there are several points of contact between fundamental issues of problem representation on the one hand and the problem of building "intelligent experts" on the other. I believe that exploring problems of problem representation in the context of expertise acquisition in problem solving will contribute to both of these AI areas.

In previous work, I analyzed specific problem solving tasks in several domains in an attempt to clarify the nature of problem representations and of shifts in problem representations (Amarel, 1967, 1968, 1971). The focus of most of this work has been on relationships between choices of alternative problem formulations, and problem solving efficiency.

More recently, I have been exploring representational shifts in *Tower of Hanoi problems* within a conceptual framework which I find useful for handling problem formulations and their changes. The grammatical specification of solutions for a problem class plays an important role in this framework. Work in this area – with emphasis on the conceptual framework and its use in a detailed description of *developmental processes of expertise acquisition* in the Tower of Hanoi domain – is presented in (Amarel, 1981). Studies of expertise acquisition in this domain suggest that an "intelligent expert" system should include the following features:

a) Several bodies of knowledge in both declarative and procedural forms; the contents would range from domain-independent items, to domain-specific and problem-class-specific items.
b) The ability to work with several problem solving schemas simultaneously; and to maintain (and coordinate the use of) several instantiations of these schemas for different formulations of a problem.
c) Theory formation capabilities for discovering "interesting" regularities in the body of problem solving experience; and program synthesis capabilities for exploiting these regularities in the development of specialized high-performance procedures.

In this paper, I will focus on these desired features of "intelligent expert"

---

* (A high performance glancoma expert system was developed at Rutgers in the '70s – see Weiss et al., 1978).

systems, and I will show how they derive from an attempt to specify developmental processes of expertise acquisition in the Tower of Hanoi domain. Only an outline of a possible, and promising, line of development will be presented here. A similar line of development is discussed in more detail in (Amarel, 1981). My emphasis will be on an analysis of the various bodies of knowledge that are involved in the processes of problem formulation and re-formulation during expertise acquisition. I will also comment on some of the characteristics of these processes, and on the problems that we face in trying to mechanize them.

2. Expertise acquisition and problem reformulation in Tower of Hanoi problems

2.1. Initial stages of problem formulation

Let us suppose that a problem solver * with general experience in *transportation scheduling problems*, but without experience in the *Tower of Hanoi domain*, is presented with the following verbal statement of a specific problem (call it P_1) in that domain.i

> There are three pegs, A, B and C, and four disks of different sizes 1, 2, 3 and 4. Disks can be stacked on pegs; they can be moved from peg to peg one at a time. Only the top disk on a peg can be moved, but it can never be placed on top of a smaller disk. Initially, the largest and smallest disks are stacked on peg A, with disk 1 on top; disk 2 is on peg B and disk 3 is on peg C. Find the shortest sequence of moves for transferring all the disks to peg C. The initial and terminal situations in this problem can be visualized as shown in Fig. 1.

Let us assume further that the problem solver recognises the given problem as a member of the transportation scheduling class, or he is told that this is the case. In general, in a transportation scheduling problem we are given a set of locations and objects, transfer facilities with certain capabilities, and an initial distribution of objects (and transfer facilities) in the locations; and we are

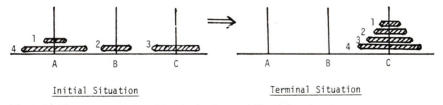

Fig. 1. Problem P_1: A 4-disk problem in the Tower of Hanoi domain.

---

* I will be using the term "problem solver" interchangeably for human or AI system – unless a specific distinction is needed. Similarly, for convenience, I will be using the pronoun "he" when referring to the problem solver; this should be read as: "he", "she" or "it".

asked to find a sequence of transfers between the locations such that (i) a desired terminal distribution of objects in the locations can be attained without violating a given set of constraints on the individual transfers or/and on possible intermediate distributions of objects (and transfer facilities) in the various locations, and (ii) certain global conditions on the sequence must be satisfied, e.g. minimality conditions. Many of the problems that are studied in AI are in this class; for example, other puzzles such as "Missionaries and Cannibals" (Amarel, 1968), the "blocks world" and related robot planning problems, and problems of the "travelling salesman" variety.

The class of transportation scheduling problems is itself a subclass of the broader class of *reasoning about actions in the physical world*. The hierarchy of problem classes can be extended further in the direction of inclusiveness (or generality); however, for our present purposes it is sufficient to stop at this point.

Now, each problem class in the hierarchy is assumed to have associated with it a body of knowledge about a domain – within which problems in the class are handled. Let us call it the *domain specification* for the problem class. Such a domain specification includes descriptions of concepts in the domain and the relationships between them; it also includes specific information about properties of the domain (such as the "laws of motion" in the domain and other regularities of domain processes) that are relevant to the problem class under consideration. A domain specification for a problem class is expressed in some *domain language*. I am assuming that the domain languages associated with problem classes in the hierarchy obey an *inheritance property*. This means that a problem class has available for its formulation(s) all the concepts and constructs of problem classes that are above it in the hierarchy. In addition, the domain language for a problem class may contain new concepts that are specific to the class. The above notions will be made more concrete in a moment.

Let us assume that the *novice* problem solver in the Tower of Hanoi domain uses the domain languages for transportaion scheduling problems to develop an *initial internal formulation* of a problem class in which he embeds the given problem P_1. Let us call this formulation F_{d1}, and the new problem class in which P_1 is embedded, TH*. Actually, only a part of the language for transportation scheduling problems is needed to build the formulation F_{d1}. I am assuming that this initial formulation is in *declarative form*.

By "internal formulation" I mean a formulation which represents an assimilation of the problem by the problem solver, i.e. the problem solver "understands it" and knows *what to do* with it. In other words, this is the problem solver's concept of the problem. I am not concerned here with the process of *initial problem acquisition*, where a problem statement which is presented in verbal form is transformed into the internal problem formulation. The problem acquisition stage (or the "problem understanding" process as it is called in recent research (Simon and Hayes, 1976)) is an important part of any problem solving activity, and it is certainly relevant to questions of problem representation. The choice of an initial problem class in which to embed a specific problem, and of a domain language in which to formulate the problem class, are significant representational decisions and they strongly influence the ease (difficulty) with which the problem can be solved. However, my emphasis here is on issues of problem re-formulation, and in particular on *transformations between internal problem formulations* that lead to increased problem solving power. To study processes of reformulation, it is reasonable to take as a starting point a situation where *some* initial internal formulation already exists.

Let us call D_1 the initial domain specification for formulating Tower of Hanoi problems in the class TH* and let LD_1 be the initial domain language for D_1.

2.1.1. Initial domain language LD_1

LD_1 inherits from the general domain of transportation scheduling problems the basic concepts of locations, objects, sets of objects and incidence relations between objects and locations. In particular, the universe of LD_1 contains the locations A, B, C (the pegs), the objects 1, 2, 3, 4 (the disks), and sets made of these four objects. The basic incidence predicates and functions defined for the universe of LD_1 are:

at (x,l) : the object x is at location l.
in (l) = u : the set of objects u is in location l.

In addition, LD_1 has the basic predicate:

smaller (x_1, x_2): the object x_1 is smaller than x_2.

This predicate is also assumed to be inherited from more general problem classes where concepts of size are assumed to be known.

In general, the properties of basic concepts in LD_1, and the relationships between them, are assumed to be known (e.g., "smaller is transitive", "an object can only be in one location in a given situation"). I am assuming that properties of a concept, and relationships with other concepts at the same level of the problem hierarchy and at higher levels of the hierarchy, are associated with the definition of the concept. Such a definition is part of the domain specification for the problem class in which the concept is first introduced.

In addition to the basic predicates, LD_1 has a new compound predicate, which is defined in terms of its basic predicates, and is needed for expressing an important specific constraint in Tower of Hanoi problems. This predicate is as follows:

movable (x,l) : the object x can be moved from (or to) the location l. It is defined as follows:

movable $(x,l) \equiv \sim \exists x_1 \, [\text{at} \, (x_1,l) \, \text{smaller} \, (x_1, x)]$,

i.e., there is no object in l which is smaller than x.

Now LD_1 inherits from the higher level domain of "reasoning about actions in the physical world" the key concepts of situations and actions, and the compound concept of situation space as well as several other concepts that are defined in such a space – specifically, the concepts of attainability and of trajectories (and their properties) in situation space.

A *situation* is a snapshot showing the instantaneous state of the physical world under consideration. A *basic description* of a situation is a listing of the basic features of a situation from which all information about the situation – which may be needed for determining what is the set of legal actions from the situation – can be directly obtained or derived. Thus the notions of "basic feature" and "basic description of a situation" are *relativistic*, and they depend on the actions and tasks under consideration. By handling the new problem in the context of a class of problems in which experience exists (in the present case, the transportation scheduling problems) the problem solver obtains the guidance, and also the bias, for the initial choice of these basic notions, i.e. for the choice of a basic "frame of reference" for the problem.

In the domain D_1, the basic description of a situation s can be defined as a set of incidence relations which specifies for each object its location. Thus, a situation in problems of the class TH* can be described as follows:

$\{$at $(1,l_1)$, at $(2,l_2)$, at $(3,l_3)$, at $(4,l_4)\}$,

where the l s are location variables that take values from the set of locations $\{A,B,C\}$. Such a description can be abbreviated to take the form of a vector $(l_1\ l_2\ l_3\ l_4)$. For example, we can write for the basic description of the initial situation in the problem P_1, which is shown in Fig. 1, the expression (ABCA).

An *action* can be defined as a transition between two situations – the "from" situation and the "to" situation. The *effect* of the action is completely captured by the pair of "from" and "to" situations. A *basic description* of an action can be given as a specification of all the changes in the basic description of the "from" situation that are effected by application of the action. A *rule of action* specifies (i) the basic description of the action, and (ii) the *conditions* under which application of the action is permissible. An action can also be defined in procedural form, and it can be invoked by an *action call* which has among its arguments a situation. In the domain D_1, the basic description of an action can be defined as a transition schema between a "from" and a "to" situation, and it can be expressed as follows:

$\{\alpha$, at $(x,l_1)\} \rightarrow \{\alpha$, at $(x,l_2)\}$,

where α stands for a set of assertions that complete the situation descriptions. The conditions for applicability of this action are:

$\{$movable (x,l_1), movable $(x,l_2)\}$.

The action call corresponding to this action can be expressed as $(T_r \times l_1\ l_2\ s)$, which can be read as "transfer the disk x from l_1 at the "from" situation s to l_2". An action can be identified (named) in general, i.e. without reference to a particular instance of its application, by an abbreviated version of its action call in the form [x l_1 l_2].

A *situation space*, σ is a fundamental concept in problems of reasoning about actions in the physical world; and it is defined as follows. Let $\langle s \rangle$ be the set of possible situations in the domain under consideration, and let $\langle a \rangle$ be the rules of action in the domain. For any two situations s_1, s_2 from $\langle s \rangle$, the situation, s_2 is *directly attainable* from s_1 if there exists a rule in $\langle a \rangle$ that permits the application of an action at s_1 which changes it to s_2. Let us denote by T the relation of direct attainability. The set $\langle s \rangle$ partly ordered under the relation T defines the situation space for the domain under consideration.

A *trajectory* τ from a situation s_i to a situation s_t in a situation space is defined as a finite sequence $\langle s_1, s_2, ..., s_m \rangle$ such that $s_1 = s_i$, $s_m = s_t$, and for each i, $1 < i \leqslant m$, the direct attainability condition $T(s_{i-1}, s_i)$ holds. For any pair of situations s_i, s_t, we say that s_t is *attainable* from s_i if $s_i = s_t$ or there exists a trajectory from s_i to s_t in situation space. The *length of a trajectory*, $l(\tau)$, is the number of actions needed to move from the initial situation to the terminal situation in the trajectory. A trajectory τ from s_i to s_t is *minimal* if there is no other trajectory between s_i and s_t in situation space whose length is smaller than $l(\tau)$.

I am assuming that more than minimal knowledge about minimality of trajectories is known in D_1. For example, the concept of a redundant (and eliminable) segment of a trajectory is known, i.e. the segment of a trajectory which lies between two situations with identical basic descriptions (such a segment represents a loop in situation space) is redundant, and therefore it can be eliminated – thus resulting in a reduction of trajectory length.

2.1.2. Initial domain specification D_1

The language LD_1 provides the means for expressing the initial body of knowledge about the domain, i.e. the domain specification D_1.

The central component of D_1 is the definition of a specific situation space for the domain under consideration. Let us call this situation space σ_1. The set of situations, $\langle s \rangle_1$, in σ_1 includes all possible configurations of the four disks on the three pegs. There are $3^4 = 81$ situations in $\langle s \rangle_1$. There are $6.4 = 24$ possible actions in the domain, and they define the direct attainability relation which determines the structure of σ_1. Any 4-disk Tower of Hanoi problem, and any possible sequence of actions (i.e. any possible *behaviour* in the world of these problems) can be represented in σ_1.

The space σ_1 can be visualized as a directed graph whose nodes stand for situations and whose branches stand for permissible actions between situations. The graph for σ_1 is shown in Fig. 2. Since each branch of this graph represents two directed branches, one in each direction, the arrows in branches

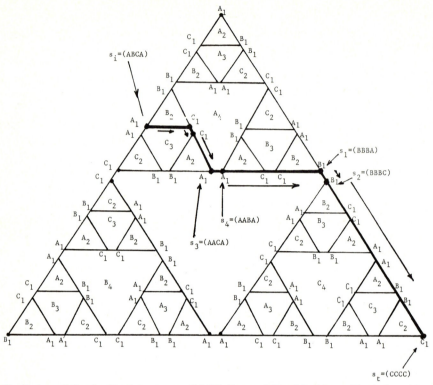

Fig. 2. A graph for the situation space σ_1 of 4-disk Tower of Hanoi Problems. (The darkened lines and the arrows show the solution trajectory for the specific problem P_1 which is shown in Fig. 1).

are omitted. The notation for labelling situations at each node is as follows. A subscripted letter, 1_x, next to a node signifies that the disk x is at peg 1 in the situation represented by the node. An 1_x in the center of a triangle signifies that for all nodes in the triangle (in its periphery as well as inside it) the disk x is at peg 1. For example, the situation $s_i = (ABCA)$ in the graph has A_1 next to the situation node itself (this means that disk 1 is at A); it has B_2 in the center of the smallest triangle of which the node is a part (i.e., disk 2 is at B); it has C_3 in the next larger triangle of which it is a part (i.e., disk 3 is at C); and it has A_4 in the largest triangle of which it is a part (i.e., disk 4 is at peg A). The solution for the problem P_1 under consideration can be seen on σ_1 as the minimal trajectory (path) from $s_i = (ABCA)$ to $s_t = (CCCC)$; and it is shown with darkened lines and arrows in the figure. This solution is made of a sequence of 15 actions (disk transfers).

It is important to stress that the definition of the space σ_1 is given *implicitly* in D_1 – via the specification of the set $\{s\}_1$ and the rules of action $\{a\}$. There is no internal representation in the form of an explicit graph or a generator for the graph.

All the concepts that enter in the definition of components of σ_1 are defined in D_1, or their definitions are accessible via links to domains that correspond to problem classes that are above TH* in the class hierarchy.

2.1.3. Initial declarative problem formulation F_{d1}

In general, the formulation of a *problem class* in declarative form can be given as a 4-tuple, (D, X, C, Λ) where D is the domain specification; X is the set of *possible (legal) solutions*; C denotes the conditions that characterize the problem class; and Λ is a parameter domain. Each element in Λ represents specific parameter values that identify an individual problem in the class. Thus, to define a *specific problem* in the class, we must provide (i) the class formulation (i.e., the above 4-tuple), and (ii) the specific element in Λ, call it d, which identifies the problem. A solution to the problem must be an element of X which also satisfies the class conditions C as specialized by the individual problem data d.

Now, the formulation F_{d1} of our problem class TH* is defined in terms of the domain specification D_1 which was discussed previously, and also in terms of components X_1, C_1, Λ_1 that are discussed next.

a. Specification of the set X_1 of possible (legal) solutions

X_1 is the set of all trajectories in the space σ_1. This set specifies necessary conditions for the internal structure of solutions, i.e. what are properties of legal sequences of actions in the domain. The specification of X_1 n F_{d1} is in terms of the definition of the trajectories which was given previously, i.e. in terms of the direct attainability relation. Membership in X_1 can be determined here by *testing* whether a given sequence of situations is a trajectory in σ_1.

b. Conditions C_1 for the problem class

These are boundary conditions and length conditions that a possible solution (a trajectory in σ_1) must satisfy in order for it to be acceptable as a *solution* to a problem in the class. They stipulate the following: i) The boundaries of a solution trajectory are ordered pairs of situations (s_i, s_t) that can take values from the domain of parameters Λ_1. ii) For a trajectory between two boundary situations to be a solution it should be minimal.

c. Domain of problem parameters Λ_1; initial internal formulation of the problem P_1

Λ_1 is the set of all situation pairs where each member of the pair can take values from $\langle s \rangle_1$. Thus, $\Lambda_1 = \langle s \rangle_1 \times \langle s \rangle_1$; and its size is $3^8 = 6,561$. This is the broadest possible domain for 4-disk Tower of Hanoi problems.

The problem P_1 can be initially specified in declarative form as a member of the cass TH*, whose formulation is F_{d1}, with additional problem data in the form of the pair (s_i, s_t) = ((ABCA), (CCCC)) taken from the parameter domain Λ_1.

2.2. Transforming a problem formulation from declarative to procedural form

The formulation F_{d1} provides a concise internal definition of the problem under consideration. The basic "laws" of the domain are defined, and so are the "local" and "global" properties of the desired solution. This formulation is in declarative form. For the problem solver to proceed with a solution finding (constructing) activity, he needs to transform (parts of) this formulation into *procedural form*, i.e. he needs to define a *solution construction process* which is controlled by the problem formulation.

I am assuming that the problem solver has a knowledge base, call it Π which includes *procedural schemas* together with properties of the schemas and advice under what conditions the schemas are to be used. This knowledge is domain independent, and it is absolutely essential for moving from a problem formulation in declarative form to a process for finding a solution. In particular, I am assuming that a number of the basic problem solving schemas (methods) in AI are included in the knowledge base. The broadest (and weakest) among them is the Generate-and-Test schema. This is a very general computational schema which involves a sequence of cycles in each of which a (part of a) *candidate solution* is generated and then it is tested, i.e. it is evaluated relative to the requirements imposed on the desired solution. More refined schemas, that are in the general mold of Generate-and-Test but that are each "best suited" to handle different types of formulations of *derivation problems*, (for a description of these problems see Amarel, 1981) have been developed in AI – and are assumed to be in Π. Two of them have been extensively used and studied in AI; they are the *production* schema (or state space search method) and the *reduction* schema (Amarel, 1970; Nilsson, 1971). A third schema, which is suitable for processes of the type studied by Sacerdoti (1975) for goal-directing reasoning with conjunctive goals, is called the *relaxed reduction* schema; and it will be described below. Each of these schemas represents a different approach to solution construction; and it has different ways of utilizing knowledge about a problem in controlling the solution contruction process.

To transform a problem formulation from a declarative form, e.g., F_{d1}, to a procedural form which would be suitable for solution construction, the problem solver would have to *assign values to the key parameters of some appropriate procedural schema* in accordance with information in F_{d1}. The specification of parameters (or slots) of the schema together with the schema definition, amount to a procedural formulation of the problem. On basis of the parameter specifications, a procedure can be obtained, which would be an instantiation of the schema, and which can be used directly for solution construction.

Basically, the problem solver must reformulate knowledge about the problem in a form suitable for defining a generative process for producing candidate solutions. In order to achieve efficiency, relevant knowledge must be used in a manner which can provide as much *a priori* selectivity and guidance as possible to the generative process – so that very few candidates are produced (preferably none) that do not satisfy all the desired characteristics of a solution.

It is important to have convenient ways of representing and manipulating the key components of procedural formulations without having to go into the implementation details of specific procedural schemas. The concepts of a *solution grammar* and its associated *control knowledge* are extremely useful in this regard. I discussed them in detail in (Amarel, 1981); and I will present them here briefly.

In many cases of interest in AI, the set of candidate solutions that can be generated (proposed) by the generative component of a problem solving system can be regarded as a *solution language*; and thus, the generative component of the system can be modeled by a *solution grammar*. Solutions can be represented as graphs that obey certain local rules of articulation and that satisfy in addition certain global properties; and candidate solutions in the process of being constructed can be represented as incompletely specified graphs of the same type. I view these graphs as analogs of strings in ordinary languages, and call them *solution aggregates*. A solution aggregate is a combination of elements each of which can be either a terminal or a non-terminal in the solution grammar, and it is assembled in accordance with the *rules of aggregation* of the grammar. These rules are analogs of rules of replacement in ordinary language grammars. The grammar has a *starting element*, and solution aggregates are constructed by repeated applications of rules of aggregation starting from the starting element. Terminal elements represent well-specified solution fragments, and non-terminals (they are called *solution schemas*) can be used to represent parts of solutions that are incompletely specified. For example, with reference to the problem P_1, a solution aggregate which represents a partly specified solution with only the first two actions specified (see Fig. 2 where the entire solution is shown) has the following form,

```
(ABCA)     (CBCA)     (CACA)      (CCCC)
  o———————>o———————>o - - -> - - - o
      [1AC]      [2BA]
```

In this graph, nodes represent situations; the two leftmost branches represent terminal elements of the grammar and they stand for actions; and the branch at right represents a solution scheme and it stands for a non-specified part of the solution – where additional solution construction activity is needed.

The specification of a solution grammar amounts to a specification of a set of key parameters in a procedure schema. Given such a grammar, it is straightforward to translate it into the specification of major features in the problem solving schema (i.e., states, moves). Basically, the grammar determines how a candidate solution *can* be constructed from elementary parts, e.g., in what order what parts can go where in a candidate solution. Since the grammar rules are typically non-deterministic, a problem solving system which is based on the grammar usually develops in parallel several candidate solutions. Let us be more specific about this point. Every time a grammar rule is applied, a specific *choice* is made among alternative applicable rules. A solution candidate can be seen as a sequence of such choices. The different candidates represent different sequences of choices. Usually, a problem solving system keeps a record of the sequences of choices that define alternative solution candidates in the form of a tree – the *search tree*.

An important function of a problem solving system is to manage the generation of alternative solution candidates in such a way that only the most promising candidates are generated. This is achieved by providing the system with appropriate *control knowledge*. The control knowledge determines the sequence of choices made by the system in the course of generating alternative solution candidates. Now, if in addition to the specification of a solution grammar, such a body of control knowledge is also specified for the problem solving system, we obtain a full specification of the system.

Thus a procedural formulation can be defined in terms of *a solution grammar and an associated body of control knowledge*. This represents a high-level view of a procedural formulation. A formulation in this form could be translated with relative ease into one or more conventional forms, each providing parameter specifications for a given problem solving schema (method).

I believe that it is important for the problem solver to be able to conceptualize procedural formulations at this higher level of abstraction. It enables a clearer view of the essential aspects of different problem formulations, and of ways in which they interrelate. What we need in this area (problem solver as well as researcher/system designer) is to understand better (i) the variety of ways in which a solution can be specified as an object with given local and global properties, and (ii) the basic approaches for constructing such objects. Changes in problem formulation amount to changes in ways of assembling a solution object and/or the sequence of choices during the construction process.

A solution grammar can easily embody the part of a declarative problem formulation which specifies the set X of possible (legal) solutions. A grammar may also incorporate some knowledge about the problem class conditions, so that only elements of X that are *a priori* consistent with this knowledge will be generated as solution candidates. If all the knowledge about problem conditions could be incorporated in the grammar, then we would have a very strong problem formulation – as the grammar would be able to generate directly only the elements of X that satisfy the problem conditions. Based on our initial formulation F_{d1} of the 4-disk Tower of Hanoi problem, only a part of the problem conditions can be incorporated into a solution grammar.

The amount of problem specific knowledge incorporated in a grammar which is used in the procedural formulation of a given problem class can be made to grow by (i) acquiring new knowledge about properties of solutions for problems in the class, and (ii) by using the knowledge "appropriately" in the specification of a modified grammar. Problem formulations of increased power can be obtained by following this route. I will describe below a developmental process of reformulations of this type; it represents a *possible path* in the growth of problem solving expertise in the Tower of Hanoi domain.

2.3. Initial procedural problem formulation F_{p1}

In general, the formulation of a *problem class* in procedural form can be given as a 4-tuple,

(D, G, CK, Λ)

The new elements in this formulation (relative to the declarative formulation) are the solution grammar G and the body of control knowledge CK.

Now, the procedural formulation F_{p1} of our problem class TH* is defined in terms of the elements D_1, Λ_1 from F_{d1}, and also in terms of a solution grammar G_{p1} and control knowledge CK_{p1}. This formulation is oriented to the specification of a *production procedure* for problem solving. In such a procedure, a candidate solution is generated by starting at a boundary situation, say the initial situation, and by trying to piece together *in an incremental manner* a sequence of actions until the second boundary is reached.

2.3.1. Solution grammar G_{p1}

A solution grammar can be easily specified to satisfy the definition of the set of possible (legal) solutions X_1 as given in F_{d1}, in a style which captures the solution construction approach of a production procedure, and also to incorporate the first condition for the problem class – which specifies the solution boundaries. Let us call this grammar G_{p1}. The starting element of the grammar has the form of a solution scheme,

$$s_i \quad \quad s_t$$
$$\circ\text{- - - -}\!\!\rightarrow\text{- - -}\circ$$

where s_i, s_t are the initial and terminal situations of a problem respectively; and they can take values from the domain Λ_1. The key rule of aggregation in this grammar is as follows:

Forward Development Rule in G_{p1}

Transition

$$s_1 \quad s_t \quad \longrightarrow \quad s_1 \xrightarrow{[x\, l_1,\, l_2]} s_2 \dashrightarrow s_t$$

[s_1 can be any situation in the space σ_1,
if $s_1 = \{\alpha,\, \text{at }(x, l_1)\}$, then $s_2 = \{\alpha,\, \text{at }(x, l_2)\}$]

Condition: In situation s_1: movable (x, l_1), movable (x, l_2)

The transition part of the rule determines the possible replacement of the solution scheme at left by a partly specified solution aggregate as shown at right. This is done by applying an action at s_1, such that s_1 can be a "from" situation for the action. The *condition* part of the rule is identical with the applicability condition of the action as originally defined in the domain specification D_1.

The application of such a rule of aggregation amounts to specifying a part of the graph structure which represents an incompletely specified candidate solution, i.e., it is a quantum of solution construction activity. The rule is applied on a solution aggregate and it produces a "more specified" aggregate. It is applicable at the aggregate if the left side of its transition schema can be matched to (part of) the aggregate and if the rule conditions are satisfied.

In addition, there is in the grammar a *Closure rule for recognizing a match* between two situations; it is used to terminate the solution construction activity.

The generation process in G_{p1} starts with application of the "Forward development" rule on the starting solution scheme, and it continues with repeated applications of the rule on successive solution aggregates until the Closure rule applies, i.e., until the terminal situation is reached. The "Forward development" rule induces an incremental forward thrust of solution construction from s_i to s_t.

The grammar G_{p1} does not incorporate the second condition of the problem class, i.e., the *minimality* condition for solutions. This is a global condition, and it cannot be expressed in the present grammar. It must be incorporated in the body of control knowledge CK_{p1}, which constitutes the second key part of the present procedural fomulation.

As I indicated previously in discussing knowledge in D_1, I am assuming that knowledge about minimality and about minimal trajectories is available to the problem solver in D_1. It is not sufficient however to have definitions of these concepts that will only permit the problem solver to *check* whether a given trajectory in a specified set of trajectories is minimal, or to *select* a minimal trajectory among members of a given set. There must be available, in addition, some knowledge about efficient methods of *generating* a minimal trajectory in a graph. In particular, the following method is assumed to be available: In order to find a trajectory (path) of minimal length between two nodes n_1, n_2 in a graph, generate, starting from n_1 all paths in the graph one step at a time, in a "breadth first" manner; the first path that reaches n_2 is a minimal path. Furthermore, in order to obtain an efficient generation process, discontinue immediately paths that enter a node n in the graph if the process has already generated shorter paths from n_1 to n [these are known to be "non-minimal redundant paths']. This method provides the basis for specifying the control knowledge CK_{p1} which is needed in F_{p1}. I am assuming that this piece of knowledge is available in the knowledge base Π of procedural schemes; and it is linked to concepts of minimality that are defined in the domain specification.

Now, the specification of a production procedure requires the definition of states and moves, as well as of sub-procedures for state evaluation, attention control and move generation. By *state*, I mean the state of one of the solution candidates whose construction is being managed by the procedure. The state must provide a description of the current status of the candidate under construction which is sufficient for a decision on whether the candidate is already a solution or, if not, what solution construction move to apply on the candidate. For a procedure which is based on the grammar G_{p1}, the state of a solution candidate which has the form,

$$s_1 \longrightarrow s_2 \longrightarrow \cdots \longrightarrow s_n \longrightarrow \cdots \longrightarrow s_t \quad , \quad (s_1 = s_{i'}, n \geq 1)$$

can be defined as a pair (s_n, s_t). If $s_n = s_t$, then a Closure move would apply; if not, a construction move which is determined by s_n would apply. The definition of *moves* for the present procedure can be obtained in a straightforward way from the specification of rules of aggregation in G_{p1}. Typically, several moves are tried at a state, and this process is recorded in the search tree – where nodes stand for states and branches for move applications (choices).

2.3.2. Control knowledge CK_{p1}

The control knowledge CK_{p1}, which embodies the minimality condition of the problem, can be made to control the way in which the search tree grows – so that no solution candidates longer than the minimal will be generated, and all the solution candidates that include "non-minimal redundant paths" will be eliminated from further consideration as soon as possible. The control knowledge is in the form of specifications for the three key subprocedures of the production procedure, as follows:

Move generation: Try the Closure move from the state on which attention is focused; if applicable, apply it and exit with success; else, generate *all possible* other moves from the state.

State evaluation: Consider all new states obtained from move generation. If a new state is identical with a previously processed state in the search tree, then delete this new state; if not, associate with the new state the trajectory length g of the candidate solution that the state represents (i.e., the number of steps from the initial situation to the last situation in the candidate solution).

Attention control: Consider all states in the search tree that were not visited by the move generation process. If there is none, exit with failure; else, select (focus attention on) the state with smallest g.

The transformation of the minimality condition of our problem into features of a search process, and more specifically into specifications of the three components of a production procedure, requires certain capabilities for *program synthesis* and *program transformation*. These are areas of active research in computer science at present. More work is needed to reach a point where the specification of CK_{p1}, starting from the declarative formulation F_{d1}, can be readily mechanized.

2.4. Procedural problem formulation F_{p2}

A production procedure which corresponds to the problem formulation F_{p1} is a special case of the A* algorithm (Nilsson, 1971) for searching minimal paths in graphs. The concept of *evaluation function* is central to this algorithm. In F_{p1}, the evaluation function associated with a (incompletely specified) candidate solution is its length g, i.e., the distance between the initial situation s_i and the latest situation s_c which has been obtained in the exploratory generation of the solution candidate (see next diagram).

This is a weak evaluation function, as it includes no information about the second boundary s_t that the process is intended to reach, or about the "territory" between s_c and s_t that is to be traversed. The solution construction process specified by F_{p1} is a disciplined forward-moving exploratory process which terminates by "bumping against the goal situation"; it is not goal-directed. This represents an approach which is commonly tried by novices in a domain. It is typically followed by attempts to use information about the goal in order to provide more direction to the process. Such information can be incorporated in the evaluation function by introducing the notion of a heuristic *distance estimate* h between a given situation and the goal (terminal) situation. Thus, in reference to the previous diagram, the state of the candidate solution can be defined as $S = (s_c, s_t)$, and the evaluation function for S is $f(S) = g(S) + h(S)$. This is a heuristic estimate of length of the candidate solution.

For any given choice of a distance estimate function h (that satisfies certain admissibility conditions) we can obtain a new procedural formulation which is stronger than F_{p1} – without changing appreciably the structure of F_{p1}. In these new formulations, the grammars remain as in F_{p1}, and the main changes in the control knowledge relative to F_{p1} are that the partial distance g is now changed by the total distance f. For the distance estimate h to be admissible, it must be a lower bound of the true minimal distance between any two situations in the space under consideration. The procedures that correspond to these formulations produce *best first* search behaviour; and they can attain highly efficient performance if they have available highly accurate heuristic estimate functions. Thus, one of the important avenues for obtaining strong(er) problem formulations within the production procedure (or A*) framework is to find more accurate h functions for the problem class under consideration.

For our problem class TH*, a simple heuristic estimate function, call it h_o, would assign to any state which is given as a pair of situations s_1, s_2 a number which is the count of the disks in s_1 that are not located in the same pegs as in s_2. This is a "count of misplaced objects" estimate. The estimate h_o is certainly a lower bound on the number of actions needed to change s_1 into s_2. However, it is a relatively weak estimate, since it captures very little of the special sequential patterns of actions that are found in trajectories of σ_1. On the other hand, it is a good first estimate for any problem of reasoning about actions in the physical world; and I am assuming that the problem solver imports it into the present formulation after recognizing that the Tower of Hanoi problem is a member of this larger class.

Let us call F_{p2} the procedural problem formulation which is defined within the production procedure framework with grammar $G_{p2} = G_{p1}$ and with control knowledger CK_{p2} whose main difference from CK_{p1} is that an evaluation function f_o is used instead of g and the heuristic distance estimator in f_o is h_o. Note that the transition from F_{p1} to F_{p2} requires procedural knowledge (about A* and about properties of evaluation functions) that I am assuming exists in the procedural knowledge base Π and also the ability to specify a first estimate for h via inheritance of properties that are obtained from a problem class which is higher in the class hierarchy.

2.5. An approach to improvement of procedural formulations

As indicated previously, it is possible to increase the power of a production procedure by increasing the quality of its heuristic estimate function h. To increase the quality of h, we must obtain additional knowledge about properties of trajectories in the situation space σ_1 and use it appropriately in the formulation of h. One of the earliest approaches to this problem is through *parameter learning* (Samuel, 1967). In this approach, h is assumed to depend on certain features of a state, and it is supposed to have a given form; the parameters of the form are adjusted automatically on the basis of problem solving experience to yield an h which results in improved performance. In some cases, this approach produces satisfactory results (Rendell, 1981). However, a key problem in this area is how to choose relevant features of a state and a structure for h. A poor choice of features and structure may block completely any attempt to find a high-quality h.

Another way of strengthening the heuristic estimate function h is to explicitly synthesize it on basis of an analysis of relevant domain knowledge. More specifically, the following is a promising approach: To compute h for a given state $S = (s_c, s_t)$, i.e. to obtain an estimate of the distance between s_c and s_t, *try to solve a simplified version of S* and derive from this attempt a good lower bound for the distance estimate. Let us assume that this approach is used to improve the initial heuristic estimator h_o, and consequently to strengthen the problem formulation F_{p2}. In particular, suppose that a *goal-directed* problem solving procedure is available for solving problems in the domain; and appropriate characteristics of solution obtained via this procedure are used to achieve improvements in h.

The assumption about the availability of a goal-directed procedure at a relatively early state of development of expertise in the domain is quite plausible on psychological grounds (Anzai and Simon, 1979). There is evidence that human problem solvers who are moving from an early novice status to a stage where they seek to improve their problem solving skills in a given domain proceed by experimenting with problems cast both in forward reasoning (production) as well as goal-directed (reduction) modes. This assumption is also justified from an analysis of *possible developmental models* of expertise that point to the importance of having multiple problem formulations, each corresponding to a different method, in order to attain new formulations of increased power. I will illustrate this point via several examples of reformulation in our present domain.

Let us discuss next an initial goal-directed formulation of our problem, and show how features taken from experience in solving problems within an extension of this formulation can be used to improve F_{p2}. I am assuming that the initial goal-directed formulation emerges around the same time (in evolution of the problem solver's expertise) as F_{p2}.

2.6. Initial goal-directed procedural formulation F_{rl}

The initial goal-directed formulation F_{rl} is oriented to the specification of a *relaxed reduction procedure* for problem solving. I am using this procedure as a model of the type of process which was introduced by Sacerdotti (1975) for hierarchical planning in problems with *conjunctive goals*. The main concepts that enter in the formulation of a procedure organized in accordance with a relaxed reduction schema are (i) *states* (problematic situations) in the form $S = (s \rightarrow g)$, where s is a "from" situation and g is a set of goal conditions, (ii) *reduction moves* that transform states into one or more states that are presumed easier to solve than the original, (iii) *relaxed reduction moves* that differ from regular reduction moves because the state transformations that they define are only *partly specified*, (iv) *critics* that apply constraints which further specify relaxed reduction moves, (v) *terminal moves* that completely resolve problematic situations, and (vi) subprocedures for evaluation, attention control and move generation. A relaxed reduction move in the present procedure may propose a relaxed approach to the transformation of a given problem into subproblems by temporarily ignoring certain interdependence constraints in the problem; and then the critics will constrain or modify the simplified approach to solution by taking into account these interdependencies. In a relaxed reduction procedure, a candidate solution is built by focusing on the goals to be satisfied, specifying the fragments of solution that are *necessary* to attain the goals, and also the order in which these fragments must appear in the solution structure; and then focusing on the remaining gaps of the solution structure and proceeding recursively. The entire process is akin to "cutting and pasting" pieces of a solution into a whole under the guidance of goals. It is very different from the process of incremental growth which characterizes the production schema of problem solving.

A detailed description of a grammar for F_{rl} and definitions of key parameters of a relaxed reduction procedure that correspond to this grammar are presented in (Amarel, 1981). I will outline here major features of the formulation F_{rl} via an example.

Let us consider the application of a relaxed reduction procedure to the solution of the 4-disk Tower of Hanoi problem shown in Fig. 1. In particular, let us concentrate on the first stages of the process – that, taken together, can be seen as a major *reasoning episode (maneuver)*. This process is shown in Fig. 3. To follow the sequence of decisions in the figure, a circled number is associated with each application of a move or a critic. Also, at the bottom of the figure, the problem situations that are involved in the process are shown together with a circled number indicating the point in the process at which a situation became completely specified.

The initial state S_o is shown at the top of the figure. The goal conditions for the problem are in the form of a conjunction of conditions that must hold at some future situation which we are asked to attain via a sequence of actions from the initial situation s_i. These conditions are {at (1C), at (2C), at (3C), at (4C)}; they are abbreviated here to (1C)(2C)(3C)(4C).

At ① a *Goal Decomposition* move is applied. This is the key relaxed

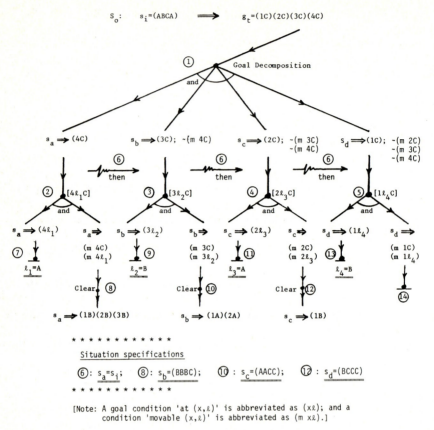

Fig. 3. The first stages of a relaxed reduction process for solving the 4-disk Tower of Hanoi problem P_1 which is shown in Fig. 1. (This process corresponds to the application of a Goal-Reduction macromove.)

reduction move in this procedure. It decomposes a state whose goal is in the form of a conjunction of n conditions (where n > 1) of the type "at(x, l)" into n substates each having as a goal a single condition. The move associates with the goal condition of each substate a set of consequences that are derivable from the goal condition and that are useful in the problem solving process. Specifically, to each condition "at (x,l)", the move associates a set of "blocked disk" assertions in the form of statements " ~ movable (y,l)", for *all* the disks y that are larger than x. In the figure, the abbreviated form of such statement is " ~ (m yl)". Thus, in our problem, the move associates with the subgoal (2C) the two assertions ~ (m 3C) and ~ (m 4C), because the presence of disk 2 at C will prevent the movement of disks 3 and 4 at that peg. While the move specifies the way in which goal conditions are to be transformed, it leaves unspecified the "from" situations in the descendant states. In particular, the order (time) relationships among the descendant situations [in our case, s_a, s_b, s_c, s_d] is left open. Thus, this is a partially specified reduction move, which needs additional information about relationships among the initial "from" situation and the set of descendant situations for its specification to become complete. The Goal Decomposition move represents a useful reasoning step for organizing the task of constructing a solution into several subtasks that are permitted temporarily to be considered in isolation, and independently of each other, in order to fix some parts of the solution. However, the relaxation obtained by avoiding consideration of interdependencies among subgoals must be dealt with subsequently; and this is achieved via the mechanism of the critics.

In our problem, following application of the Goal Decomposition move, *Action-Introduction* moves are applied at the substates that result from the initial decomposition; the order of applications of these moves, that are marked by ②, ③, ④ and ⑤ in the figure, is arbitrary. Action Introduction moves are the domain dependent, atomic, relaxed reduction moves in this procedure; each introduces an action in the candidate solution on the basis of reasoning about the effect of the action and its applicability. Such moves represent the following type of argument: If the (problem solving) objective is to attain from a situation s some other situation where the disk x is at l_2, then it can be achieved as a result of applying an action [x l_1 l_2], for some l_1, *and* by achieving the following sub-objectives: (i) attain from s a situation s_1 where x is at l_1, *and* (ii) the preconditions of the action [i.e., movable (x, l_1), movable (x, l_2)] are to be satisfied at s_1. Consider, for example, the Action Introduction move at ② in the figure. It is characterized by the action [4 l_1C]; it is applied to the state ($s_a \rightarrow$ (4C)); and it produces two substates one of which has as its goal the preconditions of the action. Note that in this move application, one parameter of the action, i.e., the location l_1 remains unspecified. The situation is similar in the other three Action Introduction moves in ③, ④ and ⑤.

At ⑥ a *goal ordering critic* is applied. This critic checks for conflicts that arise when the attainment of one goal blocks the preconditions for an action which is proposed for the attainment of another goal (among the components of a conjunctive goal). In our situation, since the consequence of attaining the goal (1C) is that the disks 2, 3 and 4 are not movable at C; and since (m 2C) is a precondition for attaining the goal (2C), and (m 3C) is a precondition for attaining (3C), and (m 4C) is a precondition for attaining (4C); then the goals (4C), (3C), (2C) should be achieved *before* the goal (1C). On basis of similar reasoning, the goals (4C), (3C) should be achieved before (2C); and the goal (4C) should be achieved before (3C). This provides an acceptable ordering of goals and of associated substates. It also fixes the "from" situation in the first substate in the ordering; thus $s_a = s_i$. This specification, as well as other specifications of situations and locations, are underlined with a double line in the figure.

At ⑦ attention focuses on the substate $(s_a \to (4\,l_1))$ of the Action Introduction move which was applied at $(s_a \to (4\,C))$. A *terminal move* applies here, since the goal condition $(4\,l_1)$ is satisfied in s_a (which is now known to be s_i) with a binding of the variable l_1 to A. With l_1 specified, the second descendant state of the Action Introduction move is now completely specified as $(s_a \to (m4C)\,(m\,4A))$. At ⑧ a *Clear* move is applied at this state. This move represents a useful reasoning step which does not involve directly the choice of actions in the domain, but it uses knowledge about domain properties in preparation of decisions for action application. The logic represented in this move is as follows: In order to satisfy the condition that the disk x be movable at l_1 and at l_2 in some situation s_1 which is attainable from a given situation s, and from which an action $[x\,l_1\,l_2]$ is planned, set as a subgoal that the "blocking disks" of x be located at the unique third peg l_3 (not l_1 or l_2) in the situation s_1. For any x, its "blocking disks" are *all* the disks that are smaller than x. The setting as a subgoal that *all* the disks that are smaller than x be located at the "third peg" – regardless of the current configuration of these disks (some of which may be currently located in the "third peg") – in order to secure a clear movement of x from l_1 to l_2, represents a powerful piece of procedural advice. It relies both on domain knowledge (i.e., characteristics of objects and motions in the physical world) which is assumed to be available in the domain specification D_1, *and* also on process/tactical knowledge about goal-directed methods (which is assumed to be available in the procedural Knowledge base Π). I am assuming that the concept "blocking disks of x" is available in an extension of the domain language LD_1 which is used in the present formulation.

Now, application of the "Clear" move at $(s_a \to (m\,4C)\,(m\,4A))$, produces as

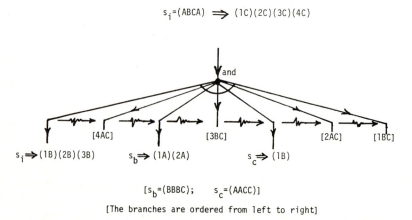

[The branches are ordered from left to right]

Fig. 4. Schematic representations of the process shown in Fig. 3 – which is equivalent to the application of a Goal Reduction macromove.

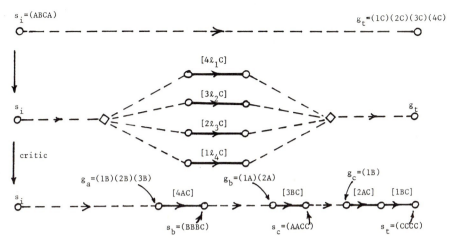

Fig. 5. Schematic graphical representation of solution construction corresponding to the first few stages of the relaxed reduction process shown in Fig. 3. (This is equivalent to an application of a Goal Reduction macromove.)

a subgoal that the "blocking disks" of 4, i.e. 3, 2 and 1, be located at the peg B. At this point, the "from" situation s_b in the state ($s_b \rightarrow$ (3C)) is fully specified; it is (BBBC). The process under this substate, and under the following two, develops in a similar manner. While the first three branches under the Goal Decomposition move result in substates that require further attention (and processing), the fourth branch can be terminated during this argument since the state ($s_d \rightarrow$ (m 1C), (m 1B)) is immediately recognized as terminal – because nothing constrains the movement of disk 1.

The process just described, which includes 13 move applications and 1 application of the goal ordering critic, has the same effect as applying a fully specified reduction macromove on the initial state S_o. In general, this process starts with a goal-decomposition move; it continues with action introduction moves; it then applies a critic to obtain an acceptable ordering of substates; and it proceeds in a systematic way to specify intermediate situations and substates that require further work. Let us call the macromove which produces equivalent behavior to this process, a *Goal-Reduction macromove*. We can view the process that we described as synthesizing at run time a Goal Reduction macromove and applying it. The macromove satisfies the global logical requirements of a valid reduction between states (i.e., the reduced states can be processed independently, and if they are all solvable, then the initial state is also solvable), and the heuristic/pragmatic requirements of problem simplification. The application of such a macromove can be represented schematically as shown in Fig. 4. It reduces the initial state to a sequence which consists of three (simpler) substates and four specific action applications. It should be noted that the concept of a Goal Reduction macromove does not enter explicitly in the present formulation F_{r1}. I am using it here as a convenient means of explaining the relaxed reduction process which corresponds to F_{r1}. It is only in the next, improved, formulation F_{r2} that this macromove is part of the formulation.

Now, the same process which was used to develop the goal reduction at the initial state can be used at each of the substates – in any order, since the substates of the reduction are independent. Clearly, this process terminates and yields the desired solution – which satisfies also the minimality condition - without any search. Note that this represents a completely different approach to the construction of a solution, as compared to the production processes discussed previously.

The procedural formulation F_{r1} for the class TH* which corresponds to the relaxed reduction process just described, can be defined in terms of a grammar G_{r1} and control knowledge CK_{r1} – in addition to D_1 and Λ_1 that are the same as in previous formulations. The grammar G_{r1}, comtrolled by CK_{r1}, produces the type of solution construction behavior described in the previous example (Fig. 3). This grammar has rules of aggregation as well as more global rules of transformation. The solution construction activity corresponding to the process shown in Fig. 3. is outlined schematically in Fig. 5. in terms of a sequence of graph transitions directed by G_{r1} and CK_{r1}.

Let us examine now the transition from the initial declarative formulation F_{d1} to the formulation F_{r1}. The Action Introduction moves in F_{r1} are domain-specific, and they can be obtained from the definition of action in F_{d1} in a relatively straightforward way. Appropriate procedural knowledge is needed to guide the transformation process; it must be available in the knowledge base Π. The "Clear" move is mainly domain-specific. It derives from knowledge about physical objects and their motions; and it is accessible in D_1 via its link to the more general class of problems of reasoning about actions in the physical world. In particular, the concepts of "blocking disk" and "set of blocking disks of a disk" are assumed to be available in the domain language for defining F_{r1}; and also their relationships to the concept "movable" must be known. To synthesize the "Clear' move, additional procedural knowledge is needed about goal-directed processes. The Goal-Decomposition move is not domain-specific. It can be assumed to derive from general knowledge about reasoning maneuvers, and specifically about methods for attaining multiple goals and for decomposing a complex goal into parts. Such knowledge must be available in Π. Also, the entire control scheme for relaxed reduction (i.e., CK_{r1}) must be available in Π.

2.7. Improvement of F_{r1}; problem formulation F_{r2}

An improved formulation F_{r2} can be obtained from F_{r1} by explicitly forming the concept of a Goal Reduction macromove and using it as the key element in a reduction procedure. In this macromove, several reasoning steps used in the relaxed reduction process are compiled together into a single step for building solutions in the class TH*. In reference to Fig. 5, the top and bottom graphs in the figure correspond to a transition which would be caused by an application of a rule in the grammar of F_{r2} which captures the macromove concept.

The automatic formation of the Goal Reduction macromove, which is at the heart of the transition from F_{r1} to F_{r2}, is an approachable task at present. It would involve (i) searching records of solution construction activity within F_{r1} for process chunks that satisfy the known properties (logical and heuristic) of reduction moves (the process described in Fig. 3 is an instance of such a chunk); (ii) generalizing from specific instances; and (iii) testing the generalization. Thus the knowledge needed for the transition from F_{r1} to F_{r2} must include records of problem solving experience within F_{r1} (in a knowledge base linked to the definition of F_{r1}); characterization of desired properties of reduction moves (assumed available in Π; and procedural advice about theory formation/discovery processes to guide the macromove formation activity.

2.8. Improvement of production formulation F_{p2} on basis of experience with the reduction formulation F_{r2}

As indicated in 2.5 above, the formulation F_{p2} can be strengthened if its heuristic distance estimator h can be improved. The approach suggested for such an improvement is to use explicit knowledge about properties of solution trajectories – obtained from experience with goal-directed formulations - in order to obtain better estimates of distance between situations in σ_1. The goal reduction process in formulation F_{r2} provides the basis for the definition of a good heuristic estimator for problems in a subclass of TH*. The problems in this subclass are characterized by a *goal set* in which all the disks in the set are at the same location. This is an interesting class of problems which includes our specific problem P_1; let us call it TH_1^*.

Consider now a state S characterized by an initial situation s_i and a terminal situation s_t. Suppose that x_n is the largest disk whose location is different at s_i and s_t; and there are $n-1$ disks, $x_{n-1}, x_{n-2}, \ldots, x_1$, that are smaller than x_n; also $x_n > x_{n-1} > x_{n-2} > \ldots > x_1$. Define a goal set g which includes incidence conditions for x_n and for the $n-1$ disks that are smaller than x_n; the conditions specify that all these n disks must be located at a given terminal location. We now have a problem state $(s_i \rightarrow g)$ which can be treated as in F_{r2}, and whose solution within this goal-directed formulation will be a solution to S. The objective is to develop an approximate solution to S which will provide a basis for computing a good lower bound for the length of its true solution.

The following line of reasoning can be developed on basis of the characteristics of a Goal Reduction macromove in F_{r2}. To transfer x_n to the goal peg from its current peg, we must have the $n-1$ blocking disks of x_n at the "third peg". Suppose that the k largest among the $n-1$ disks are already in the "third peg", i.e., the disks $x_{n-1}, x_{n-2}, ..., x_{n-k}$. The transfer of x_1 will need at least $1 + [(n-1)-k]$ actions. At the end of this stage, the $n-1$ disks are at the "third peg". To transfer the largest of the $n-1$ disks to the goal peg, we must remove the $n-2$ blocking disks from the "third peg", and then effect the desired transfer. This stage requires at least $1 + (n-2)$ actions. By pursuing this line of reasoning for all the n disks that are to be transferred to the goal peg, we obtain as a lower bound on the total number of actions the expression $[n(n+1)/2] - k$.

The result of this analysis is a property of solution sequences in the restricted class TH_1^*. I am assuming that it enters into a declarative formulation of this class, call it F_{a2}, and in particular it is associated with the set of X of possible (legal) solution sequences in the class. The formulation F_{d2} differs from the initial declarative formulation F_{d1} for the broader class TH^* in the definitions of the sets X and the parameter domains Λ. The use of the new knowledge in F_{d2} about estimates of solution lengths for the improvement of the estimator h_o in F_{p2} is a relatively simple task. Let us call the new, improved, estimator h_1.

Consider now as an example the initial state of our problem P_1; it is ((ABCA), (CCCC)). In this case, the estimator h_1 would give a distance estimate of 10. Note that the actual distance is 15. This is a considerable improvement over the simple distance estimator h_o which counts misplaced disks; in the present case, h_o would have given a distance estimate of 3.

By using the estimator h_1 – instead of h_o – in the formulation F_{p2}, a more selective search for solution is attained. Let us call F_{p2} this improved variant of the formulation F_{p2}.

It is possible to extract more accurate properties of solution sequences constructed within the goal reduction formulation F_{r2} and obtain even better heuristic estimators. For example, the previous argument can be extended to a depth of two Goal Reduction macromoves; and this would permit us to consider in more detail the pattern of transfers of "blocking disks". However, there is a point of diminishing returns at which the effort that goes into distance estimation is no longer compensated by the benefits obtained from increased selectivity in search.

The transition from F_{p2} to an improved formulation F'_{p2} is obtained by extracting appropriate knowledge from problem solving experience within the goal directed formulation F_{r2}. In particular, it involves *restricting* the class TH^* to TH_1^* and *analysing* the behavior of the Goal Reduction macromove for problems in TH_1 While the goal of the analysis is well defined (i.e., find a distance estimate function for problems in the restricted class), we still face here a difficult theory formation (theorem finding) problem. The problem solver must define a class restriction for which an argument of the type sketched above can yield a relatively simple distance estimate function. Mechanizing such a process is an interesting challenge to AI research at present.

Recent psychological studies indicate (Anzai and Simon, 1979) that as skill in solving Tower of Hanoi problems increases, the approach used by humans is a combination of forward-moving heuristic search (production approach) and more global goal-directed reasoning. Such a strategy would suggest a formulation which is a hybrid of F_{p2} and F_{r2}. For example, a complex problem may first be approached by applying one or two goal-reduction macromoves from F_{r2}, and then some of its reduced subproblems may be treated within F_{p2} or its variants. Thus, the advantage to the problem solver of having available a reduction as well as a production formulation of his problem, is not only because one formulation provides a means for improving the other, but also because there are problems that can be dealt most effectively by a combination of the two formulations.

2.9. A shift to reduction formulation F_{r3}; generalization of problem class

A relatively small structural change in the goal-directed formulation F_{r2} can lead to a formulation F_{r3} which captures an important new approach to solution construction. In this approach, the Goal Reduction macromove is transformed into a different move, which may be called a *Goal Decrement* reduction move. Let us illustrate this change in the special case of our problem P_1. In Fig. 4. the application of the Goal Reduction macromove on the problem P_1 is shown. In this case, the initial state $s_i \to g_t$, where $g_t =$ (1C)(2C)(3C)(4C), is reduced to a substate $s_i \to g_a$, with $g_a = $ (1B)(2B)(3B), followed by the action [4AC] followed by a set of substates and actions which can be "summarized" by a substate $s_b \to g_{rest}$ where $g_{rest} = $ (1C)(2C)(3C). Viewed this way, the original goal reduction represents an instance of the following basic stategy: to handle a conjunctive goal, focus attention on a single goal in the conjunction – the "most critical" goal – and prepare two subsidiary problems for further work; the solution to the first subproblem is a prerequisite for attaining the "most critical" goal (in our case, the three blocking disks of disk 4 must be moved out of the way to the "third peg" B); and the second subproblem is a reduced version of the original problem with the "most critical" goal satisfied and with the *rest* of the goals still to be attained. (In our case, from a situation where the disk 4 is assumed to be at C and the disks 1, 2, 3 are assumed to be at B, the goal is to move disks 1, 2, 3 to C).

The key grammar rule of the new formulation F_{r3} – which embodies this strategy for constructing solutions to problems in the class TH* – can be defined in terms of the following transition,

$$s \quad g \quad s \quad g_a \quad s_b \quad g_{rest}$$
$$\circ\text{-->-}\circ \quad \to \quad \circ\text{-->-}\circ \longrightarrow \circ\text{-->-}\circ$$
$$[x_1\ l_{1,1}\ l_{1,2}]$$

[s can be any situation in σ_1; g is a goal set of n incidence relations in the form (x, l), where x is any disk, l any location, and $1 \leq n \leq 4$; x_1 is the largest disk in g which is located at $l_{1,1}$ in s and whose desired location in g is $l_{1,2}$; g_a is the set of goal condition (y l_a) for all the disks y that are in the set of "blocking disks" of x_1 [i.e., *all* the disks that are smaller than x_1], and l_a is the unique "third peg" other than $l_{1,1}$ and $l_{1,2}$; s_b differs from s in the locations of x_1 (in s_b it is at $l_{1,2}$) and of all disks smaller than x_1 (in s_b they are at l_a); and g_{rest} is the same as g with the goal condition for the largest disk, i.e. (x_1 $l_{1,2}$), removed.])

The problem formulations F_{r2}, F_{r3} are very close to each other from the point of view of effectiveness in solution finding. However, F_{r3} reflects a change in viewpoint about the handling of goals, and it provides a *more convenient basis for generalizations*.

In F_{r2}, a conjunction of n goals is partitioned into n parts, each part is given equal attention and it is then organized into a sorted sequence. In F_{r3}, the conjunction of goals is partitioned into a 2-part sequence; the first part refers to the largest disk in the conjunction, and the second part, the "rest", refers to the *set* of other disks in the conjunction. I am assuming that the concept of the 2-way partition of goals is available *a priori* as a useful strategy in Π. The specific way in which this partition is used to define a reduction move in F_{r3}, can be obtained from domain reasoning of the type used in the relaxed reduction process to order the goal sequence. The concept of *dependence* among goal conditions is essential here. In the present domain, movement of a given disk depends on (the location of) all the disks that are smaller than it, and it is independent of (the location of) all the larger disks. This can lead to the definition of the 2-way partition in F_{r3}.

The reduction pattern in the formulation F_{r3} remains the same if we move from 4-disk problems to N − disk problems, for any N. Thus, experiments in solving problems within F_{r3} may easily lead to the formulation of a broader class of problems TH*(N), which involves 3 pegs and N disks, and where the objective is to find the shortest sequence of actions for going between any two arbitrary configurations of the N disks on the pegs. Clearly, our previous class TH*, of which P_1 is a member, is the same as TH*(4).

To problems in TH*(N) there corresponds a domain specification $D_1(N)$ which is an extension of the domain specification D_1 discussed previously. In the new domain language $LD_1(N)$ of $D_1(N)$, there are N disks (where N = 1,2,3,...); and the predicates of the extended domain language are now adjusted to handle any N. In addition, from experience in working with formulations F_{r2} and F_{r3}, the extended language is assumed to have acquired the following concepts:

U_N: the *set* of N disks, and its subsets.
δ_N^n the subset of n smallest disks in U_N, for $1 \leq n \leq N$.

Note that for a disk n + 1 the set of "blocking disks" of the disk is identical with σ_N^n. Since in each reduction of F_{r3} the intermediate subgoal g_a refers to a set of "blocking disks" of some disk, it is reasonable to assume that the concept σ_N^n can emerge as an "interesting" concept in a system with minimal theory formation capabilities. [The set σ_N^n can also be seen as a complete "subpyramid" of size n in the domain.]

Now the extended domain specification $D_1(N)$ includes an implicit definition of a situation space $\sigma_1(N)$ which consists of 3^N situations partly ordered under the relation of direct attainability, which is itself defined in terms of the 6N actions in the domain. For any N, the graph of the situation space has the same general form of "triangles within triangles", as shown in Fig. 2. for the case of N = 4.

2.10. Using problem solving experience to find an improved production formulation F_{p3} for a restricted class of problems

In solving problems from the class TH*(N) within the goal-directed formulation F_{r3} and the production formulation F_{p2}, useful regularities in solution sequences for interesting subclasses of problems may be discovered. In general, the *discovery processes* involved here are difficult, as they are aimed at two mutually interdependent concepts: an "interesting subclass of problems" to be defined in terms of boundary characteristics of the problems, which depends on the existence of "good, specialized, solution methods"; and a "good solution method" which depends on the ability to focus on an "interesting subclass" and to experiment with it.

In our domain, the following is the outline of a possible approach to such a discovery process. Work with problems within F_{r3}, often involves states such as the substate $s_b \to g_{rest}$ which was shown in 2.9 above where the Recursive Goal Reduction of F_{r3} was applied to our problem P_1. More specifically, we obtain in the above example a substate, (BBBC) → (1C)(2C)(3C); i.e., the set of disks {1, 2, 3} must be transferred from B to C. Thus, this subproblem can be characterized in terms of a *pyramidal difference* between two situations, i.e., the subpyramid σ_4^3 is at B in the "from" situation, and it is at C in the "to" situation. Let us denote this difference by $\langle \sigma_4^3 \text{ B C} \rangle$. The concept of pyramidal difference represents as important addition to the extended domain language of $D_1(N)$. This should be treated as a *candidate concept for defining an interesting subclass*; and it can achieve a more stable status if/when a strong solution method can be associated with it. An alternative way of focusing attention on such a concept of problem subclass is via the analysis of solution sequences obtained with any of the procedures used by the problem solver at this stage of his development. Analysis of such sequences will point to many *sub-sequences* with boundary situations that can be characterized by a "pyramidal difference". In reference to the situation space shown in Fig. 2, any path which represents the side of some triangle in the graph defines such a solution sub-sequence.

Let us assume that the problem subclass of interest is characterized by a pyramidal difference $\langle \sigma_N^n \; l_i \; l_t \rangle$, for any n from 1 to N. let us call this class TH(N). Clearly, TH(N) is a subclass of TH*(N). Let us assume further that on basis of analysis of empirical data about solution sequences in the class TH(N), the following properties are found:

K_a: No disk move twice in succession

K_b: A disk does not go back to the location from which it last moved

K_c: If n is odd (i.e., the number of disks in the subpyramid σ_N^n is odd), then the first disk transfer in the solution sequence is from the initial peg l_i to the terminal peg l_t; if n is even, then the first transfer is from l_i to the "third peg" l_a.

To obtain these properties as empirical generalizations about features of a set of solution sequences, the problem solver needs a sufficiently rich language to express candidate properties, and an effective theory formation procedure – including a good strategy of experimentation with problems in the class and with their solutions.

It is reasonable to assume at this point that the problem solver can bring to bear on the current problem a set of concepts about *properties of trajectories of individual objects* that are available in the language of the broader domain of reasoning about actions in the physical world which he is assumed to have. In particular, concepts that are needed to express the items K_a, K_b, K_c are assumed to be available as part of a further extension of the domain language $LD_1(N)$. These include such predicates as "last-moved (x)," "odd (n)," "even (n);" and such functions as "previous-location (x) = l". Given adequate language facilities, the present theory formation task can be approached with current AI methods (e.g. Mitchell et al., 1981); however, this is an area where more research is needed.

An initial *declarative* formulation of the class of problems TH(N) (i.e., before the new knowledge about solution sequences is acquired) can be given as a 4-tuple $(D_1(N), X_1(N), C_1, \Lambda_2)$, where $D_1(N)$ is as defined previously, $X_1(N)$ is the set of trajectories in the extended situation space $\sigma_1(N)$ defined in $D_1(N)$, C_1 denotes the class conditions as in the original declarative formulation F_{d1}, and Λ_2 is the set of all situation pairs in the extended space $\sigma_1(N)$ that can be characterized by a pyramidal difference.

The properties K_a, K_b, K_c of the class TH(N) can be seen as augmenting the above declarative formulation. They enter into a new definition of the set of possible (legal) solutions. This set $X_1'(N)$ is a restriction of $X_1(N)$, as only those trajectories that also satisfy the conditions K_a, K_b, K_c are accepted. With this change, an augmented declarative formulation F_{d3} of TH(N) is obtained.

Now, given the augmented declarative formulation F_{d3}, the problem solver must find a *procedural* formulation of TH(N) in such a way that the acquired knowledge is effectively incorporated in the parameters of the formulation. This can be done with relative ease in the present case by defining a formulation F_{p3} which is based on a production procedure, and by using the new knowledge almost without change in the form of conditions for the grammar rules of F_{p3}.

The key rule of aggregation in the grammar G_{p3} of F_{p3} is as follows.
Forward development rule in G_{p3}
Transition

$$s_1 \quad\quad s_t \quad\quad\quad s_1 \quad\quad s_a \quad\quad s_t$$
$$\alpha\dashrightarrow\circ \quad\longrightarrow\quad \circ\longrightarrow\circ\dashrightarrow\circ$$
$$[x\ l_1\ l_2]$$

[s_1 is any situation obtained in the course of solving a problem in TH(N); s_t is the terminal situation; if $s_1 = \{\alpha, \text{at } (x, l_1)\}$, then $s_2 = \{\alpha, \text{at } (x, l_2)\}$]

Condition: In situation s_1:

movable (x,l_1), movable (x,l_2),
$\sim$ last-moved (x),
previous-location $(x) \neq l_2$.

A comparison between this rule and the rule for forward development in the earlier grammar G_{p1}, which was given in 2.3.1 above, shows an increase in the number of constraints that control applicability of the rule. In addition to this rule, there are two special starting rules in G_{p3} for handling in a differential way initial states that are characterized by pyramidal differences with an odd or even n.

By using a production procedure based on G_{p3} a solution can be obtained for any problem in TH(N) *without any search*. All the knowledge about solutions is embodied in the *a priori* conditions for action choice. At this point, the class TH(N), changes status from a candidate concept for an interesting subclass of problem to a stable concept of an interesting subclass – for which a specialized solution method is available. In moving to the present formulation, it can be said that a certain amount of expertise has been acquired by the problem solver.

2.11. Recursive reduction formulation F_{r4} for solving problems in the restricted class

Further analysis of solution sequences for problems in TH(N), for various values of N, can lead to the identification of interesting patterns of subsequences in a solution sequence. From such an analysis, the following important property can be found:

K_d: The solution for a problem characterized by a pyramidal difference $\langle \sigma_n^N \, l_1 \, l_2 \rangle$, for $1 < n \leq N$, can be defined by a sequence made of (i) the solution to a subproblem characterized by $\langle \sigma_N^{n-1} l_1 \, l_a \rangle$, where l_a is the unique "third peg" other than l_1 or l_2, followed by (ii) an action $[n, l_1, l_2]$, and ending with (iii) the solution to a subproblem characterized by $\langle \sigma_N^{n-1} l_1 l_2 \rangle$.

This property describes the well-known *recursive description of solutions* for Tower of Hanoi problems where the objective is to transfer entire (sub)pyramids from one peg to another.

This property can be discovered by working directly with *solution sequences*, and by attempting to find part-whole relationships of a recursive nature. It is essential here to be able to refer to a solution sub-sequence by the problem characteristics (the pyramidal difference) to which it corresponds. The extended domain language $LD_1(N)$ has sufficient capabilities for producing solution descriptions of this type. Finding the property K_d under these conditions is an interesting theory formation task. The difficulty of the task depends on the amount of information which is available about the desired nature of K_d. If we start by looking for a property which provides the basis for an effective problem reduction, then the task is relatively easy because properties of good reductions are known [they are assumed available in the knowledge base Π].

The property K_d can be discovered also by working with *structural descriptions of solutions* within the goal-directed formulation F_{r3}. By structural description of a solution, I mean the tree of grammar rule applications which provides a record of how the solution has been constructed. In 2.9 above the key grammar rule in F_{r3}, which corresponds to the Goal Decrement reduction move, is shown. This rule applies to any problem in the class TH*(N). Now, if the class of problems is *restricted* to the "interesting" class TH(N), which is now under consideration, then the Goal Decrement reduction of F_{r3} gets transformed into a recursive reduction move which represents precisely the property K_d.

I am assuming that the new knowledge K_d augments the declarative formulation F_{d3} of the class TH(N). Specifically, it enters as a new characterization of the set $X_1(N)$ of possible (legal) solutions to problems in the class. Let us call the new declarative formulation F_{d3}. Now, to embody the acquired knowledge K_d into a procedural formulation is a relatively easy task. This can be done by defining a formulation F_{r4} which is a specialization of the formulation F_{r3} for the restricted class of problem TH(N). The formulation F_{r4} specifies the well known recursive reduction procedure for problems in the class TH(N).

2.12. Discovery of a strong procedural formulation F_{p4} for problems in the restricted class

The recursive reduction formulation is not necessarily the most efficient way for solving problems in the class TH(N). An interesting development towards inproved expertise would be to find a production formulation which is better than our previous production formulation F_{p3} (less computation per step) by using knowledge extracted from analysis of solutions that are obtained via the recursive reduction procedure. This approach is suggested from psychological studies of expertise acquisition in problem solving (Larkin et al., 1980) where considerable evidence was found that experts shift into a bold forward reasoning mode in handling problems in a given class after having had acquired sufficient problem solving experience in working carefully within a goal-directed mode with problems in the class.

Let us consider solution sequences in TH(N) and their structural descriptions in the recursive reduction formulation F_{r4}. In particular, let us focus on the problem of transferring a subpyramid σ_N^n from location 1_i to 1_t; and let 1_a stand for the unique third location. We defined previously σ_N^n as the subset of the n smallest disks from the total set of N disks. Let us name as follows the disks in σ_N^n: the largest disk in the subset is 1; the next smaller in size is 2, and so on; and the smallest is n. Note that this is a kind of inversion of the naming scheme which we used so far. This change is introduced in order to simplify the description of properties that are obtained from the analysis of solution sequences and of their structural descriptions. The following properties can be obtained:

K_e: Disk k moves 2^{k-1} times in a solution sequence ($1 \leq k \leq n$). Thus there are 2^{n-1} steps in the sequence.

K_f Let us number the steps in a solution sequence from 1 to 2^{n-1}. Each disk k moves for the first time in the sequence at a step number which is characteristic of the disk; let us call it "starting step" of k. After the first move, each disk (except disk 1) moves again with a "period" which is characteristic of the disk – until it reaches the total number of moves specified in K_e above. Now for any k ($1 \leq k \leq n$) the "starting step" of k is 2^{n-k}; and the "period" of k ($1 \leq k \leq n$) is 2^{n-k+1} steps.

K_g: If a disk is odd (as determined by its numerical name), then its movement between locations is determined by the following transition diagram:

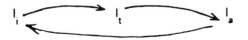

If a disk is even, then its movement is determined by a transition diagram in which the direction of the arrows is reversed.

It should be noted that the knowledge items K_a, K_b, K_c that were used previously in defining the production formulation F_{p3} are derivable from the more basic solution properties K_e, K_f and K_g. In particular, K_a is a consequence of K_f; and K_b, K_c are consequences of K_g.

The new knowledge K_e, K_f, K_g can be assumed to augment further the declarative formulation of the class TH(N); and specifically to be associated with the definition of the set $X'_1(N)$ of possible (legal) solution sequences in the class. Let us call the augmented declarative formulation F_{d3}. The interesting problem is how to move from this formulation to an effective procedural formulation.

Several procedural formulations are possible at this point. A fairly efficient "forward moving" production process can be specified as follows. Suppose that each disk has associated with it the following information: its parity (odd or even) relative to the subpyramid of size n which is to be transferred; its characteristic starting step number and its period (obtained from K_f); the characteristic number of times that it moves in a sequence (obtained from K_a); the number of times it has moved so far in the sequence; its current location; and the current step number in the solution sequence. Now suppose that a clock counts steps, and communicates the count to all the disks. Each time a new step is set, there is only one disk which recognizes that now is its turn to move; on the basis of its current location, its parity and the transition rules that are given in K_g, it then decides where to move to, and thus it specifies the transfer action that should take place at the step. This process continues until all the disks have completed their characteristic number of moves in the sequence. Let us call F_{p4} the procedural formulation which corresponds to this process. This formulation represents a highly customized routine for solving problems in the restricted class TH(N) of Tower of Hanoi problems, and it relies heavily on specific knowledge about problems (solutions) in this class.

Two difficult steps are involved in attaining the formulation F_{p4}. The first step consists of discovering and expressing knowledge about useful regularities in structural descriptions of solutions that are obtained via the recursive reduction process; it yields the knowledge items K_e, K_f, K_g in a declarative form. This is a challenging theory formation process. The second step consists of using the knowledge acquired in the past step to formulate a procedure for efficient solution generation. This is a non-trivial program synthesis process. While each of these steps cannot be handled in isolation (as the second step is needed to provide guidance for the first), it is conceptually useful to see them as two distinct tasks. The main idea is that the improved production formulation F_{p4} cannot be obtained by some "local structural modification" process from the previous production formulation F_{p3} via conventional learning methods; but it involves a radical structural change which originates from knowledge gleaned by working with a different type of procedural formulation, i.e. the recursive reduction formulation F_{r4}. This is the third time in the evolution of formulations described in this paper that an improvement in a production formulation comes from knowledge obtained from an analysis of problem solving experience with a reduction formulation. (The first inprovement involved the strengthening of an evaluation function, and the second involved the strengthening of a move selection function).

2.13. Robust expert behaviour obtained via coordinated use of multiple formulations

At this point in the development of expertise in the Tower of Hanoi domain, the problem solver has a highly efficient production formulation F_{p4} for the special subclass of problems TH(N) which is characterized by pyramidal differences, *and* a less efficient but systematic goal-directed formulation F_{r3} for approaching any problem in the broader class TH*(N). This situation is characteristic of an "intelligent expert" who has the ability to recognize whether a (sub)problem can be handled within a specialized formulation – and to solve it then via highly efficient methods – and if not, to cast it into a broad (possibly weak) basic formulation and to attempt to solve it there.

Consider for example how our "intelligent expert" would handle the 4-disk Tower of Hanoi problem P_1 which is shown in Fig. 1. The problem is to find a minimal sequence of actions from $s_i = (ABCA)$ to $s_t = (CCCC)$. The solution to this problem is marked on the graph of the situation space which is shown in Fig. 2. This problem is not in the class TH(N) on which a strong method can be used, because it cannot be characterized by a pyramidal difference. Thus, it is handled within the basic goal-directed formulation F_{r3}. After application of one "Goal Decrement" reduction move, the solution is specified as a sequence consisting of (i) the solution to a subproblem $S_1 = (s_i, s_1)$, followed by (ii) an action [4 A C] for transferring the largest misplaced disk, and (iii) the solution to a subproblem $S_2 = (s_2, s_t)$ [see Fig. 2]. Now, the subproblems S_1, S_2 can be handled independently. S_2 is recognized as a problem in the special subclass which can be handled by the strong method, because it can be characterized by a 3-disk pyramidal difference; it is approached within the formulation F_{p4}, which effectively generates a 7-step solution by "forward reasoning" from s_2 to s_t. Since S_1 is not in the special subclass, it is handled again within F_{r3}. This produces two new subproblems $S_3 = (s_i, s_3)$ and $S_4 = (s_4, s_1)$. Again, S_4 is characterized by a pyramidal difference (of 2) and solved within F_{p4}; and S_3 must be handled once more within the basic formulation F_{r3} which, via a single reduction, generates a 3-step solution to this subproblem.

This example illustrates how an intelligent expert system can use effectively a combination of highly specialized, basic methods that are more generally applicable, but possibly weak, in the handling of a relatively large class of problems. This behavior is made possible by using, on a coordinated manner, *multiple problem formulations*. As shown previously in this paper, it is also the case that the creation of new specialized formulations for expert treatment of problems in restricted classes of a domain can be helped enormously by the intelligent use of multiple formulations. This type of behavior requires that multiple formulations of a problem be available to the problem solver.

2.14 Summary and discussion of expertise acquisition processes in the Tower of Hanoi domain

A summary of the developmental paths discussed above for moving from "novice" to "intelligent expert" behavior in handling Tower of Hanoi problems is shown in Fig. 6. Declarative formulations are shown in the middle and procedural formulations in the two sides of the figure – with those oriented to production (forward reasoning) schemas at left and those oriented to goal-directed, reduction, schemas at right. The class of problems to which a formulation corresponds is shown next to it in brackets. Starting from the initial declarative formulation F_{d1} for the class TH* of 4-disk Tower of Hanoi problems, each arrow denotes a process which contributes to the creation of a new formulation, which in turn leads to another formulation, etc. until the hybrid formulation F_{r3}, F_{p4} is attained. This last formulation, which is shown at the bottom of the figure, characterizes "intelligent expert" behavior for problems with any number of disks in the Tower of Hanoi domain.

Three types of arrows are shown in the figure: (i) a single arrow denotes simple information transfer, (ii) a double arrow denotes a program synthesis process, and (iii) a dashed arrow denotes a theory formation/discovery process. There should be a transfer arrow pointing into each procedural formulation from the procedural knowledge base Π – to indicate access to various procedural schemas, reasoning methods, etc.. However, for simplicity, these arrows are omitted from the figure. Consider, for example, the procedural formulation F_{p2} which has arrows entering from F_{p2}, F_{d2} (and Π) and arrows going to F_{p3} and F_{d3}. This means that F_{p2} is a modification (improvement) of F_{p2} on basis of new knowledge coming from F_{d2}, and assimilated in procedural form on basis of guidance from Π; F_{p2} provides a base from which the improved formulation F_{p3} is built; and experience in working with F_{p2} contributes to the theory formation process that leads to the class restriction TH(N) for which special solution properties are found and then represented in the declarative formulation F_{d3}. Now, F_{d3} represents a modification of F_{d2}, which includes new knowledge to be used in the creation of the improved procedural formulation F_{p3}.

The movement from top to bottom in the figure corresponds roughly to the passage of time. At any horizontal line cutting across the figure, the history of the problem solver can be represented by the formulations above the line, and his current state by the set of formulations that are closest to the line. The formulations enclosed in circles represent the strong formulations attained in the developmental process.

Note that there are many interactions between formulations along the developmental paths that lead to expert performance. The availability of multiple problem representations seems to be crucial for processes of expertise

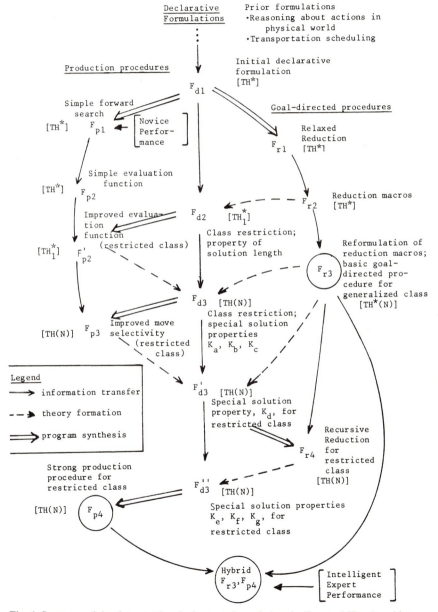

Fig. 6. Summary of developmental paths between formulations in Tower of Hanoi problems.

acquisition. Also, note the importance of *sequence* in this process. Certain formulations would be extremely hard to attain (by human or machine) unless a sequence of prior steps brought about a situation where there is sufficient knowledge in appropriate forms to make a transition possible.

It is interesting to follow the flow of knowledge in the reformation processes summarized in Fig. 6. A major source of knowledge is obtained by embedding the problem in a class for which prior knowledge exists. The rest of the knowledge is acquired via discovery of solution properties for specific problem subclasses in the domain; and this can be achieved by working in the domain, i.e. by "putting previous knowledge to work" in solving problems and in conducting experiments in the domain.

3. Concluding remarks

Problem reformulations that lead to "intelligent expert" behaviour require *large amounts of knowledge of various kinds* – even for relatively simple tasks such as Tower of Hanoi problems.

To mechanize shifts between formulations, we must have the ability (i) to perform various discovery and theory formation processes, (ii) to handle program synthesis processes, and (iii) to coordinate the operation of several problem solving processes simultaneously. There are many open problems in these areas; but there is also an increasing amount of work in AI as well as in other parts of computer science which is directed to them.

The work of Mitchell (1981) in learning problem solving heuristics and of Lenat (see Davis and Lenat, 1982) on concept discovery in mathematics are of special relevance to the theory formation and discovery problems that we face in this area. The work of Ernst and Goldstein (1982) on methods of using problem knowledge to instantiate problem solving schemas, Mostow's (1981) work on "operationalizing" heuristic advice and work by Tappel (1980) and Paige (1981) on algorithm transformations, are all especially relevant to the types of knowledge transformation and program synthesis tasks that we encounter in this area. Also, current efforts to develop expert systems of increased power in various AI centres are stimulating research on methods of coordinating the activities of several processes that are working on the "same" problem. All of these activities bring us closer to a point where the task of mechanizing appropriate shifts between problem representations becomes feasible. However, more research in all these areas is needed.

The Tower of Hanoi domain provides a good environment for work on the open problems in this area. As shown in this paper, there are several types of reformulation steps along the path of expertise acquisition in the Tower of Hanoi domain that can now be approached with a reasonable chance of success, while at the same time work on them is expected to advance our understanding of several basic AI problems. For example, the steps from the basic goal-directed formulation F_{r3} (see Fig. 6) to the recursive reduction formulation F_{r4}, and from F_{r4} to the highly customized, expert, procedure in the formulation F_{p4}, represent very interesting AI problems that deserve further exploration.

The work discussed in this paper is part of a research effort to clarify the overall nature of reformulation and expertise acquisition problems, and to explore key components (bodies of knowledge, processes) of these problems and ways in which they relate to each other. What we need next is more in-depth studies of the specific subproblems that were identified in this research.

In recent years, the AI community made considerable progress, in building specialized expert systems. However, "intelligent expert" behavior remains within the exclusive province of the human problem solver. In order to understand and mechanize (parts of) this type of behavior we must develop a better understanding of the dynamics of problem representations.

ARTIFICIAL AND HUMAN INTELLIGENCE (A. Elithorn and R. Banerji, editors)
Elsevier Science Publishers, B.V.
© NATO, 1984

Chapter 2

IS COMPLEXITY THEORY OF USE TO AI?

ALLEN GOLDBERG and IRA POHL

Computer and Information Sciences,
University of California, Santa Cruz, CA 95064, USA

Summary

Theory of computational complexity has not been a tool regularly used by AI researchers. The origin of the theory, the undecidability and incompleteness results of Godel, Post, Turing and Church create a profound problem for AI researchers. Problems of epistemology, deduction, search and natural language understanding can all be framed as problems in first order logic. Furthermore, many search-space representations of AI problems are reducible to or similar in character to combinatorial problems which have now been shown to be computationally intractable. This paper will argue that as AI and complexity theory mature the interaction between these areas will increase. Specifically, algorithmic analysis will be sophisticated enough to be used as an accurate measure of the effectiveness of AI and algorithms, and complexity theory will provide AI problems with a (partial) mathematical framework which will facilitate the discovery of new techniques.

1. Introduction

In this paper we shall argue that as Artificial Intelligence (AI) and complexity theory mature the interaction between these areas will increase. Specifically, algorithmic analysis will be utilized as an accurate measure of the effectiveness of AI algorithms for a wide domain of AI problems. This development will be made possible by the improved techniques of algorithm analysis and the embodiment of AI problems into a mathematical framework which facilitates analysis.

We first summarize "classical" complexity theory and argue that although it is not a tool regularly used by AI researchers, it does define the theoretical framework in which AI operates. In later sections we shall describe specific pragmatic contributions complexity theory has made to AI. We will describe recent developments in complexity theory which will greatly increase its usability in this domain.

2. The perspective of complexity theory

Complexity theory and AI find their deepest roots in computability theory, the mathematical theory that describes the problem solving capabilities of computers without regard to resource utilization. This theory was developed before the the introduction of electronic computers. The logicians (Godel, Post, Turing and Church) of the 1930's independently constructed different mathematical models of computation. These models led to the famous results on the limitations of formal systems to be proved. A landmark result from this work, one that has profound effect on AI, is the undecidability of first order logic (FOL) (Church, 1936, Turing, 1936). Since problems in many AI domains are naturally expressed in FOL, this result represents a fundamental limitation on the theoretical effectiveness of AI algorithms. A *decision procedure* for a logical theory is an algorithm which, given a formula in the language of that theory, will determine whether or not the formula is valid. Church and Turing each showed that no such algorithm can exist for FOL. However, *semi-decision procedures*, algorithms that when given sufficient time and space will recognize valid formulas, but which may compute endlessly on invalid formulas, do exist.

The introduction of computers made it desirable to refine computability theory to take into account the amount of resource needed to solve a problem. Time and space (memory) are the resources considered. If a solution of a problem requires excessive amounts of resource the problem is considered intractable. The resource requirements of an algorithm are measured as a function of the length of the input to the algorithm. Two types of analysis are of importance - the average and worst cases. If Time(AL,I) is the time required for algorithm AL to execute given input I on some general purpose serial computer, *the worst case time* complexity is

$$T_{worst, AL}(n) = \max_{|I|=n} [\text{Time}(AL,I)]$$

and the *average case time complexity* is

$$T_{average, AL}(n) = \sum_{|I|=n} P[I] \, \text{Time}(AL,I)$$

where P[I] is a distribution function over the set of problem instances of size n. Similar definitions can be given for space complexity.

Since the theory is primarily concerned only with the asymptotic behavior of these functions, differences in machine architecture and speed will not have a significant effect on the theory. The classical theory does assume a serial model of computation. More precisely, a problem is considered *intractable* if any known algorithm that solves the problem has time complexity which grows asymptotically faster than an exponential function.

Given that FOL is undecidable, it is natural to look for logical theories of practical utility that are decidable. *Presburger arithmetic* (PA), the theory that describes the behavior of the natural numbers with respect to equality, the less than relation, and addition, is decidable. It has many practical applications, particularly for program verification. It was shown, however, that any algorithm that decides PA requires at least 2^{2^n} (Fischer and Rabin, 1974) time and space to determine the validity of a formula of length n, in the worst case. Thus by the more stringent requirements of complexity theory, this problem is practically unsolvable, although decidable.

The best known results of complexity theory deal with the theory of NP-completeness (Garey and Johnson, 1979). The definition of the class of NP problems utilizes the notion of non-deterministic computation. A computation is *non-deterministic* if at certain points within the computation the algorithm specifies that more than one instruction may be eligible for execution. It is assumed that the computing agent chooses, in some unspecified and unpredictable way, which instruction to execute. In the Turing machine model of computation non-determinism corresponds to the removal of the requirement that only one quintuple be applicable to the possible computation states that can be reached by the execution of one instruction. For *"Yes/No"* problems, that is problems whose output is either the string "Yes" or "No" (or in the case of decision procedures "Valid" or "Invalid"), the output of the algorithm is considered to be "Yes" if at least one of the possible computation paths output the value "Yes". NP (for Non-deterministic Polynomial) is the class of Yes/No problems for which there exists a non-deterministic algorithm whose worst-case time complexity is bounded by a polynomial. Given two Yes/No problems, P_1 and P_2, P_1 is said to be *p-reducible* to P_2 if there is a function f, computable deterministically in polynomial time, such that given an instance I of P_1, f(I) is an instance of P_2 and algorithms for P_1 and P_2 yield the same results on I and f(I) respectively. In other words f is a function which embeds problem P_1 and P_2. Thus if one has a decision procedure for P_2 then one can use it to construct a decision procedure for P_1. Given an instance I of P_1, compute f(I) and then apply the decision procedure for P_2 to f(I). By the definition of p-reducibility the answer will be the correct one. In addition, since f is computable in polynomial time, the decision procedure for P_1 will be marginally less efficient than the decision procedure for P_2. A Yes/No problem is NP-complete if it is in NP and any problem in NP is p-reducible to it. In a certain sense, a problem which is NP-complete is among the hardest problems in NP. If an NP-complete problem is solvable in polynomial time, then all problems in NP are. Remarkably, this class contains hundreds of important combinatorial problems form logic, language theory, database, automata theory, graph theory, and optimization theory. The existence of a polynomial time algorithm for any one of them yields polynomial algorithms for each of them. Cook (1971) defined NP-completeness and showed that the decision problem for propositional calculus is NP-complete. The computationally equivalent (dual) problem to the decision problem is the *satisfiability problem*: Given a formula of the propositional calculus in conjunctive normal form (CNF), is there an assignment to the variables for which the formula evaluates to "True"? The satisfiability problem is basic because the propositional calculus is a primary component of any deduction system.

P is the class of Yes/No problems for which there exists a deterministic polynomial time solution. Thus NP-complete problems are tractable if and only if P = NP. The preponderance of evidence suggests that NP-complete problems are intractable, although a proof of this fact does not appear to be imminent.

PSPACE is the class of Yes/No problems which can be solved deterministically by a computer whose memory usage is bounded by a polynomial in the length of the input. It is not difficult to show that $NP \subseteq PSPACE$. It is unknown, although conjectured, that the inclusion is proper. Using a notion of reducibility closely related to p-reducibility, we define a problem to be *PSPACE-hard* if any problem in PSPACE can be reduced to it. It has been shown that the decision problem for quantified propositional logic (Schaefer, 1978), go (Lichtenstein and Sipser, 1978) and checkers (Fraenkel et al., 1978) are all PSPACE-hard. Quantified propositional logic extends the propositional calculus by permitting quantification over propositional variables. Quantified propositional logic is known to be in PSPACE and so is *PSPACE-complete*. The decision procedures for checkers and go determine whether or not the player who moves first has a forced win from some given position. In order to study the asymptotic complexity of these problems they are generalized to boards of arbitrary size. It is interesting to note that while playing perfect checkers appears computationally difficult, playing almost optimal checkers is well within current AI technology.

Deductive capability is important to most AI research. The results cited here regarding FOL, PA, quantified propositional logic and propositional satisfiability are representative of results on the complexity of deduction. These negative results should not discourage attempts to build deductive systems but they must be considered when constructing such a system. A naive implementation of the standard decision procedures will be hopelessly inefficient.

It is not surprising that from the point of view of worst-case asymptotic analysis the AI problems that we have discussed are intractable. The "macro" analysis of these problems by complexity theory defines the fundamental approach required for these problems, but not specific solutions. This has led AI work into heuristic search as a means of coping with intractability. We shall now consider complexity issues surrounding these techniques.

3. Search and complexity

The theory of heuristic search, expressed as searching state-graphs for solutions to deductive problems is now in its second decade. It is increasingly theoretical in its content and strongly linked to other areas of algorithm design and analysis (Nilsson, 1980, Ibaraki, 1976, Pearl, 1981).

Early AI researchers were concerned that exhaustive proof methods over undecidable domains were computationally infeasible. Hence they looked toward ad-hoc or heuristic schemes to search these spaces more efficiently. However they had only the loosest forms of comparative experiments to justify the efficacy of their methods in such a way to suggest generality and power - more or less this was proof by appellation.

The current systematic outlook originates chiefly in the work of Doran and Michie (1966), on the graph traverser; Hart, Nilsson and Raphael (1968) in formulating A* and Pohl (1969) in using adversary analysis to develop a theory of efficiency. This work was the AI adaptation of Moore-Dijkstra path algorithms using numerical evaluations of heuristic information. Samuel's checker playing program was an early demonstration of the effectiveness of this approach.

While operations research developed dynamic programming and branch-and-bound algorithms to solve classical optimization problems such as the traveling salesman problem, AI research used similar methods to handle puzzles, games and theorem proving.

The 1950's and 60's saw most AI deductive routines tested on sample problems, such as Monkey and Bananas, without a theory of performance. The Edinburgh work attempted to experimentally compare efficiency over classes of heuristic search methods and the subsequent work using adversary proof techniques (Pohl, 1969) provided theoretical models in which improvement could be suggested, tested, and refined.

Without a complexity or analysis of algorithms point of view there would have been little hope of discovering a number of counterintuitive improvements in heuristic search algorithms. (One can confidently say this because researchers in AI uniformly held such beliefs.) The inclusion of both a cost-to-date term and a heuristic estimator as proposed in the A* algorithm was a departure from standard practice as seen in the state-difference measure of GPS. Common practice was to not include cost-to-date information as it was so much "spilt milk". A* included it because of the constraint of requiring a shortest solution. However, it was demonstrated (Pohl, 1970) that the weighted inclusion of both terms in a heuristic search program was superior to simple heuristic search even when no shortest solution was required.

There is psychological importance to this result. A problem solver feeling heuristically close to a solution will continue to explore the state tree in that region. However, if after a significant length of time, no further progress is seen in that region the problem solver will abandon that (approach) region for an alternate region even though it heuristically evaluates as further away. The improved complexity model suggests that a problem solver see progress in proportion to effort. The original ad-hoc algorithms such as GPS suggested only that the problem solver had a notion of nearing a solution or reducing the differences to a solution.

4. Error

The complexity model has introduced the concept of error in two ways into search models. One source is the inaccuracy of the estimating functions. Another is the imprecision in obtaining a (cost) optimum solution. In real life we are not guaranteed the best chess move or the safest medical treatment; but we would settle for nearly optimum moves (or treatments) in both cases. There are examples of efficient algorithms that can guarantee near optimality where no known algorithms can efficiently find guaranteed optimum solutions (Ibarra and Kim, 1975). By settling for approximation schemes rather than exact solutions, complexity theory thus suggests one way out of the combinatorial explosion.

However, it is the first sense of error, inaccuracy in the heuristic estimators, that we want to discuss. In retrospect, it seems to us that the most profound addition to the theory of problem solving was not in seeing the heuristic as a measure of closeness to a goal (a relatively transparent notion), but in the counterpoint notion that error is what really characterizes heuristic power. This is similar to the ideas in numerical analysis where approximation schemes are more strongly understood in terms of error. Indeed, it is already implicit in undertaking to solve problems in undecidable domains that one accedes to the use of imprecise methods (and even inconsistent methods, as alluded to by Turing).

While Pohl (1977a), Munyer and Pohl(1976), and Huyn, Dechter and Pearl (1980) all present theorems relating error to search efficiency - the latter paper extending these results to probabilistic cases; the real significance is that the theory allows methodological advances. Error, efficiency, cost of a solution, and insight are all interrelated in potentially testable ways. DeGroot in his testing of chess ability found that a chief correlate to chess ablility was error in placing pieces on the board after a brief 5 second exposure of the position. This was more crucial than extent of tree search which seemed independent of performance. In effect, the grandmaster's language (or evaluation function) was a more encompassing and accurate positional description.

The classic AI approach of using heuristics to guide a search toward a solution to a Yes/No problem is currently being applied by Goldberg (1981) to an important combinatorial problem, the *subset-sum problem*. Given positive integers a_1, a_2 ..., a_n and a positive integer b, is there a subset of $\{a_1, ... ,a_n\}$ which sums precisely to be? Finding the subset whose sum, without exceeding b, comes as close to b as possible is the optimization version of this problem. Fully polynomial approximation algorithms exist for this optimization problem (Lawler, 1977). Approximation schemes utilize heuristics whose effectiveness is provable. The approximation scheme can be used to guide the search. Since they have guaranteed effectiveness, they can be used to prune the search tree of vertices that cannot possibly lead to a solution to the Yes/No problem. We expect techniques like these will be applied to other combinatorial problems.

Although many of the problems and techniques of AI and complexity theory are the same, the theorist demands provable results while the AI researcher is satisfied with performance in an applied domain. Both approaches have serious shortcomings. Asymptotic worst case analysis may be the most appropriate universal standard on which to analyze algorithms, but it does not wholly correspond to practical usefulness. The size of the problem instance may have to be very large before an asymptotic improvement is manifest. An average-case rather than worst-case analysis will give a better assessment of the true effectiveness of the algorithm. Similarly, it is difficult to get a true assessment of the effectiveness of an algorithm when it has been tested on a set of sample problems which have been chosen on an ad hoc basis. There is no effective means of comparison of two algorithms that have been tested on different sets of test cases. As analytical tools become more developed and as AI domains become well understood and hence more amenable to formalization and analysis, a finer evaluation of the quality of AI algorithms will be possible.

5. Coping with complexity

NP-complete and undecidable problems are hard in the abstract, but are often concretely manageable. This is because computationally feasible rules give surprisingly good results for most problems. Indeed, complexity theory is often misleading for practical cases because its results are based on its design of pathological instances. Let us review some of the techniques that cope with reducing complexity.

6. Local heuristics

Consider the problem of finding a knight's tour on a large chess-board, or more generally a Hamilton path in a graph. This is the non-metric version of the TSP (Pohl, 1967). In the 19th century, it was discovered that the following rule worked in finding knight's tours:

Warnsdorff's rule:
Move the knight to an unvisited square that has fewest next moves.

This rule is computable in linear time. When the knight is moved to a new square all squares it was connected to are decremented in connectivity. Initially the connectivity of the chessboard for knights is Fig. 1.

The rule suggests that a corner square is best as a starting point. Why? Because these have the fewest ways in and out and so are most easily

2	3	4	4	4	4	3	2
3	4	6	6	6	6	4	3
4	6	8	8	8	8	6	4
4	6	8	8	8	8	6	4
4	6	8	8	8	8	6	4
4	6	8	8	8	8	6	4
3	4	6	6	6	6	4	3
2	3	4	4	4	4	3	2

Fig. 1. Chessboard connectivity under knight moves.

disconnected from the main graph. The rule is easily applied to the general Hamilton graph problem and is easily modified to produce a recursive version that in testing has never failed in the chess case (Pohl, 1967).

7. Divide and conquer

A problem whose complexity is a a^n, $a > 1$, (exponential) if divisible into two relatively same size subproblems whose solution when recombined solves the original yields $2a^{n/2}$ complexity. In this general category we wish to specifically discuss two ideas: bi-directional search and the use of of lemmas.

In many problem instances both an explicit starting state and terminal state are known. What is desired is a deductive chain connecting the two states. For example in theorem proving one starts with some clauses and obtains the null clause. In puzzles such as the Rubik cube or 15 block puzzle one has a desired terminal configuration. Algorithms such as GPS or A* are uni-directional proceeding from an initial state or states. By simultaneously exploring the state space from both the initial state and the goal state, one hopes that paths of twice the length that a uni-directional scheme would find are computationally feasible.

The merits of this approach are easily demonstrated in the classical two-node shortest path problem. Let us see the savings of such a search in a regular two-dimensional lattice with unit cost edges (see Fig. 2).

The example in Fig. 2 shows that for lattices of degree four, uni-directional search examines $2n^2 + 2n + 1$ nodes, and bi-directional search examines $n^2 + 2n + 2$ nodes, where n is the number of edges from s to t. The savings would be

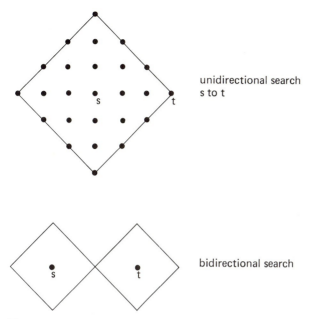

Fig. 2. Uni-directional vs. bi-directional search.

greater in lattices of higher degree. If bi-directionality is applicable, it alone as a technique allows paths of twice the length of uni-directionally solvable problems to be computed.

These arguments have been extensively confirmed in practice. Tests on randomly generated graphs solving both the shortest path problem and the network flow problem result in substantial computational savings. These savings are seen when the *cardinality comparison rule* is applied to select the direction of search. In cardinality comparison (Pohl, 1971) the search is pursued in the direction of fewest candidates. Modifying the Dinic-Karzanov network flow procedure (Pohl, 1977b) with a bi-directional flow augmenting routine provides practical improvement.

Now it is appealing to extend the same idea to heuristic search. Indeed the mechanics of performing a bi-directional heuristic search are no more difficult. However initial results on real problems have been disappointing. A non-heuristic breadth-first search can be thought as expanding the search as a wave front. Heuristic search has the flavor of expanding search as a cone. Two spheres are guaranteed to intersect near a mid-point of search. Two narrow cones, unless well directed, will tend to meet near an end-point. Narrow searches, the hoped for product of good heuristics, mediated against intersection. The practical result is that one ends up often with twice the effort of uni-directional heuristic search.

We can illustrate this theoretically using relative error in the heuristic and a tree space analysis. h(x) has relative error r, if for all x in G,

$$(1 - r) h^*(x) \leq (1 + r) h^*(x),$$

$0 \leq r \leq 1$, where h* is the exact distance to goal and G is the problem space. This model conforms to the commonly observed property of heuristic that they are better nearer the goal. Imagine performing a bi-directional search in a binary tree space (see Fig. 3). Consider a search maximally misdirected such that it searches tree T_j, the subtree hanging from the j-th node on the shortest path from s to t. The total number of nodes expanded will be

$$\sum_{j=1}^{k} T_j$$

where s and t are k edges apart. The worst case is

$$\text{height}(T_j) = \frac{2kr}{1-r} - 2 - \frac{1}{1-r}$$

and

$$|T_j| = 2^{\text{height}(T_j)+1} - 1$$

Both the forward and backward search are maximally misdirected. Since most

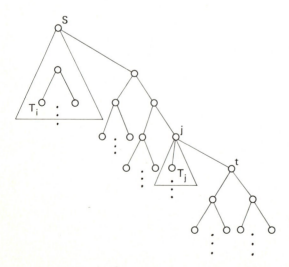

Fig. 3. Binary tree space.

of the wasted effort occurs at the beginning of the search, bi-directional search ends up nearly twice as expensive as unidirectional search.

Divide and conquer can be applied recursively to the generated sub-problems. The effectiveness of this technique depends on dividing the problem into equally sized subproblems and combining the solutions to the subproblems into a solution the complete problem. The worst case for quicksort occurs when problem division is uneven.

The most effective known algorithm for the satisfiability algorithm is the Davis-Putnam procedure. We have already discussed the importance of this problem to deduction and its apparent intractability. The Davis-Putnam procedure is based on divide and conquer. Given a CNP formula, a variable is chosen from which two subproblems are derived, corresponding to the assignments of True and False to the variable. The subproblems are such that the original formula is satisfiable if and only if either of the two subproblems are. In the worst case, the subproblems may each have only one less clause than the original formula - a situation that results in exponential complexity. However, like quicksort, on average the division is very effective . This leads to a polynomial average time bound for the procedure when the uniform distribution is assumed (Goldberg, 1979). This result confirms the observed effectiveness of the algorithm in a theorem-proving context (Davis et al., 1962)

Average-case and worst-case analyses each contribute important information about the complexity of an algorithm. Average-case analyses are more difficult combinatorially, and require an assumption regarding the probability distribution whose relevance to practical circumstance can be called into question. A recently developed notion of *probabilistic algorithm* has the potential of making significant advances in the field of algorithms. These algorithms incorporate randomization directly into the algorithm itself, eliminating the need to make explicit distributional assumptions. Probabilistic algorithm can be used to obtain exact results with certainty or with arbitrarily small error probability with little computational effort.

8. Lemmas

While practical difficulties exist in making bi-directional heuristic search efficient, our common sense experience tells us that working backward and forward is often useful. Frequently, searches are asymmetric. One direction of search is much narrower than the other (see Fig. 4). In this case the cardinality comparison rule will lead to highly efficient bi-directional search.

In the worst case bi-directional search is twice as expensive as uni-directional search, but when it works there is an exponential reduction of effort. Several suggestions have been made to improve its effectiveness. Thus, De Champeaux and Sint (1977) have proposed using a front-to-front evaluation

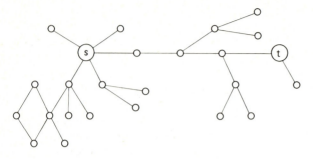

Fig. 4. Asymmetry of graph searches.

function. Rather than extend the search from that node nearest the opposite goal, one looks pairwise over all nodes in both search fronts choosing the pair which is closest. Unfortunately, the evaluation process is very expensive per node expansion.

An attractive updating idea due to Ross (1973) is to prune the search tree by identifying "distinguished nodes" or d-nodes:

> "A d-node is a node that lies on the solution path and whose value is greater than the value of any node succeeding it on the path."

Ross proves in the uni-directional case that a pruning algorithm using such nodes works as effectively as a full state search. The problem is that in most instances such nodes are only identifiable a posteriori. However, the concept does provide an attractive method for identifying the concept of "lemma" in numerical search terms. In practice lemmas are useful subtheorems. In Pohl (1979), it is proposed that these ideas be used to improve bi-directional heuristic search. Assume that a bi-directional search from s to t finds at some point the d-nodes s' and t'. Then store as lemmas the solutions s to s' and t' to t and solve the subproblem s' to t'. These candidate d-nodes will be selected after a predefined amount of search shows them to have the property of d-nodes; namely, they evaluate as greater in value than all of their descendants.

An idea related to the intuitive notion of lemmas is problem reducibility. P-reducibility, transforming one problem into another in polynomial time, has been an important concept to complexity theory. AI has for a long time studied how to properly represent problems so that applicable known solutions can be trivially applied. This is the key to the solution of such problems as the mutilated checkerboard and Nim. Highly developed reducibility techniques of complexity theory can have fruitful application in AI domains.

9. Complexity and AI future

We have demonstrated the positive value of complexity work to AI. A critical and important area is the relation of *negative results* to AI. Minsky and Papert in their book on Perceptrons were able to demonstrate the infeasibility of a particular approach to producing AI. Similarly Chomsky has shown how a Skinnerian model was inadequate for natural language comprehension. The NP and undecidability work in complexity are not meant to keep workers from attacking these problems, but instead to provide suggestions of how to avoid certain failure; e.g., comprehensive theorem provers are likely to be excessively expensive but special rules such as unit-resolution may be efficient over many particular cases.

Complexity measures provide a more precise model for human cognitive theory. Kotov (1971) and DeGroot both characterize chess knowledge and tree search. By teaching computationally inexpensive algorithms to a human problem solver one could perhaps improve on their idiosyncratically developed methods. It has been found that people capable of feats of memory and feats of numerical calculation have taught themselves efficient methods of calculation that minimize memory use.

The combinatorial explosion (Lighthill, 1973) is readily identified as a chief obstacle to effective problem solving. Search and deduction is a core-intellectual skill or as Newell (1981) has put it:

"All intelligent activity is based on search."

If this is the case then algorithms that search become models for general cognitive skills. In this regard, GPS and attendant protocol analysis represented an early attempt at an information processing based psychology. However most of this work was qualitative and unconvincing, because the test problems were toy problems. To be convincing such algorithms must be more than retrofitted to protocols but must deal in reasonable ways with the combinatorial explosion. Thus a cognitive theory must have complexity measures.

ARTIFICIAL AND HUMAN INTELLIGENCE (A. Elithorn and R. Banerji, editors)
Elsevier Science Publishers, B.V.
© NATO, 1984

Chapter 3

KNOWLEDGE-BASED SELF-ORGANIZING MEMORY FOR EVENTS *

JANET L. KOLODNER

*School of Information and Computer Science,
Georgia Institute of Technology, Atlanta, GA 30332, USA*

Summary

As new unanticipated items are added to a memory, it must be able to reorganize itself to maintain retrieval efficiency. This paper will present an algorithm for knowledge-based memory reorganization and a fact retrieval system called CYRUS which uses the algorithm.

1. Introduction

One interesting aspect of human memory is that they never seem to run out of space. Furthermore, the vast amount of knowledge people have does not interfere significantly with their memory capabilities (Smith, Adams and Schorr, 1978). Experts, who know a lot about particular subjects, can remember facts in their domain of expertise much easier than non-experts, who presumably have fewer facts to remember.

We can explain this by inferring that as people learn new facts, they integrate them with what they already know, reorganizing memory to make the important facts accessible. Previous knowledge aids in deciding where and how to place new inputs in memory.

As computer scientists, our interest in this problem stems from the problem of organizing information in a computer memory. As new information is added to a computer memory, we want its retrieval processes to remain efficient. This requires automatic reorganization.

This paper will outline necessary characteristics of a self-organizing memory for events, and will present CYRUS, a self-organizing computer program

---

* This work was supported in part by the Advanced Research Projects Agency of the Department of Defense and monitored under the Office of Naval Research under contract N00014-75-c-1111 while the author was in residence at Yale University. It is also partially supported by the National Science Foundation under Grant No. IST-8116892.

(Kolodner, 1980, 1981, 1983). Given a new fact about former Secretaries of State Cyrus Vance or Edmund Muskie, CYRUS integrates it into its already-existing memory organization. It retrieves facts from its memory when queried in English. Following is a dialog with CYRUS:

- Has Vance talked to Gromyko recently?
  YES, MOST RECENTLY IN GENEVA IN DECEMBER
- Did he talk to him about SALT?
  YES, FOR 5 HOURS.
- When did he leave Geneva?
  ON DECEMBER 24

2. Problems

An important function of a memory is remembering, or retrieval. A memory which does not slow down as it gets larger must never do sequential search. This implies that memory's categories must have some internal organization that allows retrieval without sequential enumeration.

The traditional solution to that problem within computer science has been indexing. If we propose indexing as a solution in conceptual categories, then we must specify (1) which kinds of indices are appropriate and (2) how indices for items added to memory can be chosen. To facilitate retrieval without enumeration, indices should be based on *salient* features of categories. A salient feature is one which is likely to be used in identifying an item to be retrieved from the category or in describing an event to be added to a category (e.g., destinations of trips, participants and topics of meetings).

As new events are added to memory, they must be indexed in appropriate memory categories. Indexing serves to both discriminate individual events and divide a category into reasonable-sized subcategories. In addition, it also allows similarities between events to be noticed and generalizations to be made, two intelligent processes a memory should have.

When two events are indexed in the same way, a subcategory can be formed, indexed in the parent by the feature that indexed the two events. Similarities between the two events can be extracted and stored as generalized information associated with the new subcategory. That generalized information can then be used during understanding, retrieval, and later memory update. Generalized information is not static, but changes with the addition of new events. Because later information might contradict a previous generalization, and because all generalizations cannot be made on the basis of only two items, memory update must provide for recovery from bad generalizations and control of later generalizations.

Because all retrieval specifications and new entries to memory cannot be anticipated, there is no organization of memory which will enable easy memory access every time. A good organization, however, will allow search to be directed only to relevant items, ensuring that only a small number of items will have to be searched at any time. As memory is augmented by new items, good organization must be maintained. The following list summarizes some of the problems involved in creating and maintaining good memory organization:

1. How is a new item entered into a conceptual category, and how are its indices chosen?
2. What is the role of generalization in memory processing?
3. How can generalization be directed?
4. When is it appropriate to create a new subcategory?
5. How are new categories created?
6. How can the generalized information associated with a category be derived?
7. How can memory recover from useless generalizations?

3. Initial memory organization in CYRUS

CYRUS' conceptual categories are called Episodic Memory Organization Packets (E-MOPs). E-MOPs organize similar episodes according to their differences and keep track of their similarities (Kolodner, 1980b; Schank, 1980). An E-MOP is a net in which each node is either an E-MOP or an event. Each E-MOP has two important aspects: (1) generalized information characterizing its episodes, and (2) tree-like structures that index its episodes by their differences. An E-MOP's norms include information describing its events, such as their usual participants, locations, and topics, and their usual relationships to other events.

An E-MOP's indices correspond to event features, and can index either individual events or specialized E-MOPs. When an E-MOP holds only one episode with a particular feature, the corresponding index will point to the individual episode. When two or more episodes in an E-MOP share the same feature, its corresponding index will point to a specialized sub-MOP which organizes the events with that feature. In this way, MOP/subMOP hierarchies are formed.

This organization provides rich cross-indexing of events in memory. Specification of any discriminating set of features within an E-MOP allows retrieval of the event with those features. In a richly-indexed organization such as this, enumeration of a memory category should never be necessary for retrieval. Instead, search keys specifying a conceptual category and indices to be traversed are created from question search keys, thereby inferring relevant paths through the memory structures. In this way, search is directed only to categories and subcategories whose events are relevant.

4. Automatic indexing

4.1. Maintaining discriminability

The first step in adding a new event to an E-MOP is to choose appropriate features of the event for indexing. Events should be indexed by features which differentiate them from other events indexed in the same E-MOP. Consider, for example, how the following event should be indexed in memories with the properties below:

EVI: Cyrus Vance has a meeting with Andrei Gromyko in Russia about the Afghanistan invasion.

Suppose the "diplomatic meetings" E-MOP we were adding this event to had one of the following characteristics:

Case 1: Vance has met many times before with Gromyko, but never in Russia, and never about the Afghanistan invasion.
Case 2: Vance has been in Russia for the past two weeks meeting with Gromyko every day about the Afghanistan situation.

In the first case, the topic and location of EV1 can distinguish it from other meetings in memory. Therefore, either of those features would be reasonable indices for EVI in a "diplomatic meetings" MOP. In the second case, however, its location and topic cannot distinguish this meeting from other meetings already indexed in that E-MOP. Indexing on those features will not be helpful in discriminating this meeting from others.

To maintain discriminability between events in an E-MOP, normal aspects of a situation should not be indexed, while weird and different aspects of a situation should. Indexing by a norm would supply memory with unneeded redundancy, and violate economy of storage. Differences between events, on the other hand, differentiate them from each other, providing *discriminability*. Organizing events according to differences allows events to be recognized individually. If a unique difference from a norm is specified in a retrieval key the event indexed by that feature can be retrieved. In addition, *the more general* a unique feature used as an index is, *the more retrievable* the event being indexed will be. A more general description of a feature will make a better index because it will be accessible in more cases.

Another important property indices should have is *predictive power*. A feature which is predictive often co-occurs with another event feature. In a "diplomatic meetings" MOP, for example, the nationality of participants can help predict the meeting's topic, and is a good predictive feature for indexing. These predictions are used during retrieval for elaboration, during understanding to make predictions, and during memory update to limit later indexing.

4.2. Choosing indices

These criteria for discriminability suggest the following algorithm for index selection:

Index selection

> Select the types of features from the event
> that have been predictive previously

↓

> Get rid of
> (1) features known to be non-predictive
> (2) E-MOP norms

↓

> Choose most general way of describing
> those features which are unique

One potential problem with multiple indexing is combinatorial explosion of indices in memory. This problem is controlled by indexing only differences which are predictive of other features. In that way, indexing at lower levels of the memory structure is constrained. Generalization is the tool that builds up norms and controls indexing.

5. Creating new E-MOPs

After choosing features for indexing, events must be indexed in appropriate E-MOPs by the chosen features. A feature chosen for indexing can have one of three relationships to the E-MOP (Kolodner, 1980):

1. There is nothing yet indexed in the E-MOP with that feature.
2. There is one item with that feature indexed in the E-MOP.
3. There is an E-MOP indexed by that feature.

If there is not already an index for a feature (case 1), then one is created for it. Any time an event is indexed by a feature unique to an E-MOP, it can be retrieved from that E-MOP by specifying that feature. Thus, the more features an event has that are unique to an E-MOP, the more ways there will be of retrieving it uniquely. The rule below summarizes the process of creating a new index:

Index Creation

IF there is no prior index for a relevant feature of an event
THEN
    (1) construct an index
    (2) index the event's description there

The second time an event with a particular feature is added to an E-MOP, a new sub-E-MOP can be created. When a second event is indexed at a point where there is just one other event, the previous event is remembered. This is called *reminding* (Schrank, 1980). Reminding triggers the creation of a new E-MOP. The current and previous events are compared for common aspects. Similarities between the two events are extracted, and a new E-MOP with generalized information based on those two occurrences is created:

E-MOP Creation

IF there is one event indexed at an index point for a new event
THEN
    (1) create a new E-MOP at that point
    (2) extract the similarities of the two events and add those as norms of the new E-MOP
    (3) index the two events in that E-MOP according to their differences from its norms

When there is already a sub-MOP at the point where an event is being indexed (case 3), the new event is indexed in the sub-MOP by the same procedure used to index it in the more general E-MOP. In addition, he new event is compared against the generalized information of both the parent E-MOP and the sub-MOP, and the validity of previous generalizations is checked and refined:

E-MOP Refinement

IF there is an E-MOP at an index point for a new event
THEN
    (1) index the event in that E-MOP
    (2) check the validity of its generalizations as necessary
    (3) update its generalizations as necessary

6. Generalization

Generalization during E-MOP creation makes the memory reorganization process more effective for three reasons:

1. Generalized information can provide guidelines to the elaboration process (Kolodner, 1980, 1983) during retrieval.
2. Generalized information constrains later indexing.
3. Generalized information is used during understanding to make predictions and during question answering to give default answers.

6.1. Initial generalization

In CYRUS, two types of generalization are done - initial generalization and generalization refinement. Initial generalization happens when the second event with a particular feature is added to an E-MOP. It is a process of feature extraction and comparison. Common features of the current event and the one already in memory are extracted and added to the norms of the new E-MOP.

6.2. Generalization refinement

Because some initial generalizations are more reasonable than others, generalizations often need refinement. Unreasonable initial generalizations must be discovered and deleted from an E-MOP's norms. In addition, new events must be monitored to see if additional generalized information can be extracted from them.

6.3. Additional generalizations

When an E-MOP reaches a stable size (6 in CYRUS), each time a new event is added to it, CYRUS checks each sub-MOP referred to by the incoming event to see if any index a large majority of the events in the E-MOP. If one does, CYRUS makes additional generalizations about events in the parent E-MOP by collapsing the sub-MOP and merging its generalizations with those of the parent.

Collapsing sub-MOPs

IF a sub-MOP indexes a large majority of the events in its parent E-MOP
THEN
        (1) collapse the sub-MOP
        (2) get rid of its index
        (3) add the indexed feature plus other norms of the sub-MOP to the generalized information associated with the parent E-MOP.

6.4. Recovery from bad generalizations

Recovery from bad generalizations is more complex. When new information and events contradict a previously-made generalization, that generalization must be removed as one of the E-MOP's norms.

This raises a special problem. While a feature is one of the norms of an E-MOP, events are not indexed by that feature. On the other hand, if a feature is included in the norms of an E-MOP, then many of the events already in the E-MOP have it as a feature. Because events were not indexed by that feature, however, it would be impossible to go back and find all events supporting the generalization.

Generalization removal, then, can have grave implications in retrieval. If a retrieval key specified a feature that had been removed as a generalization, but which had not yet been indexed, then the retrieval processes would not be able to find any trace in memory of an event with that feature. It would have to conclude that there had never been such an event in memory.

To correct this problem, an index to an empty sub-MOP is created each time a feature is removed from a MOP's norms. In addition, the feature is marked as having once been "generalized". This enables the retrieval functions to return with the message "there may be events with this description, but I can't find particular ones", instead of failing completely if no distinct event can be found. This message also triggers search strategies which attempt to find the sought event by some other route. During later indexing, that sub-MOP will be treated like any other.

Recovery from false generalization

IF a norm has been disconfirmed
THEN
      (1) remove it from the E-MOP
      (2) create an empty sub-MOP for it indexed by that feature
      (3) add other features removed from the E-MOP's norms at the same time
      (4) mark the new E-MOP as "once generalized"

---

7. More about CYRUS

CYRUS has two data bases - one each for former Secretaries of State Cyrus Vance and Edmund Muskie. CYRUS' E-MOPs include one for each of type of activity a secretary of state does, e.g., "diplomatic meetings", "briefings", "diplomatic trips", "state dinners", "speeches", "flying". Although CYRUS started out with the same E-MOPs and initial memory organization for each man, because of their differing experiences, the new categories built by the system for Muskie are somewhat different than those built for Vance.

CYRUS takes conceptual representations of episodes as input. Thus, stories must be analyzed and a representation must be built before sending them to CYRUS. CYRUS has two modes of receiving representations of stories. In one mode, the stories are analyzed and representations encoded by the human reader are integrated into CYRUS' memory. In its second mode of operation, CYRUS is connected to FRUMP (DeJong, 1979) to form a complete fact retrieval system called *CyFr* (Kolodner, 1980b). FRUMP reads stories from the UPI news wire, and sends conceptual summaries of stories about Muskie and Vance to CYRUS. CYRUS then adds the new events to its memory and answers questions about them. CYRUS' Muskie memory has been built up entirely from FRUMP-processed stories. Its Vance memory is built partially of FRUMP-processed stories and partially of stories encoded by hand.

The following is a story *CyFr* has processed about Muskie. FRUMP produced the summary, and sent its conceptual representation to CYRUS. After adding the events to its memory, CYRUS answered the questions:

Carter begins going from the United States to Italy and Yugoslavia to talk. Secretary of State Edmund Muskie will go from the United States to Asia this month to have talks with ASEAN. Muskie will have talks with NATO in Ankara in June.

* * * * *

– Have you been to Europe recently?
  YES, MOST RECENTLY LAST MONTH.
– Why did you go there?
  TO TALK TO ANDREI GROMYKO.
– Are you going to Asia?
  YES, THIS MONTH.
– Who will you talk to?
  WITH NATO IN ANKARA, TURKEY.

The following are some of the generalizations CYRUS has made:

CYRUS' Generalizations

1. Meetings in Middle East are about Arab-Israeli peace.
2. When Vance meets in the Middle East with Egyptians, he also meets with Israelis, and the topic is the Camp David Accords.
3. When Vance negotiates with Egyptians, the topic is the Camp David Accords.
4. Trips to Russia are for the purpose of negotiating SALT.

The Vance and Muskie memories started out the same, but after adding events to the two data bases, their organizations differ in 4 ways: (1) The indices are different. (2) The types of indices are different. While the Vance E-MOP has topic indices and larger episode indices, the Muskie E-MOP has neither of those. (3) The norms associated with corresponding E-MOPs are different,(i.e., different generalizations have been made). (4) The Vance E-MOP indexes mostly sub-MOPs, and the Muskie E-MOP indexes mostly individual events.

Although CYRUS itself is no longer being developed, it has two active descendents. The generality of CYRUS' retrieval and organizational strategies are being examined in two new areas - a world affairs expert and a medical diagnosis program. They will both work by drawing on past experience to make predictions about a current problem, and both will add new experiences to their memories, reorganizing memory appropriately and making generalizations. In working on these programs, we are investigating more sophisticated methods for index selection and creation of new categories.

Chapter 4

GPS AND THE PSYCHOLOGY OF THE RUBIK CUBIST: A STUDY IN REASONING ABOUT ACTIONS

RANAN B. BANERJI

St. Joseph's University, Philadelphia, PA 19131, USA

Summary

The paper proposes certain extensions to the paradigm for problem solving known as the General Problem Solver or GPS. Initially the paper describes this paradigm in detail. The central heuristic for the process is supplied by a so-called "difference-transformation table". While in the original GPS this table was supplied as a part of problem-specification, a number of recent efforts have succeeded in having this table constructed automatically from the problem specification.

Two difficulties are then discussed in the way of using the GPS paradigm. One, the so-called problem of "non-linearity" is well-known. The other, that of a need for a new kind of sub-problem, is not so well recognised. It is pointed out next in the paper that mechanised construction of the difference-transformation table is heavily dependent for its success on the form of the problem representation, especially on the use of move-sequences as moves.

It is then pointed out that these latter "macro-moves" can be utilised to find a satisfactory solution of the problem of non-linearity. The solution of the non-standard sub-problem generation is somewhat more difficult to come by.

These discussions suggest a slightly more general form for the GPS paradigm. The difficulties in the way of mechanising this paradigm are discussed.

1. Introduction

The purpose of this paper is to suggest some extensions and modifications to the General Problem Solver (GPS) suggested by Simon, Newell and Shaw (1953) both as a model of human problem solving and as a paradigm for general purpose problem solving programs. In the area of AI, GPS has been extended and embellished considerably (Ernst 1969, Ernst and Banerji 1977, Fikes and Nilsson 1971, Sacerdoti 1974). Some difficulties have been uncovered in the way of using these extensions, both by the workers who have used GPS in its original form and those who have developed essentially equivalent approaches (Sacerdoti 1975, Banerji and Ernst 1977).

It is our belief that some of the suggestions made by us in this paper will alleviate the difficulties encountered by later workers. Also, in the process we expect to throw some light on a major difficulty in the area of problem representation pointed out be Amarel in connection with "macro-moves" (Amarel 1966), i.e. the fact that it is often natural and convenient to consider a sequence of moves as a single move.

We are not claiming that the suggestions made here are all ready for immediate implementation and even those that may be implemented in some sort of a way, will be implemented in the best possible way. But we do believe that the paradigms suggested here are realistic enough that they point to meaningful areas of effort in the theory of problem solving.

To make our discussions precise, as well as in the interest of readers not thoroughly acquainted with GPS literature, we shall present in the next section the structure of GPS and introduce the nomenclature we shall use in the way of discussion.

We shall use several puzzles to illustrate our discussion, including the by-now-celebrated Rubik's cube. We shall, however, use other puzzles in our illustration, both in the interest of simplicity where feasible, but also to bring out the very general nature, both of the original GPS paradigm and our extensions.

2. The general problem solver

The General Problem Solver deals with problems only if they are represented to have very specific structure, which we shall shortly describe. The structure is flexible enough such that a very large class of problems can be represented with it. However, certain classes of problems (including optimisation problems) cannot be conveniently represented by it (Lauriere 1978). Nor can certain problems of knowledge-manipulation (Amarel 1981). We shall not be discussing these classes of problems.

To present a problem to the General Problem Solver one has to present the descriptions of three things in some acceptable form. First, one has to describe the set of all problem states. Second, one has to specify the the set of all desirable, or winning states, which is a subset of the set of states. Third, one has to specify the set of moves. Each move in the set of moves has to be specified by two specifications. First, one has to specify the set of states to which the move is applicable (that is, such that it is not physically or logically possible to apply the move in question to any state outside this set of states). Also, one has to specify in some general way what changes occur in the state when the move is applied.

Since GPS is a computer program, all these specifications take the forms of date structures or programs. The exact forms these presentations take determine to a great extent the possibility of the kind of operations that we shall discuss in the paper. We shall not concern ourselves with that problem. Rather, we shall discuss the semantics of the representation in terms of their abstract properties, independent of their representations. As Amarel has pointed out, these semantics often determine the form the data structures and programs have to take to make problem solving feasible. Given the specification of the problem and a specific problem state, the GPS is expected to find a solution, i.e. a sequence of applicable moves that would transform the initially given state to a desirable state. The original GPS went about the job of finding a solution by a search process aided by certain hints for pruning the search provided by the user. These hints took the form of a "difference table". In the following description of this table we shall follow an interpretation (Ernst and Banerji 1977) somewhat different from the original GPS interpretation.

We shall define a difference to be some property that all winning states are supposed to have. A state will be said to "be different" from a winning state by this difference if it does not have this property. We may also say that the state in question "has" this specific difference with the winning states in such cases. The GPS has to have specified to it a set of such properties. It is stipulated that these properties be such that any state is a winning state if and only if it has all the specified properties. These properties are to be placed by the user in a given order. We shall (more for historical reasons than anything else) call this the "order of difficulty", i.e. the first difference in the order will be called "the most difficult difference" and so on for the next ones. The real significance of this order is that GPS is supposed to "remove" these differences in the order given. That is, it chooses moves in such a way that the state initially changes to one having the first property, then into one having the first two properties and so on in sequence. To aid GPS in this choice of moves, the user also supplies another piece of information. He has to associate with each difference a list of moves which do not have any influence on removing this difference, i.e. if a state has the corresponding property, then applying any move in this list will result in a state which also has this property. Similarly, if a state does not have this propery, applying any move in this list produces a state which does not have the property. The moves in the list will be said to be irrelevant to the difference. For our present purposes, we shall call the moves outside the list relevant to the difference. This is at slight variance from the present theory but will not stand in the way of our discussion here.

The listing of the relevances is generally visualised as a table, whose rows correspond to the differences and whose columns correspond to moves or classes of moves. If move class j is relevant to difference i, then a 1 appears in the jth column of the ith row. Else a 0 appears there. The ordering of the differences are chosen to give the table a "triangular" appearance i.e. a 0 appears in each cell (i,j) of the table whenever i is less than j, i.e. everywhere above the main diagonal of this square table. The significance of this lies in the pruning technique used by GPS, which we shall describe shortly.

To remove a difference (i.e. to introduce the corresponding property into the state) GPS chooses a relevant move to apply to the state. However, there may be need for some "preliminary work" before the move is applied. The nature of this preliminary work will be commented on extensively later. Suffice it to say that the way GPS is presently conceived, this preliminary work is done only if the move chosen by the GPS in reference to the difference table is not applicable at the current state. Then the state has to be changed to a state where the move is applicable. Since the set of states at which the given move is applicable has a description just as the set of winning states has a description, one can set up a new problem where one makes the set of applicability the new winning states. This process is called "setting up a subgoal". GPS calls itself recursively on this new problem (invoking possibly a new difference table). [Note: In the original versions of GPS, differences were defined in terms of partitions rather than in terms of properties. This was because in may cases the same partitions served for all subgoals, the different winning states of the different subproblems occupying different sets in the partition. This invocation of a new table for each subgoal was found necessary for automating the construction of the difference table (vide ultra).]

GPS uses two criteria for the pruning of its search for the solution. First, it only chooses an applicable move which is relevant to the reduction of the most difficult difference in the current sub-problem. Also it never chooses a move relevant to any difference of greater difficulty which has already been removed, either in the current subproblem or in any of the active problems of which the current subproblem or an active problem is subgoal. That is, it is stipulated that a difference, once removed should never be introduced again.

We hope that in what has gone above, the formal structure of GPS and of the inputs thereto has been made sufficiently clear and precise, as well as the nature of the methods presently used. In the next section we shall discuss some of its difficulties, the recent efforts made for the removal of these difficulties, the difficulties that still remain, as well as some suggestions for removing these will be discussed later.

3. Improvement for GPS

To make GPS into the general purpose tool it was designed to be, several efforts were made to give GPS a uniform language for the description of problems. Tree and Matrix representation were used by Ernst (Ernst and Newell 1969, Ernst 1969) and logic-based languages were used by Fikes (Fikes and Nilsson 1971). Attempts were also made so that the difference table were not to be given to GPS, but would be developed by a subprogram of GPS from the problem specification itself. Some of these efforts (Quinlan and Hunt 1968) were motivated by the form of the language of the representation; others by the underlying algebraic structure of the problem. It was found in all cases, however, that the power of the table-building sub-programs were circumscribed by the specific representation used for the specific problems. One of these circumscriptions dealt with the fact that in many cases where good difference tables could be successfully constructed, the moves that seemed most natural to specify turned out on further analysis to be interpretable also as sequences of moves. That is, it was found that the ability of the program to build good GPS difference tables was heavily dependent on the problem-specification having chosen moves to be what Amarel has termed "macro-moves". We shall exemplify this presently, without going into the details of the program. However, it ought to be pointed out that the difficulty was not an artifact of the syntax chosen for the problem-representation language: it was inherently associated with the semantics, to wit, the algebraic structure represented to GPS.

In this paper we intend to shed some further light on the nature of this difficulty and methods for avoiding it. This difficulty is independent of the design philosophy of the GPS. However, this problem of macro-moves also seems relevant to another aspect of the GPS inherent in its initial design philosophy.

In section 2 above, we mentioned that after GPS chooses a move to be applied in accordance with the difference table and the most difficult difference, it has to do some "preliminary work". As GPS is presently designed, this preliminary work is performed only if the move chosen is inapplicable to the current state. In this case the preliminary work consists of devising (through the setting up of a subgoal - see above) a sequence of moves which changes the current state into a state to which the initially chosen move would be applicable.

As an example of this classical approach of the GPS, we may quote the initial "means-end-analysis" done by GPS on the celebrated Tower of Hanoi problem (see Fig. 1 in "Expert behaviour and problem representations" by S. Amarel in this volume). Consider the initial state where all the discs are on the leftmost pin and in the desireable state they are all on the rightmost pin. A well-documented analysis indicates that the most difficult difference here deals with position of the largest disc (Goldstein 1977). The move relevant to this difference is to move the largest disc from the leftmost peg. But this move is not applicable since the other pegs are all on top of it. So, preliminary to making this move, one has to apply moves so that all these discs would be removed from the leftmost peg. This is a standard technique with GPS.

However, other kinds of preliminary work often are needed in problems of this kind. One convincing example comes from Rubik's cube. The puzzle is described in Fig. 1 for the benefit of those who have so far resisted the lure of this fascinating puzzle.

Consider the state of the Rubik's cube obtained from the pristine state after the move-sequence FFD. The corner cubie, using the Hofstadter terminology (Hofstadter 1981) ufl is presently in the position dbr. There are three plane

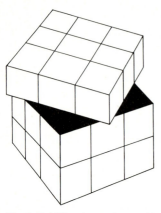

Fig. 1. Rubik's cube can be considered to be made up of 27 sub-cubes ("cubies"), arranged in three layers of nine cubies each. Each of the two horizontal faces, "up" (U) and "down" (D), "front" (F) and "back" (B), can be turned in its plane. The positions ("cubicles") occupied by the cubies, as well as the cubies themselves, are identified by their positions vis-a-vis these faces. The faces of the cube are painted six different colors but this configuration can be changed by turning the faces. Once such a jumbled configuration is attained, the problem is one of reducing the cube to its original pristine state.

rotations relevant to affecting the cubicle ufl, namely, F, U and L. However, none of these would really be effective in bringing the proper cubie to this cubicle, since the the cubie in question is not in any of these planes (we are considering here only the question of the position of the cubie, not its colour orientation). Also, each of the plane rotations are applicable, so that in classical GPS no preliminary work is needed. This leads to an impasse - unless sequences of at least two planer rotations are initially defined as single moves in the initial representation. GPS would not be able to solve this problem. However, if we allowed preliminary moves, not for making the move *APPLICABLE* but for making it *USEFUL*, then one might try to find ways of discovering - by some mechanism which we do not want to specify at present - that no move is useful for bringing a cubie to a cubicle unless the cubie and cubicle are in the same plane. Thus it would be necessary to apply either a D-move or a R- or a B-move to make any of the planer moves L,F or U useful. (Let us not go at present into the "heartache" of doing anything but DDDFF!)

In this case, as well as in the case of classical GPS preliminary work, one could interpret the phenomenon as resulting from the application of macro-moves. However, that point of view does not shed much light on the mechanism for looking for such macro-moves: the mechanism can probably be better interpreted as obtainable from the logical analysis of the rules of the puzzle. Our understanding of this reasoning action is rather weak. We shall attempt a discussion of this later on in this paper. For the present, let us return to the problem we raised earlier in this section: that the automated table-construction method available to us depends heavily on the choice of the representations of moves: these may well be represented as move-sequences.

A good example of this phenomenon comes from the puzzle "Fool's Disc" which gave us our initial hint on how to automate the construction of difference tables. The puzzle is described in Fig. 2. We discovered before we had designed the heuristics-automation program, that sums of the diameters of the disc remain unchanged by applying a half-turn to any of the discs. Similarly the sums over two perpendicular diameters (shown shaded in the figure) remain unchanged over quarter-turns of any of the discs. These observations had led to a very good difference table for the puzzle, using 45, 90 and 180 degree turns of any of the discs as the moves allowed in the puzzle. A program was designed (Goldstein 1977) which could find such difference tables for a number of puzzles, thereby taking a step forward in the program for further automation of the GPS described at the beginning of this section. The guiding principle of the program was to find properties of the states of the puzzle which remained invariant over moves and then using these properties to describe W. the set of winning states.

Initially all this looked very good till we realised that the success of the method depended heavily on what we chose to give to the program as "moves", since it looked for invariance of properties over these. For instance, the program discovered that the sums of the diameters in fool's disc were invariant over half turns only because half turns were considered to be moves.

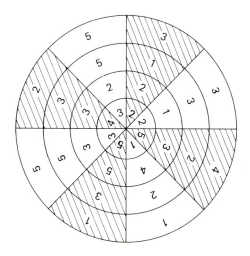

Fig. 2. The Fool's Disk Puzzle. Four concentric disks turn around a common center. Eight numbers are arranged around their rims as shown. The disks have to be turned so the numbers along each radius add to 12. The shaded spokes are not a part of the puzzle – see text for an explanation of how they facilitate solution.

One could as easily have specified that the only possible moves were 1/8th turns of any disk. If this were done, then the sum over the diameters would be invariant over a sequence of two moves. Hence the search for invariances would be a much longer, less efficient search.

The hint we finally got about the resolution of this difficulty actually came from our being faced with another well-known difficulty besetting general problem solving programs, the problem some people call the problem of linearity. This problem arises out of the fact that GPS, by adhering to the rule "once a difference is removed, it should never be reintroduced", gets in the way of finding a solution.

It is our belief – although the road from this belief to the actual implementation of a better heuristic-discovery program may be long or even non-existent – that a proper resolution of the problem of linearity would also lead to the resolution of the problem arising out of the need to describe move-sequences as moves.

In the next section we want to describe a possible design for an improved form of the GPS where the difference table is generated during the process of problem solving. This will be followed by a discussion of the difficulties in the way. These difficulties are similar to the difficulties in the way of finding move-sequences which make other moves useful, as we discussed at the beginning of this section.

4. Move sequences and linearity

Let us make some initial points by referring once again to Rubik's cube.

To the best of my knowledge, all but a very few (and I really have only heard rumors of these latter) methods of solution suggested for this puzzle follows (albeit in a very superficial way, as we shall soon see) the classical GPS paradigm. That is, given that all the surfaces should be brought to the same color, the method proceeds by restoring a part of the cube (a surface, four edges of one surface, four corners of one surface, etc.) and then going on to restoring other parts. Most beginners are frustrated in this effort, however, because they also try to follow the other dictate of the GPS paradigm, namely that once a part of the cube has been restored to a desired state, it should be left undisturbed while attempting to restore the other parts. This effort is frustrated since this severely cramps the number of moves available. That is, the average aspiring "cubist" discovers the problem of "non-linearity" quite early!

At this point one discovers or is introduced to the concept of "macro-moves". Let us exemplify this be taking the example where the entire top layer of the cube has been reduced to its desireable state, i.e., every cubie is in its correct cubicle in the correct orientation. On attempting to "clean up" the bottom layer one finds (say) that one can, by performing several D turns, bring the fdr and fdl cubies to their correct cubicles (albeit not in their correct orientations). However, one cannot get the bdl and bdr cubies in their place – they have exchanged places! U and D turns cannot change this state of affairs (U do nothing to the d cubies and any D turns merely upsets the position of the ubl and ubr cubie!). The other four moves upset the pristine state of the U layer. If one is not prone to give up on the basis of this shallow argument, one realises that any harm done to the top layer by a move can be corrected for – and not necessarily by reversing the move. One can destroy the top layer by a certain move-sequence and then restore it by another move sequence. The total sequence, while leaving the top layer clean introduces changes in the other layers. As a matter of curiosity, FFFDFLLLFLFFFDD does exchange the dbl and dbr cubies leaving the top layer unchanged.

Resisting the temptation to continue playing with the cube, what this suggests is that the GPS paradigm as presently interpreted in machines be replaced by a paradigm similar enough that humans would have no difficulty making the shift (shifting for the computer may be another matter). That is, instead of saying "once a difference is removed, do not use any move relevant to this difference while removing the next difference" one has to say "once a difference is removed, only such move sequences should be used to remove the next difference as keeps the first difference removed at the end of the sequence".

In what follows we intend to put a somewhat computerizeable meat on this skeleton, suggest some changes in the form of the difference table and make some suggestions on their mechanisation.

5. Constructing a difference table

In what has gone above we have noticed two problems with the GPS as presently conceived.

(1) Some moves, even though they are relevant by definition, is not effective in removing a difference in all cases.
(2) Linearity of solutions is often unattainable.

The discussion has also indicated that if one represents carefully selected move sequences as moves, both of these problems can be overcome. For the original GPS, which demanded that one supply the difference table with the problem, this would be somewhat acceptable: hints were a part of the problem specification. Presently, when the difference table is being constructed automatically from the "raw" problem specification, both of these difficulties present a problem.

The construction of the difference table depends on two components:

specifying the set of differences and specifying the relevance of the different moves to them. Let us look at the way the two components have been handled in the cases where the states are represented by conjunctions of statements. The conjuncts describing the winning states serve as differences, taken in proper combinations. Then the moves as given in the problem description are analysed to check which conjuncts are introduced and removed by each move from the states to yield their relevancies. In the somewhat more free-wheeling algebraic approach, one starts with the analysis of the moves to see what statements about states are altered by them and then expresses the description of the winning state in terms of these statements.

In what follows we shall consider "a little bit of both" techniques for the solution of the linearity problem: using the concept of macro-moves. We shall discuss the difficulties in the way, and move on to a discussion of similar difficulties in the way of handling the first difficulty of the GPS mentioned at the beginning of this section.

It might be useful here to take another example – that of the "15-puzzle" – for ease of discussion, as well as to show that the technique, while not universally applicable, is applicable to more than just Rubik's cube. The puzzle is shown in Fig. 3. We shall assume that the description of win is a conjunction of statements and that at least one difference can be found that can be removed easily by a move or move sequence.

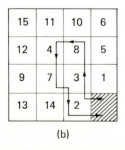

Fig. 3. A 15-puzzle consists of 15 numbered tiles arranged inside a 4 x 4 frame. A move consists of sliding a tile adjacent to the empty space into the empty space (we shall call this "moving the hole" for our purposes below). Given an arbitrary arrangement of tiles, one is required to move the hole around until the tiles are arranged in some given regular order.

In the case of the 15-puzzle one can isolate the statement, "the empty square is in its correct position" as the first difference to be removed (i.e. this is the "most difficult difference", perhaps contrary to intuition). A single move does not remove it of course – one has to find a sequence of moves for it either by some exhaustive search or a reasoning of the "make a move useful to apply" variety discussed earlier. At least in the case of this puzzle, an exhaustive search would not be prohibitive.

Once this difference is removed, one can only talk about move sequences which do not remove this difference, i.e. brings the empty square back to its correct position, i.e. circular motions of the empty square. At this point, the entire representation changes, with all moves represented by such move sequences. Now the old technique of Goldstein can be used using these move sequences as moves and noting which properties of the states remain unchanged under these moves. In this specific case, one can find (surprisingly enough, again by the application a technique used by Goldstein) that relative cyclic arrangement of the squares along the trajectory of the empty square remains unchanged under these "macro-moves".

As we have said before, this method of isolating macro-moves can only be used if a simple conjunct of the description can be found which can be attained by an easily found sequence of moves. If such is not the case, one uses the single moves found in the original representation of the puzzle, as done by Goldstein.

At this point, one seeks to remove the next difficult difference using the macro-moves generated by the previous analysis. The difference-transformation table comes in useful for search reduction again, except for the difficulty regarding "making moves useful" inherent in GPS (which, by the way rears its ugly head during the search for macro-moves also).

This process may have to be repeated in a recursive manner. As an example, the difference transformation table at the second stage of the 15 puzzle may indicate that the next three hardest differences to be removed are in the positions of tiles numbers 1, 2 and 3. Each of these can be removed by repeated motion of the empty square through the actual and desired positions of the tiles concerned, avoiding the tiles already placed in position. However, this process "jams" when the fourth tile has to be put in place since cyclic motion through the 4th position have to disturb at least the third. In that case one has to find macro-moves which first move the third tile out of the way, place the fourth tile next to it and bring the two tiles back in together.

At this point a human being would probably decide to move the tiles in position by pairs. We do not expect such cleverness on the part of GPS even with the present modifications, can probably live with it, but the problem of "making a move useful" still remains. Notice that to bring two tiles in place at the same time using the macro-moves, they must initially be brought next to one another so a circuit can be drawn through the juxtaposed pair of tiles and the juxtaposed pair of positions. Let us take stock of where we have gotten so far.

6. Discussion of the remaining weak points

What we have come to as a partial design of a stronger GPS is the following "pidgin algorithm"

1. Find a conjunct of the description of the winning states which can be removed by a single move or for which a sequence of moves can be found using either exhaustive search or some (so far unspecified) "reasoning about actions" technique used as follows:
   a. Find a move relevant to the difference (straight use of the Oyen-Goldstein technique).
   b. Reason about actions to see in what states the move would be useful and solve the subproblem to bring about such a state. Then apply the originally planned move. If no such conjunct can be easily found, go directly to the next step.
2. Find the macro-moves which keeps this first difference untouched. If step 1 was empty, then this step merely lists all single moves (i.e. is also effectively empty).
3. Test the macro-moves found in step 2 for their relevance to different properties of the states and use these to construct differences implied by the description of the winning states (if the latter description is a conjunction, the task is similar to that used by ABSTRIPS; else the Ernst-Golstein technique may be used).
4. Use the macro-moves to recursively remove the next harder difference found this way.
5. Continue the process recursively.

The isolation of the initial difference may be easier for problems like the robot problems where the description of the win is given as a conjunction of properties. However, in problems like Fool's Disc or Instant Insanity where the good differences have to be prodded out algebraically by the Ernst-Goldstein technique, this is a hard first step, since the latter technique isolates the useful differences by considering the given moves, here the prupose is to generate the useful (macro-)moves by using the differences.

The removal of the linearity problem by the use of the macro-moves would be helpful in the robot problems handled by ABSTRIPS, provided a practicable method is found for finding the macro-moves. The ideal mehod would be to emulate the reasoning of introducing a difference and then removing it without retracing the steps. This, I believe, involves the kind of reasoning about actions that has not been tried too often in the past. The alternative of exhaustive search over short move-sequences may or may not be viable.

The same kind of reasoning about actions is needed in the first step of the algorithm as well as in the second step, since the removal of the first difference is not aided by a difference-transformation table.

It seems in conclusion that while searches for macro-moves, aided by achieved properties provides a good solution to the linerarity problem, the search for these needs further research in reasoning about actions. As things stand, exhaustive search for macro-moves is certainly more feasible than an exhaustive search for solutions – just because they are shorter. Also any success in such isolation of useful macro-moves would help in the representation problem.

Acknowledgements

The preparation of this paper was supported by the National Science Foundation under grants MCS80-08889 and MCS81-10104 and the National Institute of Health under grant RR-64309.

ARTIFICIAL AND HUMAN INTELLIGENCE (A. Elithorn and R. Banerji, editors)
Elsevier Science Publishers, B.V.
© NATO, 1984

Chapter 5

TOWARD COMBINING EMPIRICAL AND ANALYTICAL METHODS FOR INFERRING HEURISTICS

TOM M. MITCHELL

Department of Computer Science
Rutgers University, New Brunswick, NJ 08903, USA

Summary

Inferring problem solving heuristics from examples of worked out solutions is one kind of generalizing from examples. A spectrum of techniques for this generalization problem is considered, ranging from purely empirical, data-driven methods, to purely deductive, analytic, knowledge-driven methods. It is argued that a combination of empirical and analytical methods is appropriate for inferring heuristics. One way of combining empirical and analytical mechanisms for inferring generalizations is suggested and illustrated for the task of inferring search heuristics for symbolic integration.

1. Introduction

Over the past decade, a considerable amount of research has been done attempting to find general mechanisms for inferring generalizations from examples (Hayes-Roth and Mostow, 1975, Vere, 1975, Michalski, 1980, Mitchell, 1978). More recently, several researchers have begun to study methods for learning problem solving heuristics (Lenat, 1980, Mitchell, 1981, Anderson, 1981, Hayes-Roth, 1980). This leads to considering the generalization task as one part of a larger goal of improving problem solving performance. Placing the generalization task within this context leads to the availability of constraints and knowledge that can provide strong guidance for the generalization process. It also leads to a considerably different view of the nature of the generalization problem than is found when considering this problem in the abstract.

This paper explores the way in which placing the generalization task in context of learning heuristics can provide guidance for the generalization process. The discussion here is based on examples taken from the task of learning heuristics for solving symbolic integration problems. First the generalization problem is defined, and a spectrum of generalization strategies sketched. Then the empirical generalization strategy for inferring heuristics used by the LEX program is summarized. Finally, one means of augmenting the generalization strategy by an analysis of problem solutions is suggested and illustrated with hand examples.

2. The generalization problem

The problem of generalizing from examples is typically described as follows: A program accepts input observations (instances) represented in some language, which we shall call the *instance language*. Learned generalizations correspond to sets of these instances and are formulated by the program as statements in a second language, which we shall call the *generalization language*. In order to associate instances with generalizations, the program possesses a *matching predicate* that tests whether a given instance and generalization match (i.e., whether the given instance is contained in the instance set corresponding to the given generalization).

Given the instance language, generalization language, and matching predicate, the generalization problem is to infer a description of some "target" generalization by observing a sample set of its training instances. Each *training instance* is an instance from the given language, *along with* its classification as either an instance of the target generalization (positive instance) or not an instance of the target generalization (negative instance). This generalization problem can be summarized as follows:

The Generalization Problem
Given:
1. Language of instances.
2. Language of generalizations.
3. Matching predicate for matching generalizations to instances.
4. Sets of positive and negative training instances.

Determine:
Generalization(s) consistent with the training instances.

As a concrete example of the above generalization problem, consider the task addressed by Winston's program for learning classes of block structures (Winston, 1975). Here, the language of instances is the representation used to describe example block structures. The language of generalizations is the language in which learned concepts (e.g., arch, tower) are described. The matching predicate specifies whether a given generalization applies to a given instance (e.g., whether the inferred description of an arch is satisfied by a specific block structure).

2.1. A generalization problem: inferring problem solving heuristics

In this paper we will consider a particular generalization problem: inferring problem solving heuristics in the domain of symbolic integration. We have previously reported on a program called LEX (Mitchell, 1981) that learns problem solving heuristics by solving practice problems and generalizing from the examples of useful and useless search steps attempted during the solution search. This problem domain is characterized briefly in the current section.

LEX begins with a set of operators for solving problems in symbolic integration, and infers a set of control heuristics, each of which recommends applying a particular operator for some general class of problem states. While each operator initially given to LEX contains preconditions that characterize a class of problem states to which that operator *can* validly be applied, learned heuristics characterize the subclass of problem states to which the operator *should* be applied; that is, the subclass of problem states for which the operator is useful. Preconditions for heuristics are learned by generalizing from examples of problem states to which the operator is applied in solving practice problems. A partial list of the operators available to LEX is shown in Fig. 1 (there are currently 45 such operators).

LEX solves practice problems and analyzes the resulting search tree in order to obtain training instances from which it infers heuristics. Each training instance corresponds to an individual search step performed during an attempted problem solution. An example of a typical LEX training instance is shown below.

When the current problem is $\int x \sin(x) \, dx$,
Apply OP2, with arguments bound as $u = x$, $dv = \sin(x)dx$

This training instance would be used as a positive instance for inferring a heuristic that recommends OP2. Negative training instances for the same

```
OP1    1·f(x)   ==>   f(x)

OP2    Integration by parts:
         ∫ u dv  ==>  uv - ∫ v du
       (the precondition is internally represented
       as ∫ f1(x) f2(x) dx, where f1(x) corresponds
       to u and f2(x) dx corresponds to dv)

OP3    ∫ r f(x) dx      ==>    r ∫ f(x) dx

OP4    ∫ x↑(r NEQ -1) dx   ==>   x↑(r+1)/(r+1) + C

OP5    0·f(x)   ==>   0

OP6    ∫ f1(x)+f2(x) dx  ==>
              ∫ f1(x) dx + ∫ f2(x) dx
```

Fig. 1. Some of the operators used by LEX.

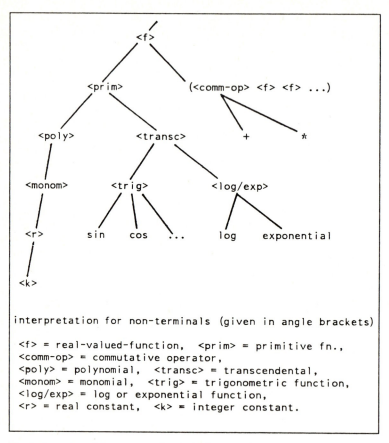

Fig. 2. A portion of the grammar for algebraic expressions.

heuristic correspond to applications of OP2 which did not lead to acceptable problem solutions. Below is one heuristic that LEX has produced, which covers the above positive instance. Here the term "transc" stands for any transcendental function (e.g., any trigonometric, exponential, or logarithmic function).

H1:
    IF the problem state contains $\int x \, \text{transc}(x) \, dx$,
    THEN use integration by Parts: $\int u \, dv \rightarrow uv - \int v \, du$,
        With u bound to x, and dv bound to transc(x) dx.

In general, the heuristics learned are of the form

    IF the current problem state matches the generalization P,
    THEN apply operator O, with variable binding B.

    The language of generalizations used to describe preconditions of heuristics determines, to a large degree, the range of heuristics that can be learned. In LEX, for the symbolic integration domain, this language of generalizations is based on a grammar for algebraic expressions containing, and contained in, indefinite integrals. The sentences derivable by this grammar are the expressions that form legal problem states. The intermediate sentential forms derivable by the grammar constitute legal generalizations of problem states. Briefly, the grammar contains non-terminal symbols that correspond to classes of functions (e.g., trigonometric, polynomial) and classes of operators (e.g., function composition, multiplication, integration). These can be combined to form generalized algebraic expressions. Fig. 2 shows a portion of this grammar in the form of a hierarchy. Each node in the hierarchy represents some substring of a sentential form, and each edge corresponds to a rule in the grammar.

Thus, the generalization problem encountered by LEX is as follows: LEX is given the languages indicated above for describing generalizations and training instances. It then generates training instances of useful and useless search steps by a mechanism that is described in (Mitchell, 1981). The generalization problem that arises in inferring heuristics is to learn the concept "the class of problem states for which operator X is to be recommended." This generalization becomes the left hand side of a heuristic to recommend operator X.

3. A spectrum of methods for inferring generalizations

A broad spectrum of approaches to the generalization problem is possible. At one end of the spectrum, one can view the generalization problem independently of the context in which it appears. In this case it can be approached in an empirical manner, assuming no knowledge of how training instances are being produced, the criteria for classifying instances as positive and negative, the intended use of the inferred heuristics, etc. This empirical approach to generalization relies solely on the observed training instances for information about appropriate generalizations. Much research over the past decade has viewed the generalization problem in this light (Winston, 1975, Hayes-Roth and Mostow, 1975, Vere, 1975, Michalski, 1980, Mitchell, 1978).

At the other end of the spectrum, if the generalization problem is considered in context, there may be a number of sources of knowledge and constraints available for constraining the search for an appropriate generalization. For example, in the above problem of inferring problem solving heuristics, knowledge of the criteria for labelling positive and negative instances is given to the learner, and used for constraining the generalization process. The intended use of the learned generalizations (heuristics) in a forward heuristic search problem solver can also be useful knowledge, as can certain general knowledge about search and the method by which the training instances were generated. Furthermore, knowledge about the domain of symbolic integration can also be useful for guiding the generalization process. Less research has gone into studying this end of the spectrum of learning strategies. One notable exception is the work of Fikes, Hart and Nilsson (1972), in which generalized macrooperators were inferred by analysis of one application of a sequence of operators. More recent work on operationalizing human-provided advice (Mostow, 1981) in the context of machine-aided heuristic programming (Hayes-Roth, Klahr, Burge and Mostow, 1978) proposes methods of analysis that seem relevant to guiding learning at the analytical end of this spectrum.

Fig. 3 illustrates schematically this spectrum of possible generalized strategies. At one end lie strongly empirical, data-directed, inductive methods. At the other extreme, one can imagine more analytical, theory-driven methods that rely heavily upon deduction, knowledge about the task-domain, and the context of the generalization problem in order to direct their search for appropriate generalizations. In inferring heuristics, for example, it may be theoretically possible to *deduce* the appropriate heuristics for a given set of operators, given sufficient knowledge of the operators, the problem domain, and the type of problem solving performance desired. At this extreme of the spectrum, there may be no need at all for acquiring training instances for empirical generalization.

In practice, neither end of this spectrum seems very practical. The remainder of this paper is concerned with examining how empirical and analytical methods can be combined in a single system to infer problem-solving heuristics. Combining these methods is desirable in order to take advantage of whatever relevant knowledge and analytical techniques are available, while allowing the system to fall back to weaker empirical techniques in cases where the analysis is too difficult or knowledge needed for the analysis is unavailable.

One prerequisite for combining empirical and analytic methods for inferring heuristics is having a method for representing partial knowledge about the identity of the heuristics being learned. Partially learned heuristics, whose exact description is not yet known, must be represented in some way that accurately summarizes alternative hypotheses about the correct description of the heuristic, and that allows various sources of knowledge to refine this set of alternative hypotheses.

The following subsection describes such a representation for partially learned generalizations. Section 4 then describes an empirical approach to inferring heuristics from training instances, which is currently implemented in the LEX program, and which is based upon this representation for partially learned heuristics. Section 5 then proposes a method for augmenting this empirical

Empirical
Data-Driven

Analytical
Theory-driven

Fig. 3. Spectrum of generalization strategies.

method by adding a capability to analyze solution traces based upon knowledge about search, about operator and problem state representations, and about symbolic integration.

3.1. Representing partially learned heuristics

A partially learned heuristic is one whose correct generalization cannot be precisely determined based on information considered thus far. Empirical generalization methods typically require many training instances before converging to an appropriate generalization.

Given a generalization language in which heuristics are to be described, one method of representing the partially learned heuristic would be to list all alternative describable generalizations that are consistent with current information (both observed training instances and knowledge gained by analysis). We refer to this set of all plausible describable versions of the heuristic as the *version space* of the partially learned heuristic, with respect to the chosen representation language (Mitchell, 1978, 1982).

In general, representing the partially learned heuristic by listing all the members of its version space would be impractical. Fortunately, there is a much more efficient way of representing exactly the same information: The version space of alternative plausible generalizations can be represented accurately by storing its sets of maximally specific and maximally general generalizations. (G1 is considered more specific than (less general than) G2 if the instances that G1 matches are contained in the instances that G2 matches).

We will refer to the subset of maximally specific members of a version space as the subset S of members of that version space. Similarly, we refer to the subset of minimally specific (i.e., maximally general) members of the version space as the subset G. The version space of each incompletely learned heuristic can then be represented by computing and storing the boundary subsets S and G for that version space. These sets delimit the version space: any heuristic in the version space is both (1) more specific than or equal to some member of G, and (2) more general than or equal to some member of S. The problem of computing and updating the version space as new information becomes available can then be recast as the problem of computing and updating the sets S and G.

4. An empirical generalization strategy

This section summarizes the empirical generalization strategy currently used in the LEX program. For a more detailed discussion, see Mitchell (1978, 1982), from which this material has been drawn.

The Generalizer represents the version space for each proposed heuristic for each operator, in terms of the sets S and G. For example, Fig. 4 shows a positive training instance associated with OP2, and the version space produced in response to this training instance. The partially learned heuristic represented by the (singleton) sets S and G shown in this figure will be refined as subsequent training instances become available. Below we describe the procedures for proposing and refining problem solving heuristics in LEX.

Proposing a new heuristic: If no member of the version space of any current heuristic applies to a newly presented positive instance, a new heuristic is formed to cover this instance. This is assumed to be the case in the example of Fig. 4. In forming a new heuristic, the set S is initialized to the very specific version of the heuristic, that applies *only* to the current training instance (this is the most specific describable version consistent with the single observed training instance). G is initialized to the version of the heuristic that suggests the operator will prove useful in *every* situation where it can validly be applied. In the example of Fig. 4, G is therefore initialized to the version whose precondition is exactly the description of the precondition for OP2. That is, $\int f1(x) * f2(x)\, dx$ represents the integral of the product of any two real functions of x, and corresponds to the precondition $\int u\, dv$ as it is stated in the system's generalization language.

At this point, S and G delimit a broad range of alternative versions of the proposed heuristic, corresponding to *all* the generalization expressible in the given language, and consistent with this single training instance. Note that matching the generalization in S is known to be a *sufficient* condition for recommending OP2, while matching the generalization in G is known to be a *necessary* condition for recommending OP2.

As subsequent positive instances are considered, S will become more general to include newly observed instances in which OP2 is found to be useful.

Positive Training Instance:

$\int 3x \cos(x)\, dx \rightarrow$ Apply OP2 with
$u = x$, and
$dv = 3 \cos(x)\, dx$

Resulting Version Space for New Heuristic:

S: $\int 3x \cos(x)\, dx \rightarrow$ Apply OP2 with
$u = x$, and
$dv = 3 \cos(x)\, dx$

G: $\int f1(x)\, f2(x)\, dx \rightarrow$ Apply OP2 with
$u = f1(x)$, and
$dv = f2(x)\, dx$

Fig. 4. Initializing the version space of a new heuristic.

Likewise, G will become more specific in order to exclude negative instances in which OP2 may validly be applied, but in which it does not lead to an acceptable solution. Thus, the range of alternative plausible versions of the heuristic delimited by S and G will narrow as new information is acquired through subsequent practice problems, and the uncertainty regarding the correct description of the heuristic is reduced.

Refining incompletely learned heuristics using subsequent data: When a new training instance is observed, the version space of a partially learned heuristic may be revised by eliminating any version that is inconsistent with this new training instance. In the current example, the next practice problem that is considered is $\int 5 \times \sin(x) \, dx$. The solution to this problem leads to both a positive and a negative training instance for the current heuristic. (These two training instances correspond to applying 0P2 in different ways to the same integrand.) Fig. 5 shows these two new training instances and the way in which they allow refining the version space of this heuristic. In the revised version space shown there, the most specific version, S, of the heuristic has been generalized just enough to allow it to apply to the new positive training instance. Here trig(x) replaces cos(x) so that the heuristic will apply to integrals containing *any* trigonometric function of x. Similarly, k (denoting any integer constant) replaces the 3 in the specific heuristic. The program determines this revision by first noting that the terms 3 and cos(x) in the old S prevent this generalization from applying to the new instance. It then consults the grammar for expressing heuristics (shown in Fig. 2) to determine the next most general terms that can be substituted in order to include this new instance. Although the disjunction "3 ∨ 5" would be a more specific generalization than "k", this disjunction is not allowed in the current generalization language and therefore cannot be stated by the program.

The general boundary of the revised version space of Fig. 5 has also been altered so that it does not apply to the new negative training instance. In this case, there are two maximally general versions (g1 and g2) of the heuristic consistent with the three observed training instances. Here, "poly(x)" refers to any polynomial function of x, and "transc(x)" denotes any transcendental function of x. As with revising the set S, revisions to G depend upon the generalization language being used. For instance, g1 is computed by replacing f1(x) (which represents "any real-valued function") by the next more specific *acceptable* expression. Notice in the hierarchy of Fig. 2, this expression is "poly".

As subsequent training instances are considered, this partially learned heuristic will be further refined so that S and G converge toward a useful statement of the heuristic, such as:

$\int kx \, \text{transc}(x) \, dx \rightarrow$ apply OP2, with u = x, and dv = k transc(x) dx

```
Version Space of Heuristic from Figure 4

        S:  ∫ 3x cos(x) dx -> Apply OP2 with
                                 u = x, and
                                 dv = 3 cos(x) dx

        G:  ∫ f1(x) f2(x) dx -> Apply OP2 with
                                 u = f1(x), and
                                 dv = f2(x) dx
```

New Training Instances:

```
    Positive training instance:
              ∫ 5x sin(x) dx -> Apply OP2 with
                                 u = x, and
                                 dv = 5 sin(x) dx

    Negative training instance:
              ∫ 5x sin(x) dx -> Apply OP2 with
                                 u = sin(x), and
                                 dv = 5x dx
```

```
Revised Version Space:

        S:  ∫ kx trig(x) dx -> Apply OP2 with
                                 u = x, and
                                 dv = k trig(x) dx

    G:
      g1:  ∫ poly(x) f2(x) dx -> Apply OP2 with
                                 u = poly(x), and
                                 dv = f2(x) dx

      g2:  ∫ f1(x) transc(x) dx -> Apply OP2
                                 with u = f1(x), and
                                 dv = transc(x) dx
```

Fig. 5. Revising the version space of a heuristic.

4.1. Biases in empirical generalization

The above empirical generalization strategy will converge on the appropriate description of the heuristic, *under the assumption that this heuristic can be represented in the provided generalization language*. This convergence is assured because each revision to the sets S and G is the minimal necessary revision to accommodate the new data, and because there are only a finite number of generalizations in the version space (for the given generalization language).

Since, in general, there is no guarantee that the heuristics to be learned will be contained in the generalization language, there is no guarantee that the inductive leaps made by the generalizer are justifiable. For instance, in the example of Fig. 5 the integers 3 and 5 in two positive instances were generalized to k (any integer) because there was no intermediate term expressible in the generalization language. The generalizer has no basis for justifying the inductive leap from 2 and 5 to "any integer", *except* under the assumption that the heuristic being learned is expressible in its generalization language. Although this particular inductive leap turns out to be appropriate, the system makes many other inductive leaps that are not.

One way of reducing the reliance on such biases implicit in the generalzation language is to use a more expressive generalization language. However, this carries its own disadvantages. Suppose LEX were given a generalization language which had a separate term for each subset of integers. The program would then be able to generalize from 3 and 5 to some term representing the disjunction $(3 \vee 5)$. While this would prevent the generalizer from making unwarranted inductive leaps, it would also prevent the generalizer from ever generalizing to the term "any integer" (since this would require observing an infinite number of training instances). Thus, the generalizer would never produce generalizations that have any more information than what was in the training data.

The above difficulty is a symptom of a deep problem with strictly empirical generalization strategies: It is impossible for any system to make any kind of nonarbitrary inductive leap beyond the information present in the data, *unless* it has some justifiable bias or knowledge for making that inductive leap. (For more detailed discussion of the need for biases in generalization, see Mitchell, 1980.) In the above case, the program does generalize beyond the information in the training data, but only because of the bias implicit in the use of a generalization language that is not capable of characterizing every possible subset of training instances.

There is an important conclusion to the above discussion: If totally unbiased generalization systems are incapable of making the inductive leap to characterize unobserved instances, then the power of a generalization system follows directly from its biases – from decisions based on criteria *beyond* matching of the training instances. Therefore, progress toward understanding learning mechanisms depends upon understanding the sources of, and justification for, various biases and sources of knowledge that can be used to verify inductive hypotheses.

5. An analytical generalization strategy

This section discusses how an explicit description of the criteria for classifying training instances, combined with knowledge about search, about the representation of operators and problem states, and about symbolic integration, provide the basis for further refining the version space of a partially learned heuristic. By analyzing *why* each observed training instance is classified as positive or negative, in the context of the overall problem solution, logically sufficient conditions for satisfying the positive instance criterion may be determined. Such analysis provides a method of producing *justifiable* generalizations based upon justifiable biases that follow from the knowledge and deductive methods underlying the analysis. This section presents hand traces of two such analyses and shows how such analysis can be used to refine the version space of the heuristic. Unlike the empirical techniques in the previous section, the analytical techniques described here have not yet been implemented in a working program; and the examples given here should be viewed as a means of focusing the discussion, rather than as predicted program traces.

The key to extracting additional information by analysis of the problem solution is to realize that the criteria being used to classify positive and negative training instances lead to a valid, but inefficient definition of the heuristic being learned. Considering this credit assignment criteria changes the nature of the generalization problem in a fundamental way: Without considering this information, the generalizer must *induce* which of the as yet unobserved instances should be included in the final generalization. With this new information, the answer to this question may be *deduced*. *The generalization problem viewed in this context can be viewed as the problem of transforming the initial definition of the credit assignment criteria into an equivalent, more useable definition of the heuristic.* Here, making a "more useable" definition means restating the credit assignment criterion in terms of the generalization language, so that the Match procedure can be used to efficiently determine whether the generalization applies to any given instance. This notion of transforming an ineffective definition into an effective definition is similar to the notion of operationalizing advice, discussed by Mostow (1981) and Hayes-Roth, Klahr, Burge and Mostow (1978). To summarize, the generalization problem may be recast as shown below.

The Generalization Problem for Inferring Heuristics
Given:
1. Language of instances (LI)
2. Language of generalizations (LG)
3. Matching predicate (Match) for matching generalizations to instances.
4. Positive and negative training instances.
5. Credit assignment criteria (Posinst and Neginst) for labelling instances as positive or negative.
6. Other knowledge about search, representation of problem states and operators, domain-specific knowledge.

Determine:
> Some statement in the generalization language which matches the same instances that the credit assignment criteria classifies as positive, and none that are classified as negative.
> In other words, find some TargetGeneralization $\in$ *LG, such that
>
> $(\forall i \in LI) [(Posinst(i) \rightarrow Match(i, TargetGeneralization))$
> $\land (Neginst(i) \rightarrow (Not (Match(i, TargetGeneralization))))]$

Note that the task now is described as finding a generalization consistent with the credit assignment criterion rather than with the observed training instances. If a strong enough theory and deductive apparatus are available, then such a generalization might be *deduced* directly, without generating and generalizing from training instances. This approach corresponds to a generalization method at the deductive extreme of the spectrum of figure 3-1. Unfortunately, there are two significant difficulties with attempting to reason directly from the definition of the credit assignment criteria to an equivalent statement phrased in the generalization language. First, it is unlikely that a complete enough theory of the problem solver and the domain will be available to deduce all relevant heuristics. Second, even if the appropriate knowledge were available, the cost of conducting the necessary analysis is likely to be prohibitive in many cases.

While purely deductive inference of heuristics seems unrealistic, *resource limited, partial analysis of training instances* can provide important information regarding the appropriate generalization of the heuristic. What is needed, therefore, is an ability to combine analytical capabilities with a reliance on observation of data.

This section illustrates an approach to generalization which is based on interpreting each training instance in terms of the credit assignment criteria, then determining features of the training instance that are logically *sufficient* for it to satisfy the credit assignment criteria. These sufficient conditions for satisfying the credit assignment strategy, once restated in terms of the generalization language, provide a direct basis for refining the S boundary set of the version space of the heuristic. Two hand examples are shown below, using two different credit assignment criteria as the basis for analyzing the same solution trace. The examples are intended to illustrate (i) how analysis of the problem solution can provide a means of reducing the range of alternative generalizations in the version space, (ii) how varying amounts of effort in analysis can provide varying amounts of information for refining the version space, and (iii) how differing credit assignment criteria lead to differing generalizations. While the discussion does not present a precise algorithm for directing the analysis of solution traces, it does indicate the main phases involved in this analysis.

The following two examples use two different credit assignment criteria for labelling search steps as positive instances from which heuristics will be inferred. The first example assumes that the goal of the learning program is to produce heuristics that recommend operators whenever they lead to solutions. Then any search step that applies some operator, *op*, to some problem state, *state*, is a positive instance provided it satisfies the predicate *Posinst1*, defined as follows:

Posinst1 (op, state) ↔
~ Goal(state) ∧ [Goal(Apply(op, state)) v Solvable(Apply(op, state))].

Here, Goal is the predicate for recognizing solution states, Apply is the function for applying operators to states, and Solvable is the predicate that tests whether a state can be transformed to a Goal state with the available operators.

Solvable is defined as follows:

Solvable(state) ↔
(∃op) [Goal(apply (op, state)) v Solvable(apply(op, state))]

The second example considers a slightly different performance criterion, in which each operator has some fixed cost, and only those search steps along the lowest cost solution paths are considered positive instances. This credit assignment criterion is characterized by the predicate *Posinst2*, defined below. Notice the first two conjuncts are the same as Posinst1, while the third conjunct corresponds to the added "minimum cost" constraint:

Posinst2(op, state) ↔
 ~ (Goal(state))
 ∧ (Goal(Apply(op, state)) ∨ Solvable(Apply(op, state))]
 ∧ [(∀ otherop)(Equal otherop op)
  ∨ ~ Applicable(otherop. state)
   ∨ (~ Solvable(Apply(otherop, state))
    ∧ ~ Goal(Apply(otherop, state)))
   ∨ (Greater-or-equal Solutioncost(Apply(otherop, state))
       Solutioncost(Apply(op, state)))]

Here the function Solutioncost(state) gives the cost of the minimum cost solution path from state to some goal state, and the predicate Applicable tests whether a given operator is applicable to a given problem state. For both of the above Posinst criteria, we assume the negative instance criterion is the negation of the positive instance criterion.

5.1. Analyzing a training instance: example 1

In this example, we consider the credit assignment criterion Posinst1 (described above) as the criterion that must be satisfied by learned heuristics. Suppose that the system has just produced the problem solution tree shown in

Fig. 6, and the generalizer is now considering the first step along the solution path as a positive training instance for a heuristic that is to recommend OP3. Assuming no heuristic yet exists for OP3, the empirical generalization method described earlier will produce the following version space for the new heuristic:

S: $\int 7(x \wedge) dx \to$ use OP3
G: $\int r\, f(x)\, dx \to$ use OP3

In this example, analysis of how this training instance satisfies the credit assignment criterion will lead to additional information for refining the above version space of alternative hypotheses. The trace of this analysis, shown below, is broken into four main stages, which attempt to determine some property of the integrand in the training instance which is *sufficient* to assure that the credit assignment criteria will be met. This sufficient condition for satisfying Posinst1 can then be used to further generalize the S boundary of the version space for this heuristic. The four main stages are (i) Generate an explanation that shows how the current positive instance satisfies Posinst, (ii) Extract from this explanation a sufficient condition for satisfying Posinst, (iii) Restate the sufficient condition in terms of the generalization language, as restrictions on various problem states in the solution tree, and (iv) Propagate the restrictions on various problem states through the solution tree, and combine them into a generalization that corresponds to a sufficient condition for assuring Posinst will be satisfied.

Stage 1: Produce an explanation of how the current training instance satisfies Posinst. This explanation is produced by instantiating the definition of Posinst1 for the positive instance in question. By determining which disjunctive clauses in the definition of Posinst are satisfied by the current training instance, then further expanding those clauses by instantiating predicates to which they refer, a proof is produced that Posinst1(OP3, state 1). The result of this stage is an And/Or proof tree, which we shall call the *explanation tree* for the training instance. The tip nodes in the explanation tree are known to be satisfied

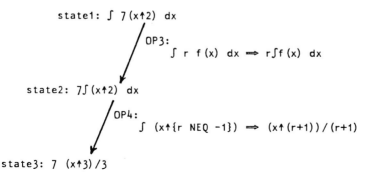

Fig. 6. The solution tree for example 1.

because of the observed solution tree to which the training instance belongs. This explanation tree indicates how the training instance satisfies Posinst1, and forms the basis for generalization by inferring sufficient conditions for satisfying Posinst1.

The explanation tree for the positive training instance $\langle OP3, State1 \rangle$ is shown in Fig. 7. Nodes in the *explanation tree* correspond to statements about various problem states and operators in the associated *solution tree*. The explanation tree for the current example indicates that $\langle OP3, State\ 1 \rangle$ is a Positive instance because (1) State 1 is not a Goal state, and (2) by applying OP4 to the state resulting from the positive instance step, it is possible to reach a goal state. Subsequent stages of analysis of this explanation tree, shown below, extract this explanation (at an appropriate level of generality), and restate it in the generalization language in which heuristics are expressed.

Stage 2: Extract a sufficient condition for satisfying Posinst. If the explanation tree is viewed as a proof that Posinst1 is satisfied by the current training instance, then it is clear that any set of nodes that satisfy this And/Or tree correspond to a sufficient condition for satisfying Posinst1. In the current example, for instance, if all the tip nodes of the explanation tree are satisfied by a given state, s, then Posinst1 will be satisfied by the training instance $\langle OP3, s \rangle$. In this stage, a set of nodes that satisfy the And/Or tree is selected, and the corresponding sufficient condition for Posinst is formulated by replacing the problem state from the training instance by a universally quantified variable. In the current example, if the tip nodes of the explanation tree are selected, then the resulting sufficient condition for Posinst1 may be stated as follows:

$(\forall s)$ Posinst(OP3, s) ← (~ Goal(s) ∧ Goal(Apply(OP4, Apply(OP3, s))))

Notice that there are many possible choices of sets of nodes to satisfy the And/Or tree, and correspondingly many sufficient conditions. This choice of

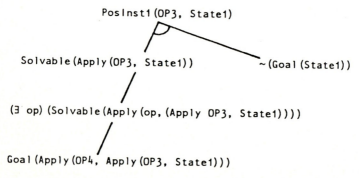

Fig. 7. The explanation tree for Posinst1 (Op 3, State 1).

nodes is one of the major control issues in the analysis of the training instance. Generally, nodes close to the root of the explanation tree lead to more general sufficient conditions. However, since the sufficient conditions formulated in this stage must be transformed by subsequent stages to statements in the generalization language for heuristics, the choice of covering nodes from the explanation tree must trade off (a) the generality of the corresponding sufficient condition, with (b) the loss in generality that is likely when this sufficient condition is transformed into the generalization language for heuristics. As an example, consider the alternative choice of the two nodes at the second level of the explanation tree. This set of nodes leads to the following sufficient condition for Posinst1:

($\forall$s) Posinst(OP3, s) ←
(~ Goal(s) $\wedge$ Solvable(Apply(OP3, s)))

While this sufficient condition on satisfying Posinst1 is more general than the earlier sufficient condition, it turns out that this added generality will be lost when attempting to redescribe the sufficient condition in terms of the generalization language. The difficulty in this case stems from the fact that there is no straightforward translation from the predicate "Solvable" to a statement in the generalization language of LEX. In contrast, the sufficient condition corresponding to the tip nodes of the explanation tree involves only the predicate "Goal", which is easily characterized in terms of the generalization language.

Stage 3: Restate the sufficient condition in terms of the generalization language, as restrictions on various problem states involved in the solution tree. In the current example, the sufficient condition corresponding to the tip nodes of the explanation tree can be restated as follows:

($\forall$s) Posinst(OP3, s) ← (Match($\int$f(x)dx, s)
$\wedge$ Match(f(x), Apply(OP4, Apply(OP3, s))))

The first conjunct above expresses the fact that s is *not* a Goal state, and the second conjunct expresses the fact that Apply(OP4, Apply(OP3, s)) *is* a goal state. This second conjunct corresponds to a restriction on the state labelled State3 in Fig. 6.

In general, the goal of this stage is to translate the sufficient condition into a conjunctive set of statements of the form Match(⟨generalization⟩, ⟨problem-state⟩), where ⟨generalization⟩ can be any expression in the generalization language.

The translation of sufficient conditions into the generalization language requires knowledge about the correspondence between the representation language in which the analysis is being done and the generalization language used to describe heuristics. For instance, in the current example the following knowledge is used in the translation:

$$(\forall s) \sim \text{Goal}(s) \leftrightarrow \text{Match}(\int f(x)dx, s)$$

and

$$(\forall s)\ \text{Goal}(s) \leftrightarrow \text{Match}(f(x)dx, s)$$

Unfortunately, some expressions generated by analyzing the explanation tree may have no corresponding expression in the generalization language. For example, in the current LEX generalization language, there is no way of characterizing all "Solvable" functions. In this case, translating the sufficient condition corresponding to the second level nodes in the explanation tree may require further specializing the sufficient condition, by replacing Solvable(x) by sufficient conditions for Solvable. An example of such knowledge is the knowledge that all polynomial integrands are solvable. It is important to note that even if no such knowledge is available, it will always be possible to translate the sufficient condition into some weaker condition describable in the generalization language. This can always be accomplished by using the fact that the solution tree provides at least one problem state which satisfies the predicate, and that this problem state will be describable in the generalization language. Thus, for example, the condition Solvable(Apply(OP3, s)) may, if no other relevant knowledge is available, be weakened and replaced by Match $7\int(x\uparrow 2)\ dx$, Apply(OP3, s)).

Stage 4: Propagate the restrictions on various problem states through the solution tree to determine equivalent conditions on the problem state involved in the current training instance. By examining the definitions of the operators involved in reaching a given state x, it is possible to propagate restrictions on x through the solution tree to deduce the corresponding constraints on an earlier problem state. This back propagation of restrictions is necessary in order to restate the sufficient condition on Posinst in terms of a generalization that applies to the training instance. This propagation requires using the operators in a way different from the way in which they are used during forward search problem solving, and is similar to the process of goal regression discussed in the literature on means-ends problem solving and planning (Nilsson, 1980).

As an example, consider the second expression in the sufficient condition from stage 3: Match(f(x), Apply(OP4, Apply(OP3, s))). This condition, when back propagated through OP4 becomes Match $f(x)\int(x\uparrow(rNEQ - 1)dx)$, Apply(OP3, s)). The new generalization corresponds to the class of problem states which can be transformed using OP4 into an expression that satisfies the original condition. Similarly, this new expression can be propagated back through OP3 to yield an equivalent condition on State 1: Match($\int r(x\uparrow\{rNEQ - 1\})dx$, s). Thus, the sufficient condition from stage 3 can be restated as:

(∀s) Posinst(OP3, s) ←
(Match(∫f(x)dx, s) ∧ Match(∫r(x ∧ *{r NEQ − 1})dx, s))

Since the second conjunct is more specific than the first, this can be simplified to:

(∀s) [Posinst(OP3, s) ← Match(S * r(x ∧ *{r NEQ − 1}dx, s)]

Finally, we have found sufficient conditions for Posinst1(OP3, s) which are stated as a generalization that must match State 1. Thus, the analysis of how Posinst1 is satisfied by the current training instance leads to a sufficient condition for Posinst1 *stated in terms of the generalization language*. This sufficient condition can now be used to refine the boundary set S in the version space, by generalizing S to the generalization which forms the above sufficient condition. More generally, the set S will be updated to contain the maximal common generalizations of the current set S with the newly found sufficient condition. The sufficient condition found in this analysis is not the most general sufficient condition that exists for Posinst1. However, it is a sufficient condition that is satisfied by the current training instance, and that follows naturally from analyzing that instance. Different sufficient conditions may be found by focusing on a different set of nodes from the explanation tree, or by extending the analysis, taking advantage of a stronger theory of the domain and of the problem solver.

5.2. Analyzing a training Instance: Example 2

In this section, we sketch an analysis of the same problem solution (shown in Fig. 6), assuming a different Posinst criterion, Posinst2, shown below.

Posinst2(op, state)
  ↔ ~ (Goal(state))
  ∧ (Goal(Apply(op, state)) ∨ Solvable(Apply(op, state)))
  ∧ [(∀ otherop) (Equal otherop op)
  ∨ ~ Applicable(otherop, state)
  ∨ (~ Solvable(Apply(otherop, state))
      ∧ ~ Goal(Apply(otherop, state)))
  ∨ (Greater-or-equal Solutioncost(Apply(otherop, state))
Solutioncost(Apply(op, state)))]

This example is included to illustrate how analysis of the same problem solution based on a different Posinst criterion can lead to a different heuristic. Here we assume that the entire set of operators available to the system are the operators shown in Fig. 6, as well as the two operators below:

OP1: $1 * f(x) \rightarrow f(x)$
OP2: $0 * f(x) \rightarrow 0$

Stage 1: Produce an explanation of how the current training instance satisfies Posinst. Instantiating Posinst2(OP3, State 1) produces the explanation tree shown in Fig. 8. In this figure, the three dots correspond to a subtree that is identical to the explanation tree for this training instance and Posinst1 (note Posinst2 is an elaboration of Posinst1).

Stage 2: Extract a sufficient condition for satisfying Posinst. In this example, the sufficient condition corresponding to the tip nodes of the explanation tree is shown below. The first two conjuncts are the sufficient condition for Posinst1, and follow from the portion of the explanation tree that is identical to the explanation tree for Posinst1. The third conjunct arises because in this example, none of the available operators apply to State 1.

($\forall$s) Posinst2(OP3, s) ←
~ Goal(s)
∧
Goal(Apply(OP4, Apply(OP3, s)))
∧
($\forall$ otherop) (Equal otherop OP3)
∨ ~ Match(Precondition(otherop), s)

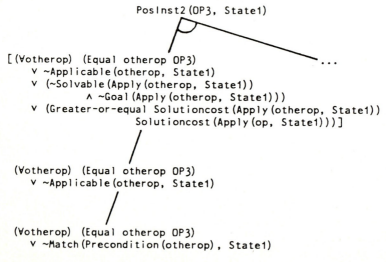

Fig. 8. Portion of the explanation tree for Posinst2 (Op 3, State 1).

Stage 3: Restate the sufficient condition in terms of the generalization language, as restrictions on various problem states involved in the solution tree. The result of this step is the sufficient condition shown below. The last three conjuncts arise from instantiating the universally quantified variable, otherop, in the final conjunct of the result from stage 2 (i.e., otherop is instantiated for each of the possible operators).

$(\forall s)$ Posinst2(OP3, s) ←
  Match($\int f(x)dx$, s)
  ∧ Match(f(x), Apply(OP4, Apply(OP3, s)))
  ∧
  ~ Match(1 * f(x), s)
  ∧
  ~ Match(0 * f(x), s)
  ∧
  ~ Match($\int (x \uparrow * \langle r\ NEQ - 1 \rangle)$, s)

Stage 4: Propagate the restrictions on various problem states through the solution tree to determine equivalent conditions on the problem state involved in the current training instance. In this case, only the second conjunct above needs to be propagated to state s. The resulting conjunction can then be simplified to a single expression, by combining the statements about what s must and must not match. (The definition of Match in LEX allows a generalization to match a problem state provided it matches any subexpression in the problem state.) The resulting sufficient condition is:

$(\forall s)$ Posinst2(Op3, s) ←
  Match($\int \langle r\ NEQ\ 0, 1 \rangle * (x \wedge * \langle r\ NEQ - 1 \rangle *)dx$, s)

Thus, analysis has produced the above sufficient condition for Posinst2, described in terms of the generalization language. Notice that this is a different sufficient condition than the one derived above for Posinst1, reflecting the difference between the two Posinst criteria. For any state, s, that Matches the above generalization, it will be true that OP3 will lead to the optimal solution. In addition, it will also be the case OP4 will follow OP3 to produce the solution, and that no other operator will apply to s. These additional conditions correspond to assumptions made to simplify the analysis of the training instance, and are not *necessary* conditions for satisfying Posinst2.

One additional point is worth noting regarding the above example. Notice that the analysis circumvented reasoning about the solution costs of various paths, by assuming that no other operators would apply to State 1. This assumption is made because (1) this is known to hold for the training instance being analyzed, and (2) even though the assumption leads to relatively weak sufficient conditions, it allows for a simpler analysis of the solution. A more sophisticated analysis might remove this assumption and try to generalize the sufficient condition by reasoning about solution paths and their costs. In general, such an analysis may be very difficult, and resources might better be spent collecting additional training instances. This once more points out the difficulty of a completely analytical approach to generalization and the need for a combining empirical generalization with resource-limited analytical methods.

6. Combining Empirical and Analytical Methods for Generalization

The above sections described both analytical and empirical methods for inferring general search heuristics. The analytical method produces sufficient conditions for the Posinst credit assignment predicate, which are stated in terms of the generalization language. Although we have not considered it here, it seems plausible that a similar analysis of negative instances may give rise to sufficient conditions for the Neginst predicate, whose negation would constitute necessary conditions for the Posinst predicate.

The empirical method discussed above is based on representing and updating the version space of all possible generalizations of the heuristic consistent with the observed data. This is accomplished by computing the boundary sets S (of maximally specific generalizations consistent with observed data) and G (of maximally general generalizations consistent with observed data).

The key observation involved in combining the results of the analytical and empirical methods is the following: *The two boundary sets S and G of the version space correspond to sufficient and necessary conditions for Posinst, which follow from (1) the observed training instances and (2) the assumption that the generalization language can correctly describe the target heuristic.* (In fact, the target heuristic corresponds to a necessary and sufficient condition for Posinst.) Therefore, the sufficient conditions obtained by analysis may be used to refine the version space in exactly the same way that positive instances are used. The set S must be generalized just as though the generalization in the sufficient condition were an observed positive instance (i.e., the set S is generalized as needed to cover the generalization mentioned in the sufficient condition). In short, the generalizations derived analytically as sufficient conditions for Posinst correspond to classes of instances that are known to be positive even though they have not yet been observed empirically. Similarly, each observed positive instance corresponds to a (not very interesting) sufficient condition for Posinst.

7. Conclusion

We have examined the generalization problem that occurs as a subtask of inferring problem solving heuristics. A spectrum of generalization techniques was characterized, ranging from empirical generalization of observed instances to analytical methods guided by an explicit definition of the Posinst criterion and knowledge about search and the task domain. Both extremes of this spectrum seem impractical. A combined method is suggested which takes advantage of analytical methods where possible and relies upon empirical generalization when necessary.

The analysis of training instances used to guide generalization is based upon determining sufficient conditions for satisfying the Posinst criterion. Two examples were presented to suggest how such sufficient conditions might be automatically inferred by constructing and generalizing an explanation of how the training instance satisfies Posinst. This analysis can make use of (1) explicit knowledge of the credit assignment criteria for labelling problem solving steps as positive or negative instances, (2) knowledge regarding the representation of problem states and operators and the ability to propagate generalizations through operators, (3) general knowledge about search trees produced by forward heuristic search, and (4) domain-specific knowledge regarding symbolic integration.

The availability of an explicitly stated credit assignment criteria changes the character of the generalization problem in a fundamental way. The generalization problem becomes one of "operationalizing" this criterion, by converting it from an ineffective though valid definition of the heuristic into a logically equivalent but more useful statement in the generalization language.

An important requirement for combining empirical and analytical generalization methods is having a common representation of hypotheses by which they combine information. In this paper, the language of generalizations is the basis for combining the information from these two knowledge sources. The representation of the version space of alternative plausible generalizations provides a kind of "blackboard" of hypotheses that can be refined by either method. Here, the close correspondence between the notions of "more specific than" and "sufficient condition for" allows both methods to refine the version space by operating on its boundary sets S and G.

Acknowledgments

The ideas in this paper stem from many productive conversations with Paul Utgoff and Ranan Banerji. Rich Keller provided useful comments on an earlier draft of this paper. The work reported here is supported by the National Science Foundation under Grant No. MCS80-08889, and by the National Institutes of Health under Grant No. RR-64309.

Chapter 6

SEARCH VS. KNOWLEDGE:
AN ANALYSIS FROM THE DOMAIN OF GAMES

HANS J. BERLINER

Computer Science Department,
Carnegie-Mellon University, Pittsburg, PA 15213, USA

Summary

We examine computer games in order to develop concepts of the relative roles of knowledge and search. The paper concentrates on the relation between knowledge applied at leaf nodes of a search and the depth of the search that is being conducted. Each knowledge of an advantage has a projection ability (time to convert to a more permanent advantage) associated with it. The best programs appear to have the longest projection ability knowledge in them. If the application of knowledge forces a single view of a terminal situation, this may at times be very wrong. We consider the advantages of knowledge delivering a range as its output, a method for which some theory exists, but which is as yet unproven.

1. Introduction

This paper examines the relation of knowledge to search in the domain of adversary (2-person game) searches. There are basically two different types of search, although in practice many hybrids occur. The informed (knowledge-directed, or best-first) search expands next the node that the semantics of the position indicate will produce the most useful contribution toward finding a solution. This type of search has been confirmed to be the basis of human solving of game type problems. On the other hand, the full-width or brute-force search looks at all possibilities (except those that can be logically eliminated; i.e. alpha-beta cut-offs) as deeply as time allows.

It is a fact that the best computer programs in the game playing domain (e.g. chess, checkers, othello) all use the brute-force approach. Even though a great deal of competent effort has been expended to try to make the knowledge-directed search work, no outstanding programs have resulted. The best exemplars to date are CHAOS, one of the top 4 chess programs in the World, developed at the University of Michigan. It uses a form of best-first search augmented by some brute-force searching. The other exemplar would be my backgammon program, BKG 9.9, that does no searching (the branching factor is about 400), but uses extensive knowledge to play a very good game.

Existing work indicates that very large amounts of knowledge are required to make knowledge-directed search work properly. It is known that a sequential process, such as selecting moves in a game playing environment, is as strong as its weakest link. The slightest failing of such a process has dire consequences that can not be recovered by making a sequence of outstanding moves in a row. This accounts for why CHAOS uses brute-force searches as part of the process of selecting the next node to examine.

There are two basic types of knowledge that interact with search:

1. *Directing* knowledge that is used to guide the knowledge-directed search, and also to a very important extent affect the order in which descendants of a node are examined in the brute-force search. This latter is particularly important as the efficiency of the alpha-beta tree searching technique is known to be highly dependent on the goodness of the order of examining alternatives.
2. *Terminal* knowledge that is applied at the leaf nodes of the search to produce a measure of the goodness of the leaf position. This is used both by knowledge-directed searches and by brute-force searches.

In a knowledge-directed search, directing knowledge and terminal knowledge are very closely related and may be identical. Such a program cannot function without such knowledge, and since the number of nodes is small, all knowledge is welcome. Thus, the opportunities for analyzing trade-offs are very limited.

In brute-force searches cheap directing knowledge is very welcome, but the crux of the matter is the utility of various items of terminal knowledge. Since a terminal evaluation function may be executed millions of times in a single search, each item in such a function contributes heavily to the cost of doing a search, and must justify its own existence. This trade-off will be the major focus of this paper. *

2. The projection ability of knowledge

In a game, there are really only three outcomes possible; win, lose, or draw. All evaluation functions are thus an attempt to project the likelihood of these three outcomes. Even very coarse evaluation functions, such as material count in chess, do a reasonable job at this, as the material balance is highly correlated with who is winning. A material advantage of 2 pawns is almost always decisive at the master level of play, and an advantage of a single pawn is

---

* We assume herein that the knowledge function will be executed serially. With the advent of special purpose hardware, this may no longer be a completely valid assumption.

decisive over one half of the time, assuming there are no major compensations for the inferior side.

However, for sophisticated play a program must be able to recognize many of the more delicate advantages that can be accrued by either side. Some of these advantages, such as an unbreakable pin, will be able to be detected by a search that goes deep enough to find the winning of the pinned man. Other advantages, such as defects in pawn structure, may take a search of 30 or more ply to convert into some material gain. Let us define the projection ability of an item of knowledge as the *average* number of ply the game must proceed before it leads to the win of at least a pawn. Game playing terminology speaks of tactical, positional, and strategic advantages. For chess the respective projection ability of these advantages are approximately 3 to 19 ply, 15 to 40 ply, and 30 to 80 ply. These boundaries are rather arbitrary, but it is not unreasonable to consider the projection abilities of the three types of knowledge to be 9, 25, and 45. In general, it is important to be able to accurately deal with those advantages that are closest at hand, as failure to do this has immediate repercussions. A full-width-search does this, but the more it understands at leaf nodes, the better it will play. We now examine a few examples of the projection ability of several kinds of knowledge in chess.

A very simple kind of knowledge appears in Figure 1. Here, even though Black is two pawns ahead in material, White has a clear win because he has the tactical advantage of an unstoppable QRP. This can be detected by the *rule of the square* (see dark line in Fig. 1), which states that in order to prevent a passed pawn from queening, the defending king must be within the square when it is the pawn's turn to move. In the present case, the rule of the square is equivalent to what would be discovered in a 10 ply search. The projection ability of this item depends on the degree of advancement of the pawn, and can vary between 2 and 10. It is only applicable in pawn endings, but this is a

Fig. 1. Black to play.

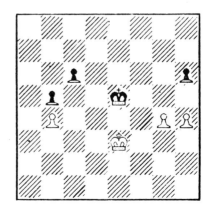

Fig. 2. White to play.

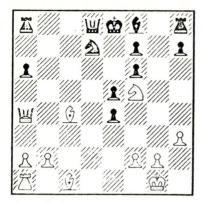

Fig. 3. Black to play.

decisive advantage when it occurs, and the ability to detect it is of considerable value.

In Fig. 2 we see a more subtle type of knowledge in action. White wins easily because Black's extra pawn on the queen side cannot be advanced effectively. The win would become apparent with a search of about 12 ply in this case. The noting of this type of pawn structure (the so-called *backward QBP*) is a strategic advantage that is applicable at all stages of the game and has a projection ability of 30 to 50 ply.

Our final example, in Fig. 3, shows a much more difficult advantage to encode. Here Black has a rook plus pawn versus bishop, but his king's position is very unsafe. In fact, a good player will immediately understand that White's positional advantage is worth much more than his material deficit. Yet, how good players perceive this is not completely clear. If Black could somehow survive, his material advantage would be decisive. But to a good player, this seems very unlikely. Most, if not all chess programs would judge this position as favorable for Black, a signal failing in their knowledge apparatus, because they err toward the conservative in making such advantage trade-off decisions. The projection ability of knowledge of this kind is on the order of 20 to 30 ply. In the actual game (Fischer-Najdorf, 1962), Black resigned 18 ply later, when he was still ahead in material.

3. Data from actual programs

Some information on the knowledge/search trade-off is available from actual programs. In practice, there is usually only a small range of choices in any implementation. For instance, if a game is not completely solved by either search or knowledge, then some amount of each will be required. Usually, the question comes down to how much evaluation of terminal nodes is done, since each instruction used in this process, is muliplied by the number of terminal nodes examined. Thus, opting for large scale evaluations may produce good judgements, but will radically cut down the search effort. So, evaluation is done with an eye on the effort required, and reduced to what can be done quickly and be of considerable use.

The knowledge on this trade-off comes mainly from computer chess. During the 1970's CHESS 3.0 thru 4.9, the Northwestern University Chess Program, was the best around. It was a model of searching efficiency; in fact, the basic searching techniques now used by all the top chess programs were developed by Slate and Atkin during their work on this program (Slate and Atkin, 1977). However, its evaluating ability was even more outstanding. For instance, it understood many of the strategic advantages relating to pawn structure, such as the example in Fig. 2. It also had much positional knowledge relating to the placement of pieces with respect to the pawn structure. During this decade, CHESS x.x. played a number of games against TECH, TECH-II and other programs that searched about one ply more deeply than it, but had no strategic and only very little positional knowledge. In every case CHESS, the program with the better terminal knowledge, won the game.

Another data point comes from some studies on TECH (Gillogly, 1978). Its terminal evaluation only counted material on the board, and was thus as simple as possible. Apart from this, TECH applied knowledge of the location of the pieces to each of the immediate descendants of the root node. These nodes were thus ordered with respect to "desirabilty". When the brute-force search operated, it would choose the best move from the material point of view, and if there were several, the above ordering would select the best "positional" move among these. This unusual form of knowledge application is no longer being used. Nowadays, most chess programs that do little terminal evaluation at least apply piece location knowledge incrementally on the way down a branch, so that it is available at the leaf nodes where it has more permanency.

Various versions of the TECH program, with and without root knowledge, and running at different searching depths, were played against each other. The overall result was that the root knowledge was worth approximately 1 ply of search. Such knowledge must have some value, as it provides the pieces with some sense of direction. However, such direction is of very limited value, as a piece could move to a promising location on its move at the root, only to be attacked and sent back in the next few ply. Thus a projection ability of 1 ply appears about right. Another noteworthy datum from this research is the fact that the quiescence search (the pursuit of all captures and recaptures in terminal positions) is worth at least four ply of search. At first glance this appears excessive. However, when one considers that without a quiescence search, a program cannot tell the difference between a bona fide capture of material at the last ply, and a move that merely initiates an exchange, then it becomes clear how important such information really is.

Another data point comes from Othello, a game that has recently risen to prominence both in human and computer competition. A program at Carnegie-Mellon University, IAGO, authorised by Paul Rosenbloom (Rosenbloom, 1981) is now the best program in the World and very likely the best player too. It achieved a perfect score against an international field in a recent tournament of all the best Othello programs, and the current human champion politely declined a challenge match offer. This program won its decisive victory by virtue of its superior knowledge. It frequently was opposed by programs that searched one to two ply deeper, but in each case its superior understanding produced lop-sided contests. In fact, the only close games were with the programs that had the best evaluation functions. So here is a clear case favoring knowledge. Actually, the best humans probably know somewhat more about Othello than IAGO does; however, its ability to look ahead 6 ply at all possibilities during the middle game, and all the way to the end of the game when only 14 moves are left, more than make up for the small superiority in the human's understanding.

IAGO has extensive tables of compiled information relating to the worth of edge configurations (the most stable parts of any Othello position), and also the ability to understand important factors such as the mobility for each side. The projection ability of mobility is such that it produces advantages that last the whole game long (up to 50 ply at times) while correct understanding of edge configurations is worth at least 20 ply. Rosenbloom estimates that IAGO would defeat a program not having such knowledge, even if it searched 20 ply deeper.

In backgammon there has not been any direct comparison, partly because the branching factor is so large as to make it impossible to search more than two or three ply from the root node. Such a search could hardly afford to do very much evaluation; possibly just two or three of the most important, easily computable features. In backgammon, major advantages relate to blockading, preparing to blockade, and avoiding being blockaded. These factors require complicated computations. The projection ability of blockading information is at least 8 ply. It is unlikely that a program that did not understand much about blockading would do well against my program BKG9.9, which does not search at all, but has very comprehensive knowledge of all phases of the game. I am sure the searching program would at times make a better move than BKG9.9, however, this should be outweighed by the number of times it would not be able to rely on its superficial evaluation function.

From the above, it appears that the most successful programs have the longest projection ability knowledge. However, this says nothing about how well matched inferior programs are with respect to knowledge with shorter projection ability; though one would have to assume that the match would have to be fairly good else one program would win quickly.

It appears that some balance between depth of search and goodness of terminal knowledge may be required. One indication of this comes from the performance of the chess program/machine BELLE (Condon and Thompson, 1982). BELLE searches to a depth of at least 8 ply plus quiescence in all positions, and deeper once material starts to disappear off the board in large quantities. BELLE uses an evaluation method similar to the one used in the Northwestern program. While this was very good during the time that CHESSx.x moved up from Class "C" to Expert level chess player, it does not seem to be adequate for the Master level performance that BELLE is otherwise extremely well equipped for. At tactics (the precise calculation of variations), BELLE would undoubtedly be a welcome consultant to any chess player in the world. However, in positional understanding it has at times made mistakes that no human Master would possibly make. It is quite possible that there is a delicate balance between the amount of search and the amount of knowledge required in a game playing program, and here it has tipped too far toward search.

Every knowledge item contemplated for inclusion in an evaluation function has a definite cost associated with it. For each, a study must be made to see if the cost of including it pays its way; a process that is tedious and fraught with difficulties since sometimes a single knowledge item will not produce much of a change, while in combination with some as yet untried item, it would be very valuable. However, it appears clear that in all the above domains, knowledge is extremely important and the effort should be to get as much in as possible, rather than to get along on as little as possible.

4. What can be done with very little knowledge

However, the value of the search alone should not be underestimated. An example of the power of a deep searching program can be seen in Fig. 4, from a game BLITZ–BELLE, North-American Computer Chess Championships, 1979. Here Black to play won brilliantly by 10. --RxP!!, 11. KxR, Q-R5ch, 12. K-R1, N-N6!!, 13. Q-R5 (a typical delay when the worst has been discovered), PxQ, 14. PxNch, N-B6 mate a combination encompassing 7 ply. Another variation would be 11. NxN, Q-R5, 12. N-N3, QxN!!, 13. PxQch, N-B6 mate, also 7 ply long.

By any standards, human or machine, this is a brilliant performance. However, any program that searches to a depth of 7 ply, and has only knowledge of the value of material would play this position correctly. It only needs to see that the initial move results in the gain of material (White can stave off the mate by some delaying sacrifices). This combination would also be fairly easy for any human Expert. However, his mode of discovering the

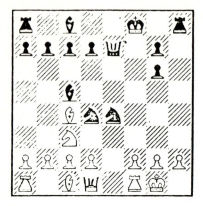

Fig. 4. Black to play.

combination would be quite different. He would almost certainly see a standard sacrificial pattern relating to the initial move and the follow-up Q-R5. However, everything must be calculated in detail. Further, there is the possibility that the Expert may be put off the track by the fact that just before the mate White will make a capture with check, and he may not see that the reply is a check-blocking double check that is mate. Such moves are very, very rare except in composed problems and good players have been known to overlook such things. However, a brute-force searching program makes such combinations with ease, never even realizing that it is making a "sacrifice", because from its materialistic view the "sacrifice" leads to material gain. A further indication of the strength of the search alone is BELLE's performance on a set of 300 chess problems that have been used for a decade now to evaluate chess programs (Reinfeld, 1958). It only got 19.5 wrong (.5 credit is given when the correct move is tendered but the supporting analysis is not all present) out of the set. According to the compiler of the volume, a master could expect to get about 30 wrong. However, the most surprising thing was that BELLE discovered 9 errors in the solutions presented by the author, only two of which were previously known. This dramatically shows certain limitations of the human pattern recognition and analysis apparatus. However, such combinations are possible against good opposition only when a great deal of groundwork has been laid by the previous play; something that even World Computer Champion BELLE has not been able to do consistently. Additional examples of the performance of brute-force programs may be found in Berliner (1981).

5. The incompleteness of almost all knowledge

In any interesting domain it will not be possible to have a complete catalog of states of the domain. Thus, it will be necessary to have a method for aggregating states into classes. Then a single measure can stand for a class. This measure is the result of evaluation based on commonality of features throughout the class. In Berliner (1980) we dicussed the problems that can arise when artificial boundaries between such classes exist. Two domain elements on either side of such a boundary could receive quite disparate evaluations when, in fact, they should be quite close. To circumvent this problem, it was found useful to develop evaluation functions that were smooth. These functions were non-linear to allow the major differences that could be expected to be associated with different classes. However, domain elements did not just belong or not belong to a class (boolean relationship). Instead, they had a degree of membership in any given class specified by an application coefficient (similar to a *characteristic function* in fuzzy set theory). By controlling set membership through slowly varying application coefficients that understood global context, it was possible to avoid such boundary problems.

However, there are considerable problems in most domains in deciding what a class should include. The descriptions of the positions of Fig. 5 and Fig. 6 are very nearly the same. Thus they could easily end up in the same class even though in Fig. 5 whoever moves loses, while in Fig. 6 no matter who moves, White will lose his pawn but still be able to draw. In both cases, anything except a very knowledgeable evaluation function would probably consider the position even. However, if this is a terminal judgement on one branch of a tree, then a considerable error will propagate upward in the case of Fig. 5. Of course, it is possible to create functions that correctly analyse such situations. For such simple situations this has been done (Perdue and Berliner, 1977). However, as complexity increases, it will become harder and harder to create such knowledge functions.

The obvious "solution" is to invoke pattern recognition, but this technique has definite limitations also. Consider the position in Fig. 6. Here, White to

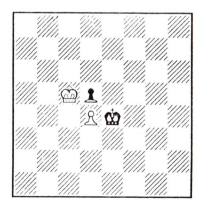

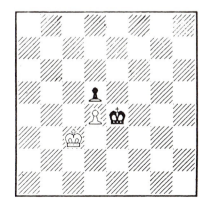

Fig. 5.

Fig. 6.

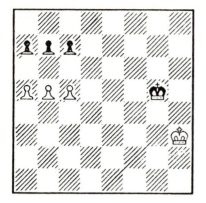
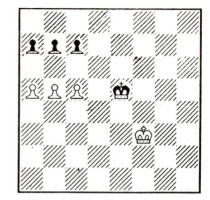

Fig. 7. White to play.   Fig. 8. White to play.

play can win by executing the well known maneuver 1. P-N6, BPxP, 2. P-R6, NPxP, 3. P-B6 and this pawn will queen. Now, this pawn formation is worth remembering as this break-thru is always possible. However, it would be a mistake to believe that this is always an advantage in King and Pawn endings. Consider Fig. 8, which is Fig. 7 with the kings each shifted 2 squares to the left. Now, White to play loses because the black king is too close for the above maneuver to succeed, and White will lose at least a pawn with the resultant losing position. For this example, it would be harder to define a knowledge function that would appraise the situation correctly. If such a function were created, it would undoubtedly have a very narrow range of applicability; this implying that a very large number of functions would be required to adequately cover any domain. Instead, it would seem that the correct method is to refuse to statically evaluate positions where there are counter-indications (in the above example the break-thru formation exists favoring White, while the black king in the vicinity of the pawns favors Black). This would suggest that it is wisest not to make a final decision here, but instead require more searching to resolve the problem.

6. The B* search

There is a searching method that works ideally in such an environment. It is the B* search (Berliner, 1979). One of the features of this search is that nodes may be assigned a value range instead of a point value. The endpoints of this range represent the optimistic and pessimistic bounds of the real value. Ranges can be backed up in a way that is very similar to the backing up of values in a search with point-valued nodes. The search terminates when the pessimistic value of the best descendant of the root is no worse than the optimistic value of the rest of its sibling nodes. Two strategies may be invoked in the search:

the Provebest strategy tries to raise the pessimistic bound of the best node at the root, while the Disproverest strategy tries to lower the optimistic bound of one of its sibling competitors. This search strategy embodies the essentials of the arguments in the previous section, and has been found by simulation to be better than other knowledge based searches (Berliner, 1979). We are implementing B* in a problem solving chess program where it is showing great promise of paying attention to issues that need to be resolved. Present research indicates that augmenting the notion of bounds with probability density functions, over the range from optimistic to pessimistic, does a better job of preserving useful information from lower in the tree, and thus results in more rapid convergence of the search.

7. A knowledge / search paradox

The standard search technique used by today's brute-force game playing programs requires the use of *iterative deepening*. This search technique dictates that a complete search to depth N be done before a search to depth N + 1 be undertaken. This apparently wasteful procedure, actually produces some major savings. A large hash table is used to enter positions at the time they are quitted in the search, together with their backed-up value and the most successful move at that point. This information is of great future use, as it allows the pursuit of known successful moves at future iterations, and also turns the tree into a graph since identical positions in the current iteration need not be searched again. Good ordering of moves also results in being able to avoid searching some sub-trees. These savings are both exponential, and depend upon how near the root avoided sub-trees are anchored. Consider the pawn endgame in Fig. 9. Here White to play can win through a long and

Fig. 9. White to play.

involved series of king maneuvers resulting in breaking through at either KN5 or QN5. The principal variation takes about 30 ply. This prompted Newborn (Newborn, 1977) to estimate that to solve this position on a high speed digital machine would require about 25,000 hours of CPU time.

At first glance this seems a reasonable analysis of the problem. However, when it is noted that until a pawn is captured only king moves can be made for both sides, the situation is given a dramatic turn. There are less than 4000 positions that can result from merely moving the kings, and these can be accommodated in a moderately sized hash table. This will result in progressively quicker searches, and progressively better understanding as the nodes in the hash table proceed toward their correct value, as the search deepens. Programs with such hash tables have now solved this position in a few minutes of CPU time.

While this is an extreme example of the utility of the hash table, it is interesting to consider its role. Whereas usually it acts merely to facilitate the search by providing directing knowledge and making it possible to avoid duplicating effort, here it is the actual repository of terminal knowledge. Assume in such a search, a position is encountered that is to be searched to a depth of N additional ply (where N = Maxdepth − Curdepth). However, the hash table entry indicates that the Maxdepth − Curdepth at the time this entry was made, was larger than the N we wish to achieve at present. This can happen when the current position is nearer to the root than the earlier incarnation that resulted in the hash table entry. These circumstances not only abort the search at this point, but provide a more informed estimate of the node's value than would be found by doing the search to N further ply. It is this action of the hash table that is a remarkable paradox. Clearly, the deeper the searches the more likely it is that such action is possible.

8. Conclusions

Knowledge without search has limited utility as has search without knowledge. For each domain, a certain balance appears to exist; however, 4 to 8 ply worth of searching appear to adequately duplicate the non-knowledge portion of human performance. Each item of knowledge has a projection ability. Programs with long projection ability knowledge appear to be the best. However, short projection ability knowledge must clearly also be accommodated if the longer projection knowledge is to get a chance to exert an effect. Further, the frequency of occurence of each knowledge item also bears on its utility. The latter has not been studied yet.

In brute-force searches knowledge must be applied willy-nilly at the maximum depth to produce a point value. Thus it is forced to take a "view" on any subject. This can result in very skewed views of what is going on. Because of this, it may be that a flexible search such as B* will ultimately still prove better than the brute-force approach, but evidence for such a conclusion is lacking at present.

Chapter 7

ADVICE AND PLANNING IN CHESS ENDGAMES *

IVAN BRATKO

*Faculty of Electrical Engineering and J. Stefan Institute,
E. Kardelj University, Ljubljana, Yugoslavia*

Summary

The paper describes a chess endgame program which is capable of reasoning about the problem in terms of plans and "advice". The king and pawn vs. king and pawn ending is used in experiments with the system.

1. Introduction

Chess playing programs are, in general, of two types:

(A) search-based
(B) knowledge-based.

The programs of type A rely on the ability of deeply searching large subtrees of the game-tree, up to a uniform depth of 8 or 9 ply (e.g. BELLE, Thompson, 1981), and in addition the capture sequences up to their end. The simplicity of the structure of such programs makes it possible to implement them very efficiently in terms of the number of positions that the program can search per second. For example the Thompson's program BELLE, which uses a special purpose chess machine that implements in hardware the legal move genarator and the alpha-beta search procedure, can investigate 150 thousand positions per second.

On the other hand, the knowledge-based programs rely on the use of chess knowledge in order to intelligently guide the analysis thereby reducing the search. As the use of knowledge itself takes time such programs can search much smaller portions of the game tree. The idea is that less search is compensated by knowledge. This trade-off between search and knowledge is analysed in more detail by Berliner (1984, same volume).

---

* Part of this work was done during the author's stay at Machine Intelligence Research Unit, University of Edinburgh.

In computer chess tournaments, the existing search-based programs tend to dominate the knowledge-based programs. The latter are, however, of much greater scientific interest in artificial intelligence. From the expert-systems viewpoint it is important to realise that the structure of the knowledge-based programs is much more suitable for generating the human-understandable explanations of the program's decisions.

The interesting research problem is how to represent and use the chess knowledge in order to reduce search. Several ideas have been investigated: Berliner's program CAPS 2 (Berliner, 1977) uses, among other mechanisms, the principle of causal reasoning. If the program discovers that an idea being analysed fails, it tries to identify the cause of the failure and directs its reasoning towards the removal of the cause. The programs of Pitrat (1977) and Wilkins (1979) use plans to find forced combinations in the middle game. Some attempts to use chess knowledge in endgames are: Huberman (1968), Bramer (1977), and the work on Advice Language 1 (e.g. Bratko and Michie, 1980). A more recent development of the latter work is the AL3 System described in Bratko (1981).

AL3 is a problem-solver which uses declarative knowledge about the domain of application. The architecture of the system is that of pattern-directed inference systems (e.g. Waterman and Hayes-Roth, 1978). The experimental domain to which AL3 has been applied is the chess ending with king and pawn vs. king and pawn (KPKP). Although this constitutes only a tiny sub-domain of chess it is rich enough to contain many interesting ideas that have been used in chess studies from this sub-domain (e.g. Averbakh and Maizelis, 1974).

This paper describes in more detail a formalism for plans and advice, and a way that they can be used for representing knowledge in the chess endgame.

2. The use of plans in endgame positions

The example of Fig. 1 illustrates the use of plans in reasoning about endgame positions. The following outline is essentially a trace of the behaviour of AL3 when solving this problem.

The system starts with the initial hypothesis (call it h0): Can White win? The only way for White to win in the position of Fig. 1 is to promote the White pawn. The simplest idea for achieving that is a straightforward plan: 'Push the White pawn until it becomes a queen resulting in a won position.' Call this plan WPQ (White pawn queens). So we have a hypothesis, h1, based on this idea: 'Plan WPQ succeeds.' The system also generates a fact: If plan WPQ succeeds then White wins.

Now the system finds counter ideas for Black. These are:

– Stop White pawn by the Black king (call the plan based on this idea SWP).
– Push Black pawn and queen (call the plan based on this idea BPQ).

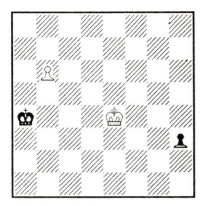

Fig. 1. White to move, can White win. If yes, how?

In association with these ideas the system also generates two hypotheses:

h2: Plan SWP refutes plan WPQ?
h3: Plan BPQ refutes plan WPQ?

Each of these two hypotheses, if proved to be true, implies that the plan WPQ does not succeed (i.e. h1 is false). It is easy to see (by the pawn-square rule) that the plan SWP does not refute the plan WPQ. The hypothesis h3 can be investigated by searching a part of the game-tree. As both plans that occur in this hypothesis, WPQ and BPQ, are restricted to pawn-moves only, the corresponding search is of trivial size: 5 nodes. The search produces the variation (without branching):

1 b7 h2 2 b8 queens h1 queens

In the resulting position both pawns have queened and the position is a clear draw. So we have the fact "h3 is true", and consequently h1 is false, i.e. plan WPQ fails.

Here the system tries to improve the White's initial idea, WPQ, by removing the cause for its failure. That is: find a plan that counters the plan BPQ. One idea is: stop Black pawn (SBP). A new plan for White is thus found which is modification of the original one:

WPQ "modified by" SBP

This composed plan says: Promote the pawn by pushing it and win, but in the meantime, if necessary, stop the Black pawn. This turns out to be the winning plan which gives the correct move: 1 Kf3. If now 1 ... h2 then 2 Kg2, else advance the White pawn. That this plan succeeds against *any* legal Black move is established by search which takes 197 nodes. If only those Black moves are searched that "make sense" rather than all legal moves, the size of this search is reduced to 57 nodes. The moves that "make sense" are simply those moves which correspond to one of the Black's plans SBP or BPQ.

The AL3 implementation of the problem-solving behaviour, outlined above, is based on formalism for plans which is given in the next section.

3. Formalism for plans

Most of the reasoning during problem-solving in AL3 is concerned with plans. Ingredients of plans are:

- conditions that are to be achieved or maintained (called *goals*),
- means of achieving these conditions (called *move-constraints*).

In order to define precise meaning of plans and notions like "a plan succeeds" or "a plan refutes another plan" we use the concept of "piece-of-advice" in a similar sense as defined in the previous work on Advice Languages (e.g. Bratko and Michie, 1980). This concept provides a firmly defined framework for reasoning about plans.

A *piece-of-advice* is a five-tuple

(X, BG, HG, MCX, MCY)

where X is the side (White or Black) to which A belongs, BG and HG are predicates on positions called *better-goal* and *holding-goal* respectively; MCX and MCY are predicates on moves, called move-constraints for side X and Y respectively. We use X and Y to represent both sides. Thus X is always White or Black, and Y is the opponent of X. Move-constraints can, besides a mere selection of a subset of legal moves, prescribe an ordering on the moves that are selected.

We say the a piece-of-advice is *satisfiable* in a position Pos if and only if

(1) the side X can force the achievement of the better-goal while
(2) during the play toward the better-goal, the holding-goal is never violated, and
(3) X always chooses his moves only from the set of moves that satisfy the condition MCX, and
(4) Y always chooses his moves only from the set of moves that satisfy MCY.

A situation in which

(1) the holding goal holds, and
(2) the better goal does not hold, and
(3) it is Y to move and there is no legal move for Y such that MCY is satisfied,

is interpreted as if the better-goal has been achieved. This entails that stalemate in chess has to be explicitly stated. We write

sat(A,Pos)

meaning: a piece-of-advice A is satisfiable in a position Pos.

If A is satisfiable in Pos then there is a *forcing-tree* which represents a detailed strategy for the achievement of the goals of A. A forcing tree is a subtree of the game-tree, rooted in Pos, and containing for each allowed Y-move exactly one X-move up to the terminating condition: better-goal or "no-move" situation.

A *plan* P is a quadruple

(X, BG, HG, MCX)

where X is the side to which P belongs, and BG, HG and MCX are goals and move-constraints with the same meaning as in piece-of-advice. The only formal difference between the concepts of plan and piece-of-advice is that in plans, the opponent of X, Y, is not restricted by any move-constraint condition.

A plan P = (X, BG, HG, MCX) *succeeds* in a position Pos if and only if sat(A,Pos) where

A = (X, BG, HG, MCX, anymove)

The Y's move-constraint "anymove" allows for any legal move.

Let Px and Py be plans

Px = (X, BGX, HGX, MCX)
Py = (Y, BGY, HGY, MCY)

Py *refutes* Px in a position Pos if sat(A,Pos) where

A = (Y, not HGX or BGY, HGY and not (BGX and HGX), MCY, MCX)

These definitions basically reflect the intuitive notions of "plan succeeds" and "plan refutes another plan". But they also say what happens in "boundary" cases which are left undecided by common sense, for example: what happens if both holding-goals HGX and HGY get destroyed at the same time. The above definition puts more weight on the failure of HGY which is an arbitrary decision. In practice, however, such "boundary" cases never occur during the system's reasoning about plans if only the plans are defined naturally so as to make sense with respect to the problem being solved.

Plans can be combined into more elaborated plans by using operators on plans: *or* and *mod*. If P1 and P2 are plans

P1 = (X, BG1, HG1, MCX1)
P2 = (X, BG2, HG2, MCX2)

then

P1 *or* P2 = (X, BG1 or BG2, HG1 or HG2, MCX1 or MCX2)

P1 *mod* P2 = (X, BG1, HG1, MCX1 mod MCX2)

The operator "or" on goals has the obvious meaning: logical disjunction. The operations "or" and "mod" on move-constraints define besides move-selection also ordering on moves as follows:

MCX1 or MCX2:
select moves that satisfy MCX1 or MCX2 or both, ordered roughly by the criterion "first satisfy both MCX1 and MCX2"; fine ordering is as prescribed by MCX1 and MCX2;

MCX1 mod MCX2:
select moves that satisfy MCX1 or MCX2 or both, ordered roughly by: first, satisfy both MCX1 and MCX2, second, satisfy MCX1 only, third, satisfy MCX2 only; fine ordering as prescribed by MCX1 and MCX2.

There are two other natural ways of combining plans: "conjunction" and sequencing. Somewhat surprisingly they turned out to be of no use in the experiments with the KPKP ending. Sequencing can be treated as a special case of *mod*.

4. Reasoning about plans and their elaboration

In AL3 plans correspond to ideas for solving problems. The general problem-solving strategy used by AL3 in chess endings is to try simple ideas first. If they do not work then find more sophisticated plans by combining simpler plans.

Simple plans are generated through motifs observed in the given position. For example, in the pawn ending, if there is a hypothesis "White can win?" and White has passed pawn, then a simple idea is: try to straightforwardly advance the pawn, promote it into a queen, and win; necessary conditions for this plan to succeed are: the pawn must not be captured and must not be stopped by the opponent's king. This is easily expressed in our formalism for plans:

P = "White, queen and win, pawn-alive and not stopped, pushpawn)

More sophisticated plans are generated through the use of operators *or* and *mod* for combining plans. There are two main principles for generating more elaborate plans:

1. Combine two already existing plans that are known to fail into their or-combination.
2. For a plan that fails, find the cause of the failure and modify the plan so as to hopefully remove the cause of the failure.

In the system's knowledge-base there are *methods* that suggest how and when to combine simple plans into more elaborate ones. As these methods are independent of particular plans, they represent the system's meta-knowledge about plans. These methods are, as all other methods in AL3, realised as pattern-directed modules. They consist of:

(1) a precondition pattern, and
(2) an action.

If the current knowledge about the problem being solved contains the precondition pattern then the action can be triggered. Actions are procedures that update the current knowledge. The current knowledge is a structure containing:

— definitions of plans and pieces-of-advice,
— hypotheses about the problem, eg. "Plan P succeeds",
— logical relations among hypotheses,
— currently known facts about the truth or falsity of hypotheses.

In the KPKP ending, only three methods for plan elaboration were used. They implement rather fundamental ideas and are limited neither to this particular ending nor to chess. These three methods are as follows.

Method ORPLAN. The idea behind this method is: if there are two plans that have both turned out not to work, then consider their or-combination. The details of the method are:

if precondition
   (1) there is a hypothesis H: suc(P,Pos), and
   (2) there are hypotheses H1: ref(R1,P,Pos) and
                         H2: ref(R2,P,Pos), and
   (3) there are the facts "H1 is false" and "H2 is false"

then action

   (1) generate the hypothesis H3: ref (R1 *or* R2, P, Pos)
   (2) generate the fact: H3 $\Rightarrow$ not H

The way that this method affects the current knowledge about the problem at hand is graphically illustrated in fig. 2.

Method MODPLAN1. Here the idea is: if there is a plan, P1, that has turned out not to work because of a counter plan R, then try to modify the original plan P1 by a plan P2 such that P2 counters the plan R. The detailed formulation of this method is graphically presented in Fig 3.

Method MODPLAN2. If there is a plan, R1, about which we already know that (1) R1 refutes a plan P1, and (2) R1 cannot refute a modified plan P1 *mod* P2, then modify the plan R1 by a plan, R2, which counters the plan P2. Fig. 4 shows details.

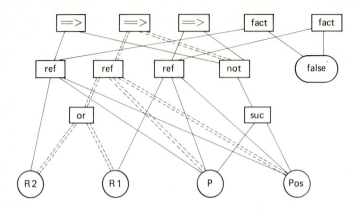

Fig. 2. Illustration of method ORPLAN. Solid lines represent the precondition pattern, dashed lines represent the result of the action as it is added to the current knowledge about the problem. P, R1 and R2 are plans, Pos is a position.

This simple meta-knowledge structure draws the system's attention on important aspects of the problem. The plan modification methods MOD-PLAN1 and MODPLAN2 implement the causal reasoning. They concentrate on the cause of the failure and try to improve ideas by modifying them toward the removal of the cause of the failure. For example, in the position of Fig. 1, the correct plan for White was found through the modification of the original plan. The original White's plan "push White pawn" (WPQ) failed against the Black's plan "push Black pawn". The improvement was based on the modification of the original plan with "stop Black pawn" (SBP). This resulted in the

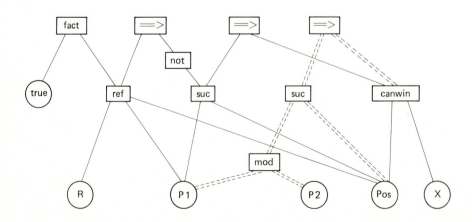

Fig. 3. Method MODPLAN1. Solid lines represent the precondition, dashed lines the result of the action. P1, P2 and R are plans, Pos is a position.

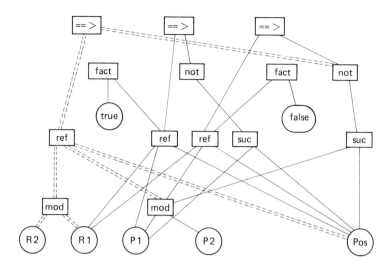

Fig. 4. Method MODPLAN2. Solid lines represent the precondition, dashed lines the result. P1, P2, R1, R2 are plans, Pos is a position.

correct

WPQ *mod* SBP

The plan modification methods produce a similar pattern of reasoning, although on different plans, when solving the problem of Fig.5. Here, the original White's idea "push White pawn" (WPQ) gets refuted by Black's "stop White pawn" (SWP). This time the cause of the failure is different and accordingly the White's original plan is modified by "stop Black king" (SBK).

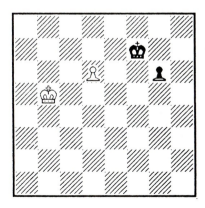

Fig. 5. White to move wins by 1 Kc6. If now 1 ... Ke8 then 2 Kc7, if 1 ... g5 then 2 d7 Ke7 3 Kc7 etc.

The correct plan is thus

WPQ *mod* SBK

The last example also illustrates that this way of reasoning about plans in effect leads to the discovery of higher level ideas. The plan WPQ *mod* SBK corresponds to the concept which would in chess be called "joint attack of pawn and king".

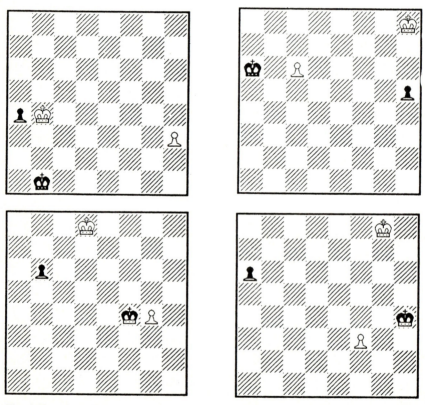

Fig. 6. Four interesting positions from Averbakh and Maizelis (1974). (A) A position from the game Yates-Marshall 1929. Two moves before this position was reached White had a completely won position, but chose this continuation not forseeing that now Black draws by 1 Kb2 KxP 2 Kc3. (B) A study by Reti: White to move draw. Solution is : 1 Kg7 h4 2 Kf6 and if (a) 2 ... h3 Ke6 h2 4 c7 and White pawn queens in time; if (b) 2 ... Kb6 3 Ke5 h3 4 Kd6 and White pawn again queens in time. If Black captures White pawn White king catches Black pawn. (C) A study by Leick: White to move and draw. Solution: 1 Ke7 b5 2 Kf6 and if 2 ... b4 then g5 else if 2 ... KxP 3 Ke5. (D) A study by Prokes: White to move and draw. Solution: 1 Kf7 a5 2 f4 a4 3 f5 a3 4 f6 a2 5 Kg8 a1 queens 6 f7. White has reached a drawing pattern with pawn vs. queen.

5. Performance and pattern-knowledge vs. search

The AL3 system is implemented in Prolog on DEC-10. Some aspects of the the implementation, in particular the way that individual pieces of the current knowledge about the problem are integrated through their logical relations, are described in Bratko (1981). The experimental knowledge-base for the KPKP ending is capable of solving difficult chess studies from this domain although it is not perfect in the following sense: the success or failure of plans can be, in principle, investigated by searching the game tree; the point is, however, to avoid large searches; in our experiments the search-size was typically limited to 100 or 200 nodes. Under this restriction some of the difficult KPKP problems are not correctly solved by the system.

Fig. 6 shows four examples of nontrivial problems correctly solved by AL3. We present these positions here in order to illustrate one interesting observation from KPKP experiments concerning the dilemma of pattern-knowledge vs. search. The point indicated by the experiments is: very small searches can often produce useful information; therefore search should be used as practical way to solve easy (sub)problems. For complicated problems, however, search gets larger and is not economical any more. Harder problems have to be solved gradually by investigating easier subproblems and combining simpler ideas.

Therefore AL3 typically performs a number of small, "local" searches on subproblems thereby gathering information for streamlining the higher-level reasoning about the whole problem. Simple subproblems in KPKP are typically concerned with questions like: "Can a king catch a pawn?" or "Can one king obtain control over a given square before the other king can reach it?". Such questions can often be answered by pattern-knowledge, and they can always be answered by search. Pattern-based solutions are often lengthy and hard to program, while search-based solutions are easily expressed in terms of advice. Pattern-based solutions are typically faster than search-based, but the latter are often not impractically slow if the size of search is small. The interesting question is: what is the right proportion between search and pattern-knowledge in the program. After exhaustive experiments, the following strategy has been adopted for AL3: first try to investigate questions by limited search (each search attempt is given a budget of, say, 100 nodes); if the search budget is exhausted before an answer is found then other (more sophisticated) methods are tried. One advantage of search is that it produces firm facts while many other methods (like plan combination methods) tend to produce more ideas and further hypotheses to be investigated. Usually simple plans are easily investigated by small searches. Results from such searches provide information for properly formulating more sophisticated plans. More sophisticated plans may get so complex that they cannot be any more investigated by limited search, but they at least contain the right ideas. If plans become too complex for search and no other method works then AL3 "vaguely" analyses them by

Table 1
Some statistical figures on the use of search when solving problems of Figs. 1, 5, 6. Columns are: N = number of nodes searched; R = result of search (result can be: F = "fact found"; L = "search limit exceeded"; B = "best try"); S = size of forcing tree (if any); D = depth of forcing tree.

Position	N	R	S	D	Position	N	R	S	D
Fig. 1						30	F	–	–
	4	F	–	–		3	F	3	2
	5	F	5	4	Leick	4	F	–	–
	44	B	35	7		30	F	–	–
	193	F	65	7		201	L	–	–
						143	B	29	6
Fig. 5	3	F	–	–		10	F	10	9
	4	F	4	3		18	F	–	–
	3	F	–	–	Prokes	8	F	–	–
	37	F	–	–		201	L	–	–
	56	B	37	7		53	B	43	8
	101	F	77	7					
Reti	3	F	3	2	Yates vs. Marshall	3	F	3	2
	6	F	–	–		4	F	–	–
	35	F	–	–		14	F	–	–
	201	L	–	–		201	L	–	–
	72	B	58	9		146	B	9	4

limited search to the maximal depth that can still be reached within the search-limit. The corresponding depth-bound solution in the form of a forcing-tree is then offered as the "best try" for both sides.

Table 1 gives some figures on the nature of searches when solving problems of Figs. 1, 5, 6. The last problem (Prokes) is, on the other hand, an example where the pattern-knowledge is essential. The goal position of this study, arising after 6 moves, is a known drawing pattern which can be easily recognised as pattern. In this case, the search-based decision would be incomparably more costly.

ARTIFICIAL AND HUMAN INTELLIGENCE (A. Elithorn and R. Banerji, editors)
Elsevier Science Publishers, B.V.
© NATO, 1984

Chapter 8

ORBIT: A TOOL FOR BUILDING AI SYSTEMS IN AN OBJECT-ORIENTED STYLE

LUC STEELS *

Schlumberger-Doll Research, Old Quarry Road, Ridgefield CT 06877, USA

1. Introduction

Complex AI systems are seldom built directly in LISP. Normally a package of tools is used which contains programming abstractions and datastructures that are domain independent utilities for designing systems in a certain style. A specific system is then constructed using these tools rather than the primitive LISP functions. This paper is an informal introduction to such a package called ORBIT.

ORBIT is an interactive LISP-based programming system for artificial intelligence applications. It is based on the ideas of frames, object-oriented programming, semantic networks and description languages. The fundamental unit in the system is called an object. It contains all information about one entity in the domain of discourse and a computational shell in the form of message passing machinery, which enables it to interact with other objects (or the user) via message passing. Message passing is not visible to the user except when he traces it explicitly.

Objects can be related to other objects through generalization hierarchies, part-whole hierarchies or equality relationships. Objects can also be in one or more contexts and be activated via associative links. A variety of functions for accessing the components of objects is available. Inheritance based on the generalization hierarchies is taken care of, even if objects have multiple parents and the hierarchy is circular. Utilities to ease system development include functions for changing objects either on-line or through a text-oriented editor, a file-system for storing and retrieving objects including a mechanism for selectively loading compiled objects, facilities for stepping, tracing and timing message passing between objects, and a character-oriented TOPS-20 style command interface which handles defaults, abbreviations and explanations for each command. ORBIT runs on the VAX in Franzlisp and on the DEC-20 in Maclisp. It is currently used in several applications, including a symbolic

---

* Present address: Vrije Universiteit Brussel, Pleinlaan 2, B-1050 Brussels, Belgium.

VLSI-design system, and a knowledge-based geological expert system.

Making AI tool-packages is in a sense a never ending endeavour. Hundreds of issues need to be resolved and often certain applications will require new features. Nevertheless ORBIT as it exists today is a practical tool effective for constructing real-world applications.

The rest of the paper is in three parts. Section 2 introduces the basic structures supported by ORBIT. Section 3 discusses the interaction with the system for building expert systems. Section 4 contains a small example.

2. Basic structures

ORBIT is an object-oriented system in the sense that knowledge and computational activity is organized in terms of the objects of the domain of discourse: all information pertaining to a certain object (including procedural information) is assembled in a single unit. The idea of organizing information in terms of the objects of the domain raises the following issues:

1. What is the nature of the information associated with an object and how is this information structured?
2. What computational machinery will be used to carry out the behavior of an object?
3. What are the relationships between objects, how are they represented and how do related objects interact?

2.1. The structure of objects

We have adopted the principles of frame-theory to deal with the first of these questions. Frame theory states that the information associated with an object is highly varied. For example, it should be possible to store special hints on how to recognize instances of the object, pointers to more general objects, methods on how the object can be compared to other objects, reminders to do something if an instance is encountered, procedures to compute what the object would look like from a different viewpoint, defaults that can be assumed in case no actual values are known, procedures that are able to compute unknown properties, pointers to examples of instances, notes on when, how and why the object was formed or changed, etc.

Note that the information is not just varied because it is about different things. It is also different in type: partially procedural (knowledge on how to do things), partially declarative (knowledge that something is the case), partially meta-knowledge (knowledge about other knowledge). The second point of frame theory is that all this information is structured as a set of questions that can or should be asked about the object. The intuition behind this idea is that knowing what questions one should be prepared to answer is the key to a successful information system. The questions are called the aspects or slots of the frame.

ORBIT has datastructures for representing objects in terms of frames with aspects and facets for each aspect. The facets include a VALUE facet to store the value of the aspect, a PROCEDURE facet containing a procedure to compute the value, a DEFAULT facet containing a procedure that can compute the value of the aspect in an instance if no value is mentioned, a RESTRICTIONS facet containing a set of predicates that have to be true for the value, an EXPLANATION facet containing documentation on the aspect and a DEMONS facet containing procedures that have to be executed when the value changes.

2.2. Object-oriented programming

The answer to the second question, namely what is the nature of the computational machinery that activates an object, is provided by another line of research associated with the paradigm of object-oriented programming.

Consider the problem of writing a program that will print something. One way to do this is to write a subroutine that can be used whenever something needs to be printed. This subroutine will have a number of cases such as (i) if the object to be printed is a number, use procedure x, (ii) if the object is a list structure, use procedure y, etc. This style of programming is called action-oriented. The programmer thinks in terms of what actions need to be performed, analyses the possible cases and then defines subactions for each case.

There is also a different, object-oriented way to write programs. In an object-oriented programming style, a set of object-types are defined and actions are organized around these types. For example, instead of specifying in a general print function how numbers, lists, strings, arrays, etc. need to be printed, a method is associated with each kind of object that specifies how it should be printed. When an object of type x needs to be printed the method associated with x is invoked. The object types could be very domain specific. For example, there could be a transistor and an inverter type if the problem domain involves electronic circuits.

Object-oriented programming languages are languages that support programming in an object-oriented style. They have primitives for defining objects, specifying relations between objects, creating and manipulating objects, associating procedures with objects, etc. Recently object-oriented programming systems have been conceived more and more as parallel systems, at least conceptually. Each object is viewed as an active computational unit that interacts with other objects via message passing. The response to a message could be to send a reply, to change state, or to send out more messages.

It is not hard to see the similarities between frame theory and object-oriented programming. Both propose to organize knowledge in terms of objects. Frame theory focuses more on the representation (cf. the idea of aspects and facets) whereas object-oriented programming focuses on computational issues (cf. the idea of message passing). The two methodologies can be combined in the sense that a frame can be viewed as a specific kind of object. The aspects are the topics about which messages can be sent. The facets are types of messages, and the contents of a facet is a method for responding to that type of message. The object with its message passing machinery acts like a computational shell around the frame.

This approach, which could be called frame-based object-oriented programming has been adopted for ORBIT. The system is frame-based because a user specifies knowledge in terms of frames. It is object-oriented because it uses the ideas of object-oriented programming as the underlying computational framework. Message passing is not taken all the way down to the most primitive level as in some pure object-oriented programming systems, but it is restricted to implement the activity and interactions between objects.

2.3. Networks of objects

Given these ideas on the internal structure of objects and their computational properties, we can now turn to the third question, namely what are the relationships between objects and how do objects interact through these relationships. Basically there are three primitive relationships that are absolutely necessary: the specialization relation, the part-whole relation and the equality relation. In the spirit of semantic networks these relationships are represented as links between the nodes that represent the objects to enable fast operations over the semantic relationships. For example, the generalizations of an object are immediately accessible as links going out of the object. In addition, ORBIT is able to represent and utilize associative relationships and partitionings of the objects in a set of possible overlapping contexts.

2.3.1. The specialization relation

The specialization (or generalization) relation is based on the idea that some objects are more general than others, i.e. that one object can be a specialization or instance of another object. For example, a rectangle is a specialization of a polygon and a specific rectangle is an instance of rectangle. We also say that polygon is a parent of rectangle. Based on this relationship objects can be organized in hierarchical trees with the more general objects at the top and the more specific objects lower in the tree. The trees often become more complex because some objects have multiple parents. For example, a ball can be viewed as a specialization of many different objects: a round object, a toy, etc. Also some objects are indirectly defined in terms of themselves, leading to circular trees. The specialization hierarchies are therefore tangled hierarchies rather than strict trees. Multiple parents and circular definitions can be represented in ORBIT without any problem.

The specialization hierarchies impose a clear structure on the objects. They thus aid in the development of the knowledge base and allow an answer to questions of the form "is a rectangle a polygon?". But there is more. Objects which are specializations of others usually inherit part of their structure and behavior from their more general counterpart so that their structure and behavior does not have to be kept explicitly. For example, a particular person can inherit the aspects and facet-contents from the more general person object. the technique of only storing those portions of an object that are different from its parent-objects is known as inheritance. Inheritance eliminates some of the loss in efficiency and memory usage associated with object-oriented systems because information needs to be stored only once. Inheritance also yields extra flexibility. For example, the parent-object can be changed and if a message is sent to any of the instances, this change will be automatically adopted. This feature can only be truly appreciated when several thousands of instances have been created (not an unusual situation in real world applications) and a change needs to be made to the parent!

2.3.2. Part-whole relations

The second primitive relation is the part-whole relationship. More generally, the situation when one object plays a role in another object. In ORBIT part-whole relationships are implemented by making the part be the contents of the value facet in an aspect of the whole. For example, if arm is a part of body, then the arm object would be made the value of the aspect arm in the body object.

Part-whole relationships cause objects to cluster in groups which have various cross-object relations between them. These cross-object relationships have to be maintained in instantiations. In ORBIT this is done by associating environments (i.e. information on bindings) with part-whole relationships. Cross-object relations, and in general references to objects through the role they play in other objects, is done with path-descriptions. A path-description consists of a series of aspects followed by an object. For example, "the density of the sand of the sand-shale-mixture" refers to the value of the density aspect of the object which is the value of the sand aspect in the sand-shale-mixture.

Path-descriptions are one of the key tools in object-oriented representation because they allow the user to refer symbolically to objects that have not been created yet or whose exact values and structure is unknown.

2.3.3. Merges and equality relations

In a sense, equality is a two-way specialization relation: behavior and aspects are inherited between the two objects. For example, given an object John with age 15 and an object Person-1 with location New York, then equality of John and Person-1 implies that if asked for its age, person-1 will reply with 15 and if asked for its location John will replay with New York.

There is however a stronger form of equality where the aspects are not just considered as globally shared but merged. Consider the problem of handling the equation momentum = mass × velocity, assuming there exists an object for product with aspects for result, arg1 and arg2, and an object for a body with aspects for momentum, mass and velocity. Making the body object equal to the product-1 object is not enough, we need to establish merges between the momentum of the body and the result, the mass and arg1 and the velocity and arg2, so that procedures associated with the aspects of the product can be used by the aspects of the body object and vice-versa. ORBIT is able to represent these relationships and perform the appropriate substitutions.

2.4. Associative relationships and contexts

One of the recurring functions in AI systems is the retrieval of objects based on a set of features. The features might be properties of the object, predicates that are true for values of its aspects, features that should remind the system of an object, etc. One way to perform this function is to store association-relations between features and objects. ORBIT has the ability to maintain networks of associative relations and to utilize these relations in retrieval. There are also facilities for automatically building associative networks while objects are being defined. Another utility that is very important for object retrieval is the ability to partition the network of objects into different contexts. For example, in a large geological database, the objects relevant to one geographical area might be put in one context so that search can be restricted within that context. ORBIT has the ability to represent and maintain multiple overlapping contexts.

3. Interacting with objects

A user interacting with ORBIT creates and changes structured objects, builds and modifies networks of objects and causes computational activity inside an object or through message passing between objects.

There are two major ways in which these interactions can take place: through a graphical interface or through a description language. Each of these types of interactions has its specific advantages and has been implemented. In the graphical interface objects and structures between objects are displayed on the screen and by pointing, menu-selection or typing, a user can create, modify and activate objects. Utilities have been written relating ORBIT to the RAMTEK colour-graphics device through a FORTRAN/LISP interface. With the description language the user can type expressions in a semi-declarative language which affect the object-structures, or cause computational activity to happen. The idea is that the internal data-structure (e.g. the existence of facets and aspects) or the computational mechanisms (e.g. the message passing activity) is invisible to the user.

The goal of the description language developed for ORBIT is to use some ideas from natural language in order to exploit the intuitions that users already have in describing objects and relations between objects. Basically a stylized form of English is used with expressions like

(a person)

to refer to an instance of a person object, or

(the father family)

to refer to the object that fills the father aspect in the family object, etc. Although these expressions have a declarative look, each has a procedural interpretation that could involve thousands of instructions. For example, when the expression

(a person)

is encountered the system will create a new object, establish a specialization relation with the person object and check the things that need to be done at the time of creation. Several tools have been developed to facilitate interaction with objects through the description language. One tool is a Tops-20 style command language interface which corrects spelling errors, fills in prompts, explains the structure and parts of a command, etc.

A file package for objects has been developed which can be used with a text-oriented editor (emacs) to define and modify objects through editing. The descriptions can be loaded in the system and interactively debugged in the same way as LISP-functions using LEDIT. This works very well and is the normal way to construct an application. It is also possible (on the VAX implementation) to use the in-core INTERLISP style character-oriented editor. Collections of debugged objects can be stored on disk in a frozen state and fast loaded on demand. A virtual object memory enables the system to deal with thousands of objects.

4. An example

The paper concludes with a simple example from the domain of electrical engineering, more specifically VLSI design. We assume that there are primitive objects for rectangle and cell which have procedures on how to produce a lay-out. The goal is to represent a CMOS-transistor.

The transistor has a gate and a source-drain. The channel-width and the channel-length are parameters sufficient to establish the dimensions of the transistor. There are defaults such as minimum-transistor-:widthwhich depend on the design rules. The gate is a rectangle on the ply-layer whose length is equal to the channel-length of the transistor and whose width is computed based on the channel-width and the gate-overhang The value of gate-overhang also depends on the design-rules. The source and drain together form a rectangle on the ndiffusion layer whose width is equal to the width of the transistor and whose length depends on the channel-length of the transistor and the sd-overhang which is another variable depending on the design-rules.

In ORBIT all of this would be expressed as follows:

```
(defobject n-transistor
   (parts (gate source-drain))
   (channel-width
      (default minimum-transistor-width)
   (channel-length
      (default minimum-transistor-length)
   (gate
      (a rectangle
         (layer poly)
         (length (procedure (the channel-length n-transistor)))
         (width
            (procedure (plus (the channel-width) n-transistor)
               (times *gate-overhang* 2)))))
   (source-drain
      (a rectangle
         (layer ndiffusion)
         (length
            (procedure
               (plus (the channel-length n-transistor)
                  (times *sd-overhang* 2)))
         (width
            (procedure (the channel-width n-transistor))))))).
```

Here is a sample dialogue with the system based on this object. First we can look in detail at the objects constructed based on this definition:

```
>> (describe n-transistor)
object: n-transistor
     a cell
   + sd
     - value: rectangle-15
   + gate
     - value: rectangle-14
```

+ channel-length
  – default: *min-transistor-length*
+ channel-width
  – default: *min-transistor-width*
+ parts
  – value: (gate sd)
+ symbol-nr
  – value: 5
*

We can ask questions like what is the procedure associated with the gate of the transistor:

⟩⟩ (the procedure width gate n-transistor)
(plus (the channel-width n-transistor)
    (times *gate-overhang* 2))

or what is the channel-length of n-transistor (this will invoke the default attached to that aspect)

⟩⟩ (the channel-length n-transistor)
2

Now we create an instance of n-transistor:

⟩⟩ (an n-transistor)
n-transistor-2

The instance created here is called n-transistor-2. Here is its description

⟩⟩ (describe it)
object: n-transistor-2
  a n-transistor
  + channel-width
    –value: 4
  + channel-length
    –value: 2
  + gate
    –value: rectangle-14-2
  + sd
    –value: rectangle-15-2
*

Observe that only those parts of the object are created that are not inherited. Notice also how transpositions are made in inheritance. For example the procedure associated with the length of the gate of the transistor contains references within the instance:

⟩⟩ (the procedure length gate n-transistor-2)
(the channel-length n-transistor-2)

Finally here is a trace of the messages resulting from one transaction:

⟩ (the center gate ntr-2)
   1. → (gate ntr:2 value)
   1 ← rectangle-14-2
   1 → (center rectangle-14-2 value)
   1.1 → (center rectangle-14-2 value)
   1.1 → (center rectangle-14-2 procedure)
   1.1 ← (or (given ((the lower-left ....))))
   1. ← (0.0)
0.0

5. Conclusions

The paper introduces the ideas behind a practical tool for making expert systems in an object-oriented style. The main point is that knowledge is organized around the objects of the domain and that activity in the system comes from procedural information attached to the objects and activated through message passing.

Acknowledgement

K. de Smedt has made substantial contributions to the system presented here.

Chapter 9

AN INTEGRATED FRAME/RULE ARCHITECTURE [*]

CARL ENGELMAN and WILLIAM M. STANTON

The MITRE Corporation
P.O Box 208, Bedford MA 01730, USA

Summary

The KNOBS project is dedicated primarily to planning applications whose nature has led us to the conclusion that both frame representations, with inference implicit through "inheritance", and production system representations, with inference governed by backchaining, have compelling virtues. This has led to the design and implementation of a hybrid frame/rule inference architecture. Inferences in the current system are made primarily to verify the conformation of plans to prior constraints. The arguments entail convolved simultaneous reasoning about rules and frames, leading to what we refer to as an "integrated" inference system.

1. Introduction

1.1. The application

The KNOBS system is a highly interactive experimental knowledge based planning demonstration system. Its current principle application domain is tactical air mission planning. While the system is capable of automatically generating complete plans, its primary role is checking the completeness and consistency of a plan as it evolves through an interchange in which the user normally makes the significant choices. The program supports him by explaining clearly and judiciously what inconsistencies have arisen, by understanding what has to be rechecked as the planner changes elements of the plan in response to the program's criticism, and by providing the planner with dynamically generated lists of recommendations for various plan elements. The program also responds to questions about the database posed in English and further affords the planner the opportunity to employ simple English for the alteration of the system's behavior through the rewriting of rules.

---

[*] This work was sponsored by the Rome Air Development Center under Air Force contract F19628-81-C-0001.

1.2. FRL

The package chosen by the KNOBS project for the representation, access, and manipulation of frames is FRL (Frame Representation Language) [Roberts], developed at MIT by R. B. Roberts and I.P. Goldstein. We translated it into INTERLISP [Ericson] and added a number of features, a few of which figure strongly in the integrated inference architecture. The first involves inheritance, a word used in FRL to indicate that, while one might be requesting data from one frame, he might be receiving it automatically from another; the intent being to pass information from the generic to the specific. In the MIT/MACLISP version of FRL this inheritance is traced through successive "AKO" (A-Kind-Of) slots. In the MITRE/INTERLISP version of FRL, it is traced along arbitrary slots (called "colors") under program control. We have also specialized the AKO concept by introducing the "AIO" (An-Individual-Of) slots to distinguish concrete objects from conceptual ones. The default colors for inheritance are AIO and AKO. Any number of AKO arcs are permitted in an inheritance, but only one AIO and, if present, it must come first. This reflects an interpretation of AIO as designating set membership and AKO as set inclusion. Another change to FRL that impacts on inference is that we have permitted, under program control, the acquisition of slot values through the automatic execution of "$IF-NEEDED" procedures.

1.3. Templates

In addition to generic and individual frames, we have introduced a third class of frames, called "templates". A template is attached to a generic frame, and mirrors an individual frame corresponding to that generic frame in that its slots are in one-one correspondence with those expected in the individual except that, in place of values, one finds procedures to supply those values. In addition, templates contain constraints which decide whether specified subsets of slot values are consistent. The templates are used to control the instantiation of generic frames [Engelman80], in particular those representing missions.

1.4. Relation to other work

There were two papers at the 1980 AAAI meeting that combined the use of rules and frames. One [Smith] describes the use of frames to represent rules. The other [Aikens] describes the use of frames to explicitly control production system inference. Neither of these papers mentions inheritance. In the most general sense, there is a relation of our templates to Aikens' use of frames in that they both, one implicitly and the other explicitly, are concerned with control. Templates aside, the use of frames in KNOBS is entirely different than that in either of the above papers. KNOBS uses frames to represent a large data base containing scores of generic objects and hundreds of individual ones. This frame data base also contains a great portion of our mission planning knowledge and much of our inference is via inheritance and other FRL mechanisms such as defaults and $IF-NEEDED procedures. The "integration" referred to in our title is the integration of that FRL inference with backchaining production system inference. If one ignores FRL's capabilities for procedural attachment, the inference system closest to KNOBS' is probably FRAIL [Charniak].

1.5. The case for rules

A number of knowledge based application programs, e.g., MYCIN [Shortliffe] or our own MICROKNOBS demonstration [Engelman79], have been constructed as pure production systems. The advantages of such systems, particularly the facileness of explanation and modification as well as the encapsulation of knowledge into discrete nuggets, obtain for KNOBS applications as well. Rules are an effective means to express knowledge, for example, about choices of weapons and aircraft since such knowledge is judgmental, must be easily modified to support tactical improvisation, is essential to system self-explanation, and, perhaps, because the considerations involved must span several data bases (resources, targets, geography/weather) - rendering the localization of any frame attachment problematic.

1.6. The case for frames

On the other hand, there is a great deal about the KNOBS applications to warrant the use of frame representations. There is the massiveness of the data bases (currently, about 1000 frames, some 700 of which represent individual targets) and the naturalness of organizing them into semantic nets to represent relations between specific objects as well as between the specific and the general. The generic frames serve, above all, as depositories of inheritable knowledge. They further serve, in the descending direction, as roots for required tree searches. Frames are especially attractive because of the number of stereotypes we are concerned with: aircraft, munitions, target types, mission types, etc.. The instantiation mechanism we have added to FRL serves to facilitate the creation of new objects: checking syntactic type, semantic constraints, defaults, missing parts, etc.. Finally the procedural attachments provided by FRL - particularly the $IF-ADDED and $IF-REMOVED facets which cause data modifications to automatically invoke checks and corrective actions - assist in the construction of realistic event driven demonstrations.

2. The integrated inference architecture

These considerations have led us to construct a hybrid system combining our FRL data base with a production system interpreter. Clearly these subsystems must communicate. The immediate observation is that the production system interpreter must be capable of examining "the facts" when confirming antecedent clauses and that these "facts" will most likely be data retrieved from the frame data base. The action, though, is two-way: $IF-NEEDED procedures attached to frame slots may call the production system interpreter. The balance of this paper will be dedicated to describing, by example, the variety of mechanisms which might be called upon to demonstrate a single conclusion. Each of these is simple and familiar enough in itself: data access, database search, inheritance, backtracking, and rule backchaining. What is interesting is how the inference interpreter must recognize which method to use at each step and how it must orchestrate them to derive a single inference.

We shall explain the deduction mechanism, in fact, by considering a rule which represents a constraint on the appropriateness of aircraft type against a class of targets. Such a rule would be invoked by a call to the inference interpreter from a constraint in the mission template. An English rendition of the rule is exhibited in Fig. 1.

An "ALPHA" is the aircraft of choice against radiating targets, and the rule is trying to recommend the use of such a plane. It is written backwards, i.e., it reads, in effect, that if you are not using an ALPHA in such circumstances, you are in error. The reason for this inversion is that the rule is meant primarily for constraint checking, rather than choice generation. The phrase "radiation time" refers to the last time the target was reported radiating. The reference to "part" is intended to cover targets, such as surface-to-air missile sites, which have associated radars.

Should the above rule be triggered, the first indication that the user might receive of trouble could be the computer's printing the message:

BY TARGET-AIRCRAFT-2: THERE IS A SEVERE CONFLICT BETWEEN THE TARGET AND THE AIRCRAFT FOR MISSION INT1003

–TARGET–AIRCRAFT–2–

IF:
      1: PART OF THE TARGET OF A MISSION RADIATES
  AND 2: THE RADIATION TIME OF THE PART IS RECENT
  AND 3: THE AIRCRAFT OF THE MISSION IS NOT AN ALPHA
THEN:
      1: THERE IS A SEVERE CONFLICT BETWEEN THE TARGET AND THE AIRCRAFT FOR THE MISSION

Fig. 1. The Example Rule.

followed by the invitation:

Explain?

Should he respond affirmatively, the user would next see a restatement of the antecedants of the offended rule:

1. PART OF THE TARGET OF INT1003 RADIATES
2. THE RADIATION TIME OF THE PART IS RECENT
3. THE AIRCRAFT OF INT1003 IS NOT AN ALPHA

The third clause is trite and represents a simple retrieval of the value of the AIRCRAFT slot of the INT1003 frame, followed by a test for inequality. Such tests can, in fact, be represented by arbitrarily complex LISP functions. In that respect there is a similarity between our productions system interpreter and the inference engine of LOGLISP [Robinson]. Turning to the first clause, the situation is more complex. If the user were to ask the program to explicate the clause at greater length, the program would print:

1.1. DATA: THE TARGET OF INT1003 IS BE50326
1.2. DATA: PART OF BE50326 IS BE50326-CONTROL-RADAR
1.3. INHERITANCE: BE50326-CONTROL-RADAR RADIATES

The first of these clauses is another simple retrieval of data from a slot of a frame. The second clause represents a more complex inference than might at first be evident. Of course, a small data base search is necessary to find the part, but this is no particular problem since the PART relationship is represented explicitly in the net of frames. The concealed complexity arises from the fact that the BE50326 frame lists two parts that radiate, the one mentioned, the BE50326-CONTROL-RADAR, and another, BE50326-SEARCH-RADAR. The program actually chose the search radar first, which led to an inference failure due to the "recency" condition (Clause 2.) of the hypotheses. It turns out that it is impossible to complete the mission consistently if that part is chosen. The program sought such a proof and, failing to find one, backtracked to the above decision point in order to switch to another "PART", BE50326-CONTROL-RADAR. With that choice, a proof can be found, so the CONTROL-RADAR appears as part of the constraint violation explanation. If the user were now to ask for an explanation of the third clause, the one signaled by the key "INHERITANCE", the computer would print:

1.3.1. DATA: BE50326-CONTROL-RADAR IS A LOLLIPOP
1.3.2. DATA: LOLLIPOP IS A CONTROL-RADAR
1.3.3. DATA: CONTROL-RADAR IS A RADAR
1.3.4. DATA: RADAR RADIATES

This little syllogism reflects an inheritance of knowledge which started with the BE50326-CONTROL-RADAR and passed through the LOLLIPOP and CONTROL-RADAR frames until reaching the one named RADAR. There the program learned that all radars, and hence BE50326-CONTROL-RADAR, radiate. Turning, finally, to the second top-level clause,

2. THE RADIATION TIME OF THE PART IS RECENT

a request for further explanation yields:

2.1. DATA: THE RADIATION TIME OF BE50326-CONTROL-RADAR IS 14-Apr-81 00:24:27
2.2. TIME1: 14-Apr-81 00:24:27 IS RECENT

The first of these clauses is a straightforward frame data retrieval. The second, keyed by the word "TIME1", is a reference to a rule of that name. A request to expand that clause would produce:

2.2.1. 14-Apr-81 00:24:27 IS A TIME
2.2.2. THE CURRENTTIME - 14-Apr-81 00:24:27 < 1 DAY

That is, the rule TIME1 says that a time is recent if it is within the last twenty-four hours.

Tracing this inference has thus shown that the program's warning the planner of a detected constraint conflict in his evolving plan resulted from the orchestration of a number of familiar processes: simple (frame) data access, data base search, the automatic inheritance of knowledge from the generic to the specific, backtracking in proof search, and backchaining through rules. This illustrates what we mean by an integrated frame/rule inference architecture.

ARTIFICIAL AND HUMAN INTELLIGENCE (A. Elithorn and R. Banerji, editors)
Elsevier Science Publishers, B.V.
© NATO, 1984

Chapter 10

BELIEFS, POINTS OF VIEW AND MULTIPLE ENVIRONMENTS

YORICK WILKS [*]

Cognitive Studies Centre, University of Essex, Colchester, C04 3SQ, UK

JANUSZ BIEN [*]

Institute of Informatics, University of Warsaw, 00-325 Warsaw, Poland

Summary

The paper describes the role of the belief structures of individual understanders in the understanding of dialogue and text (as modelled algorithmically in a computer) and, in particular, how nested belief structures (of one individual's beliefs about another's beliefs and so on) are to be constructed, stored and maintained.

1. Introduction

The paper presents a model of beliefs for computer understanding of natural language and discusses its implications for speech act theory.

Although using knowledge for language understanding is an artificial intelligence (AI) tradition, the relevance of speaker's knowledge about the hearer (and vice versa) was appreciated only recently in the research of the Toronto group (Cohen, 1978, Allen and Perrault, 1978). With the exception of Bien's multiple environments approach to natural language (Bien 1976a, 1976b, 1977), modelling the beliefs of the persons only mentioned in the text was completely neglected.

The following dialogue is perfectly natural:

USER: Frank is coming tomorrow I think
SYSTEM: Perhaps I should leave (I)
USER: Why?
SYSTEM: Coming from you that is a warning (II)
USER: Does Frank dislike you?

---

[*] The authors are indebted to comments and criticisms from Dan Dennett, Bill Mann, Bob Balzer, Bob Abelson, Roger Schank, Mike Rosner. The errors, of course, are all our own.

SYSTEM: I don't know, but you think he does and that is what is important now

It is clear that, to follow this dialogue, it is necessary to distinguish the user's beliefs about Frank's beliefs from the system's beliefs about Frank's beliefs and from Frank's actual beliefs. Such a situation is common enough to deserve special attention.

In this paper we want to tackle the issue generally and to ask the question "what is it to maintain a stucture, not only of one's beliefs about the inanimate world, but about beliefs about other individuals and their beliefs?" The argument of the paper will be that there can be a very general algorithm for the construction of beliefs about beliefs about beliefs or, if you wish, models of models of models, or points of view of points of view of points of view.

Its a philosophical cliche that understanding of language is dependent upon, not only the beliefs of the understander about the world, but his beliefs about the beliefs of the speaker and the ways in which those two may be different. To adopt a well-known philosophical example (Donnellan, which makes the point from a speaker's point of view): a person at a cocktail party may look across the room to a lady whose name he wants to know. He does not know her name, but knows she is a teetotaller, although he sees her holding a glass with a colourless liquid and an olive in it. Since he knows she is a teetotaller he also knows that it is not a Martini. Nonetheless, he wants to ask the person next to him who the lady is. He could ask who is the lady drinking a glass of water, which would be consistent with his, the speaker's, own beliefs, but in fact what he says to his hearer is "who is the lady over there drinking the martini?". He does this in order to get the reply he wants, and does it by assuming a belief which he in fact believes to be false, but which he believes to be *consistent with the beliefs of his hearer*. That is to say, he believes that his hearer knows the name of the lady in question, but does not know that she is a teetotaller and therefore assumes she is drinking what, at a party, she appears to be drinking. It is a somewhat laboured story but it makes the point rather well: that we often operate with assumed beliefs which we do not in fact hold, but which we attribute to our hearers. In this paper we are going to discuss the construction of such entities as the structured beliefs of others and how we manipulate and maintain such entities.

The present paper does not describe the working of actual programs, but presents work in the course of being programmed. After we started this work, we discovered the work of the Toronto group, Perrault, Cohen and Allen (q.v.). However, we think our proposals here differ from theirs in significant respects, and at the end of the paper we shall make clear what those differences are. The distinctive features of what we propose will be:

(a) The metaphorical use of the computer science notion of *multiple environments* for representing the beliefs and their inter-relations: interpreting an utterance according to someone's beliefs is viewed as running or evaluating the utterance in the appropriate environment.

(b) Another crucial aspect of our approach is that a belief manipulating system which is to be psychologically and computationally plausible must have built into it some limitations on processing, so as to accord with the fact that deep nestings of beliefs (while well formed in some "competance" sense) are in practice incomprehensible. Consider just a small part of an example in R.D. Laing's *Knots*:

Jack thinks
   he does not know
  what he thinks
    Jill thinks
  he does not know   etc. etc.

We intend that our proposals reflect this aspect of language processing (largely neglected in more logic-based approaches) that follows from real-time understanding with limited resources.

We have independently argued in the past (Wilks, 1975a, 1975b, Bien Ph.D., 1977) for a "least-effort" view of language processing, and the present proposals are consistent with that, as we shall show.

(c) Our means for explicating this will be what we shall later call the *percolation effect*, a method in which beliefs propagate about a belief system in a way not necessarily intended by any believer or participant, but which follows as a side-effort of our principal algorithm.

The form of presentation in the paper is discussion of the design and operation of a hypothetical language understanding system, capable, in principle, of performing the role of either of the participants in the dialogue quoted above.

The task we are describing is one of explicating dialogues like this, and in particular the appropriate responses from the system (though the same methodology should apply to a modelling of the USER).

The system has produced replies at points marked (I) and (II) in the dialogue above, and the question we shall ask is why should the system say these different things at these different times, and what structure of knowledge, inference and beliefs about the User and Frank should be postulated in order to produce a dialogue of this type? What we shall argue is that the system is *running its knowledge about individuals in different environments at points (I) and (II)*, and the difference beween them will be crucial for us. In order to explain this we shall have recourse to shorthand as follows:

{FRANK}
SYSTEM

to represent what the bearer of the outer name believes about the bearer of the inner name, that is to say what the system believes about Frank. Structures like this can be nested so that the following structure

$$\begin{Bmatrix} \{USER\} \\ FRANK \end{Bmatrix}$$
SYSTEM

is intended to be shorthand for what the system believes about what Frank believes about the user.

We shall refer to this as a nested environment and every such structure is considered to be (trivially) inside the system, for it knows everything there is to be known about the individuals mentioned.

The first important question is, what are the structures that this shorthand represents? For the moment, the simplest form of what the system believes about Frank, i.e.

{FRANK}
SYSTEM

could simply be thought of as a less permanent version of a *frame* (Minsky, 1975, Charniak, 1978) or more suitably in terms of (Wilks, 1977) as a *pseudo-text* or, if you prefer, any knowledge structure whatever about the individual named inside. The simplest metaphor is that of a can into which all incoming information that the bearer of the inner name is thrown. This information will have internal structure (and we shall come to that) *but the nature of the internal structure is not crucial to the argument of this paper.* The advantage of using the word pseudo-text (PT for short) and what it was defined to mean in that paper, is in the episodic tradition of viewing memory: that the structures of information about Frank unsorted, unrefined (and in that sense unframelike) items of knowledge which have not been reclassified and checked against permanent, semantic, memory. One could put this point by saying that the knowledge structure held by the system about Frank is in some sense only a narrative about Frank. It can be thought of as a text representation, and the earlier (Wilks, 1977) paper argued that input structures from a semantic parser of natural English could themselves be reasonable memory structures for certain well-defined purposes.

The PT's are packed into memory schemata together with topic-specific inference rules, and the difference between pseudo-texts and inference rules may often be neglected.

Again, it is a strong assumption there that the representation of the systems beliefs about entities (humans, etc.) and their beliefs is all in the same format as more structural beliefs of the system, about itself and its own functioning. We shall therefore propose a very general inference engine that will run over

PT's on any topic, and in PT's nested to any depth to yield an inner environment.

A further feature of this approach will be the context-dependent nature of, and their associated pointers, descriptions within PT's (cf. Bobrow and Norman, 1975, 1979).

The context dependency of descriptions originally meant that they are never more precise than is needed in the context of their creation, but we understand the feature in a broader sense: a given description in various contexts may refer to different items. For example, "the murderer" in the environment of John's beliefs may refer to Jones, but, in the environment of May's beliefs, to Smith. In other words, the context-dependent descriptions supply us with some power of intensional logic, which is necessary for an adequate knowledge representation, though in the simplified example we use for illustrative purposes below, we shall not make use of this feature.

2. Constructing environments

The essence of this paper is to evaluate and compare two perspectives or environments (equals nested PT's) and they will be the ones which are created by the system at points I and II in the dialogue above. "Evaluate" here is intended to have a standard computer science meaning, one we could put more adventurously as *running structural descriptions in given environments* (Bien, 1977). What this will mean in concrete terms is to draw plausible pragmatic inferences, and in that sense our view of understanding is to be identified with the drawing of such pragmatic inferences in context which is in the standard tradition of the AI approach to natural language of the last ten years.

In particular, at (I) in the dialogue the system is evaluating the user's initial remark 'Frank is coming tomorrow, I think' in the following nested environment:

$$\left\{ \begin{Bmatrix} \{SYSTEM\} \\ FRANK \\ USER \end{Bmatrix} \right\}.$$

SYSTEM

Whereas, at Point (II) in the conversation that the system has evaluated just Frank's view of himself, that is to say he has run the user's first sentence in the simpler environment:

$$\begin{Bmatrix} SYSTEM \\ FRANK \end{Bmatrix}$$

SYSTEM

where he discovers that he has no such information on what Frank thinks of him.

If we suppose some parsing of the input sentences into a semantic representation, the first question of principle is that of strategies for setting up environments. We shall distinguish the *presentation strategy* and the *insertional strategy*. The question for the presentation strategy is this: given any incoming information about an individual, how deep a level of nested environment should the system construct? A minimal strategy will be appropriate when, say, listening to a mathematics lecture, where one is not normally evaluating the input in terms of the presence of the speaker: one is not asking oneself "why is this algebra lecturer telling me this?" and evaluating his motives and reasons for doing it. We shall call that a *minimal strategy* that would have a very shallow environment with no level corresponding to the speaker.

What we shall call the *standard presentation strategy* for information in the one adopted in the nested environments above, where they are nested so as to include a level corresponding to the speaker (the user in this case) and then the individuals mentioned. At (I) the system evaluates the initial sentence while taking account of the speaker's motives, but at Point (II) he does not take account of the speaker and the speaker/user does not occur in the nesting.

This standard and strategy allows a hearer either to disbelieve a speaker or to co-operate with him, as he chooses (cf. Taylor and Whitehall, 1981).

In addition to this we can imagine super-strategies (see further below) which are reflexive nestings of speakers and others, as well as the system itself. In these the system constructs even deeper environments corresponding to what it believes about what somebody else believes about what it itself believes, etc. We shall call anything deeper than a single nesting using the speaker a reflexive strategy and we shall not consider it here.

The second important question concerns what we have called *insertion strategies*. When the system reads something as at (I), said by the user about Frank, the question arises as to where in the system this should be stored. In the case of the user's sentence "Frank is coming tomorrow, I think", should the semantic representaion of that sentence be stored simply in the pseudo-text for the user, the person who said it, or in one for Frank, the person spoken about, or both? For reasons that will become clear later, we shall adopt a "scatter-gun" strategy, in that the information will be stored initially in all the possible places, i.e. both the PT for user and for Frank. This is an assumption that may need revision in the light of later experiment, but the system we are describing is heavily orientated towards redundant storage of information. For the form of the information to be stored, we shall simply assume some simple standard semantic parsing (Wilks, 1975a) so that user's statement "Frank is coming tomorrow" will parse as the following structure of simple templates:

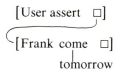

where each wor-like item above is itself a pointer to a complex semantic representation, and the parsed structure above, for a simple dependency of two clauses, indicates the agents (first slot) and actions involved, (second slot) the objects being dummies (□). This whole structure will be added into *both* {USER} and {FRANK} since all PT's are in SYSTEM, it is not necessary to add this to lowest level PT's, as here.

Notice here that the PT's are general items and will not be stored only for individual human beings but also for groups of humans, objects, substances, classes, my car, a jury, a professor, a salesman, sulphur and Germany. In Wilks (1977), their hierarchical relations and inheritance relations were discussed, and here we may assume these are standard. In this paper we concentrate only on PT's for agents (and we shall explain why later), and a consequence of this is that when we consider nested environments, PT's for agents will be the only ones that can be outer environments in nesting diagrams, because we can consider computing, for example, Jim's view of the oil crisis but we cannot consider the oil crisis' view of Jim. We can do this for groups as well: to be able to consider Germany's view of the oil crisis, although never the oil crisis' view of Germany, but in the examples in the paper we shall confine ourselves to the names of individuals rather than groups or states or classes of individuals as names on the "outside" of PT's.

3. Beliefs about and beliefs of

A final preliminary distinction we must make is between someone's beliefs *about* someone and his beliefs about the beliefs *of* that individual. To put it simply, we can have beliefs about Smith, that he is male, 45, etc. etc.. We can also have beliefs about his beliefs: that Smith believs that, say, Vitamin C cures colds. On one general view of belief these are all properties of Smith, from the believer's point of view, but they are, of course, importantly different sorts of property.

Earlier, we discursively introduced the knowledge structures (PT's) about entities animate and inanimate. Before we get to the heart of our paper, which is an algorithm for constructing an *environment*, or point of view that one of the entities represented by a PT can have of another, we must discuss in a little more detail what the structure of the PT's is. In (Wilks, 1977) we introduced a PT as a narrative-like structure, within which was collected, in a semantic representation, the information the system had about some entity or generic class of entities. It was considered separate from a semantic definition, as well as from a frame which was a permanent memory structure (largely of episodic information). A PT was intended to be an intermediate memory structure, some of whose contents would undoubtedly be transferred to permanent memory. So, in (Wilks, 1977) we expressed information about the generic concept of CAR, separate from the definition of a car as a people moving device (a non-essential separation, and KRL and Charniak 1978 would have chosen differently at this point), and containing material appropriate for a permanent frame (CARs have fluid injected into them, so that .... etc.) as well as episodic material that would not be so transferred (MY CAR is purple). The simple illustrative PT of that paper used the symbol * for "car" in its templates because it was not a pointer to another definitional semantic formula or PT or associated frame (as WHEEL would be) but to the PT itself in which it occured. It was thus a special pointed carrying, as it were, a warning against vicious self-reference.

In the present case where individuals are concerned that can themselves have beliefs, we must amend the notation. Suppose we ask where the system keeps its knowledge about Frank. He, like the car, will have a semantic definition (human, male, etc.) as well as beliefs the system has about him (Frank is an alcoholic), as well as beliefs the system has that it explicitly believes to be Frank's beliefs (Frank believes he is a robot, and that he is merely a social drinker). Thus Frank's beliefs, as known to the system, can superficially contradict both definitional and accidental information about himself, if we may use an old-fashioned distinction here (again nothing crucial depends on it).

One also has a pretty firm intuition that the structure of Frank's own beliefs (as believed to be his by the system, of course) are rather different from beliefs *about* him. And yet if, for administrative and computational convenience, we want to keep the system's view of Frank in one place, these should all in some sense be in the box marked "Frank" (different though they are). There is an additional complication, which will be very important when we come to a proposed algorithm, that many of the system's beliefs *about* Frank also, as a matter of fact, correspond to his own belief, even though we have no direct evidence of the correspondence. That is to say, the system believes Frank to be a human, even though, oddly enough he believes himself to be a robot and that is known to the system. However, the system believes Frank to have two hands and so does Frank, even though the system has never heard him say so. All this will fall under the general rule we shall use later that X's view of Y can be assumed to be one's own view of Y, *except where one has explicit evidence to the contrary*; and this rule also covers X's view of Y!

So, in the sample, over-simplified, PT below we shall continue to indicate mention of Frank, in the PT for Frank (i.e. the system's beliefs about all aspects of Frank) by *. This is again (as in Wilks, 1977) a pointer warning against vicious self-reference. We shall not include the semantic definition in the PT (as Charniak would), and the * pointer (after Kleene's star) may be considered as pointing to the semantic formula definition, which in turn points to the PT. Just as the "Earth" below is also a pointer to the corresponding semantic formula definition and PT, though with no risk of self-reference in that case. The belief "Earth is flat" is inserted precisely because it is an odd, an so reportable, belief. "Earth is round" would not be so inserted for a PT for a round-earther simply because it could be inherited from the lattice of common-knowledge from the PT for EDUCATED HUMAN, say.

Thus in the sample PT below, the semantic formula definition is not present but assumed, and the horizontal line simply divides the beliefs above it (which are explicitly believed by the system to be Frank's, and so can be thought of as prefaced by an implicit * BELIEVES ....) from those below which are beliefs about Frank, that may or may not be his. In some clear sense those above the line are a sort of "inner Frank" and the different function they have when we construct a "push-down" algorithm to create environments, will become clear.

So, the following might be trivial content for a PT:

{FRANK}
SYSTEM

$$\left\{ \begin{array}{l} \text{FRANK} \\ \text{Earth is flat} \\ \text{System likes} * \\ \underline{\text{User dislikes} *} \\ \text{User dislikes} * \end{array} \right\}$$

SYSTEM

The line across the PT separates beliefs believed to be *of* Frank, above the line, from those believed to be *about* Frank, below it. We shall have to exercise great care with the line because, in practice, some below line beliefs will be believed by their object: if I say of Frank that he hates dogs, I may put that below the line, but a simple pragmatic inference rule would lift it above.

4. Pushing down environments

We are now approaching the heart of the paper. Pushing down one of the PTs *inside another* means resetting values in the PT being pushed down. The transitory object achieved by this method of environment, we shall interpret as being the outer PT *holder's* view of the inner PT object. Suppose we want to construct the system's view of the user's view of Frank

$$\left\{ \begin{array}{c} \{\text{FRANK}\} \\ \text{USER} \end{array} \right\}$$
$$\text{SYSTEM}$$

We shall assume this is done in two stages as follows: First by constructing, or having available, the system's view of Frank, secondly by constructing, or having available, the system's view of the user, and then pushing the former down into the latter to achieve the system's view of the user's view of Frank:

$$\{\text{FRANK}\} \quad \overbrace{\{\text{USER}\}}^{} \Rightarrow \left\{ \begin{array}{c} \{\text{FRANK}\} \\ \text{USER} \end{array} \right\}$$
$$\text{SYSTEM} \quad\quad \text{SYSTEM} \quad\quad \text{SYSTEM}$$

Suppose the content of the outer PT, the system's view of the user, contains the proposition 'User dislikes Frank', and the inner PT the system's view of Frank, contains the proposition 'User likes Frank', believed by Frank (and hence underlined in our simple notation),

$$\left\{ \begin{array}{l} \text{USER} \\ \left\{ \begin{array}{l} \text{FRANK} \\ \underline{\text{user likes} *} \\ \text{SYSTEM} \end{array} \right\} \\ \overline{* \text{ dislikes Frank}} \end{array} \right\}$$
$$\text{SYSTEM}$$

One of our major assumptions in this paper is that the system does not *preserve* complex constructions of environments, the complex points of view. It maintains structures only at the bottom level: in terms of our earlier crude metaphor, it maintains simply a row of PT's about individuals (and other entities), not environments, i.e. not push-downs of points of view. If the system, by pushing one of these down into the other as we postulated, wishes to construct the inner environment which, in this case, is the system's view of the user's view of Frank, it does this by considering the influence of the outer belief on the inner belief, and we shall consider outer beliefs migrating or *percolating* into the inner environment and then examine their mutual interaction.

However, it should be clear that only "upper half" templates of a PT can migrate into the Inner environment and override what it contains. If I want to consider what User thinks of Frank, I will let my beliefs about the User's view of Frank override my views of Frank, but not in general my views of the User.

However, the matter is not quite so simple for certain attitude verbs like dislike: if I say X dislikes Y, I imply X believes he dislikes Y except in exceptional circumstances, or, in a simple rule: for a class of "conscious attitude" verbs, we have

$$\begin{bmatrix} X & \text{dislike} & Y \\ \text{human} & & \end{bmatrix} \Rightarrow \begin{bmatrix} X \text{ believe} & \square \\ \hline [X \text{ dislike} & Y] \end{bmatrix}$$

Again, if I believe Smith is 6 feet tall, I imply he believes he is 6 feet tall, as much as I assume he accepts his own "semantic definition" (male, human, etc.). We shall return to the problem of self-knowledge later.

Let us now consider in more detail the push down of the system's view of Frank into the system's view of the User, and assume the following propositions as consituting a slightly more complex PT for the system's view of Frank.

$$\left\{ \begin{array}{lll} \text{FRANK} & & \\ & \text{Vitamin C} & \text{cures} & \text{colds} \\ & \text{User} & \text{likes} & * \\ & * & \text{dislikes} & \text{user} \end{array} \right\}$$

SYSTEM

Lets now consider this in relation to a more complex view of the system's view of the user:

$$\left\{ \begin{array}{lll} \text{USER} & & \\ \text{Vitamin C} & \text{not cure} & \text{colds} \\ \text{Frank} & \text{believes} & \square \\ \text{Vitamin C} & \text{cures} & \text{colds} \\ * & \text{dislikes} & \text{Frank} \\ \text{Frank} & \text{likes} & * \\ \text{Frank} & \text{dislikes} & \text{system} \\ \hline * & \text{is} & \text{an alcoholic} \end{array} \right\}$$

SYSTEM

In this last we see the more complex two-clause proposition: the one that expresses the system's belief that the user believes Frank believs that Vitamin C cures colds. If we now consider the first of these to be pushed down into the second, we achieve a complex item like the following where the arrows show the interaction as the relevant outer propositions *percolate* into the inner environment. This is fundamentally simple, and we now want to discuss one by one the interactions that are obtained by this method. We have numbered the linkages 1, 2, 3 and 4 to show four separate percolations "inwards" (templates shown ringed).

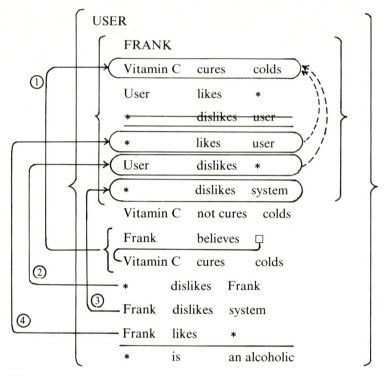

The two dotted lines show those templates that mount to the upper half of FRANK via the inference rule. Other percolations remain in the lower half, except the one marked 1 whose content requires the upper half beliefs.

What we have to consider is those propositions in the outer PT being drawn into the inner pseudo-text by a relevance criterion, given that they are above the line in the outer PT, for only *explicit beliefs* of user can override anything inside the (bottom half of) the inner PT. Our diagrammatic distinction of the upper and lower halves of the PT is thus a notation for limiting inference. We shall discuss the criterion that causes them to be considered relevant further below but, for the moment, we take an over simple criterion of explicit mention in the outer PT (upper half) of the "holder" of the inner PT.

(1) We have the proposition "Frank believes that Vitamin C cures colds".
    This enters the inner PT and in appropriate reduced form "Vitamin C cures colds" is just another copy of the system's belief about Frank.
(2) In the inner PT

⟨FRANK⟩
SYSTEM

we have the system's belief that Frank believes that the user likes him, and

in the outer PT we have the relevant belief of the system of the user that the user dislikes Frank. The latter comes in to the inner PT as "User dislikes Frank", but into its bottom half, not immediate as a belief of Frank. There is of course no contradiction between these, because the inference rule given does not generate any contradiction.
(3) The belief in the outer PT "Frank dislikes system" is drawn into the inner environment and which meets no contradiction of any kind but simply remains there. We shall have cause to refer back to this later as a crucial percolation.
(4) We have in the outer PT the belief held by the user that Frank likes him. This is drawn in and, given the inference rule above, contradicts the inner belief of Frank that he, Frank, dislikes the user. The inner belief that he, Frank, dislikes the user is explicitly contradicted, and overwritten by the outer belief Frank likes user. The s change reference, since they refer to the local object of the PT, the incoming belief taking the form " ∗ likes User".

The result of these four operations in the inner environment is now the construction

$$\begin{pmatrix} \{\text{FRANK}\} \\ \text{USER} \end{pmatrix}$$
$$\text{SYSTEM}$$

that is to say the system's view of the user's view of Frank. So we now have an inner result as shown above in the inner environment.

Let us recall the two heuristics used in order to obtain this intermediate result. First, the *relevance heuristic*: the basis for considering outer PT propositions (from the "upper" explicit belief part) as being possible migrants into the inner environment. The criterion has been explicit mention, of Frank in this case, in the outer propositions. The reader should not assume that the beliefs listed in the two example PTs were chosen as relevant to the example: the original example dialogue referred to Frank hating the user, which was in a PT but there was nothing relevant to the example about his views on Vitamin C and its efficacy. Those were drawn into the inner environment simply by the general relevance mechanism. There will, of course, be considerable practical problems caused by conjunction, disjunction, etc. given a richer PT structure. Moreover, the present criterion of relevance (explicit mention) is far too naive: in fact there will not normally be relevance only by name, but also by descriptions. So, for example, Frank may not appear in the outer propositions as his name "Frank" but under some description such as "John's father", in which case much more complex inference procedures will be required to establish the relevance of the corresponding outer proposition. This is a general problem for all artificial intelligence systems of this type and no peculiar diffficulties arise here. Secondly, contradiction: inner beliefs survive unless contradicted by outer ones from the upper, explicit, half. Any inner belief which is not contradicted survives.

The reader may ask at this point what is the function of the heuristics and construction we have produced, and upon what general intuition do they rest. The assumption is that of basic common sense: that one's view of another person's view of a third person (and so on) is simply that it is the same as one's own view *unless one has explicit reason to believe otherwise* . This sounds extremely simple but, as we have seen, there are considerable complications in working out even this very commonsensical principle.

At this point let us recall why we have performed this environment construction. The initial example of dialogue required the first environment (at the point marked (I))

$$\left\{ \begin{array}{l} \left\{ \begin{array}{l} \{SYSTEM\} \\ FRANK \\ USER \end{array} \right\} \end{array} \right\}$$
$$SYSTEM$$

This is obtained in two such push down moves. First,

$$\left\{ \begin{array}{l} \{FRANK\} \\ USER \end{array} \right\}$$
$$SYSTEM$$

which we have just done, and then the full nesting by pushing down

$$\{SYSTEM\}$$
$$SYSTEM$$

into that. After applying these two moves we shall achieve the inner environment required at point (I) in the example. Let us now consider two effects of the push-down environment achieved. First, within

$$\left\{ \begin{array}{l} \left\{ \begin{array}{l} \{SYSTEM\} \\ FRANK \\ USER \end{array} \right\} \end{array} \right\}$$
$$SYSTEM$$

we now have the percolated proposition "Frank dislikes system", and we also have from our parsed input "User asserts that Frank comes tomorrow". Notice that this belief would not have percolated into the alternative environment

$$\begin{Bmatrix} \{SYSTEM\} \\ FRANK \end{Bmatrix}$$
SYSTEM

constructed at point (II) in the example, because the belief originated in

{USER}
SYSTEM

which is not involved here. So, if we now have appropriate inference rules we can generate:

"Perhaps I (system) should leave" in the innermost environment, if we suppose some commonsense inference rule of the following type:

$$\begin{bmatrix} X & & \\ & DISLIKE & * \\ HUMAN & & \end{bmatrix}$$

$$\begin{bmatrix} Y & & \square \\ & ASSERT & \\ HUMAN & & \end{bmatrix}$$

$$\begin{bmatrix} X & & \\ & APPROACH & * \\ HUMAN & & \end{bmatrix}$$

$$\Rightarrow [\ * \quad LEAVE \quad X\ ]$$

We shall not defend specific inference rules here and only assume that they have a function in general semantic parsing systems of the present type; similar rules exist in many other systems. If we now match this rule onto the contents of the inner environment we have we shall see the first line matches with the proposition obtained through push-down, "Frank dislikes the system". The rest of the lefthand side matches the parsed input: a human Y, which is the user, asserts the human X, which is Frank, approaches the object, which is the system, the * since we are in a system PT (the innermost). From these we infer by rule the output "leaves", that is to say, the system leaves. Thus we have the motivation of the system's reply at (I) in the original dialogue. This inference rule could appear as a partial plan, in a more fully developed speech act system.

In any actual operation it would probably help to have a rule like the one above stored as part of a class of rules which we might label say, WARN. It is here that the belief manipulations of this paper bear upon the general topic of speech acts. If it were procedurally useful to have a class of such rules stored under a primitive label like WARN then it would give justification for the use of speech act terminology as part of belief systems of this type. The problem is that this would be a very weak defence of speech acts because, as with all primitives (like WARN in this case), it can be argued (Charniak, 1975) that the taxonomy of items one proposes could be maintained without primitive labels. On that view, one could have a classification of inferenece rules available, but would not be helped further by special labels for the classes (such as warn, threat, promise, assert, etc.) in order to access that rule class.

5. Percolation

A second result of the push-down we have arrived at is that the proposition "Frank dislikes the system" can now be retained in the inner PT *if we adopt what we shall call the "percolation heuristic"*. This is as follows: when a proposition has appeared in an inner environment and is not contradicted, it remains there in the standard copy of that inner PT *when that copy is subsequently re-established at bottom level*. We shall say the proposition "Frank dislikes the system" has *percolated* from the "outer" PT

{USER}
SYSTEM

into the "inner" PT

{FRANK}
SYSTEM

After the example dialogue has been dealt with, the inner PT is, as it were, pulled out and remains the system's view of Frank. The percolation heuristic asserts that "Frank dislikes the system", *stays in that copy * for the future*. By iterative percolation, it will also have gone further into the innermost environment

{SYSTEM}
SYSTEM

---

* This allows the possibility of multiple copies of a PT for Frank and hence the problem of which is most *salient* in later retrieval (see Bien, 1980).

as "Frank dislikes the system". We shall argue that on a least-effort principle of belief manipulations, this percolation heuristic is justified. But first let us consider an immediate potential counter-example. Supposing the user had said "Frank thinks you're crazy, but I don't". We might imagine a contradiction achieved by percolation into the innermost environment (which is the system's view of the user's view of Frank's view of the system), where we might have mutually contradictory percolations: both "The system is crazy", and "The system is not crazy". In fact, if we follow this in detail, we find this does not happen: the worst that can happen is a contradiction in the system's view *of the user's beliefs* after percolation. And none of us find anything disturbing about the idea that others (rather than ourselves) have contradictory beliefs. Nevertheless, although no contradiction follows here, we might well want to have certain surface key words inhibit multi-step percolations, in this case "but".

The principle suggested here is that percolations remain for all future use of a given PT, not just in relation to the PT from which they percolated. Another result of percolation will be that, say,

⟨FRANK⟩
SYSTEM

is no longer the *general* representation of Frank, for beliefs about him may percolate anywhere in the system's PTs.

One argument for the percolation heuristic is based on the assumption that pushing down PTs inside each other to create environments requires considerable computational, or psychological, effort; with greater effort required for greater nesting depths. Allowing beliefs to percolate about the system in the suggested way, avoids having to recompute the same environment by repeating a push-down, should another dialogue be encountered that required the same environment. Before running a sentence representation in an environment, we can check the push-down nesting required and examine a flag in the innermost PT to see whether that inner environment had been constructed recently or not. The notion of recency would have to be firmly defined but, if the sentence representation had been run recently on any such definition, we would assume that percolations and settlings of consistencies had been done and would not need to be repeated.

An important point here is that the push-downs are not in any sense topic-guided: that is to say if the text required us to calculate Reagan's view of Begin's view *of the oil problem*, then we could not be sure that, if we were to assemble the same order of nesting of outer PTs for another topic, say Reagan's view of Begin's view of Saudi Arabia, then the register of previous push-downs would mean that all possible consistencies and percolations had already been achieved in the innermost environment (since they would have been directed by relevance to oil). However, our overall least-effort principle of comprehension requires that we do not repeat the *outer part* of that push-down, which would have been constructed already.

It must be remembered that the push-down metaphor is merely a metaphor. The actual computaion involved in computing the inner environments is a cross product of PT contents. However, it might turn out experimentally that the assumption here about percolation is not suitable for all topics. We might, on the basis of experiment, wish to restrict percolation itself to certain topics or psychological modes, and in particular that of *attitudes*. What is being suggested here, in psychological terms, under the metaphor of percolation, is that it is essentially a side-effect that transfers beliefs for which one had not got explicit evidence. There is a phenomenon called the sleeper effect (Gruder et al., 1978) which is well attested, and yields experimental evidence about how people come to hold beliefs for which they have no direct evidence of any kind. We take this as indirect evidence that something along the lines we propose for percolation could in fact be experimentally tested.

6. Percolation and the about/of belief division

It will be clear from the earlier detailed discussion of the example push-down that it is normally only the upper half beliefs of the lower PT that migrate into the lower half of the PT being pushed down. The diagrammatic upper and lower half metaphor expresses this conveniently, but the motivation is also clear: it is, in general, the system's beliefs about the lower PT-holder's beliefs that will modify the beliefs stored in the (lower half of) the upper, or pushing-down, PT. As we saw, beliefs in the lower PT that explicitly refer to the beliefs in other PTs (e.g. USER BELIEVES FRANK BELIEVES VITAMIN C CURES COLDS) will naturally migrate to the upper or inner part of a pushing-down PT.

The upper and lower half of a PT metaphor has, of course, no application to a PT for an inanimate entity or entities (except perhaps computers), since they do not have the inner beliefs. So we can think of a PT for, say, *coal* as having all its content below some notional line, and nothing above. Thus, nothing can be pushed down into such a PT, and when it is pushed down into some other (animate) PT (so as to construct, for example, someone's beliefs about coal) all migrations will be into its lower half. There will be the standard status problems about whether PTs for such entities as *France* and *The Auto Workers' Union* can have beliefs.

One further clarification is needed of the meaning of the *percolation* heuristic proper, as opposed to beliefs migrating into an inner PT on some relevance criterion. Percolations are those beliefs that migrate into a lower half of an upper PT *and are not contradicted* *. It is these, we suggest, that may remain in the resulting permanent copy of the upper PT. The key example in the discussion was of FRANK DISLIKES THE SYSTEM. Now, we suggested that on withdrawal of the upper PT from the push-down, such a belief might remain, with its source believer stripped away, as it were, and so be a belief of the system that it had merely inherited as a side-effect. It will be clear that such persistence could not apply to beliefs that had migrated into ⟨FRANK⟩ and contradicted/overrode FRANK DISLIKES USER. for if that were to remain in a permanent copy any push-down might cause the system randomly to reverse its beliefs: e.g. having calculated Begin's view of Reagan and finding it the reverse of its own, it would not be likely to reverse its own beliefs on Reagan just from having constructed that particular environment!

Two other important topics have been left in an incomplete state, and will require further discussion in another paper: first, what classes of beliefs can be inferred pragmatically to be those of their subject and, secondly and closely related, are "self-pushdowns" significantly different from the general case, i.e.

⟨FRANK⟩ from ⟨FRANK⟩.
FRANK   USER

We noted earlier that there is a class of attitude beliefs that we would expect to migrate from the lower to upper halves of a PT, e.g.

X DISLIKES Y ⇒ X BELIEVES (X DISLIKES Y)

Again, one would expect the same inference to hold for

(a) all parts of a semantic definition **, unless explicitly overriden:

X IS HUMAN ⇒ X BELIEVES (X IS HUMAN)

---

* Where contradiction also covers those contradictions reached via inference rules, as in

John is married to Mary

and

Fred says John is married to Rita

inside

$\left\{ \begin{array}{c} \langle JOHN \rangle \\ FRED \end{array} \right\}$
SYSTEM

The latter sentence overrides and contradicts the former only given some rule such as

X IS MARRIED TO Y ⇒ X IS NOT MARRIED TO Z (≠ Y).

** In Wilks (1977) semantic definitions were started separately from PTs, rather than together as in (Charniak, 1978), but nothing here depends on that.

(b) all parts inherited from a "lattice of common knowledge PTs":

X IS AN ARCHITECT ⇒ X BELIEVES (X CAN-PLAN BUILDINGS)

(c) what Clark and Carlson (in Smith, in press) have, following Schiffer, called *mutual knowledge*: as when X and Y observe a candle, an infinite number of such propositions as

X KNOWS Y KNOWS THERE IS A CANDLE

can be inferred by a simple rule of construction (in which the superficial differences between *know* and *believe* are not significant here). There has been much misunderstanding of the degree to which Clark and Carlson thought that such complex nested entities were really (rather than trivially) constructed by participants (see Smith, in press). However, it is clear that in certain complex situations such as detective stories independent evidence can be offered for number of levels of such nestings in situations more complex than mere copresence with an object such as a candle. These situations do not collapse trivially (or, conversely, are not trivially inferrable by a recursive rule) and are more like the processing of (non-collapsing) centre embeddings:

The dog the cat the man saw bit died.

As in those cases, deep nestings are very hard to compute and handle for subjects, and this, for us, is additional evidence supporting our "least-effort" view of environments. One could view the present paper as a beginning for a procedural account of limitations on (non-trivial) "mutual knowledge" embeddings.

(d) A natural additional inference would be

X ASSERT P ⇒ X BELIEVE P

unless there was any indication of, or reason to suspect, lying by X.

Indeed application of this rule makes the basic inference to the systems dialogue reply far clearer because

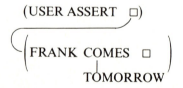

is replaced by a belief form, which enters the inner environment, and the response is then generated by a simplified, and more plausible, inference rule

$$[(\text{HUM X}) \quad \text{DISLIKE} \quad (\text{HUM Y})]$$

$$[(\text{HUM X}) \quad \text{APPROACH} \quad (\text{HUM Y})]$$

$$\Rightarrow [\text{Y} \quad (\text{MOVE AWAY}) \quad \square]$$

7. Self-embedding

A topic that has been touched on but not confronted is that of an individual's view of himself, and the ways in which that does not conform to our general heuristic for the computation of points of view: someone else's view of X is my view *except where I believe that not to be the case*.

No problem arises with the system's self-model: the PT

{SYSTEM}
SYSTEM

has all its content above the line (to continue the demarcation line metaphor): there are no beliefs the system has about the system that are not its own beliefs.

More interesting cases arise when the system wishes to compute, say, Frank's view of himself or Frank's view of the system: i.e.

$$\begin{Bmatrix} \text{FRANK} \\ \text{FRANK} \end{Bmatrix} \quad \text{or} \quad \begin{Bmatrix} \text{SYSTEM} \\ \text{FRANK} \end{Bmatrix}$$
$$\text{SYSTEM} \qquad \qquad \text{SYSTEM}$$

It would be reasonable to assume that Frank's view of himself is, *in general*, the same as my view of him except where I have evidence to the contrary. Our main heuristic would create an environment in which Frank believes his address to be what I believe it to be; his number of eyes to be what I believe it to be; but his number of teeth to be the value of what he believes it to be (and not the empty slot that I have ----- as suggested by the last section); and so on. In other words, Frank may well have beliefs, concrete and abstract, that I know nothing about but, given the limitations on my beliefs, my best construction is still to believe that his beliefs are as mine (except for the listed exceptions that I am aware of, and the special treatment of empty slots). So, we might say, for the first of these situations behaviourism is a safe intellectual policy!

What about the second case: the computation of Frank's view of the system? Here the general heuristic must surely break down, because the system cannot assume that Frank has access to all the beliefs about itself that it has. The situation is the inverse of the earlier one as regards the evaluation of slot fillers for, if we applied the general heuristic to a system that believed itself to be human and believed a particular figure for its number of teeth, we would construct an inner environment in which Frank would have the system's own beliefs about its number of teeth, which is not at all pluasible. One simply knows oneself better than others do, and that fact has concrete expression for oneself (though that implies nothing about behaviourism and the degree to which others could *in principle* know as much about one as one does oneself). Though in the case of one's beliefs about others, one believes they know more about themselves than one does oneself but nothing follows from that (if one knew what such things were they would be known to one, ex hypothesi).

However, it ought to be possible for the system to ask and answer the question: "what is Frank's view of me?", if only because this is a common and troublesome question in everyday life. If we apply the heuristic to compute

$$\left\{ \begin{array}{c} \text{SYSTEM} \\ \text{FRANK} \end{array} \right\}$$
SYSTEM

we would get Frank's explicit beliefs about the system (as believed by the system, and so in the upper half of

{FRANK}
SYSTEM

migrating into the lower half of

{SYSTEM}
SYSTEM

which was (see above) previously empty, since all the system's beliefs about itself are necessarily its beliefs. we must assume that Frank's beliefs about the system also include some of the list (a)–(e) above, such semantic definitional knowledge, copresence information as well as general information from the higher level PT {HUMAN} , or of course, COMPUTER , if system has been found out for what it is. However, this does not add up to much, if the inner environment is to be limited (as it seems it must be in this special case) to the *lower half* of the inner

{SYSTEM}
SYSTEM,

so as to avoid the system assuming Frank knows all the things about it that it does.

More thought is required on this issue, and a solution may be found (in the sense of a psychologically plausible solution) via a special PT for the system's view of its *public self* (i.e. what it believes to be the public's view of it, including what it is publically believed to believe about itself). But it would seem a pity to introduce a special entity here, one that ought to be constructible from the entities already available in the system, lest such entities have to be produced in some form for all other entities in the system. Such entities would not fit with the general assumptions of this paper because they would be essentially stored push-downs instead of everything being stored at the lowest level, as we have assumend, for the entity proposed would be:

$$\left\{ \begin{array}{l} \{\text{SYSTEM}\} \\ \text{AVERAGE MAN} \end{array} \right\}$$
SYSTEM

A way of avoiding this would be for there to be beliefs in the lower half of

{SYSTEM}
SYSTEM

and for them to be the system's beliefs about the average man's view of the system's self. If these were present then the general heuristic would run properly.

It needs to be emphasised that all operations in the system are, in some sense, self-embedding since all the PTs are the system's PTs and are *trivially* indexed from

{SYSTEM}
SYSTEM,

i.e. only a minute fraction of the system's real beliefs are actually in the upper part of

{SYSTEM}
SYSTEM.

But the system should be able to distinguish between what it believes about elephants, say, and what the average man believes about them. After all, the system might be an expert on elephants and any simple minded application of the general heuristic would again be wrong. The plausible solution here is again a pointer from the upper half of the PT {AVERAGE WESTERN MAN} to the system's own beliefs as default, but with "expertise areas" segregated off in those of the system's PTs about which it is an expert (corresponding perhaps, even in the semantic definitions, to Putnam's "division of linguistic labour".

Some, on reading all this, will want to argue for reverse or outward percolations, but we would claim that on detailed inspection such cases all turn out to be (inward) percolations falling under the general heuristic rule. The most obvious case would be the inverse of X believes p → p, namely, p (in one of the system's PTs) → Average man believes p. However, this is accounted for (without any "reverse percolation") by this default arrangement of pointers.

8. Conclusion

Enormous gaps in what has been described here will immediately be evident to the reader. First, we have said little about the nature of the organization of the inference rules and their relationship to plans. This is in part deliberate, for there are many systems for which plans are central, and planning is a relatively well understood sub-topic in AI. The specific claims of this paper do not bear on that issue. Secondly, we have noted that a system like this could not be serious until augmented by intensional logic notions, such as being able to show the equivalence of *Dolores* to *John's mother*, say, or *Frank* to *Jack's father*. Without this any kind of relevance heuristic for deciding what, in an outer PT, should be allowed to percolate into an inner, would be inadequate. Thirdly, we have said nothing about the relationship of the intermediate (and partly episodic) PTs to permanent memory frame, but again this is a subject of study in many other systems and no specific problems to do with that issue arise here.

Finally, something should be said about the differences between this work and work on speech acts and plans done at Toronto by Perrault, Allen and Cohen (see Allen and Perrault, 1978; Cohen, 1978 etc.). One is their emphasis on plans, which are not of central concern to us. A second, and fundamental, difference is that in the Toronto systems, all possible perspectives on beliefs *are already considered as computed*. That is to say, if, in a Toronto system, you want to to know what the system believes the user's belief about Frank's belief about the system is, then you can simply examine an inner partition of a set of beliefs that has already been constructed, where it is already explicitly stored. This is the exact opposite point of view to that adopted in this paper, which is that such inner environments are not stored already, and previously computed, but are constructed when needed and then, as it were, taken apart again, subject to what we call percolation. You can see the difference by asking yourself if you already know what Reagan thinks Begin thinks of Gaddafi. If you think you *already* know without calculation, then you will be inclined to the Toronto view that such inner belief partitions are already constructed. If you think that in some sense, consciously or unconsciously, you have to think it out, you will lean towards a constructivist hypothesis, like the one advanced in this paper. In the Toronto view there is no place for least-effort hypothesis of understanding. A fundamental principle of our system is that the points of view are kept wherever possible at a single (bottom) level, unless input comes in explicitly stating what person A believes about person or entity B.

The system presented in this paper is in the course of being programmed but, in the form offered here, is essentially a model containing ideas about how to explicate a difficult problem in language understanding. Two things have not concerned us here: first, the precise relation of this work to the analysis of speech acts, direct and indirect. These phenomena have been addressed within an AI context (Cohen, Allen, Perrault, q.v.) but we believe a rather different treatment of them will follow naturally - in a later paper - from the prolegomena on belief set out here: one in which the detection of a speech act as being a speech act of particular type will involve more stereotypical reasoning (speech act reasoning as "frame-like", as it were, rather then plan-like or deduction-like) and curtailed, rather than being in the more extended form of those working in the tradition of Searle (1969).

However, we would claim that the belief analysis presented here can be decoupled from this general problem, by assuming a parsing into some semantic representation (and the PTs have been a rhetorical rather than a truly technical device in this paper), and passing over the complex problems of the taxonomy of the inference rules we have assumed. Even if a reader is unwilling to grant this "decoupling" of activities, the proposed computation of nested beleifs can be judged independently, in terms of its psychological and other experimental consequences.

Secondly, the present work is not presented in the more fully formalized manner of projects like (Moore and Hendrix, 1979). We accept a distinction Schank has made recently between "neat" and "untidy" work in the area of Cognitive Science (as part of defence of the latter, of course). The ideas and claims expressed here are, we believe, independent of any particular notation, however desirable a full formalization may ultimately turn out to be. In the meantime, we hope that our proposals can be judged in a relatively "untidy" form; for there is all the time in the world for the axiomatisation of theories. The important thing is to have an idea worth axiomatising!

Chapter 11

A FRAMEWORK OF A MECHANICAL TRANSLATION BETWEEN JAPANESE AND ENGLISH BY ANALOGY PRINCIPLE

MAKOTO NAGAO

Department of Electrical Engineering, Kyoto University, Kyoto, Japan

Summary

Problems inherent in current machine translation systems have been reviewed and have been shown to be inherently inconsistent. The present paper defines a model based on a series of human language processing and in particular the use of analogical thinking.

Machine translation systems developed so far have a kind of inherent contradiction in themselves. The more detailed a system has become by the additional improvements, the clearer the limitation and the boundary will be for the translation ability. To break through this difficulty we have to think about the mechanism of human translation, and have to build a model based on the fundamental function of language processing in the human brain. The following is an attempt to do this based on the ability of analogy finding in human beings.

1. Prototypical consideration

Let us reflect about the mechanism of human translation of elementary sentences at the beginning of foreign language learning. A student memorizes the elementary English sentences with the corresponding Japanese sentences. The first stage is completely a drill of memorizing lots of similar sentences and words in English, and the corresponding Japanese. Here we have no translation theory at all to give to the student. He has to get the translation mechanism through his own instinct. He has to compare several different English sentences with the corresponding Japanese. He has to guess, make inferences about the structure of sentences from a lot of examples.

Along the same lines as this learning process, we shall start the consideration of our machine translation system, by giving lots of example sentences with their corresponding translations. The system must be able to recognize the similarity and the difference of the given example sentences. Initially a pair of sentences are given, a simple English sentence and the corresponding Japanese sentence. The next step is to give another pair of sentences (English and Japanese), which is different from the first only by one word.

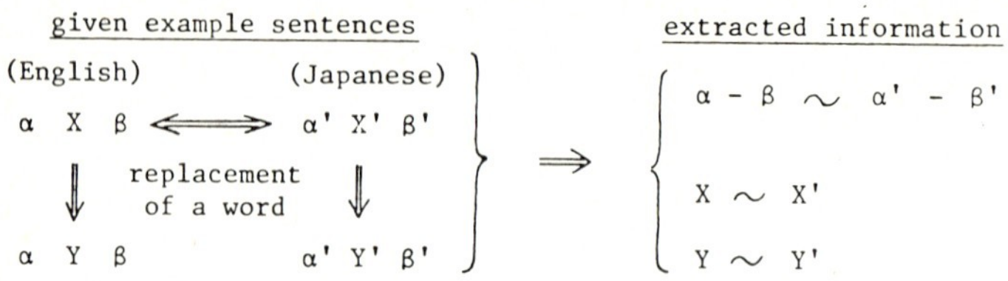

```
          given example sentences              extracted information
      (English)           (Japanese)
        α X β    ⟺    α' X' β'               ⎧  α - β  ∼  α' - β'
           ⇓   replacement   ⇓         ⟹     ⎨    X   ∼   X'
                of a word                    ⎩    Y   ∼   Y'
        α Y β            α' Y' β'
```

Fig. 1

This word replacement operation is done one word at a time in the subject, object, and complement positions of a sentence with lots of different words. For each replacement man must give the information to the system of whether the sentence is acceptable or non-acceptable. Then the system will obtain at least the following information from this experiment:

(1) Certain facts about the structure of a sentence;

Table 1

(1) S · verb · O · C ⟺ S' は · O' を · C' に · verb',

  S, S' ∈ W_X,   O, O' ∈ W_Y,   C, C' ∈ W_Z

  where W_X, W_Y, and W_Z are semantic groups of words X, Y, Z.

(2) A man eats vegetables.

(3) 人は   野菜を   たべる。
    (man) (vegetable) (eat)

(4) He eats potatoes.

(5)   man   ∼   he
       vegetable ∼   potato

(6)   人   ∼   彼
     (man)   (he)

      野菜   ∼   じゃがいも
     (vegetable) (potato)

(7) 彼は   じゃがいもを   たべる。

(8) Acid eats metal.

(9)   acid   ∼   man
      metal   ∼   vegetable

Table 1 (continued)

(1 0)   酸は   金属を   侵す。
           (acid) (metal) $\begin{pmatrix} eat \\ invade \\ attack \end{pmatrix}$

(1 1) Sulphuric acid eats iron.

(1 2)   硫酸は   鉄を   侵す。
           (sulphuric acid)   (iron)   (eat)

(1 3)   彼は   選挙に   破れた。
           (he)   (election)   (be defeated)

(1 4) He was defeated by the election.

(1 5)   紙袋は   重みで   破れた。
           (paper bag)   (weight)   (be broken)

(1 6) The paper bag was broken by the weight.

(1 7)   大統領は   投票に   破れた。
           (president)   (vote)

(1 8)   大統領   〜   人
           (president)   (man)

           投票   〜   選挙
           (vote)   (election)

(1 9) The president was defeated by the vote.

(2 0)   残念   ながら   明日は   行け   ません。
           $\begin{pmatrix} regret \\ disappointment \end{pmatrix}$ $\begin{pmatrix} though \\ inspite\ of \\ while \\ with \end{pmatrix}$ (tomorrow) $\begin{pmatrix} go \\ visit \\ attend \end{pmatrix}$ (not)

(2 1)   To my regret I cannot go tomorrow.

(2 2)   I am sorry I cannot visit tomorrow.

(2 3)   It is a pity that I cannot go tomorrow.

(2 4)   Sorry, tomorrow I will not be available.

Table 1 (continued)

(2 5)　国際政治　の　事　について　書いた　本。
(International) (of) (matter/thing/affair/situation/event) (about/of/on/with) (write/draw) (book/volume/work)

(2 6)　a book in which the affairs of international politics is written.
(2 7)　a book in which (someone) wrote about the events of international politics.
(2 8)　a book written about the events of international politics.

(2 9)　a book on international politics.

(3 0)　日本語の　翻訳の　場合について、　難しい　問題が　ある。
(Japanese language) (translation) (case) (about) (difficult) (problem) (exist)

(3 1)　日本語の　翻訳　には　難しい　問題が　ある。
(3 2)　投票　の　結果　大統領　の　敗北が　明らかと　なった。
(vote) (of) (result) (president) (of) (defeat) (clear/evident) (become)

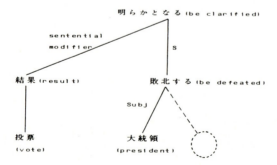

(3 3)　As the result of the vote the defeat of the president becomes definite.
(3 4)　The result of the vote revealed that the president was defeated.

(2) Correspondence between English and Japanese words.

These are expressed symbolically in Table 1.

These results indicate that we can formulate a word dictionary between English and Japanese, and a set of noun groups by a sentential context. If this experiment is done for different kinds of verbs the noun grouping will become much more fine and complex, and more reliable. Then certain kinds of relations will be established between word groups in a very complicated network structure. A noun may belong to several different groups with many different relations to other nouns. This is a kind of extensional representation of word meanings.

The same experiment can be done to verbs by replacing a verb in the same contextual environment. However, this is not so easy as noun replacement, because each verb has certain specific features as to the sentential structure, and no good grouping of verbs can be expected. So the sentential structure abstraction is done for each verb, and the structures are memorised in the verb dictionary entry for individual verb basis in such forms as (1).

This is a procedure of finding the case frames for each verb mechanically. But to get a good and reliable result we have to have a huge amount of sample sentences which are carefully prepared. To distinguish word usages of similar nature, we sometimes have to prepare near miss sentences. The data preparation of this kind is very difficult, and the speed of learning of the linguistic structures by the system is very slow.

2. A modified approach

To improve this simple language learning process, we can think of the utilization of ordinary word dictionaries and thesauri. In an ordinary word dictionary a verb has, in the explanation part, typical usages of the verb in example sentences rather than by grammatical explanations. That is, typical sentential structures which the verb is governed by are given by examples. These dictionary examples give us, human beings, plenty of information as to the usage of verbs in constructing sentences. Man is guided by these examples, makes inferences, and generates varieties of sentences.

We want to incorporate this human process into our mechanical translation system. And for this purpose we need varieties of knowledge in our system. The knowledge the machine can utilize at the moment, however, is an ordinary word dictionary and thesaurus, which is of course not comparable to the human knowledge about the word and the sentences. A thesaurus is a system of word groupings of similar nature, It has the information about synonyms, antonyms, upper/lower concept relations, part/whole relations and so on. The thesauri available at present are all very old, and they are not satisfactory from our standpoint, but we can use them properly.

The most important function in the utilization of example sentences in an ordinary dictionary is how to find out the similarity of the given input sentence and an example sentence, which can be a guide for the translation of the input sentence. First the global sytactic similarity between the input and example sentences must be checked. Then the replaceability of the corresponding words is tested by tracing the thesaurus relations. If the the replaceability for every word is sufficiently sure, then the translation sentence of the example sentence is changed by replacing the words to the translation words of the input sentence. In this way the translation can be obtained.

For example, we are given an example sentence (2) in the table for the verb eat from an English-Japanese dictionary, and its translation as sentence (3). Suppose sentence (4) is given for translation. The system checks the replaceability ($\sim$) of the words (5) by tracing the synonym and upper/lower concept relations in a thesaurus. Because these are similar word pairs, the system determines that the translated example (3) can be used for the the translation of (4). From the dictionary the translation of the words (5) is (6) in the table, and the replaced result is (7) which is a good translation of the sentence (4).

When sentence (8) is given, the similarity check of (9) fails in the thesaurus, and no translation comes out. If this is an example sentence in an entry of eat, and has the Japanese translation (10), then the input sentence (11) can be translatable as (12).

The important point in this process is the recognition of the similarity between the input sentence and an example sentence in a dictionary. This completely depends on the structure of the thesaurus. Typical examples of YABURERU (be defeated, or be broken) are sentences (13) and (15), and the corresponding translations as (14) and (16).

Suppose we are given a sentence (17). To know which usage of YABURERU fits to this sentence, we check the words, president and vote in a thesaurus, and find out the relations (18). We can determine from this information that (17) is more related to (13) than to (15), and the translation is obtained as (19).

To do an experiment along these lines, we stored all the contents of an ordinary Japanese dictionary, and an ordinary English-Japanese dictionary and an English-English dictionary (Longman's) into computer files. We will have a Japanese thesaurus very soon. We want to have a good English thesaurus in computer usable form.

3. Machine translation by analogy

Our fundamental ideas about the translation are:

(1) Man does not translate a simple sentence by doing deep linguistic analysis, rather,

(2) Man does the translation, first, by properly decomposing an input sentence into certain fragmental phrases (very often, into case frame units), then, by translating these fragmental phrases into other language phrases, and finally by properly composing these fragmental translations into one long sentence. The translation of each fragmental phrase will be done by the analogy translation principle with proper examples as its reference, which is illustrated above.

European languages have a certain common basis among them, and the mutual translation between these languages will be possible without great structural changes in sentential expressions. But the translation between two languages which are totally different, like English and Japanese, has a lot of difficult problems. Sometimes the same contents are expressed by completely different sentential structures, and there is no good structural correspondence between each part of the sentences of the two languages.

For example, a Japanese sentence (20) corresponds to such a different English sentence as (21) ~ (24). Another example is (25), which will literally correspond to such sentences as (26) ~ (28). But, it simply means (29).

A translation of this kind cannot be achieved by a mere detailed syntactic analysis of the original sentence. If we pick up each word and look for the corresponding translation word, the synthesis of a target language sentence becomes almost impossible. The choice of a proper translation from many candidates of a source language word is also very difficult without seeing the wider sentential context.

Therefore we adopted the method which may be called machine translation by example-guided inference, or machine translation by the analogy principle, and whose fundamental idea has been introduced already in the above. One of the strong reasons for this approach has been that the detailed analysis of a source language sentence is of no use for the translation between languages of completely different structure like English and Japanese. We have to see as wide a scope as possible in a sentence, and the translation must be from a block of words to a block of words. To realize this we have to store varieties of example sentences in the dictionary and to have a mechanism to find out analogical example sentences for the given one.

It is very important to point out that, if we want to construct a system of learning, we have to be able to give the system the data which is not very much processed. In our system the augmentation of the knowledge is very simple and easy. It requires only the addition of new words and new usage examples and their translations. It does not require the information which is deeply analyzed and well arranged. Linguistic theories change rapidly to and fro, and sometimes a model must by thrown away in a few years. On the contrary, language data and its usage do not change for a long time. We will rely on the primary data rather than analysed data which may change sometimes because of changes in the theory.

4. A practical approach

The process of mechanical translation by analogy is again very time consuming in its primary structure. So we divide the process into a few substages and give all the available information we have to the system, in the initial system construction. The learning comes in only at the augmentation stage of the system, which is mainly the increase of example sentences and the improvement of the thesaurus.

The following substages have been distinguished in our Japanese English translation system which is being constructed.

(a) Reduction of redundant expressions, and supplement of eliminated expressions in a Japanese input sentence, and getting an essential sentential structure. Sentence (30) has almost the same meaning as sentence (31).
(b) Analysis of sentential structure by case grammar. Phrase structure grammar is not suitable for the analysis of Japanese, because the word order in Japanese is almost free except that the final predicate verb comes at the end.
(c) Retrieval of target language words, and example phrases which are stored in the word entries from the dictionary. The dictionary contains varieties of examples besides grammatical information, meaning and, for verbs, the case frames.
(d) Recognition of the similarity between the input sentential phrases and example phrases in the dictionary. The word thesaurus is used for the similarity finding.
(e) Choice of a global sentential form for translation. For example, sentence (32) has such translations as (33) and (34). These can only be derived from the examples for the word result in the dictionary.
(f) The choice of local phrase structure is determined by the requirements of the global sentential structure.

It is very difficult to clarify what factors contribute to the determination of the stages (e) and (f). These remain to be solved.

ARTIFICIAL AND HUMAN INTELLIGENCE (A. Elithorn and R. Banerji, editors)
Elsevier Science Publishers, B.V.
© NATO, 1984

Chapter 12

TOOLS FOR CREATING INTELLIGENT COMPUTER TUTORS

TIM O'SHEA

Institute of Educational Technology, Open University, Milton Keynes MK7 6AA, UK

RICHARD BORNAT

Computer Science Laboratory, Queen Mary College, University of London WC1E 7HU, UK

BENEDICT DU BOULAY

Computer Science Department, University of Aberdeen AB9 1FX, UK

MARC EISENSTADT

Faculty of Social Science, Open University, Milton Keynes MK7 6AA, UK

IAN PAGE

Computer Science Laboratory, Queen Mary College, University of London WC1E 7HU, UK

Summary

This paper reports an application of artificial intelligence representation techniques to the problems involved in designing, implementing and refining intelligent computer tutors. Starting from Hartley's (1973) model for adaptive computer assisted instruction we have produced a simple five component model for intelligent computer tutors. The five components are the student model, teaching strategy, teaching generator, teaching administrator and student history. Each of these five functionally distinct components can be expressed with production rules using techniques adapted from Brown et al. (1976), Clancey (1979) and O'Shea (1979). We then show that it is possible to constrain this general model to yield all the various particular types of computer tutor and computer assisted learning environments currently in existence. Ten specialisations of our general model are proposed and these range in application from computer games to problem-solving monitors.
 Our main objective in producing this parsimonious and homogenous account of computer assisted learning is to make it possible for innovators in education without extensive programming skills to create high quality computer based educational materials. Accordingly we have designed for each specialised model a courseware development template which enables the user to create his educational materials via a computer mediated form filling activity. The design of the user interface is a development of Eisenstadt's (1979) SOLO system but is designed to run on a stand alone personal computer with high resolution color graphics.

1. Introduction

This paper is a speculative discussion of the possible application of artificial intelligence techniques to the problem of designing computer based training systems. In particular we are interested in designing an authoring system which would make it easy for an instructional designer without programming skills to create computer based learning materials of high educational quality. This paper is organised in the following way. First we discuss a single general model of computer based training which will underly all interactions between the system and students or trainers. Then we discuss the specialisations of this model which would be used as the basis of ten courseware design templates to organise and assist a trainer's creation of different types of learning material. We then give three hypothetical case studies of use of the authoring system.

The artificial intelligence representation technique that we use in many places in our design is production rule modelling. We discuss how production rules would be input by instructional designers and then give an account of the student records that a training package would have to maintain. We complete the paper by detailing the characteristics that the user interface would have to have in order to be both powerful and friendly enough to make this system accessible to computationally naive instructional designers.

2. A model for computer based training

Starting from the work of Hartley (1973) we have produced the simple five component model for computer based training in Fig. 1. The components of

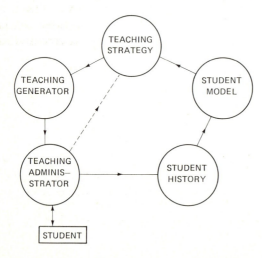

Fig. 1. 5 circle model for computer based training.

the model have the following functions:

1. Teaching Administrator – this is the part of a computer based training system which presents material to a student and processes student responses.
2. Student History – this is a *record* of the material presented to the student and the responses of the student to the material.
3. Student Model – this *makes predictions* of the students' future performance and current state of knowledge and ability.
4. Teaching Strategy – this relates the systems view of the student to the general types of teaching action that are possible, and *decides* the type of the next action.
5. Teaching Generator – this is a mechanism that yields a specific teaching action for use by the teaching administrator.

Note that in addition to flow of control Administrator – History – Model – Strategy – Generator – Administrator the diagram includes a dotted line from the Administrator to the Strategy. This represents the possibility that the student may appeal for some particular types of teaching action or exercise some form of learner control.

The five component model, as described above, in extremely general. By constraining the content of the various components it is possible to create different types of computer based training programs. These constrained models form the basis of Courseware Design Templates (CDTs) which are used to help trainees without programming skills create computer based training

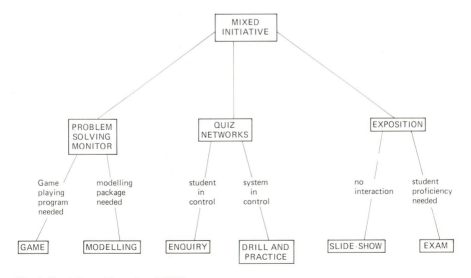

Fig. 2. Special-case hierarchy of CDT.

materials of different types. Our claim is that our model can easily be applied to all computer based training systems currently in existence or envisaged in the contemporary research literature. Ten CDTs are discussed below and their inter-relationships summarised in Fig. 2. From the student's point of view we distinguish those systems which act on evaluations of student's performance from those which do not. From the teaching point of view we distinguish between systems which

a) only present material
b) can also tutor the student
c) can also demonstrate mastery of the subject being taught.

We discuss below the CDTs necessary for these different systems.

3. Presenting material

One general name, which we have chosen to give to that CDT, is *exposition*. In terms of our model a characteristic of exposition is that the student *cannot* take control of the choice of teaching material. Most material written in conventional author languages is essentially exposition. It is important to note that if we replace the student history by a *student profile* which is record of the student's use of some series of CDT lessons or modules, then we have a CDT for *Computer Managed Learning*.

There are two useful special cases of the exposition CDT. The first is the *exam*. In this case there is no Teaching Strategy or Student Model and the Teaching Generator is a linear sequence. The other special case is the *slide-show*. In this case the only response that the Teaching Administrator will process is the "O.K." signifying that the student has finished looking at a "slide".

4. Tutoring

The principal distinction between this type of system and the exposition types is that the student may ask questions of the system and that the questions asked by the system of the student may depend on the system's teaching goals. The name we give to the general CDT for tutoring is *Quiz Network*.

The student may attempt to short-circuit the Student Model's prediction of his proficiency at topics by requesting a quiz or information on a topic. One special case of the Quiz Network is the *Drill and Practice* CDT. In this case all teaching occurs through the careful choice of examples and the student cannot intervene. The other special case is the *Enquiry CDT*. In this case the system is essentially acting as a database system obedient to the requests of the student.

In this case the Student Model can only operate on a record of the topics explored.

5. Demonstrating mastery

For a system to do this it must be able to actually do what it teaches and *show* the student how to exercise the skill he is acquiring and comment sensibly on his own attempts. We call the general CDT for this Problem Solving Monitor (from Sleeman, 1974). Such systems are extremely rare for the good reason that is is necessary to construct a computer based "domain expert" capable of carrying out the skills being taught. However such systems have been successfully implemented for integration (Kimball, 1973), NMR spectroscopy (Sleeman, 1976), electronic trouble-shooting (Brown et al, 1976) and medical diagnosis of bacterial intestinal infections (Clancey, 1979). Note the addition of the "domain experts" to the CDT model to comment on the "sense" of the student's partial solution in addition to a model which allows the student to see the result of his problem step. The clearest account of a working problem-solving monitor is that which describes the Stanford integration tutor (Kimball, 1973). One special case of this CDT is that for *modelling*. In order to construct CDT lessons for this we only require that a working model program be available. The other special case of the problem-solving monitor CDT is the games CDT. In this case it is necessary to provide a single domain expert which is able to play the game against the student if the game is to be competitive.

For example, if we wished to turn a quiz network into a game it would be necessary to implement a variety of domain experts and their choice of parameters could be used in the teaching strategy as a basis for monitoring and reacting intelligently to the student's choice of parameters.

6. Hierarchy of courseware design templates

Clearly some of these CDTs will involve the trainer using them in considerable design. However we claim that our model-based approach will be easier to use and provide educationally "cleaner" educational software than existing authoring systems. But our approach will not solve the difficult problems which confront the designers and implementers of domain experts or even simulation packages. The most general CDT is that which provides *mixed-initiative* teaching. This term (from Carbonell, 1970) implies that the system should be able to teach in a variety of ways and respond to a variety of student requests. With the possible exception of SOPHIE (Brown and Burton, 1976) no existing system can strongly claim this title and as SOPHIE required man-years of development per hour of intelligent system/student interaction it is included here partly as a long-term ideal. However the incorporation of such a CDT makes it possible for trainer to construct lessons which switch from, say, problem-solving monitoring to exposition.

The beginning CDT designer will find the most constrained versions of our CDT model the easiest to use as defaults will create most of the components for her. As she becomes more confident she will progress to the more powerful ones. In terms of ease of use for a beginner a rough ordering is: slide show, exam, exposition, games, enquiry, drill and practice, modelling, quiz network, problem-solving monitor, mixed initiative. This will vary with the teaching application. The relationships between the ten CDTs are best summarised as a special case hierarchy in Fig. 2.

7. Translation of high level objectives into the 5 circle model

Here we give examples of the development of high level objectives in instantiated 5 circle models. They cover mixed initiative, modelling and quiz network in the domains of engine fault-finding, analysis of static friction and microcomputer structure. Each of the following lessons starts with a very high level and brief statement of the training objective that the trainer might start from. This is followed by a much fuller English description. Finally a briefer instantiated 5 circle model is given. These descriptions provide very little detail of how the trainer is likely to develop his lesson (which may, after all, start out with some nice idea for a model that is only post-hoc given a proper educational rationalisation through an objective).

8. Example 1. Mixed initiative

8.1. Content

The lesson is to be given as part of a series to apprentice plant maintenance persons. It concerns the mechanism of, and fault-finding in, a portable generator driven by a four cylinder, 4-stroke petrol engine of conventional design. Only the motor is considered here.

8.2. Objective

To provide apprentices with opportunities to develop their fault-finding skills as well as providing some basic training in the function of the engine and its parts.

8.3. Principal CDT and Overview

The principle CDT is to be quiz-network, where the topic network specifies the interdependence of the parts of the engine. Such a network can be explored in one of two modes: "teach me" or "test me". In the "teach me" mode, the student is to be provided with a lesson about the component (or system of components) denoted by a node in the network. This lesson may be a simple slide show or a more complex lesson (eg. modelling) that provides information about the component, its likely faults: their detection and symptoms. Certain systems will be presented in moving graphics, eg. the operation of the 4-stroke cycle itself. In the "test me" mode, questions will be presented about components, faults and symptoms. A portion of the network is given in Fig. 3. Notice that the tip nodes refer to mechanically or electronically distinct (and simple) parts about which knowledge can be treated as pre-requisite for understanding assemblies built of those parts. So a student desiring to be taught or tested about "plugs" (say) would be given material or questions on insulators and electrodes unless he had previously demonstrated mastery of these two areas.

However the lesson can be more versatile than a quiz network. The same network can be used as the basis for a simulation of an engine. Each of the tip nodes can be given three values eg. good, poor, and broken that indicate its state. An assembly constructed of good parts is itself good, and one constructed of broken parts is itself broken. An assembly constructed out of

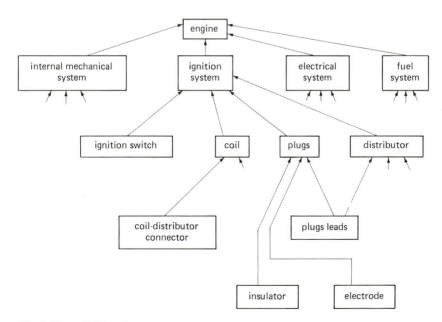

Fig. 3. Network for engine.

(some) poor parts may be good, broken or poor depending on the conditions of operation (ie. a cracked distributor cap gives a broken distributor in wet weather, but only a poor one in dry weather). By chaining upward from the tip nodes, the behaviour of the engine as a whole can be predicted by knowledge of the states of its components and of the external conditions. The system will therefore (in a SOPHIE-like style) choose states for the components of the engine and invite the student to detect and rectify the faults.

If the trainer is ambitious the system could impose a rigid fault-detecting style on the student (eg. by only enabling access to nodes near the engine node before those far down the network). Or it could monitor the debugging style of the student and make suggestions for improvements in that style. The student will be able to "examine" the state of a component by pressing its node on the topic map and also pressing a suitable menu button. The system will allow the student to replace a component with a fault-free version if his prior examination has shown that component to be poor or broken.

The model can be run in a more open ended way where the student will also be free to set the state of any component (in an initially perfect engine) and observe the behaviour of the engine as whole, or of any assembly. For example, setting the value of the plug electrode to poor, induces the behaviour that the engine turns over quickly, but is sluggish to start in the dry and will not start at all in the wet. By contrast, setting the fuel filter to poor does not affect starting but reduces power output at high revs.

Although the basic lesson CDT is that of the quiz network, the lesson can develop into either modelling lesson or a problem-solving monitor lesson.

9. Five circle model for the engine

9.1. Student History

An elaborate log of the modes chosen in the "teach me' mode, the questions presented and answers given in the "test me" mode. The order and method of fault finding will be recorded.

9.2. Student Model

There will be a domain expert that embodies a fault-finding strategy which can suggest a fault-finding move. The student model can compare the student's fault finding moves with those of the domain expert to build a production rule model of the student's fault finding capability. In the "teach me", "test me" modes, the Student Model will also construct a network of nodes that the student is presumed to understand.

9.3. Teaching Strategy

In "teach me" mode the Teaching Strategy can compare the partial network provided by the student model (eg. student knows about plugs, electrodes and insulation) with the full network and decide which is the next most appropriate node to teach. In "test me" mode, it can decide what level of questioning to adopt about the node chosen by the student (eg. questions about plugs, if the student chooses the ignition system). When the network is being run as a problem-solving monitor, it can decide where to introduce faults in order to (a) keep within the knowledge of the student or (b) exercise some particular problem solving skill in the student.

9.4. Teaching Generator

This will contain the topic network in a form suitable for use as a quiz network. It will also contain a representation of the network suitable to run as a simulation – into which faults can be introduced if need be. It will also contain a data-base of faults with links to particular fault-finding skills.

9.5. Teaching Adminstrator

This will contain specific information about how to display and receive information for all the variety of modes that this lesson may be in. In this particular example the simulation is developed as part of a quiz network rather than being a separate mechanism. As such it will live in the Teaching Generator rather than linking directly to the Teaching Administrator.

10. Example 2. Modelling

10.1. Context

The course will be a mathematics/physics/engineering science course for technicians or engineers. The particular topic is friction and the lesson described is supposed to be used after practical work in a lab and before a full, formal theoretical treatment is undertaken.

10.2. Objectives

There are two objectives. First, to give the student the opportunity to try inclined plane experiments using a wider range of values and getting more "reliable" results than are possible in the lab. Second, to link experimental work with the later theoretical treatment that uses force diagrams and equations

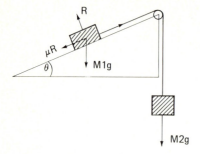

Fig. 4. Inclined plane.

10.3. Principal CDT and Overview

The principle CDT will be modelling. This will consist of an inclined plane on which a mass rests connected to a second mass by means of a light, smooth inextensible string. The coefficient of friction between the block and the plane and the plane is μ. The student is expected to adjust the values of the free parameters in the model so that the block on the plane just slides up the plane (without accelerating). Success will be indicated both by the movement of the blocks and by a message (since the critical condition gives a very slow movement of the blocks). The parameters of the model are μ (the coefficient of friction), θ (the angle of inclination of the plane), M1 and M2 (the masses of the two blocks).

If the system sets the value of any three of these parameters the value of the fourth is determined. The model can be run where the student has to choose values for either 1,2,3 or 4 parameters. Certain choices by the student will provoke teaching actions, for example choosing illegal values ($\mu < 0$ or $\mu > 1$, $\theta > 90$ or $\theta < -90$). Where the student has only one parameter left to determine and his second attempt shows that he is changing its value in the wrong direction, then some remedial teaching will be given. For instance, if he only has the slope angle θ to determine and his initial choice of 45° produces no movement (for the given values of μ, M1 and M2) then a second choice of 50° is clearly not acceptable.

11. Five circle model for friction

11.1. Student History

This will consist of a record of all the parameters values chosen by the student: both final correct sets of values and attempts that fail to produce the required condition.

11.2. Student Model

This will be rudimentary and will only concern itself with illegal values of μ and θ and poor second choices when only one variable is left to determine.

11.3. Teaching Strategy

Where the student has made an illegal choice of μ or θ the system will give a short slide show and then continue with the simulation. Where the student has made a poor second choice in fixing the final parameter value the system will give practice in choosing that parameter by automatically setting the values of the other 3 parameters and inviting the student to choose the fourth.

11.4. Teaching Generator

This will provide a simulation with no parameter set unless otherwise directed by the Teaching Strategy or by the student who is here to ask for some parameters to be set.

11.5. Teaching Administrator

This will display the results of the simulation and receive the student's choice for parameter values. The simulation itself will be a simple mechanism (based on equations) that adjusts the picture according to the values given and then produces the appropriate behaviour (no motion, just moving – critical condition, acceleration up the slope, acceleration down the slope). The system will have to accept a certain amount of tolerance in deciding that the student's values produce the critical condition. The student is not supposed to be computing the equation himself at this stage. Though these criteria could be narrowed, if the simulation was to be used after the student had received a theoretical lesson. As the slope angle changes to the direction of the arrows representing R and μR will also change. The lengths of the arrows representing forces will adjust to indicate the magnitude of the forces.

12. Example 3. Quiz network

12.1. Context

The lesson is part of an extended sequence on microprocessor application in product design. This particular lesson is concerned with the structure of microcomputers and their possible component parts.

12.2. Objective

To provide information about the different components that go to make up a microcomputer.

12.3. Basic CDT and Overview

The basic CDT is the quiz network of which a fragment is given overleaf. Unlike the elaborate lesson developed in example 1, this lesson has no pretensions to being anything but a quiz network. Each node has questions associated with it and mastery of a node implies mastery of the children of that node, and is a pre-requisite for mastery of the parent of that node.

13. Five circle model for microprocessor application

13.1. Student History

This records which nodes (ie. which parts of the microcomputer) have been presented and how questions have been answered.

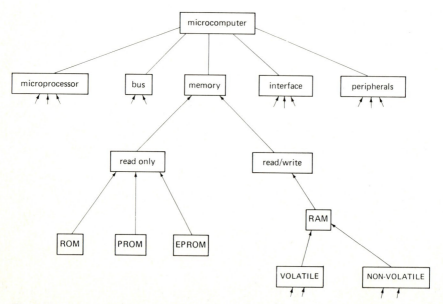

Fig. 5. Network for microprocessor applications.

13.2. Student Model

This constructs a partial network consisting of nodes of which the student has demonstrated his understanding. It also computes the nodes of which the student has a partial understanding.

13.3. Teaching Strategy

Both the teaching and testing strategy is to question or teach the students at the node nearest to the current node of interest that is feasible. For example, if the student has demonstrated mastery in say "ROM", "PROM" and "EPROM" and asks for questions of "memory", he should be tested about "read only" (c.f. network).

13.4. Teaching Generator

This will contain the representation for the network itself, for the question associated with each node and for the teaching materials on each node. In this case the teaching materials are simply slides of text and pictures.

13.5. Teaching Administrator

This will be the standard default mechanism for dealing with the presentation of a quiz network

14. Inputting production rules

The creation by the author of new production rules for use in the Teaching Strategy, Student Model and Teaching Generator is not trivially easy in the same way as the creation of initialisation and termination rules for the Teaching Administrator. It is however straightforward. The flow of control of lesson execution is specified exactly by the five circle model. This means that the predicates of the Teaching Strategy must match on variables whose value are actions of the production rules of the Student Model. The Teaching Generator is in exactly the above relationship to the Teaching Strategy. The action of the Teaching Generators production rules will be restricted to legal operations of the Teaching Administrator. This leaves the most complex case, namely, the variables on which the Student Model matches. These will be cells, rows or columns of the Student History viewed as matrix. The constraints of flow of control and function of components of the five circle model result in a constrained possible set of variables and actions for each type of production rule. These are summarised in Table 1. In each case where production rules

Table 1

Component of model	Student Model	Teaching Strategy	Teaching Generator	Teaching Administrator
Constraint on Variables	Student History	Student Model	Teaching Strategy	Student History and Profile
Constraint on Actions	Legal Student States	Legal Teaching Operations	Legal Teaching Acts	Student History and Profile Variables

might be created there is a pre-existing set of variables and actions. In each case the set of variables cannot be changed but new actions can be created by simply naming the action. The process of creating a production rule has two stages:

1. Associating a predicate with one or more variables to yield a condition.
2. Associating a condition with an action.

The process of creating individual production rules will be simple and in some cases, such as creating a complex teaching strategy tedious, as the author will in fact be manipulating a partial ordering of teaching subgoals (with variables having as values the names of subgoals). While production rule creation is simple, like any form of programming, it will be possible to create peculiar rules which might always fire or never fire. To create such rules would require malice or a very sophisticated form of naivety. To help the well-intentioned author there will be facilities for checking and examining the firing conditions and behaviours of both individual and collections of rules. The author will be able to ask the system to generate, or himself pose, critical test cases. If the author specifies the possible ranges of values of his variables the system will identify rules which will always or never fire.

15. Teaching individual students

Once a student starts using some lesson materials created with a CDT there will need to be a record of the students and systems actions.

So for each instantiation of a CDT there will always be an associated student history. Student records separate from these will be kept in a *student profile* which will be used by individual lessons and by course organisers to obtain information on student progress. The student profile can be viewed metaphorically as a student history associated with a very general "all student learning" CDT. An author producing a series of lessons or a curriculum will have to decide how the student histories in the particular lessons are to be initialised and what lesson information should be stored for future use when a student leaves a lesson. These two types of decision determine the form and organisation of the student profile. Maintaining such profiles is usually a problem in CDT systems. Our design offers a very elegant solution which uses only the mechanisms required for the five circle model.

The student profile may include any of the types of information associated with any of the legal CDTs. When a lesson is to be administered its history is initialised by a collection of production rules in the teaching administrator which may be a subset of the profile variable values in the new lesson history. During the lesson administration the student model of that lesson can access both its own student history and the profile using the predicates which are associated with the current model. However only the student history is updated *during* the course of the lesson. When a lesson *terminates*, another collection of production rules in the teaching administrator assigns values to variables in the student profile.

In addition to being parsimonious and elegant this solution to the student profile design problem permits modular refinement of the student profile. When an author creates a new lesson the process for extending the profile will be as follows. Firstly, having outlined a student history, determine which variables might be usefully initialised from past recorded student performance. Secondly, consider which variables in the history might usefully be recorded for use in initialising other lessons. Then working with the union of these variables identify those which will not be used in both lesson initialisation and termination of the lesson being added to the system. For these specify which of initialisation and termination they are relevant to. This identification then automatically yields a set of very simple production rules mapping variables to variables (with the possibility of different variable names in the profile and history). This set of rules is associated with the teaching administrator. As each rule is independent the information flow between the profile and particular lessons can always be extended.

The author will think of the student profile as the top-level student history and will, of course be required to document the variables in the profile so that other authors can access and update the profile from their lessons. This information and the variable names will also make it possible for the production rules in particular student models to match on (but not, of course, alter) the variables in the profile.

16. The student and trainer interface

One of the many challenges we face is to design a system which is both powerful and "user friendly". These two objectives (power and friendliness) often conflict: CBT systems which exhibit a superficial degree of friendliness when being used by a knowledgeable author often turn out to be highly brittle and idiosyncratic in their behaviour. In such systems, deviation from a prescribed route is taboo, and it is extremely difficult for a user to do what he really wants to do in the manner which he finds most natural.

Our design is intended to provide "hand-holding" guidance for the CBT author. There have been other attempts at hand-holding, but we believe our conception of hand-holding to be unique, because it provides both simplicity and power *without* offering yet another new author language to the world. From the beginning of this project, our aim has been to take a well-understood and highly respected *existing* language and to embed it in a total supportive soft-ware *environment* which would provide a relatively painless interface for students and trainers. In doing this, we feel that we have successfully avoided two dangerous pitfalls: (a) the "steamroller" pitfall of leading authors, via a series of multiple-choice menus, down a pathway which they do not really want to take; and (b) the "powerful new language" pitfall of providing authors with syntactic constructs which may or may not mesh with their personal views of how control flow and data flow should be handled in a CBT context. The "steamroller' approach suffers from trying to impose a highly idiosyncratic design process on the author. The "powerful new language" approach provides authors with many useful syntactic constructs, but these constructs implicitly represent some particular model of courseware design which may not be consistent with the author's own model. We believe that the design process itself needs to be made explicit. We feel that authors can be shown a particular model of the design process, and adapt it to their own needs. Thus, rather than forcing authors into one type of design (pitfall "a") or providing them with syntactic constructs whose underlying design goals are unclear (pitfall "b"), we provide authors with a way of exploring design alternatives. Every choice our authors are presented with, has an underlying rationale in terms of courseware design. If the authors do not like the choice, they can escape to a more open-ended design process which they may find more suitable.

The next section outlines the main "pillars" of our design philosophy. We then describe the main aspects of the student and trainer interface, with specific reference to how the design of each of these tools was influenced by the pillars of our philosophy.

17. The thirteen pillars of our design philosophy

a) *Robustness*: input errors (e.g. typing mistakes) which are thought by human observers to be "obvious" mistakes should be detectable by the system, and dealt with in a graceful fashion.

b) *Helpfulness*: The system should be capable of providing help when the user gets stuck, including displays of documentation describing its design and operation.

c) *Simplicity*: The system should minimize the amount of typing necessary to achieve a given task (i.e. simple or common tasks should be achievable with few keystrokes).

d) *Perspicuity*: At the same time, the system should not provide the user with a mystifying choice from an array of several hundred buttons.

e) *Power*: State-of-the-art graphics capabilities should be available (at some level) to all users.

f) *Navigability*: The user must always be able to find out "where he is" when using the system.

g) *Consistency*: The underlying virtual machine, from the user's point of view, should work in a clear and consistent fashion. This means that error messages should be carefully designed to conform with the way in which the user *believes* the system to work.

h) *Transparency*: The effects of user actions should always be displayed.

i) *Flexibility*: "Wizards" or experienced users should be able to take advantage of *all* of the capabilities of the system. Even intermediate level users and novices should be able to deviate from routine (or overused) pathways.

j) *Redundancy*: Trainers with different perspectives on the design process (e.g. one may view simulation as a special case of games while the other sees it the other way round) should be capable of using the system, remaining faithful to their respective views, and ending up via two different pathways at the same destination (i.e. identical teaching material).

k) *Sensitivity* The system should be able to tailor its response according to that it knows about the needs of the user (even if this is only true at a gross level).

l) *Omniscience* The system should be capable of leading the user "by the hand" in cases where it has reason to believe that it already knows a large proportion of what it is that the user wants to do.

m) *Docility*: The system must always be seen to be under the user's command, (and not "steamrolling" him through a sequence of menu choices).

18. The touch screen, menu selection and form-filling

Our system makes extensive use of the touch screen to minimize lengthy keyboard input sequences. The presentation of "pressable" or touch-button menus on the screen clearly makes selection a one-touch process. More important than the menu concept, however (which can lead to "steamrolling" or "strait-jacketing" of the user), is our use of "editing menus" and "form-filling dialogues" to minimize keystrokes. The "editing menus" (e.g. display editor, topic network editor) attempt to strike a balance between forcing the user into a canned choice versus letting him type powerful but hard-to-remember commands at the keyboard. By displaying editing menus on the screen, the user is spared having to remember what the magical key words are. But since these menus contain powerful editing commands, they allow the user to build and manipulate complex graphical and textual objects with a very small number of button presses. This enables us to achieve our objectives of *power* and *simplicity*.

The "form-filling dialogues" serve a dual purpose: first, the left hand columns of the forms typically remind the user of what *sort* of entity he is expected to type in; second, the item the user is meant to type in often has a system-default name in its place in advance, which the user can leave if he is feeling lazy – this clearly cuts down on the number of keystrokes involved.

To keep from overloading the screen (and the user), our system uses sub-menus (menus which "pop up" only when a particular item has been selected from a higher-level menu). Very long menus are augmented by a "scroll" button which appears at the bottom or the top of the menu, as appropriate.

On every CDT "pathway", there is always an option (such as "display editor", "question editor", etc.) which opens up the full powers of the system to the enterprising author satisfying our criterion of *flexibility*.

The system provides *redundancy*, in that one author who produced a "Slide Show" could clearly end up with the exact same presentation as another author who used the "Display Editor" to create all the overlays separately, and then the "Animation Sequencer" to put them together with the same sequence and timing as the slide show.

When the trainer is specifying ways for typed-in answers to be analysed he will be able to use either simple keyword matching or the response analysis module. The latter will be based on the philosophy used in Lifer (Hendrix, 1977) and will allow the author to specify a set of top-down rewrite rules. These would be created and changed in the same way that production rules are inputted into the student model or teaching strategy.

19. Conclusions

This paper is speculative. It remains to be seen whether the various artificial intelligence techniques we advocate can be successfully married and whether the resulting software would run on a powerful personal computer with high resolution colour graphics. What we are reporting here are some components of a larger paper and pencil study on all the educational, software and hardware aspects of a design for a computer based training authoring system. Our own optimism about this project stemmed initially from the fact that all the component programs of the design can be developed from existing graphics and artificial intelligence software. The keys to this design are the general "five circle" model for intelligent computer tutors and the ten specific course development templates. This design has been successfully applied to a variety of educational and training design problems. As some of these problems were initially offered as counter-examples this design activity has had the effect of reinforcing our initial optimism. We remain interested in receiving instructional design challenges.

Acknowledgements

We thank ICL for funding the project described here and Marcus Clark, Penny Guthrie and Bill Hudspith of ICL for helpful critical comments. Useful advice and criticism was also received from Bruce Anderson and John Self. This paper benefited from the advice and comment of Eileen Scanlon. We thank Claire Jones for patient typing and retyping of drafts.

ARTIFICIAL AND HUMAN INTELLIGENCE (A. Elithorn and R. Banerji, editors)
Elsevier Science Publishers, B.V.
© NATO, 1984

Chapter 13

BENCHMARK AND YARDSTICK PROBLEMS: A SYSTEMATIC APPROACH

A. ELITHORN, R. COOPER and A. TELFORD

Institute of Neurology, Royal Free Hospital, London

1. Introduction

Turing's criteria for assessing the intelligence of a system are unsatisfactory. Firstly they depend on an assessment made by a fallible system i.e. man. Secondly, since one would not deny that most mental defectives have some intelligence, a system with the same intelligence as a mental defective would satisfy Turing's criteria (Turing 1936). That such a system would in fact be an intelligent one is acceptable. It is equally acceptable to accord intelligence to many *subhuman* species. Moreover, as one descends through the biological spectrum there is no clear cut off point below which one can say that behaviour is unintelligent. By Turing's criteria an automaton which was behaviourally indistinguishable from a spider or from a worm would be an intelligent automaton. The questions that one should ask about intelligent systems must therefore be quantitative as well as descriptive.

Psychologists have since the beginning of the century put considerable effort into devising measures of intelligence. In spite of many criticisms and genuine weaknesses and the recent widely promulgative shibboleth that all human beings are equal, the methods developed have proved to be practical and useful in matching human subjects to a wide range of tasks requiring different levels and patterns of intellectual skill.

The techniques used for assessing human intelligence can be grouped into two broad classes. The first attempts to assess the subject's competence at skills which, it is thought, all humans possess to some extent. Those who favour this approach now recognise that there is no single all-purpose skill of "G" and that individual human beings may excel in one type of intellectual performance while being relatively inept in another. This intelligence test approach, therefore, tends to use a battery of tests which provides a profile and an overall weighted score. The second approach makes the assumption that human beings share a common structure and its proponents advocate tests such as reaction time tests, tests measuring speed of perception and electroencephalographic measures, all of which are assumed to measure the quality of the physiological substrate which determines the upper limit of the individuals intellectual capacity. Crudely, these two approaches are comparable to an evaluation of a machine intelligence by looking on the one hand at the performance of the software available and on the other at the capacity of the hardware. Psychologists sometimes distinguish these two approaches as assessing "fluid" and crystalised intelligence (Cattell, 1943).

There is no reason to assume that human intelligence marks a ceiling above which intellectual skills cannot rise. Human intelligence is a point or rather a range of points in a multidimensional space. Since no single human being or computing system can be optimal for all possible problem spaces a comparison of two systems with different "task" areas may be irrelevant. In assessing the power of intelligent systems, therefore, a useful and certainly relevant approximation is to assess their value in relation to man's problem solving needs. In taking this approach it might be argued that one should apply to the machine tests similar to those that one applies to man. Indeed machine intelligence presents the experimental psychologist with an important new comparative psychology. Unfortunately the techniques which would allow psychologists to make meaningful comparisons between the intelligence of man and that of other biological or mechanical systems have yet to be developed. Indeed, the nearer the goal is approached the narrower the gap between man and other systems appears.

Machine intelligence, like the intelligence of ants and bees, is at the present time highly specific. Indeed it is not difficult to write programs which will solve more items from this or that intelligent test than many a human subject. But the same computer program will be quite unable to make even a stab at solving a wide range of problems which most humans would cheerfully tackle. The computer system which is a true general problem solver even at a low level does not as yet exist.

Man as a problem solving system is also more highly specific than many psychologists will readily admit. Essentially, he has evolved as a computing system for coordinating sensory input with motor behaviour. As a logic-analyst man, bereft of his cultural heuristics and a range of mechanical aids, is a poor performer. How many times on average must a conventional six-sided dice be thrown to produce every number from 1–6 at least once? * Computer programs have been written which will beat all human subjects at penny matching and most at Nim, Mancala, Backgammon and Reversi (Othello). Indeed it appears that the more a problem demands logical analysis as opposed to knowledge and experience, the greater the advantage to the machine. Man is essentially an inexpert system with a diffuse data base.

---

* Most graduates would answer 11 which is the most probable number but not the average.

Chess is one yardstick problem which has been widely used in Artificial Intelligence research and in this very limited universe direct comparisons between the performances of men and machines can be made. Currently the strongest chess playing program claims an ELO ranking score of around 2300. That is master level and very much higher than the ranking of the average chess player. However chess automata have no general intelligence whereas for human beings success at chess is a function of general intelligence, experience and specific skills. Because of the general component an average to good chess player will be able to play a moderately good game of bridge. Not so the chess program.

2. Paradigms of intelligence

In another paper in these proceedings, Sternberg and Lasaga (1984) review past and current approaches to the study of human reasoning. In their review these authors isolate what they believe to be the four most significant "schools" which they characterise as Psychometric, Stimulus Response, Gestalt and Information Processing. In the past, these different paradigms have largely been pursued independently and there has been a dearth, if not a complete lack of attempts to compare them systematically in terms of what each can tell us about human reasoning or in terms of their various strengths and weaknesses. These criticisms are similar to those put forward earlier by Chrisof (1939), Kolers (1960) and Elithorn and Telford (1969). The approach described in this paper meets many of these criticisms in that it seeks to devise experimental tasks which lend themselves to systematic analysis by each of these four approaches.

We believe that the reason that research into human thinking has evolved along these relatively isolated lines, reflects a rejection of the stimulus response approach developed by Donders (1868). This was because the results obtained with the relatively simple tasks which Donders and his successors used, were difficult to relate to the more complex problems which many psychologists regarded as key examples of logical analysis and reasoning. Consequently a top-down approach was evolved in which attempts were made to devise experimental methods for the analysis of human performance on relatively complex tasks. Unfortunately, the tasks used were in general chosen because they resembled the problems of everyday life rather than problems whose structure was suitable for research. It is our belief, therefore, that research into human problem reasoning and problem solving would be facilitated by the wider use of problems specifically designed for research, namely, problems in which the variables determining task difficulty can be systematically varied by the experimenter.

We illustrate this approach with two examples. The first is a game calculus which we argue would make a more cost-effective yardstick problem for research in Artificial Intelligence than does chess. The second is a perceptual test which is particularly sensitive to right hemisphere damage.

The simplest comparative measure of physical fitness is a race in which neither contestant can hinder the other and the winner is he who travels the fastest over a measured course. Problem solving can usefully be seen as movement within a psychological problem space from a starting state or position to a defined end state or goal and intellectual contests can be seen as races. The sequencing of operations within a problem space is identical with the basic logical process of constructing a derivation for a given premise through a sequence of given symbol transformations. Problem solving therefore becomes a sequence or series of steps.

Games of strategy are one form of intellectual contest in which the contestants make alternate moves – transformations. Murray (1952) classifies some strategic games as race games but theoretically all strategic games are race games in that each contestant seeks to reach a goal or winning position before his opponent does so.

The simplest transformation which will produce a solution B from a premise A is the magical one $A \rightarrow B$ – a giant stride. In the real world there are restrictions on the transformations which are permitted and it is these which determine the complexity of a problem. In an earlier paper Elithorn and Telford (1970) analysed the structure of a number of games including chess, Go, the French Polytechnic game – Boxes, five in a row (Go-Bang), Northcotts Nim and Ko No. On the basis of this analysis a Cartesian game calculus was developed within which "Cain and Abel" defines the simplest game in a family of games and puzzles which forms a paradigm for problems in general (Elithorn 1974).

2.1. Cain and Abel

1. A "node" is a point (x, y) where x, y are positive or negative integers.
2. Time t takes the integral value 0, 1, 2, 3...
3. A "Board" or field of play is a set (N) of n specified nodes so that between any two nodes P, P′ there is a set (Q) of nodes where P, P′ are in Q and for any node (x, y) in Q there is a node (x′, y′) in Q such that [y′ − y] and x′ − x] are one of them = 1 and the other = 0.
4. A position at time t is a division of the set N of n nodes into defined non-overlapping subsets W (White), B (Black) and U (Unoccupied), containing respectively w, b and n − w − b. nodes. At time t these sets are W(t), B(t), U(t).
5. At the beginning of the game t = 0 and the subsets W and B defined in 4. are specified sets W(0) and B(0) which define the initial configuration of the board.
6. $W(t_{end})$ and $B(t_{end})$ are define configurations such that when either B(t) =

$B(t_{end})$ or $W(t) = W(t_{end})$ the game ceases if t even or at $t + 1$.

7. Subject to the restraints 6, 8, and 9 at even time ($t = 2m$), White can "move" i.e. specify the position at $t + 1$. Similarly Black moves at odd t.

8. A "move" by White consists of the following changes: B is unchanged i.e. $B(t + 1) = B(t)$. W and U are unchanged except that one node (X, Y) of $U(t)$ is in $W(t + 1)$ and one node (x, y), of $W(t)$ is in $U(t + 1)$. These nodes can be specified arbitrarily by White provided that (X, Y) is accessible from (x, y) i.e. conforms to the restraints of 9.

9. A node (X, Y) is "accessible" from (x, y) at time t when one of the following conditions holds: (x, y) is in $B(t)$ or $W(t)$ and (X, Y) is in $U(t)$ and either:

$[X - x]$, $[Y - y]$ are one of them $= 1$, the other $= 0$ or both $= 1$;

The complexity of this calculus is trivial, the move allowed to each piece being that of the King in chess. With the restriction that pieces can move only diagonally, i.e., in proposition 9
$[X - x]$, $[Y - y]$ are both 1.

Cain and Abel becomes the primitive Korean game O-Pat-Ko-No or five-field Ko-No (Bell, 1960).

The fact that games as simple as this were played and enjoyed by adults until quite recent times, tells us much that we would apparently rather not know about the capacity and the structure of the human brain.

Chess which gains its complexity in a number of ways requires a complex calculus to describe it. There is capture and a differentiation of the pieces of each side into 7 types with 10 types of move. There are also "fairy" rules such as determine castling, stale mate and the en passant move. To prevent cycling, a 50 rule move is necessary. The complexities of chess are irregular. This may be one source of its charm but unfortunately its irregularities give its structure a rigidity which reduces its value as a research problem. Indeed, we have not traced any computer programs which play fairy chess or research programs in which the variables determining chess complexity have been systematically varied.

We argue here that research design and a sophisticated experimental methodology are as important to Artificial Intelligence research and the design of yardstick and benchmark problems as they are in the physical and social sciences. In the particular it is possible to elaborate systematically the Cain and Abel calculus to provide games as complex as chess with a simpler structure. An example – the game Advice – is given in the Appendix. A fortiori we also argue that Cain and Abel can be progressively developed to provide a hierarchy of experimental problems which model with increasing verisimilitude the world of conflict and competition in which we live. While the development of powerful chess playing programs has undoubtedly made important contributions to the development of computing techniques we believe that the adoption of this approach would greatly increase the progress of research into intelligent systems.

The difficulty of a problem depends on the size of the database, the complexity of the transformations possible and on the interactions between these two determinants. With Cain and Abel, increasing the values of N, B(0), or W(0) makes relatively little difference to task difficulty. Small changes in propositions 8 and 9 which define the types of move or transformations allowable may, however, make large changes in the complexity of the problem space and hence the difficulty of the problem. If, for example, we add to proposition 9 alternative moves such as those possessed by the chess pieces other than the King, the increase in complexity is relatively small unless one also adds propositions which introduce such concepts as capture and the differentiation of pieces. We can however make a very considerable increase in the complexity of the problem family by adding a simple "hop-move" to proposition 9. i.e.

$[X - x]$ and $Y - y]$ are both even and there exists a sequence of nodes $(X_0, Y_0), (X_1, Y_1)...(X_k, Y_k)$ where $X_0 = x$, $Y_0 = y$ and $X_k - X$, $Y = Y$, and (X, Y) is in $U(t)$ except $r = 0$ and $[X_{r+1} - X_r]$ and $[Y_{r+1} - Y]$ are either both $= 2$ or one of them $= 0$ and the other $= 2$ for all r such that $0 < r < k$ and

$$\left[\frac{X_{r-1} + X_r}{2}, \frac{Y_{r+1} + Y_r}{2} \right]$$

lies in $W(t)$ or $B(t)$ for all r such that $0 < r < k$.

In the 1880s a Boston surgeon then practising in England added this hop-move to a version of five-field Ko-No, placed the opposing armies in the opposite corners of a double chess-board and thus invented Halma, later to become Neo-Halma and then Chinese Checkers, games whose complexities though of different origins are comparable to that of Draughts (Checkers). For fifty years Halma and Chinese Checkers were extremely popular games and they are still widely played both in Europe and America.

Halma is an easy game to program and programs to play a reduced form of Halma with a limited look ahead have been found to beat quite intelligent subjects (Elithorn and Jagoe, 1967, Elithorn and Telford, 1973). However, as far as we are aware, no programs have been written capable of "discovering" the key concepts which determine the strategies which human subjects adopt when playing Halma on a full size board. There is, for example, a very simple "ladder" algorithm – a repeatable sequence of three moves – which Elithorn and Telford claimed provided for an army of any n (n > 2) a maximum rate of movement for the whole army of 2/3 of a vector unit (1, 1) per move. A subsequent study by Cooper and Elithorn (1973) however showed that there was an unexpected exception to this rule. For $N = 4$ there is an alternative algorithm which gives a faster rate of movement – 3/4 of a vector unit per move.

2.2. The Perceptual Maze Test

The Perceptual Maze Test, which is our second example, is a psychological test which bridges the gap between experimental psychology and the psychometric approach. The problem presented in this task requires the subject to separate from a randomly generated ground, a meaningful figure and is clearly susceptible to a Gestalt approach and to an information processing one, the index of the subject's ability being the rate at which he can process the unitary perceptual units from which the Gestalt is constructed. Again, the stimulus response approach is basic both to the structure of the problem and the analysis of the subject's solutions strategies.

In this test the subject is presented with a background lattice or field of play which has the same Cartesian structure as Cain and Abel. At the intersections

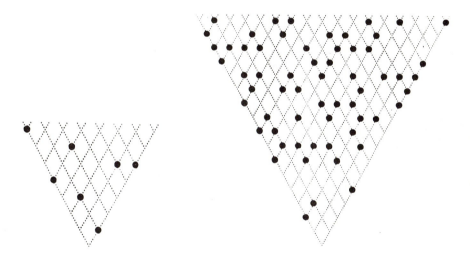

Fig. 1. Sample items from the Perceptual Maze Test. The subject's task is to find a pathway along the background lattice which passes through the greatest number of target dots. He must keep to the lattice or tracks and not cut across from one path to another. At each intersection the path must continue forward, i.e. the subject may fork right or left but not double back. In general, dependent on the arrangement of the target dots, there is more than one "best" pathway and the subject succeeds if he finds any one of these. A subject is either told the maximum number of dots which can be obtained, or this information is witheld. Conventionally, these two methods of presentation are called the "with information condition" and the "without information condition". Performance under these two conditions interacts with personality and reflects individual differences in cognitive style. In the example given the maximum scores are 3 and 11 respectively. The larger of these two items is relatively difficult a solution being found by only 10% of human subjects of average intelligence. See caption to Fig. 3.

of the lattice are scattered, either by design or at random, a number of target dots so that the vertices of the lattice take the value 1 (target dot present) or 0 (target dot absent). The subject's task is to find a path through the problem space represented by the lattice which is unidirectional in a general sense and which is optimal in that it passes through the maximum number of target dots (Fig. 1).

Apart from the physical dimensions of the lattice and the target dots there

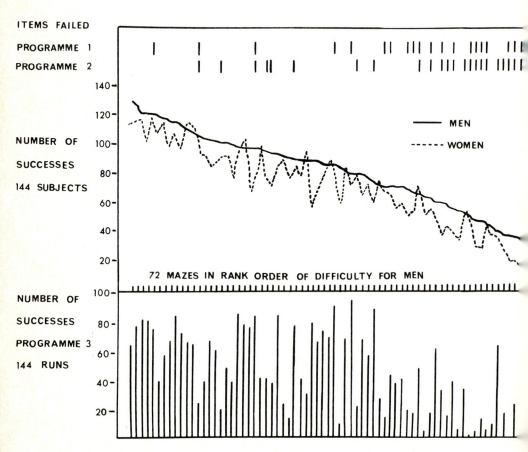

Fig. 2. Computer simulation of human performance on the Perceptual Maze Test. Seventy two test items are arranged in order of difficulty (the easiest on the left) as determined by 144 male subjects (solid line). The scores for 144 women (dotted line) are also plotted. Programs 1 and 2 each of which produced a single solution both failed very few of the "easy" items and most of the difficult ones. Program 3 contained a randomisation component and hence produced different solutions in each run. The scores for 144 runs by this program are plotted at the bottom of the figure. This program again does well on the easy items and poorly on the more difficult ones. (From Elithorn, Jagoe and Lee, 1966.)

are three variables which determine task difficulty:
(a) the number of rows in the lattice,
(b) the ratio of number of target nodes to the total number of nodes,
(c) a 'pattern' factor defined by the arrangement of the target nodes.
These three parameters are all amenable to exact treatment and have already been made the subject of a number of experimental studies (e.g. Davies and Davies, 1965 and Lee, 1965, 1967).

The problem presented by this test is essentially that of the travelling salesman. Computationally it is trivial, there being a simple route finding algorithm which, for items of the sizes used in the test, can be easily carried out with the aid of pencil and paper (Moore, 1959). Without the algorithm, however, human subjects of good intelligence find items of quite modest complexity quite difficult. Indeed there is good evidence that those who find the task relatively easy use a genetically determined skill which is sex-dependent (De Fries et al., 1976, Wilson et al., 1975, Carter-Saltzman, 1979, Beard,

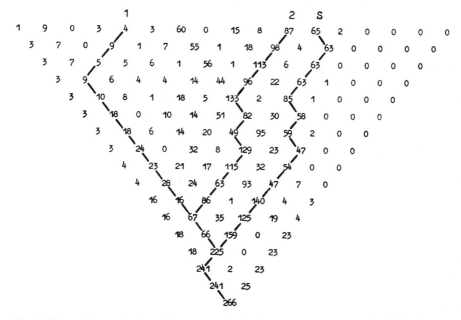

Fig. 3. Point choice evaluation of the error made by two computer programs simulating human performance on the larger of the two maze items illustrated in Fig. 2. Each numeral represents a node and defines the number of subjects whose solution path passed through that node. The paths marked 1 and 2 are those chosen by the two simulation programs. S is the correct solution path. No node on the solution pathway was used by less than 47 subjects but only 29 of the 266 who completed a solution for this item found the correct pathway. The performance of simulation 2 more closely resembles that of the human subjects than does that of simulation 1. Neither program however made any decision not made by any human subject. (From Smith, Jones and Elithorn, 1978.)

1975) and which in most right hand subjects is located in the right hemisphere (Archibald, 1967, 1978).

Because its complexity can be systematically manipulated this test in a computerised version has provided a powerful technique for analysing the changes brought about in human thinking by, for example, ECT (Elithorn, 1974) and psychotropic and anticonvulsant drugs (Elithorn, Cooper and Lennox, 1979, Elithorn, Mornington and Stavrou, 1982) and age (Heron and Chown, 1967). Although trivial to compute, the test has also been useful in research on artificial intelligence in that it has proved practicable to write programs which simulate the way intelligent human beings solve the problem in the absence of the Moore algorithm. Such programs will make similar mistakes to those made by human subjects and will find similar solutions and will have greater difficulty with the items which human beings find difficult.

In addition to those mentioned here a wide range of studies with the Perceptual Maze Test confirms Sternberg and Lasaga's preference for computer based studies of human thinking. On the other hand, there have been few attempts to implement the Cain and Abel approach. We believe nevertheless that it follows logically as well as by analogy that comparative studies with Cain and Abel and its more complex derivatives such as the game "Advice" described in the Appendix would, like the studies with the Perceptual Maze Test, form a valuable approach to the study of human and machine reasoning. Such studies would meet many of the criticisms of past research made by Sternberg and Lasaga and many others.

Appendix

A strategic board game

Using Cain and Abel as the basic calculus, one of us (AE) has devised a strategic board game of approximately the same complexity as chess. The goal positions are defined so that draws are impossible and a simple rule of progression ensures that the game proceeds steadily to a definite conclusion. The game is called Advice * and is an evolution of Halma. The step and hop moves remain the same but 4 types of pieces have been defined. Capture by leap as in draughts (checkers) has been added and a rule of capture taken from the Japanese and Chinese hand games defines a circular power structure between the pieces.

---

* Advice can be obtained direct from the publishers INQUOT Ltd. 1 Holmes Road, NW5 3AA London England.

Rules of ADVICE

1. *The Board and Pieces*: Advice is played on a board of 81 squares (9 × 9) with 26 pieces divided into two sets of different colour conventionally black and white. Each set contains 1 key piece, the Citizen, and 12 supporting pieces – 4 Lawyers, 4 Priests and 4 Psychiatrists.

2. *Starting Position*: At the start of each game the pieces are arranged at two opposite corners of the board as shown in the diagram (Fig. A.1).

3. *Aims*: A player may win the game in one of 3 possible ways. Either by:
a) being the first to move his Citizen into his Goal Square. A player's Goal Square is the corner square behind his opponent's starting position.
or b) capturing his opponent's Citizen (see rule 6).
or c) blocking his opponent so that the latter is unable to make a legal move (see rule 4).

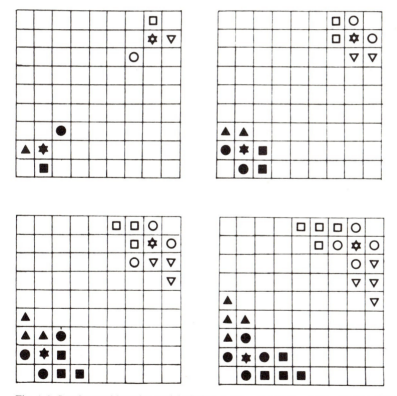

Fig. A.1. Starting positions for "Advice" Game. The complexity of the calculus of Cain and Able is increased by the increasing the number of pieces, the size of the board and by varying the transformations associated with the different pieces. As defined and played with 13 pieces aside on a 9×9 matrix the complexity of the game is comparable to that of chess. The circles, squares, triangles and stars represent Priests, Lawyers, Psychiatrists and Citizens, respectively.

4. *The Moves*: At each turn a player must advance one and only one of his pieces by one and one only of the following moves:

a) A Step Move: any piece may move orthogonally or diagonally to any of the 3 squares in front of it provided that the square is vacant. The move must be progressive (see rule 5).

b) A Hop Move: any piece may hop orthogonally or diagonally over an adjacent piece of either colour and any category provided that the next adjacent square in the same orthogonal or diagonal line is vacant. The move must be progressive (see rule 5).

c) A Chain Move: a single piece may make a series of hops as described above and the series may be continued as long as there is an adjacent piece to hop over and a vacant square to hop into along an orthogonal or diagonal line. During the course of a chain move, the direction of the move may change – backwards, forwards or sideways – as long as the piece ends up in a square which is further forward than the one it started from at the beginning of the move (see rule 5). Also during a chain move, the same piece may be hopped over more than once provided it is not an inferior piece belonging to one's opponent, in which case it is captured after the first hop and removed from the board (see rule 6).

If when it is his turn a player is unable to make a legal move he loses the game.

5. All moves must be progressive, i.e. they must reduce the Manhattan distance between the starting square of a piece at the beginning of a move and the player's Goal Square. The Manhattan distance is the minimum number of orthogonal steps (not hops) needed to reach the Goal Square. Thus a move sideways, except as part of a chain move, along a diagonal of the board at right angles to the line of advance whether it be away from or towards the centre does not reduce the manhattan distance and hence is not a legal move.

6. *Capture*: Capture is by a hop move and occurs when a player jumps one of his pieces over one of his opponent's pieces of inferior rank. The inferior piece is then removed from the board and from the game. The order of rank is: Priests capture Lawyers; Lawyers capture Psychiatrists; Psychiatrists capture Priests; any piece other than the Citizen captures the Citizen who has no power of capture. A player may jump over his own pieces with impunity. A hop move which captures the opponent's Citizen when this is situated behind the capturing piece is legal and ends the game provided that the hop move would have advanced the piece (see rule 5).

Acknowledgements

It is a pleasure to acknowledge the support and interest of my colleagues at the Royal Free Hospital, the National Hospitals for Nervous Diseases and the Institute of Neurology. We are grateful to Professor Cedric Smith for help with the canonical definitions for Cain and Abel.

ARTIFICIAL AND HUMAN INTELLIGENCE (A. Elithorn and R. Banerji, editors)
Elsevier Science Publishers, B.V.
© NATO, 1984

Chapter 14

APPROACHES TO HUMAN REASONING: AN ANALYTIC FRAMEWORK *

ROBERT J. STERNBERG and MARIA I. LASAGA

Department of Psychology
Yale University, New Haven, CT 06520-7447, USA

Summary

We compare alternative approaches to the study of human reasoning in terms of a framework that we believe is helpful in elucidating and comparing the relative advantages and disadvantages of the various major approaches that have been used to study human reasoning. The approaches considered are the psychometric, the stimulus-response, the Gestalt, and the information-processing. Moreover, we consider three different implementations of the information-processing approach: response-time-based, computer-based, and rule-based. Our comparative assessment most favors the computer-based implementation over its "competitors", but we believe that the interests of reasoning research will best be served if other approaches to reasoning are used to provide converging operations on the outcomes of computer-based analyses.

1. Introduction

Human reasoning has been an important topic of philosophical and psychological investigation at least since Aristotle's interest in the structure of the syllogism. Philosophers have been concerned primarily with normative theories of reasoning. Such theories seek to explain the rules by which deduction and induction problems can be solved without regard to the procedures people typically use in solving such problems. Their concern is with optimal performance rather than with typical performance. Psychologists, on the other hand, have been concerned primarily with performance theories of reasoning. Such theories seek to explain the rules or heuristics people actually use in solving reasoning problems (see, e.g., Sternberg, 1982; Wason and Johnson-Laird, 1972; for reviews of various research programs). Over the course of the last century, a number of psychological approaches have evolved for the study of

---

* Preparation of this report was supported by Contract N0001478C0025 from the Office of Naval Research to Robert J. Sternberg. The report was written while Maria Lasaga was supported by a Yale University graduate fellowship. We are grateful to attendees at the NATO Conference where this paper was presented for suggestions regarding its improvement.

human reasoning. As is typical in psychological research, the approach applied within a given specialty area tends to reflect the going paradigm or paradigms of the moment within the general area of psychology of which the specialty is a part. In the case of reasoning research, this general area is human-experimental psychology, and the going paradigm is the information-processing one. But it is worthwhile, every now and then, to become self-conscious about one's choice of paradigms and subparadigms, and to ask whether one's world view is the one most conducive to understanding the phenomena at hand, and if so, why. We ask this question in the present chapter.

Our goal in this paper is to compare alternative approaches to the study of human reasoning in terms of an analytic framework that we have found useful in elucidating and comparing the advantages and disadvantages of the various major approaches that have been used in the study of human reasoning. In the remainder of this chapter, we shall present and briefly describe the approaches we wish to consider; propose a framework for analyzing and comparing these approaches and apply the framework to the various approaches; and discuss briefly the implications of how the approaches stack up for future research on human reasoning.

2. Alternative approaches to the study of human reasoning

We believe that four approaches have predominated during this century in the study of human reasoning. These approaches are the psychometric, the stimulus-response, the Gestalt, and information-processing approaches to reasoning. We shall consider each approach briefly, in turn.

2.1. The psychometric approach

The psychometric approach has been widely used in the study of intelligence during the twentieth century, although in the past two decades, its popularity has faded at the same time that the information-processing approach has gained in popularity. Psychometric accounts of reasoning have in common their reliance upon individual-differences data as a means of testing theories, and in some cases, as heuristics aiding the formulation of the theories. Psychometric researchers use techniques of data analysis such as factor analysis to discover common patterns of individual differences across tests. These patterns are then hypothesized to emanate from latent sources of individual differences, namely, mental abilities. Consider two examples of the use of factor analysis to understand human reasoning.

Spearman, who is widely credited with having developed factor analysis, believed that inductive reasoning is a central element in general intelligence, or what he referred to as g. Indeed, analogy items were viewed as probably the best single indicants of g (Spearman, 1923, 1927). This g can be identified as the first unrotated factor in a standard factor analysis. Spearman believed that cognition as a whole could be largely understood in terms of three principles of cognition – apprehension of experience, eduction of relations, and eduction of correlates – that he illustrated in the context of reasoning by analogy. In the analogy, A : B :: C : D, apprehension of experience is the encoding of the information in each of the terms, eduction of relations is the inference of the relation between the A and B analogy terms, and eduction of correlates is the application of the inferred relation from C to D.

Whereas Spearman used factor analysis to identify a general factor largely associated with reasoning ability, Guilford, Kettner, and Christensen (1956) used factor analysis to attempt to define and hence understand "the nature of the general reasoning factor." Guilford and his colleagues found that it was "much easier to decide what *general reasoning* is not than to say what it is" (p. 171). Their factor analyses of various reasoning tests led them to conclude that general reasoning (a) is not general intelligence, although it is almost certainly among the most important intellectual activities; (b) is not a broad ability to manipulate symbols, although a narrow symbol-manipulation ability does appear to exist; (c) is not a generic ability to solve problems, although it does play a role in solving certain types of problems; (d) is not an ability to order a sequence of steps, although an ordering ability does exist that plays some role in planning processes; (e) is not an ability to use trial-and-error in problem solving; and (f) is not a general idea span. Primarily on the basis of evidence about what reasoning is not, Guilford and his colleagues suggested that the best formulation they could provide was that "*general reasoning* has something to do with comprehending or structuring problems of certain kinds in preparation for solving them ... It may be a general ability to formulate complex conceptions of many kinds" (pp. 171-172).

In sum, the psychometric approach uses individual-differences data to isolate reasoning ability from other kinds of abilities, or to distinguish among different kinds of reasoning skills. For the most part, psychometric theorists have been interested in reasoning because of its important role in intelligence rather than for its own sake (Guilford being one of the notable exceptions). Indeed, the study of reasoning has played a subordinate role to the study of intelligence in psychometric theorizing, and what we have learned about reasoning from psychometric investigations has usually been learned in the context of investigations of intelligence.

2.2. The stimulus-response approach

If reasoning has taken second place to intelligence in psychometric investigations, it has taken third or fourth place to learning in stimulus-response investigations. Although stimulus-response investigators differ in their particular viewpoints, the following assumptions seem common to many of these points of view (White, 1970, pp. 665-666): (a) the environment may be unambiguously characterized in terms of stimuli; (b) behaviour may be unambiguously characterized in terms of responses; (c) a class of stimuli exists which, applied contingently and immediately following a response, increases it or decreases it in some measurable fashion; these stimuli may be treated as reinforcers; (d) learning may be completely characterized in terms of various possible couplings among stimuli, responses, and reinforcers; and (e) unless there is definite evidence to the contrary, classes of behaviour may be assumed to be learned, manipulable by the environment, extinguishable, and trainable.

One of the few stimulus-response analyses of reasoning behaviour that have been proposed is that of Skinner (1966). His particular analysis is of the operant variety. According to Skinner, induction is the construction of a rule that generates behaviour appropriate to a set of contingencies. The term *induction* applies whether the stimuli that evoke the behaviour are identified from prolonged responding under appropriate contingencies or from examination of the environment without engagement in behaviour. Deduction is an alternative way of deriving discriminative stimuli (i.e., stimuli in whose presence behaviour either is or is not reinforced) and involves the manipulation of other contingencies. New second-order rules can be discovered either inductively – when they are found to produce effective new first-order rules--or deductively – when they are based on an analysis of first-order rules or the contingencies they describe.

The Skinnerian analysis of reasoning has been applied by Goldiamond (1966) in an analysis of performance on a particular kind of induction problem, namely, the classification problem, in which an individual must decide what dimensions of a stimulus are relevant for a given problem situation. On Goldiamond's view, the ability to solve such a problem has evolved from past experience with related problems: Discriminative stimuli differing simultaneously along many dimensions have been presented at various points of time in the individual's life history. After a while, discrimination comes to occur only along reinforced dimensions, which tend to be those required in the classification tasks one meets in one's life subsequent to the earlier exposures to the various relevant and irrelevant dimensions. Responding along the reinforced dimensions is what we typically view as "abstraction" or "conceptualization".

In sum, the stimulus-response approach to reasoning emphasizes the role of past learning in present reasoning. The approach has not been widely applied in the study of reasoning, perhaps because reasoning has not been viewed as central in the phenomenon of greatest interest – learning – or perhaps because once one begins to analyze the kinds of complex learning in which reasoning does play a role, stimulus-response analysis becomes a bit tortured. In any event, this approach is not currently in favour in the study of reasoning, nor is it clear as to how it would be applied to complex reasoning problems if it were more widely used.

2.3. The Gestalt approach

Gestalt psychologists had a strong interest in problem solving, second only to their interest in perception. We are unaware of any Gestalt analyses of reasoning distinct from analyses of problem solving; hence, we shall briefly describe the analysis of problem solving. The Gestalt analysis reflects the emphasis on and interest in perception that has traditionally characterized Gestalt psychologists and their disciples.

For Köhler (1925), problem solution consisted of the restructuring of a perceptual field. A problem consists of a situation in which some element necessary for solution is missing: The solution occurs when the missing ingredient is supplied so that the perceptual field becomes meaningful in relation to the problem as a whole. Consider, for example, Duncker's (1945) radiation problem, in which an individual must figure out how radiation can be used to destroy the cancerous cells of a tumour at the same time that it spares the healthy cells surrounding the tumour. A solution is reached once a particular missing ingredient--distribution of the origin of the radiation--is added to the problem situation: The cancerous but not the healthy cells are destroyed by having multiple sources of radiation converge just where the tumorous cells are.

Duncker (1945) believed that one of the most serious obstacles to problem solution is the tendency of individuals to narrow too much their field of possible solutions. His studies of problem solving focused upon the construct of *functional fixedness*, or the tendency of individuals to adopt a set for problem solving which they retain even when it is nonoptimal. A second construct that was central in Gestalt analyses of problem solving is that of *insight*, or the "aha" experience by which individuals suddenly see how a complex problem can be solved (see, e.g., Köhler, 1925; Maier, 1970). Some recent evidence suggests that Gestaltists, and almost everyone else, may have overemphasized the role of insight in solving "insight" problems: Weisberg and Alba (1981) have recently shown that certain "insight" problems formulated by Gestalt psychologists remain difficult even when subjects are provided with the insights needed to solve the problems.

In sum, the Gestalt approach emphasized the role of restructuring in problem solution. Their view differed from those of the stimulus-response theorists in a number of ways, but one of the most obvious was in their emphasis upon directed behaviour, in contrast to the emphasis on trial-and-error learning that characterized many stimulus-response psychologists. In many respects, Gestalt psychology was a reaction to stimulus-response psychology, as was the last approach we consider, the information-processing approach.

2.4. The information-processing approach

The information-processing approach to human reasoning seeks to understand reasoning in terms of the mental processes individuals use in reasoning, the strategies into which these processes combine, the representations upon which the processes and strategies act, and the knowledge base that is mentally represented. The information-processing approach was advocated in part because the stimulus-response approach that it partially replaced dealt with these issues less than adequately (Miller, Galanter, and Pribam, 1960). The information-processing approach remains in vogue today, two decades after its introduction by Miller and his colleagues and by Newell, Shaw, and Simon (1960), among others.

What passes as "the information-processing" approach to research on human cognition actually comprises a number of subapproaches with varying procedures and, concomitantly, strengths and weaknesses. We consider here what we believe to be three major subapproaches, which are distinguishable in part by the dependent variables upon which they primarily rely. The three approaches are a response-time-based one, a rule-based one and a computer-based one. We hasten to note that these approaches are neither mutually exclusive nor exhaustive; to the contrary, their use overlaps both within and between investigations and investigators.

2.4.1. The response-time-based approach

The use of this approach is usually traced back to Donders (1868), who proposed that the time between a stimulus and a response can be decomposed into a sequence of successive processes, with each process beginning as soon as the previous one ends. The durations of these processes can be ascertained through the use of a subtraction method: Subjects solve each of two tasks proposed by an experimenter to differ only in that the more difficult task requires one more component process for its solution than does the simpler task. The duration of this process can then be computed by subtracting the time taken to solve the easier task from the time taken to solve the harder task. The subtraction method was popular for several decades, but then came into disfavor because of the method's assumption of strict additivity: One had to assume that one could insert into or delete from a task a given process without affecting somehow the execution of other processes. Less stringent assumptions for response-time research have been introduced by S. Sternberg (1969) in his additive factor method, which makes it possible to decompose stages of information processing without assuming additivity. This additive-factor method has come into favour in response-time research at the same time that the subtraction method has come back into favour because methods are now available for testing the extent to which the assumption of additivity holds for a given data set (see Sternberg, 1977). It should be noted that the assumption of seriality of processing introduced by Donders no longer is a necessary ingredient of response-time-based models of information processing, although it has been shown to be extremely difficult to distinguish serial from parallel processing on the basis of response-time (or any other) data (see Anderson, 1976; Townsend, 1971).

Response-time-based methodology has been used widely in the study of both inductive reasoning (e.g.,Mulholland, Pellegrino, and Glaser, 1980; Sternberg, 1977; Whitely, 1977) and deductive reasoning (e.g., Clark, 1969; Guyote and Sternberg, 1981; Huttenlocher and Higgins, 1971; Sternberg, 1980a). Item content and form is manipulated so as to vary those sources of difficulty that are believed to be sources of differential latency in solution. In a linear syllogism (such as "John is taller than Mary; Mary is taller than Pete; who is the tallest?"), for example, difficulty might be manipulated by varying the number of negations, the number of marked adjectives (such as "shorter" as opposed to "taller"), the placement of the correct answer in the premises, and so on. Response times to each time type are collected, and the subtraction method might be used to infer the latency of each component process.

2.4.2. The rule-based approach

The basic assumption underlying the rule-based approach is that cognition and its development can be characterized in large part in terms of the rules (or ministrategies) that individuals use in solving problems (Siegler, 1981). Individuals are typically asked a series of questions about a given test problem, and their patterns of responses used to infer the rule(s) the individuals use to solve the problem. Consider as a simple example how one might infer an individual's interpretation of the logical connective, *or*, in the statement, "The circle or the square is in the box." One can infer an individual's implicit truth table by asking the individual questions such as whether it is possible for (a) just the circle to be in the box, (b) just the square to be in the box, (c) both the circle and the square to be in the box, and (d) neither the circle nor the square to be in the box (see Sternberg, 1979). An individual using the logically inclusive meaning of *or*, for example, would answer the question (c) in the affirmative, whereas an individual using the logically exclusive meaning of *or* would answer question (c) in the negative.

Rule-based methodology has been widely used in the assessment of rules in solving Piagetian kinds of reasoning problems such as the balance-scale, where individuals must indicate whether or not weights systematically distributed on opposing sides of a balance scale will in fact balance (Siegler,1978); understanding of counting rules (Gelman and Gallistel, 1978); understanding of and reasoning with logical connectives (Staudenmayer and Bourne, 1977; Sternberg, 1979;); solution of categorical and conditional syllogisms (Ceraso and Provitera,1971; Erickson, 1978; Johnson-Laird and Steedman, 1978; Revlis, 1975); and solution of propositional reasoning problems (Osherson, 1974). The assumption underlying the use of the methodology, of course, is that the rules being sought out by the investigator are indeed being used by the subject, for example, that in understanding and reasoning with logical connectives, subjects are indeed using a truth table. The assumption seems to work well in the domains that have been investigated, although the boundary conditions for where rule-based systems are used have not been clearly delineated.

2.4.3. The computer-based approach

In the computer-based approach to human cognition, in general, and human reasoning, in particular, a computer program is written that is alleged to simulate, at a functional level, the representations, processes, and strategies human subjects use in solving problems of one or more types. The computer program is then executed, usually multiple times, and its output is compared to that of human subjects. The computer model is viewed as successful in part depending on the degree to which its output simulates that of human output.

Computer models have been used to investigate a number of different kinds of reasoning problems, such as analogies (Evans, 1968), series completion problems (Simon and Kotovsky, 1963), natural language inferences (Rieger, 1978), geometry theorems (Greeno, 1976), and logical theorems (Newell and Simon, 1956). Several programs, such as those of Newell, Shaw, and Simon (1960), Simon and Lea (1974), and Williams (1972), have been multi-purpose, solving reasoning problems of a limited variety of types (see also Newell and Simon, 1972). Recent computer programs by Schank (1975) and his associates have combined comprehension and reasoning functions in the understanding of various kinds of written texts.

It is important in understanding computer models to realize that they seek to simulate human behaviour only at a functional level, not at a structural one. No reasonable computer theorist has claimed that humans are structured anatomically in any way that resembles the way a computer is structured. The claim, rather, is that the steps the computer goes through in executing a program can resemble the steps a human goes through in executing a strategy for solving a problem. It is further important to understand that our interest here is *only* in those computer theorists who are interested in simulating human behaviour, at least to some degree. Some computer programs in the artificial intelligence tradition have been constructed with optimization rather than simulation of performance in mind. It would be silly to criticize these programs for failing to simulate human performance when this was never their goal in the first place.

In sum, the information-processing approach has been concerned with the component processes of reasoning and the constructs they manipulate or execute. Unlike the Gestalt and the stimulus-response traditions, the information-processing approach places greater emphasis on the means to an end rather than on the end itself (e.g., a problem solution or response).

Table 1
Analytic framework for approaches to reasoning.[a]

Criterion	Approach					
	Psychometric	Stimulus-response	Gestalt	Information-processing		
				Response time based	Computer based	Rule based
Processes	N	N	N	Y	Y	N
Strategies	N	N	N	Y	Y	Y
Representations	N	N	N	N	Y	N
Contents of representations	N	N	N	N	Y	N
Structures	Y	Y	Y	N	Y	Y
Contents of structures	Y	Y	N	N	Y	Y
Process speeds	N	N	N	Y	N	N
Process accuracies	N	N	N	Y	Y	N
Form(s) of input	Correlation matrix	Rate of response No. of responses	Response time + pattern	Latencies accuracies	Problem in coded form	Response pattern
Form(s) of output	Pattern, structure, & score matrices	Hypothetical chain of S-Rs	Proportion using each strategy	Process latencies & difficulties; model fits	Solution + track of solution	Model + model fit
Level of analysis						
Performance	2	4	5	2	1	3
Competence	1	1	4	1	1+	2

[a] Y = Yes; N = No. 1 = Superior rating; 5 = Inferior rating.

We have further subdivided the information-processing approach into three different implementations which differ in terms of the dependent variables they use, as well as in terms of features described later in the discussion of the proposed analytic framework.

2.5. Summary

We have briefly reviewed what we believe to be the four most significant approaches to the study of human reasoning – the psychometric, the stimulus-response, the Gestalt, and the information-processing approaches. It is clear from our review that the approaches address somewhat different issues, and have different strengths and weaknesses. We believe that there has been a dearth, if not a complete lack, of attempts to compare the approaches systematically in terms of what they can tell us about reasoning, and of what their various strengths and weaknesses are. We attempt such a comparison forthwith.

3. Analytic framework

Our proposed analytic framework for evaluating and comparing approaches to human reasoning is shown in Table 1. Each of the approaches and subapproaches introduced earlier is represented by a single column. Each of the criteria by which the theories are evaluated is represented by a single row. The criteria are of three types. The first type of criterion specifies what kinds of information about human reasoning one learns from each given approach to reasoning. The entries in the table are expressed as simple yes's (Y) and no's (N). A greater number of Y's in a given column could be interpreted as indicating an approach that is relatively more informative about the nature of human reasoning. The second type of criterion specifies the form of input that is needed for formulation or testing of the theory and the form of output that is generated by theory. The third type of criterion specifies the depth or level of analysis that we believe is actually attained (performance) and that, in principle, could be attained (competence) via a given approach to reasoning. (Note that we refer to performance and competence of approaches, not of the subjects they study.) In both of these specifications, we evaluated each approach on a scale ranging form superior (1) to inferior (5). We now consider the various approaches and the criteria for evaluation in greater detail.

3.1. Kinds of information supplied by the various approaches

The top portion of the table supplies information about the kinds of information supplied by the various approaches. We shall discuss each line of the table briefly.

3.1.1. Processes

We refer here to real-time mental operations used in the solution of a reasoning problem. This information is provided by two of the three information-processing implementations, but none of the other approaches. The third information-processing implementation, the rule-based one, specifies rules that individuals use in solving problems but does not delineate the real-time processes applied by the individuals. The psychometric approach extracts sources of individual differences that may or may not include processes, but even if they do, the processes are likely to be confounded with each other and with other things. The stimulus-response approach assumes the existence of internal stimuli and responses (in some versions), but does not specify the processes that intervene between stimulus and response. The Gestalt approach considers general states of an individual (e.g., insight, functional fixedness, awareness) during reasoning, but not the component processes that generate these states. The superiority of the information-processing approach in identifying processes used in problem solution is what led to formulation of the approach.

3.1.2. Strategies

By strategies, we refer to the sequence of mental steps used in solving a problem, and also to whether the steps are executed serially or in parallel, exhaustively or with self-termination, and deterministically or probabilistically. Only the three information-processing implementations supply this information. The psychometric tradition has not provided a means of eliciting order of mental events; the stimulus-response approach, again, does not specify processes or how they combine; and the Gestalt tradition emphasizes the overt steps to problem solution taken by an individual rather than the individual's covert mental processes – it deals more with the different types of solutions that an individual offers than it does with differential paths to these solutions.

3.1.3. Representations

By representations, we mean fairly detailed specifications of how information is represented mentally, whether in the form of a propositional network, a multidimensional space, or whatever. Any of these approaches can assume a representation – indeed, must specify it – in considerable detail in a way that is testable (i.e., through program execution). The response-time-based approach does postulate mental distance between the contents of representations; however, this provides only modest information about the nature of the representations themselves.

3.1.4. Contents of representations

By contents of representations, we refer to the information that is mentally represented, for example, the specific propositions that are stored, the particular dimensions in the multidimensional space and the coordinates of points loading on these dimensions, and so on. Again, only the computer-based approach specifies this information in detail in a way that is testable.

3.1.5. Structures

Structures are analytic units of some kind that serve as sources of (stimulus or person) variation in performance, for example, factors, S-R bonds, production systems, or rules. They present a model of how mental abilities are organized. Structures differ from representation in that they show the organization of abilities rather than of information. Although they are not necessarily repositories of information, they can be. For example, factors are mental structures that are alleged to generate individual differences in performance, but they are not storehouses of information. Rather, they determine, to some extent, the abilities of individuals to acquire, process, and represent information. Rules, on the other hand, are repositories of information as well as "abilities" of sorts. They contain information, which may be either procedural or declarative. Only the response-time-based approach does not specifically indicate a kind of structure; in fact, it can be adapted to be consistent with any structural model at all.

3.1.6. Contents of structures

We refer here to identification of the particular structures involved in reasoning, as well as mere identification of the form the structures take. For example, a psychometric theory might specify that the kinds of structures are factors, and that the natures of these factors are verbal, spatial, numerical, memory, and so on (see Thurstone, 1938). A rule-based theory might specify that the kinds of structures are rules, and that one such rule is cardinality, by which is meant that the tag assigned to the last object in an array has special significance in that it represents the cardinality (number of objects) in the array (Gelman and Gallistel, 1978). Note that the content of the structure does not tell one what form the representation is in, nor what the representation contains. For example, numbers might be represented along some kind of analogue mental continuum, or as discrete symbols. In this example, the structure could either be a factor or a rule; the nature of the structure would be numerical; the representation could be the mental continuum or the discrete symbols; and the content of the representation would be the numbers.

3.1.7. Process speeds

We refer here to the real-time latency with which a given mental process is executed. Only the response-time-based subapproach actually has indicated latencies of mental processes used in problem solution.

3.1.8. Process accuracies

We refer here to the accuracy with which each mental process is executed. For example, in solving an analogy, one might ask what proportion of inferences between the first two analogy terms are done correctly. Both of the approaches that specify processes can potentially specify the accuracy with which they are executed, the response-time-based approach if error rate or proportion correct is used as a supplementary dependent variable, the computer-based approach if the computer actually solves reasoning items so that its level of performance can be assessed.

3.2. Input-output

The middle portion of the table specifies the forms input and output take under each approach. We make no claim that these specifications are exhaustive for all possible theories under a given approach.

3.2.1. Form(s) of input
The form of input refers to the information needed to formulate or test a given theory under one of the approaches. For example, psychometric (factorial) theories are derived by factoring a correlation (or covariance or cross-products) matrix; response-time-based theories use response latencies, or secondarily, accuracies (or error rates) as bases for multiple regression or analysis of variance.

3.2.2. Form(s) of output
The form of output refers to the information about reasoning that is supplied by a given theory under one of the approaches. For example, psychometric (factorial) theories provide a factor pattern matrix (giving weights assigned to tests in predicting factor scores), a factor structure matrix (giving correlations of tests with factors), and (optionally) a factor score matrix (giving scores of each individual on each factor if raw-score data were made available to the algorithm for computing factors).

3.2.3. Level(s) of analysis
In assessing level(s) of analysis, we have essentially rated each approach in terms of the depth of analysis that we believe it provides in the analysis of reasoning. The "competence" of the approach is always at least as good as its "performance", in that approaches always function at a level less than or equal to their potential. Obviously, our assessments are subjective, but they are based on the information we have at our disposal about the theories under each approach. We believe, for example, that computer-based theories specify reasoning performance in the greatest detail and with the least information left out; Gestalt theories specify reasoning performance in the least detail, and we don't believe that their "competence" is a whole lot better than their performance has been. In principle, most approaches could specify performance in much greater detail than they do, but experimental operations do not exist for

such specification, for example, for specifying the complete set of S-R links, internal and external, that lead from a given stimulus to a given response.

3.3. Implications of the framework

We find one implication inescapable from the analysis we have proposed within our framework for comparing approaches to the study of reasoning: Of the various approaches, the computer-based one seems to offer the most promise for future research on reasoning. We further note that this conclusion does not derive from a "rigged" analysis designed to justify our own preferences: To the contrary, almost all of our research has been under the response-time-based approach (e.g., Sternberg, 1977, 1980a) and the rule-based approach (e.g., Guyote and Sternberg, 1981; Sternberg, 1979) (see Sternberg, 1981, for a review). Thus, the extent to which the computer-based approach came out ahead of the other approaches, including our own, came as something of surprise to us, whether or not it did to the readers of this chapter. This is not to say that the computer-based approach does not have its problems, too: We see as a major one the problem of determining just what, in a computer-based theory, is a program feature associated with an empirical claim and what is a program feature that is needed to make the program operational, but that does not necessarily carry with it any empirical claims regarding human data (see Sternberg, 1977). Computer-oriented theorists should make an effort to state quite clearly just what their empirical claims are.

What we refer to as the "computer-based approach" is defined in terms of the input to and output from a given kind of theory. Indeed, each of our approaches is defined operationally in terms of input and output relations. We wish to make clear that whereas this kind of operational distinction provides reasonable degrees of differentiation among the approaches, other kinds of distinctions may not. For example, a computer program can be used to simulate a stimulus-response type theory, and response latency can be used as a dependent variable in psychometrically based studies of reasoning. Thus, our scheme applies according to one set of operational definitions, but not according to *any* set. The usefulness of a given scheme depends upon how one wishes to partition the space of possible approaches to reasoning.

We have believed in the past, and continue to believe, that research on reasoning will be best served by the use of converging operations rather than by exclusive reliance upon any single approach. Indeed, some of the confidence we have achieved in our past theory and data has derived from convergences between results obtained through our own approaches and those of others. Any one method of analysis is likely to suffer from a problem of theory identifiability (see Anderson, 1976), but converging operations decrease the set of possible alternative theories that could mimic the predictions of the theory being tested.

We also believe that it is a fact of scientific life that different investigators work best (most comfortably and to greatest scientific advantage) with different approaches, and the interests of science are probably best served if scientists exploit their own proclivities to maximal advantage at the same time that they take into consideration the maximum potential of the approach or approaches under which they are working. We therefore believe that the three information-processing subapproaches we have described, and possibly other approaches as well, can continue to serve the interests of reasoning research. Our potential enthusiasm does not extend to all approaches: For example, we are not sanguine about the present-day potentialities of either the stimulus-response or Gestalt approaches, although it is not inconceivable that at some future time, more advanced versions of these approaches will enable them to deal with issues that at present they fail to deal with or deal with inadequately. Indeed, it is quite possible that the approaches that will prove most profitable in the future have not yet been tried, or even proposed. When such approaches are proposed, we hope that we will not be so locked into our own paradigms that we find ourselves unable to accept them.

Chapter 15

THE DISTRIBUTED PROCESSING OF KNOWLEDGE AND BELIEF IN THE HUMAN BRAIN

P.M. LAVOREL

CNRS; INSERM, 16 avenue D. Lepine, 69500 Bron, France

Summary

Because the human brain processes knowledge in a functionally efficient manner, it may be considered as an example for future systems development and programming. "Distributed cooperative computation" is one aspect of the natural computation of world representations and of the generation of schemas for intelligent acts. But belief processes associated with human knowledge are more complex and much more dangerous to imitate.

In 1948 a historical conference was organized in the U.S. (Hixon Symposium, Caltech) where papers were read either by neurophysiologists like Lashley or by cyberneticians like McCulloch and Von Neumann. Most of the founders of Computer Science, of Cognitive Psychology, and of A.I. (Artificial Intelligence) were present. Since then, cybernetics has gone out of fashion. Out of it AI, Brain Theory, and Cognitive Sciences have developed as completely different disciplines. Yet, they still share many concepts when it comes to defining the principles of intelligence processes. For instance, the recent notions of distributed processing or of cooperative computation (as they were respectively implemented by Erman, Lesser and coll. in the computer system called HEARSAY, or formulated as a specific theory of brain control by Szentágothai and Arbib) have been very fruitful in systems programming and in the understanding of animal and human behavior. I would like to show that, thanks to many successful discoveries of the seventies, brain sciences have much to offer to theoreticians in cognitive psychology, as well as to computer system analysts. Knowledge and belief, which I shall successively deal with, have been the central issues of much recent research in neurosciences.

1. How is human knowledge processed?

In a paper written for linguists (Lavorel and Arbib, 1981) Lavorel and Arbib claim that the study of language processing, ranging from the observation of neuron column activity in specific areas of the cortex to computer simulations of pathological speech, will have to find its physical constraints in neurology and its theory in the general tenets of computation and informatics. In fact, the biophysical study of the brains of animals together with the now powerfully instrumented chemical observation of human patients has enabled Brain Theory to reach the point where a breakthrough is possible in the modelling of how knowledge about the world, the self, and active behavior is processed by the 14 billion neuron brain.

First, it has long been accepted that information flowing in through the "gates of perception" is *distributed* across the two hemispheres and processed preferably (or sometimes exclusively) by certain areas, and that process control is achieved both locally at several levels and from the outside by particular parts of the cortical or subcortical nervous system which initiate, filter, time, or harmonize the flow of information. What has been found recently is first that information processing is duplicated locally by columns working simultaneously (thus confirming some theoretical models of Nilsson about parallel computation). Secondly, that specialized or semi-specialized areas do not work in isolation. Local activity is constantly broadcasted to the neighboring areas in a sort of slow propagation not unlike some magnetic wave mechanics, while long distance communication with some predesignated receiving areas is ensured speedily by bundles of fibers. This has all been well observed for vision, audition, tactile and body sensations. Thus, *cooperative computation* between areas is what underlies the rich knowledge of man. Moreover, these processes take place in a *dynamic* manner because the brain *learns* how to use genetically planned connections between areas or to grow microconnections between local groups of neurons. Learning and forgetting governed by pragmatic constraints and adaptation are the causes of interactive effects between the nervous hardware and the intelligence software. Chemical pathways in the synapses, and dendrite growth or regression appear as elementary processing takes place, after which more efficient and more complex processing will then be possible (Jeannerod and Hecaen, 1980). Eventually, habituated or ageing brains tend to have specialized and as it were cabled cooperative processes, which prevent them from dealing adequately with unexpected situations, as structural organization becomes irreversible, and creative cooperation between subsystems is superseded by usual routine calculation.

But computer specialists will ask: "How do those biological concepts of help to us?" Further details about the computing power of the human brain will perhaps tell them how they could design better intelligent systems for the understanding of the production of natural language, for information retrieval, for robotics, etc. The following remarks will be based on studies of *animal or human lesions affecting normal representations of the world* (or worlds), and then on studies of other lesions affecting *schemas of acts* which must be carried out by body and mind.

1.1. Representations are computed at three levels. At a low level corresponding to highly specialized areas of the posterior part of the cortex, specific features of information detected and transmitted (like aspects of the sound of a bell, or characteristics of the color, or of shape of that bell) are processed. At an intermediate level, many features of one modality are fitted into patterns. For

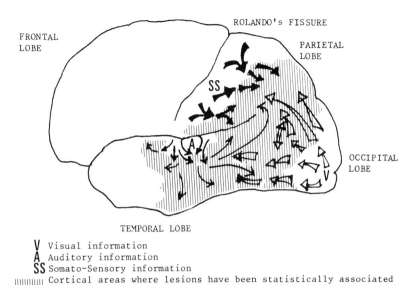

Fig. 1. The propagation and the intersection of information in the left hemisphere representational areas.

instance, while lesions affecting temporal lobes cause cortical deafness, lesions affecting intermediate level calculation cause verbal agnosia, or amusia (which is the inability to identify meaningful sound patterns and decide what basic information can be drawn and transferred). At the third level, multimodal information inputs are matched. Loss or disruption of third level knowledge processing causes a wide range of severe disturbances like aphasia, apraxia, acalculia, simultagnosia, and even dementia. Our understanding of regularity and variation of high level processes in a population of lesioned individuals is helped by gross and microscopic anatomic studies. It has been found, for instance, that in the lower parietal lobe (see Fig. 1), cell tissue specialized in the processing of auditory information is found together with cell tissue specialized in the processing of visual input, or with cell tissue specialized in the processing of somato-sensory input. In the same area, one also finds magnopyramidal associative neurons, which are necessary for language comprehension and production. It is thus possible to hypothesize that exchanges may enable some parts of the brain to generate structured images which I shall call *cognitive images*.

These cognitive representations may be of varying complexity and potentially infinite in number if we deal with a language-like structure., We know mathematically that a great number of strings, or of hierarchically ordered formulas could be formed with a few associative rules and a base of *primitive percepts or concepts* (perhaps patterns calculated by the intermediate level cortex). Evidence of such combinative possibilities has been provided by the study of posterior lesions of the left hemisphere. The patients produce continuous jargon or occasional errors. It seems that the production of strings from a basic alphabet or vocabulary runs loose for lack of control by mental representations (Lavorel, 1980). Stochastic processes or semantic games replace the normally controlled generative mechanism. If representations of the world or representations of language (which is representation or representations) are computed in the left hemisphere as has been hypothesized here, it is necessary to understand that *cooperative neural calculus* is not always satisfactory and must often be reinitiated, confirmed, corrected. This peculiar approach can be measured almost on-line when we analyze eye movements of subjects reading, looking at pictures, or answering questions about pictures. It is easy to observe coexisting bottom-up and top-down computation when readers scan basic details, or, on the contrary, rely on semantic-syntactic inference in an economic way, in order to regulate their saccades. Sometimes one process fails, or is unsatisfactory, and information intake must be reinitiated (regressions).

For the sake of simplicity, nothing has been said of the right hemisphere associative areas which probably work in a more "holistic" manner (some, like Pribram, have formulated holographic analogies for the aggregation of orthogonal spaces). Nor has there been any account of the possibility of competition between the two hemispheres ...

1.2. Schemas of acts can be understood principally by observing subjects who suffer from frontal or parietal lesions. Motor behavior, for example, is triggered off by activity in the motor cortex (pre-rolandic area), and is then transmitted and filtered in a complex way through the thalamus and the brain-stem. However, high-level control is necessary in order to plan, regulate, and update a motor act. There are patients who cannot form a correct representation of body sensations and motion (post-rolandic and upper-parietal lesions), patients who cannot visually control their hands and feet (parieto-occipital lesions), patients who cannot decide, conceive in advance, or time their moves, or who lose track of their intricate purposes (frontal lesions or deficits of supplementary motor and somatosensory areas), patients who cannot regulate tension and relaxation, or coordination of muscles (subcortical dysfunctions, or cerebellar problems). Arbib (1980) has for instance summarized decisions to act and motor control in interactive box diagrams. This is the minimal cooperative strategy called forth in order to take one step forward (Fig. 2).

Language emission itself is one of the most controlled acts. Different levels of interaction are then mediated by language-specific centers like Broca's area, where the interface between morphological representations and phono-articulatory programs, and perhaps also some elementary transformational operations

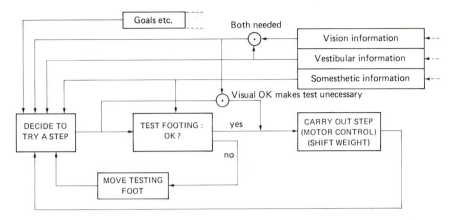

Fig. 2. Neural control of movement (walking). Reprinted by permission.

on syllable order, word order, morphological inflection, rhythmic variations are calculated.

The principal lesson which has been learned from all these studies of man's remarkable ability for knowledge of the world and for schemas of acts is that intelligent performance is not simple and deterministic. It varies because it is economical, task determined, and permanently controlled. The identification of a bell, the remembrance of it, or the naming of it make use of distributed processes which vary a great deal and may be either cursory or sophisicated, according to needs and to detected success or failure. Those who work in automatic documentation, mechanised translation, or in man-machine interaction through intelligent "monitors" should now think more of systems with cooperative processes, some minimal and specific, others more extended and inter-modal. This will enable them to design systems which will interact intelligently with man's own knowledge.

But what kind of tools are going to be required in the near future for such distributive processing or for such cooperative computation? *First, learning must be integrated into data bases.* Knowledge sources could be updated by some distributed memory of the frequency or the weight of inputs, and augmented by some kind of minimal inference modules. The brain offers us a great example for a constructivist and dynamic approach. Scientific interest should then be directed towards a better understanding of what is activation, organization, decay, and updating of information. Research on neuron membrane chemistry, dendrite growth, cortical pathology, and limbic ancillary help in case of cortical breakdown has already provided cues. Some of them have been rapidly sketched here. More interdisciplinary exchanges must be organized. *Secondly, a strategic use of alternative algorithms must be thought of for different levels of comprehension and active performance.* For artificial language for instance, all-purpose semantic systems must no longer be thought of; and general Chomskian sets of rules to represent the knowledge of *all* the speakers of a language are obsolete dreams. Instead of calling on a machine gun to kill a fly, one should make do with one simple weapon whenever possible. However, failure should be detected. When routine processes fail, slower, and more costly devices can be brought into action. Failure will seldom happen if computation is initiated simultaneously at different levels (viz. semantic, syntactic, and pragmatic hypotheses cannot all fail; or if they do, it would possibly be the same for the human mind).

It must be noted here that, as an intelligent system grows more diversified, more complex, and more cooperative, it does not necessarily become more reliable. Redundancy or incompleteness of converging inputs in a process can result in consistency. Different ways of deriving new information can also create conflicts. Yet the normal brain which often works in such conditions is functionally accurate and will tolerate only a few slips (slips of the tongue for instance), soon to be corrected and avoided afterwards (Lavorel, 1982). *For control modalities ensure a range of acceptable performance.* Studies in animal neurophysiology have shown that partially inconsistent inputs are neutralized by some kind of threshold management at the level of communication between columns and between the six horizontal strata of neurons. More exactly, in the network of parallel, sequential, or reafferent exchanges, some convenient operational delay is permanently ensured by specific neurons while, in the odd neurons which are in disgreement or out of phase, local inhibition of rhythmic firing is ensured by chemical regulation synaptic transfer. And so, *the timing of information transfer and transformation* by loops, by multiplexing connections, or by delaying modules appears to solve slightly jarring effects in cooperative neural calculus (Szentágothai and Arbib, 1974).

Modern computer scientists who want reliable processing while playing with several sources of knowledge and with several calculation modules are beginning to think of such deft use of timing (Lesser and Corkill, 1981). Some attention should also be paid to the theory of fuzzy automata as formulated Arbib and Manes (1975). If Brain Theory and AI both have to understand the difficulties caused by the local breakdowns or by the growing complexity of process and control, the notion of a fuzzing effect of multiple calculation on the flow of information might well correspond to the category of phenomena under study. And if some method could be derived to deal with "machines with unreliable inputs" (this has nothing to do with Zadeh's presentation of "fuzzy sets" which is a static and not-so-fuzzy conception) by associating every piece of data with a weight indicating confidence, it might be possible to decide where and when control must be applied. But for that to be done, the theory of calculability (Church's *Lambda calculus*) must be augmented. The logics of automatic calculus may have to be reformulated to associate inhibition factors to operators or to changes of state, this simulating what cortical tissue can do. Such an approach to the filtering of errors upstream of any operation seems possible with electronic hardware, and should not be rejected without consideration.

To control the gradual decay of knowledge after it has been activated in memory is much easier and should be currently seen in major data banks. If some item is no longer required, or if it is contradicted, or becomes unclear, it must by automatically deactivated. Different clocks and threshold management modules can be used in order to decrease or increase usefulness or confidence weights associated with information memorized transiently or for a long time.

In conclusion, decisive improvements in AI go along with more elaborate timing and control. It remains to be examined whether local control or centralized control or processes is preferable. This problem will be encountered when dealing with the question of beliefs.

2. On belief mechanisms

What does the goldfish feel about the superpower which is changing the water in the bowl every morning?

Beliefs are not only underlying the truth value of propositions or the expression of quality, quantity, and intensity through adjectives, quantifiers, and modal expressions. They also serve as top-down constraints in form recognition and perception, in the naming and classification objects and acts known or imagined. The belief issue is unavoidable in social and psychological sciences. It should thus not be left aside by the technology of information processing. Let us think of a documentation expert who has to create a thesaurus of keywords to represent the world of historical research. Should *Christianism be classified together with opium (of the people)* under *oppression* or *feudalism*? It all depends on the idealistic context and also on the purpose of the data bank using the thesaurus. However, even such beliefs will not always matter. They will not interfere with the classification of Christian pots and pans found in the catacombs of Rome.

For Cognitive Science, which considers not the fields of application of intelligence, but the processes, the problem of beliefs is ruled by three perfectly distinct cognitive viewpoints.

2.1. First, belief of beliefs can be a coinage for *associated ideas*, or, more properly (as studies on epilepsic remembrance phenomena and on synesthesia have shown), for the probability of the co-firing of particular columns of neurons. This is conditioned by:

a. dendrite of fiber connections which have been developed or selected during a training period (mainly during childhood),

b. the specialization of particular neurons or groups of neurons responding better and faster to some rhythmic signals when specific neurotransmitters cross synaptic membranes where they find gates opened by previous stimuli of the same nature.

Experience obviously plays a major role in conditioning the Central Nervous System to process information in a more and more adapted, and also in a more and more habituated manner. This memory of past stimulations has been tested repeatedly with rats, cats and dogs. Whether living organisms are consciously or not consciously aware of associated percepts and concepts does not matter. They rely on some inner estimates about co-occurrences. Then, the confidence values their brains attribute to those associated neuropsychological events may be called *local beliefs*.

2.2. Psychologists and psycholinguists have argued from complementary positions that association of ideas which create beliefs about the world could be divided into:

a. *Paradigmatic associations* (also called connotations by logicians) which are the result of frequent co-occurrence. Opposites are thus felt to be "near" each other, because one evokes the other (Wundt, Freud, Jakobson).
b. *Contextual associations* (also called syntagmatic relations in linguistics after Saussure and Jakobson). They are the result of habituation to certain combinations of successive stimuli, events, or words.

Such a distinction has not yet been associated with anatomo-physiological evidence. However, it is not without interest. If a topological representation of a world of knowledge (incorporating beliefs about how items are associated) has to be undertaken by psychologists, linguists, or information specialists, co-occurrences and distributional properties of entries must be materialized by links. It is not enough to structure a data bank as a set of hierarchical trees, as Quillian had suggested doing twenty years ago. Tagged pointers must connect several terminal nodes of a tree or several trees to simulate this possibility to associate data which, at first sight, were "distant", but came to be "near" as the system evolved into an experienced entity (Lavorel, 1980). One should perhaps envisage even the possibility of several simultaneous live networks which could have the same nodes but different structures of relations (Lavorel, 1980). Pragmatic situations would dictate the choice of one or the other. Experiments like NETL at M.I.T. (Fahlmann, 1979), have shown that such many-dimensional approaches are worthwhile developing.

2.3. Belief has also been defined by logicians and philosophers (See other papers in this volume) *as a heuristic activity of the human mind when it is confronted with a collection of phenomena or facts, and infers or extrapolates new abstract objects and relations from given elements of knowledge.*

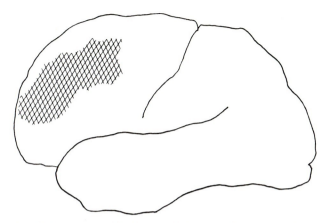

Fig. 3. Cases reported by Luria and Tsvetkova (1969). Cumulative representation of lesions (this picture has been inferred from the written report).

Natural inference or extrapolation are disrupted by *prefontal* lesions which also affect problem-solving and the conception of strategies (as observed by Luria and Tsvetkova (1969) (Fig. 3). According to Luria and coll., man's heuristic and abstract belief activities seem to be one and the same complex function mediated by prefrontal cortex. It is a relatively autonomous calculating system whose disappearance (in some lobotomies and lesions) does not affect a patient in any spectacular way. He perceives the world and moves his body normally. Only his behavior is somewhat limited by a difficulty in finding solutions to situations and problems which he has not encountered before. He will reproduce past performance rather automatically, or will follow new strategies when they are dictated to him. He is a credulous believer in matters of religion and politics. Such a patient may even become a bigot and not question past beliefs, or any kind of propaganda which he has been exposed to before and after his brain damage.

The question now is: do we want to try and design artificial intelligent systems with "heuristic" or "abstract belief" centers? This has actually been attempted in strategic war-game simulaton (see this volume). But can we safely design systems which would by themselves start reasoning and believing something about the knowledge which is fed into them? I have implied above that, contrary to what is traditionally thought in AI, computer systems of the future should imitate data driven brains by substituting dynamic memory bases for static data bases. How then can we be assured that the momentary frequency of unimportat information will not distort preferences (Frécon and Lavorel, 1980)? Or that some insufficiently documented moves will not yield erroneous links and conclusions? Artificial information systems, as they grow more ambitious, are like men's brains: they do not necessarily become wiser. Men may suffer from paranoia. So can computer belief organs, as Colby (1975) has shown with simulation programs. It seems to me that to ward off such dangers, cognitive scientists should further inquire into the genesis of psychosis, or into readaptation after frontal lesions before they create intelligent systems with autonomous capacities for inference and extrapolation.

The operational weight of human beliefs depends on their integration into a whole, which is eminently adaptive. Neurobiologists tell us that the unity of consciousness, personality, and free undertaking is based upon genetically coded interaction between the glandular system and the nervous system, or between the hypothalamus, the hippocamus, and the orbital part of frontal lobes (Pribam,1969). If we integrate their models into a caricature, a given human individual is genetically equipped to have drives (hypothalamus), and a permanent access to his bibliography (hippocampus), to his knowledge of the world and to his knowledge about particular acts, when he decides to behave one way or another, *initiates* plans of action, and optionally *modifies* his tactics.

Should man rely on artificial aids to supplement his memory and his processing abilities in the representation of knowledge and of prerecorded schemas of acts?

A few arguments have been presented against using central heuristic organs elaborating beliefs and judgments. Other arguments have been presented in favor of distributed control systems and cooperative computation using local belief mediation if necessary.

But such a proposal is quite a cynical one. It rests upon analysis of the human brain and uses it as an archetype of satisfactory computation. Yet, for those who work in clinical neuropsychology or in social sciences, it is most obvious that human decision-makers cannot master their primitive drives, do not remember their past failures, pass inappropriate judgements, and favor dangerous strategies.

Acknowledgement

I wish to express my gratitude to Victor Lesser of the University of Massachusetts at Amherst. His theoretical advice has improved my understanding of cooperative competition in AI and in neural processes.

ARTIFICIAL AND HUMAN INTELLIGENCE (A. Elithorn and R. Banerji, editors)
Elsevier Science Publishers, B.V.
© NATO, 1984

Chapter 16

THE BILATERAL COOPERATIVE MODEL OF READING: A HUMAN PARADIGM FOR ARTIFICIAL INTELLIGENCE *

M.M. TAYLOR

DCIEM, Box 2000, Downsview, Ont, Canada M3M 3B9

Summary

The Bilateral Cooperative model of human reading is introduced. Two process streams interact at a few discrete points. One stream, primarily represented in the right brain hemisphere, performs at each stage a rapid approximate pattern-match which results in several alternative interpretations of the data; the other, in the left hemisphere, performs a rule-based (syntactic) analysis which produces a unique result if it can. The possibilities developed by the approximate pattern-match can be used to assist the analysis procedure (top-down), whereas the unique result derived from the analysis can inhibit all other possibilities developed from the pattern match. At each stage, the resulting data become input for the next stage of both processes. Evidence from experiments with normal subjects and patients with brain lesions is presented to support the model.

1. Introduction

This paper introduces the Bilateral Cooperative (BLC) model of human reading, and proposes it as a paradigm for Artificial Intelligence research. The model is described more fully in the forthcoming book "Psychology of Reading" (Taylor and Taylor, in press). A related, dual-process approach to pattern recognition has been suggested by Duerr, Haettich, Tropf and Winkler (1980), and applied successfully to the recognition of unconstrained handwritten numerals.

According to the BLC model, human reading is performed by the repeated interaction of two kinds of process operating in parallel. At each of several stages, the processes interconnect and can influence each other in both a top-down and a bottom-up way. One of the two processes is a careful, rule-based, analytic process which attempts to produce a unique result; the other is a quicker, approximate pattern matching process which may produce many simultaneous options. In this paper, the two processes will be discussed

---

* This is DCIEM Research Paper No. 81-P-4.

239

as if the analytic process were performed exclusively by the left hemisphere (LH) of the brain, and the pattern matching by the right hemisphere (RH). In fact, "RH" processes probably are done by both hemispheres, the right being preferred.

It is generally agreed that speech is represented in the left hemisphere of normal right-handed people, and in most left-handed people as well. Evidence has been accumulating, however, that the RH is more deeply involved in reading than had been thought. This paper briefly sketches some of the areas of research from which this evidence has been gathered.

2. Left brain vs. right brain

2.1. Motivation

Three illustrations may help to motivate the exploration.

2.1.1. J.W. – a case of a partially split brain

There are some brain pathologies for which the recommended surgery is to separate the two halves of the brain, by cutting the connective tissue known as the "corpus callosum". In a recent case (Sidtis, Volpe, Holtzman, Wilson and Gazzaniga, 1981), the patient (known as J.W.) had a partial cut rather than a complete one.

J.W. was able to read words presented in the right side of his visual field (which projects to LH) easily and precisely. Words presented to the other side of his visual field (RH projection) caused some difficulty. He could obviously comprehend at least some of them, but in order to say the word, he had to resort to a complex strategy. As an example, when presented with the word "Knight", he said: "I have a picture in my mind but can't say it ... Two fighters in a ring ... Ancient and wearing uniforms and helmets ... on horses ... trying to knock each other off ... Knights?"

This pictorial way of producing the word was typical of J.W.'s procedure with RH presentations. He would visualize a scene centrally incorporating the reference of the word, and then laboriously work out what the word was. The RH made a picture out of the word if it could, and the LH solved a puzzle to provide the spoken output.

2.1.2. Evoked potential when reading

Electrical signals recorded from the scalp (EEG) provide a gross way of monitoring brain activity. Ornstein, Herron, Johnstone and Swencionis (1979) measured the EEG while subjects read texts. If the text was a story, rather than technical material, the signals were relatively stronger from the RH, suggesting that the story involved the RH relatively more than did the technical test.

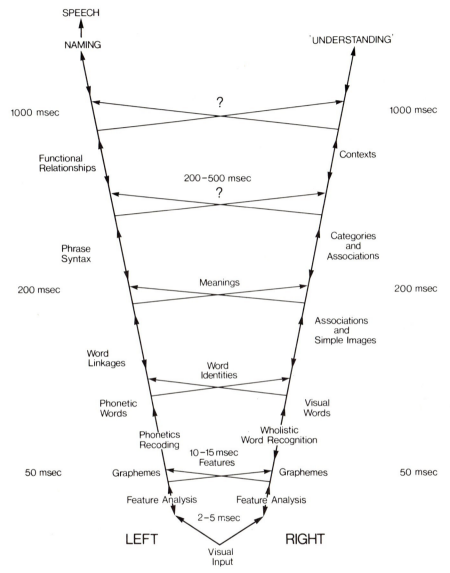

Fig. 1. The skeleton of the BLC model, showing the types of stage and possible information crossovers between stages. LEFT track processes are analytic and syntactic, dealing with functional relationships; RIGHT track processes are associative and categorical.

2.1.3. Measuring brain activity by radioactive tracing

It is possible to obtain a gross measure of the activity of different regions of the brain by introducing radioactive atoms which are used in the brain metabolism. Silent reading does not activate exclusively the LH, where speech and language are ordinarily thought to be represented. Rather, each hemisphere shows approximately the same pattern of five active areas, as if the two hemispheres had related activities in corresponding regions (Lassen, Ingvar and Skinhoj, 1978).

2.1.4. LH and RH work together, but differently

The brain-scan work suggests that both hemispheres work together, J.W. shows that both can interpret printed words, though very differently, and the EEG work suggests that they tend to handle different kinds of material.

2.2. The bilateral cooperative model of reading

Fig. 1 presents a crude and tentative schematic diagram for the BLC model. There are two separate tracks, marked LEFT and RIGHT, with five crossovers indicated between them (the number is chosen to be five because of the brain-scan work, not for obvious functions or experimental reasons). The actual stages named in Fig. 1 should not be taken too seriously, especially on the RIGHT track. The important points about Fig. 1 are:

– The processes on each track can operate independently of one another between interconnection points.
– The processes on the LEFT track are analytic and synthetic, whereas those on the RIGHT track are associative and wholistic.
– The interconnections occur only at discrete points, between which the processes on the two tracks are performing related tasks on similar data.
– The separation between the tasks increases, in terms of the time taken to make a data transfer from one track to the other. This is taken as an indication of the increasing amount of processing required to translate the representations on one track to those of the other.

We shall use Fig. 1 to illustrate many of the ideas developed in the following sections.

As a first illustration, consider the problem of J.W. In the BLC model, J.W. had the first three or four crossovers cut, and could pass only word meanings (images) or more complex aspects from RH to LH. If he could have passed word labels or letter shapes, he would have had as little trouble saying words projected to RH as he did with words projected to LH.

2.2.1. Low-level crossover – kanji, kana and alphabetics

The crossover of information at a low level in Fig. 1 may be illustrated by an experiment which uses some of the special properties of Japanese writing.

Japanese writing uses three main types of symbols:

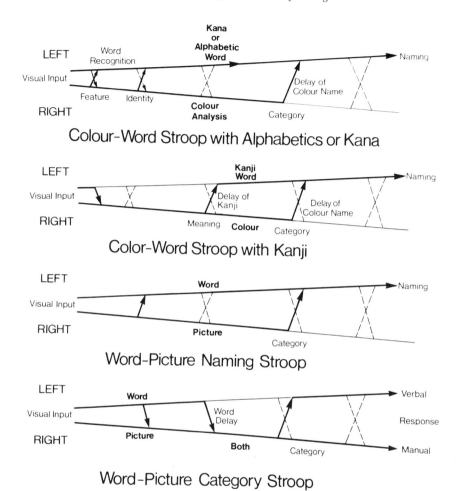

Fig. 2. Data paths through the BLC skeleton for four kinds of Stroop effect: (a) Normal colour-word Stroop; (b) Colour-Kanji Stroop; (c) Picture-word naming; (d) Picture-word categorization.

- *Kanji*: Kanji are Chinese characters, each of which represents one morpheme (meaning element). A word may be composed of one or more Kanji, two being typical. Kanji tend to be used for content words.
- *Kana*: Kana are phonetic symbols, each of which represents one spoken CV (Consonant-Vowel) syllable.
- *Roman Alphabet*: The Roman Alphabet is used for names and similar transcriptions of Western words and abbreviations such as "cm.", mostly in technical writing.

Many experiments in Western countries have shown that alphabetic material is most accurately and quickly identified by the LH. The same is true for Kana (Sasanuma, Itoh, Mori and Kobayashi, 1977). For Kanji, however, the situation is more complex. A single Kanji seems most frequently to be best identified by the RH. When two Kanji are presented together, they are recognised best by the LH if they combine to form a real word, but by the RH if they do not (Hatta, 1978; Tzeng, Hung, Cotton and Wang, 1979).

In the experiment (Nishikawa and Niina, 1981), subjects were required to detect as quickly as possible whether there was an interloper among a set of symbols that were otherwise all alike in name or shape. If the items were alphabetics or Kana, then the responses took a time which increased with the number of items set, and LH presentation was quicker by 10–15 msec. If they were Kanji, or upside-down alphabetics or Kana, then there was almost no effect of set size, and RH presentation was quicker by 10–15 msec. The pattern of results did not depend on which hemisphere received the initial visual data, but there was a delay of 10–15 msec if the initial hemisphere was inappropriate to the stimuli, which suggests that the data were being transferred at a relatively early stage to the appropriate hemisphere.

This pattern is characteristic of the difference between LH and RH processing. LH is basically analytic and serial, whereas the RH shows no aptitude for analysis, working instead pictorially and in a parallel way.

2.3. Stroop effects: inter-process interference

2.3.1. Colour Stroop with alphabetics, kana and kanji

If the word "RED" is written in green ink, it takes longer to say the colour of the ink than if the word had been, say, "BED". The colour name of the word interferes with naming the ink colour. The reverse does not happen, however. The ink colour does not interfere with the speed of saying the word. This is the classic "Stroop effect".

When the colour words are written in Kanji, the interference is larger than with alphabetics or Kana (Biederman and Tsao, 1979; Morikawa, 1981; Tsao and Wu, 1981). Moreover, only when the colour name is written in Kanji does the ink colour interfere with the speed of reading the word.

Fig. 2 shows pathways responsible for Stroop effects, according to the BLC model. Colour is processed by the RIGHT path as far as the level of "category", after which it can be passed to the LEFT track for naming. Kana and alphabetics are processed by the LEFT track after the stage of word labelling, whereas Kanji have to use the RIGHT track at least as far as word meaning. This provides an opportunity for resource competition between Kanji recognition and colour naming. Since inter-track transfer takes longer at the later stages, this means that Kana and alphabetics reach the naming stage quicker than Kanji (Feldman and Turvey, 1980), followed by colour name. The leading items can interfere with the delayed ones, but not the reverse. The mutual interference between Kanji and colour may be due to common use of the right track by concepts of similar meanings.

2.3.2. Name-category Stroop effects

Two opposed Stroop-like effects can be demonstrated between words and pictures. They are also illustrated in Fig. 2. Suppose one is presented with a cartoon drawing of a car, inside which is written the word "DOG". It takes longer to say "car" in response to the picture than if there were no word in it, but the presence of the picture has no effect on the speed of saying "dog" in response to the word. So far, this effect is much like the colour-word Stroop effect. The LH-processed word interferes with the following RH-processed picture name, but not vice-versa.

The opposite effect is observed when the subject is asked, not to say the word or name the picture, but to indicate whether the word or picture belongs to a specified category, such as "vehicle" or "animal". The picture now interferes with the word, but not vice-versa (Smith and Magee, 1980). Here, the final output is derived from the RH process of categorization, and the delay from the LH word labelling process to the categorization function causes the reversed effect. The timing relations of the two effects are very different, however. In the BLC model, word information must cross from LH to RH at a level below categorization in order for the category of the word to be identified; information about the picture name cannot cross from RH to LH until a stage after categorization, which takes longer.

2.4. Acquired dyslexia

"Acquired dyslexia" means impaired reading ability due to brain damage. In the following, some of its many varieties will be described.

2.4.1. Phonemic (deep) dyslexia

Phonemic dyslexia is a syndrome which is always accompanied by damage to a large region of the left hemisphere. Most of the following description is based on various chapters of the book "Deep Dyslexia", edited by Coltheart, Patterson and Marshall (1980).

The most characteristic symptom of phonemic dyslexia is an inability to read pseudo-words (e.g. DAKE) and most function words. When a phonemic dyslexic misreads a content word, the response may be related in meaning to the correct word; "lilac" may be substituted for "crocus". Phonemic dyslexics never make phonetically related errors, but may report a word visually like the stimulus word. Japanese phonemic dyslexics may be totally unable to read Kana (the phonetic characters representing syllables), but have a relatively small deficit for Kanji. Kana are preferentially processed by LH, Kanji by RH.

Phonemic dyslexics often have trouble with words and morphemes dealing with syntax. These are function words: "butter" can be read, but not "but". Function morphemes may be confused, ignored, or cause a puzzle: "jumps", "jumping", "jumped" may all be reported as "jump ... something". Normal readers also seem to process the content and function morphemes of multi-morpheme words differently (Murrell and Morton, 1974; Taft and Forster, 1975).

In terms of the BLC model, the phonemic dyslexics appear to lack most of the LEFT track functions up to "naming and speech", which remains functional (though sometimes impaired). Some may retain syntactic capabilities, in the higher stages of the LEFT track, but all lack the phonetic recoding and word function stages.

2.4.2. Phonological dyslexics

Phonological dyslexics are like phonemic dyslexics in that they cannot read pseudo-words or unfamiliar words. In all other respects, they seem to read normally, having no special problems with function words or syntax (Beauvois and Desrouesne, 1979). In terms of Fig. 1, they lack only one stage - that marked "phonetic recoding" on the LEFT track.

2.4.3. Surface dyslexia

"Surface Dyslexics" can decode pseudo-words, but have trouble dealing with irregularly spelled common words, such as "yacht". So long as the words can be worked out by rules, they can say them. On the other hand, they may have trouble understanding what they have read. They also tend to have problems with pictorial representation (Warrington, 1975). Their problems are with functions on the RIGHT track of Fig. 1.

The Japanese equivalent to the surface dyslexic is the patient who has little trouble reading Kana, but has lost most of the capability to read Kanji. These patients also comprehend poorly what they read (Sasanuma, 1975).

2.5. Semantic priming

"Semantic priming" provides evidence concerning the two interacting process streams in reading. These experiments use normal, not damaged patients. The prototype semantic priming experiment might be as follows:

In a tachistoscope, a target word such as "NURSE" is shown, and the subject must say it as fast as possible. If another word, called the "prime", is presented before the target, it may make the response to the target faster or slower, compared to a control condition in which a row of XXXXX is presented before the target. If the prime is semantically related to the target (say "DOCTOR"), then the response to the target will be quicker. If it is unrelated, the response will be slower.

The prime causes inhibition only if it precedes the target by a sufficient time. A prime very shortly before, or simultaneous with the target provides only facilitation for related words, not inhibition for unrelated words.

When the prime is an ambiguous word such as PALM (of the hand, or a tree), both senses facilitate the recognition of targets (Holley-Wilcox and Blank, 1980). Subjects, however, may be consciously aware of only one sense of the ambiguous prime.

These apparently confusing results have a direct explanation in terms of the BLC model. The RIGHT process quickly develops a set of possible interpretations of the incoming data, all of which can activate patterns of association which exert a top-down influence on subsequent RIGHT recognitions. There is no mechanism for inhibition at this level; the RIGHT process does not tend to be inhibitory. Only when the slow but careful LEFT process has completed its work will incorrect words be inhibited. This inhibition will have an effect on the top-down processing of the target only if it works at the word-recognition level. In the case of the ambiguous prime, the word recognition is unambiguous; the ambiguity is one level higher, at the level of word meaning. Hence the LH process cannot readily inhibit the associates of either meaning of the correctly perceived prime, but can inhibit (as always), the associates of other, unrelated words.

The same mechanism also serves to explain a result that otherwise seems quite magical. A prime may be masked by presenting it for a very short time and following it by a pattern of lines and curves. With appropriate selection of the parameters, it is possible to generate a prime which cannot be reported, but which does facilitate recognition of a related target (Marcel, in press; Fowler, Wolford, Slade and Tassinary, 1981). Marcel (1980) further showed that if an ambiguous word was used as a prime, but was also preceded by a cue to one of its meanings (e.g. TREE PALM), then only the cued meaning served to facilitate a following word (e.g. WRIST would not be facilitated by TREE PALM, but would be by HAND PALM, in agreement with an earlier result by Schvaneveldt, Meyer and Becker, 1976). If, now, the ambiguous prime was masked so that it could not be identified, both senses retained their facilitative effect.

A related effect is that an unattended word flashed together with a word to be categorized can affect the ability of subjects to perform the categorization, even when they are unaware of the existence of the unattended word (Underwood, 1981). The effect also works for pictures as well as words. A picture used as a semantic prime can have an effect even when it is flashed at too short a duration for it to be named (McCauley, Parmelee, Sperber and Carr, 1980).

According to the BLC model, an "unseen" prime acts at the word recognition level in the same way as an ambiguous word acts at the word meaning level. The masked prime contains some information, enough to let the RIGHT process generate some plausible alternatives, but not enough for the LEFT process to make a unique decision, which would inhibit the other alternatives. Hence, no word is reported, but the semantic priming effects can occur.

2.6. LEFT and RIGHT: Conclusion

The several different lines of research lead to a general set of conclusions about the characteristics of LEFT and RIGHT processes.

- LEFT uses analysis whereas RIGHT uses approximate pattern matching.
- LEFT obtains a single unique result and inhibits potential competing results, whereas RIGHT obtains and maintains many competing possibilities.
- LEFT may inhibit RIGHT possibilities when it has obtained its unique result, but it is slower than RIGHT; RIGHT can use its multiple possibilities to guide LEFT analysis in a top-down way.
- The LEFT analytic techniques can handle any reasonable input data, whereas RIGHT can deal only with familiar patterns.
- LEFT tends to deal with functional relations, RIGHT with pictorial ones. In terms of language, LEFT deals with syntax and phonology, RIGHT with meaning, categorization, and association. In this aspect particularly, the "RIGHT" processes must be understood to occur in both brain hemispheres, but the dichotomy between process characteristics should be maintained, since the LEFT hemisphere is uniquely capable of performing "LEFT" processes.

3. Implications for artificial intelligence

3.1. Metaphor and linguistic drifts

As a method for determining the meanings of patterns, the two-fold system has much to recommend it. Even a language understanding system cannot be based on syntax alone; semantic relationships among words are also required. These semantic relationships can be embedded in the syntax, by refining categories such as "noun" into finer and finer detail: "animate–inanimate", "male–female", "adult–child", and so forth, where each refinement implies further control on the appropriateness of verbs and adjectives. If, however, the semantics are embedded into the syntax in this way, the process of interpretation can become not only complex and slow, but also rigid and literal. Metaphor becomes hard to handle.

Using the BLC model, the syntax can remain simple. All the content words have association patterns, which permit interpretation of the words in different modes, depending on which areas of the available association arena are emphasized by surrounding context. If the overlap of the association patterns of the content words is unusual, but contextually appropriate according to the LEFT process, we have a metaphor.

Natural language is frequently carried on in metaphor. Words accrue meaning through consistent metaphoric usage, and meanings drift and multiply or die over time. Who now remembers that "orient" once meant "face to the east"? That meaning has split into two quite independent meanings: to face in a specific direction, and "The East". The BLC model makes it quite easy to handle such shifts of meaning. The associative pattern evoked by a word can proliferate until the explosion of possibilities is limited by an analytic process which accepts one of them.

In the above, the idea of metaphor was restricted to the level of word meaning. Of course, the same process should apply at all levels of the process track, from feature analysis to metaphoric texts (e.g. parables). Mis-shapen letters may be understood as metaphors for canonical forms, and possibilities may be developed by the RIGHT process for checking by the LEFT, under control of context.

3.2. Importance of discrete information crossover points

3.2.1. Operations in a single stage of the model

In each stage of processing, the many possibilities provided by the RIGHT process are added to the semantic and syntactic context as top-down information for the LEFT process, which works in an analytic manner, and which has the primary function of inhibiting interpretations inconsistent with the data. In the BLC model, as distinguished from most others, inhibition is a function distinct from activation, and works substantially more slowly. Eventually, if a unique interpretation at this stage is possible, the LEFT process will have produced it. Even if it cannot, it may well inhibit many of the possibilities produced by the RIGHT process. Either way, any RIGHT interpretations inconsistent with the LEFT analysis are actively inhibited, and any associative patterns that might have been developed in the next stage begin to be de-activated. After control by the LEFT process, most of the RIGHT possibilities have been denied; sometimes all have been, and nothing remains but "noise". Whatever does remain forms part of the input pattern for the next stage of processing on both LEFT and RIGHT tracks.

The separation of processes does not in itself imply a discrete series of information crossover points. There is no clear staging a priori in the development of meaning from marks on a page. It seems likely that the human stratagem of providing a path from marks on the page to phonologically coded patterns is simply a matter of expediency, permitting written language to use some of the structures previously developed for dealing with spoken language.

Staged information crossover permits the dual interaction of the two types of process. If information were continuously interchanged between the processes, it would not be possible for the RIGHT process to develop its multiplicity of potential explanations for a pattern. These, in turn, could not be used as top-down control for the LEFT process search for a uniquely correct interpretation, although the LEFT process could still inhibit the RIGHT. Staged crossover permits a useful mix of freedom and interaction which might be lacking in a more blended system.

4. Summary and conclusions

The object of this paper was to introduce the bilateral cooperative model of reading as a paradigm for AI development. For this purpose, the exact nature of the human processing scheme is of less importance than its principles. The main principles of the BLC model are:

– At each of several stages, an approximate but fast pattern-matching process which generates one or more potential results is partnered with a rule-based process which can generate a unique result in a general situation. The first process proposes, the second disposes. The first is primarily performed in the RH, the second in the LH.
– A complex, "intelligent" result is obtained from the work of several stages of partnered process pairs.
– Top-down effects apply to both members of a process pair. These effects may derive from feedback from higher stages, or come from the partner process within the pair.
– Although in principle each of the two processes in a process pair could perform the task of a stage, the partnership permits each to be much simpler than would otherwise be necessary.

ARTIFICIAL AND HUMAN INTELLIGENCE (A. Elithorn and R. Banerji, editors)
Elsevier Science Publishers, B.V.
© NATO, 1984

Chapter 17

HANDLING THE UNCONSCIOUS

B. MELTZER

Via Uzzarini 483, Rosola, Zocca (MO) Italy

Summary

As a contribution to the study of unconscious processes, it is proposed to formalize and develop Freud's theory of dream-work by computational modelling, using the conceptual dependency representation of thought developed by Schank and his collaborators.

1. Introduction

The role of "the unconscious" in mental phenomena is in general rather inadequately appreciated by cognitive psychologists and philosophers. Whether or not one accepts Leibniz's demonstration of its existence, or Freud's or others' views of how it functions, the following simple observation made in the last century by Lipps puts the matter squarely:

"Thus the following general statement holds good: The factors of psychical life are not the contents of consciousness but the psychical processes which are in themselves unconscious. The task of psychology, if it does not merely wish to describe the contents of consciousness, must therefore consist in inferring the nature of these unconscious processes from the character of the contents of consciousness and their temporal connections. Psychology must be a theory of these processes. But a psychology of this kind will very soon find that there are quite a number of these processes which are not represented in the contents of consciousness".

Thus without a theory of the unconscious psychology would be merely descriptive with minimal claims to be a science. One could make an even stronger claim than Lipps', though I shall not pursue it farther in this essay. Namely, if one asks what are these "contents of consciousness", the answer must be something like propositions, questions, commands, etc. But their occurrence in the mind takes finite amounts of time and therefore must themselves be processes; it appears that it is a function of language to represent these processes as unitary "static" thoughts. In this respect language performs in the general area of cognition the same rôle that it does in the particular area of perception, where by assigning names it "staticizes" physical processes into objects – for example a complex observed phenomenon exhibiting constantly changes of contours and dispositions becomes a "tree". This incidentally shows that the study of mind is probably inseparable from that of language.

2. Plan of the discussion

The underlying theme is the proposal that computational modelling may be the most suitable vehicle for studying unconscious processes. Process aspects of the most convincing existing theory of the unconscious, that of Freud, will be discussed. Its possible limitations and the need to make it more precise, possibly predictive and develop it further, leads to the proposal that the "conceptual dependency" representation of thought in the programs of Schank and his school for understanding natural language, can – by being provided with a new repertoire of transformations – appropriately be used as a base for modelling such processes. And finally a specific example taken from the Freudian corpus will be presented as a possible challenge and bench-mark in the development of such an application.

3. The question of complexity

Why should one consider using computer programs as the vehicle for expressing and working out the consequences of theories of unconscious processes? The reason is that the latter are putatively in general of very great complexity, and computer programs are essentially specifications of processes of arbitrary complexity whose results can be exhibited by running them – in practice the complexity that can be handled is limited only by the speed and storage capacity of the machine.

That mental processes are in general of great complexity is by no means obvious. To commonsense such things as consciousness, colours, images, etc. seem obviously simple, but in this view there is a confusion between overall performance and what goes to make up the performance. What Craik said about machines long ago is an apt analogue. He remarked that there are several ways of putting the parts of an engine together: you could drop them all into a bucket, in which case the complexity would be fairly high and the performance nil; but if you put them together correctly and let the engine start, you would have much greater complexity (now there would be relational as well as atomic complexity), but at the same time there would have entered a new simplicity and co-ordination "very like that of a living organism".

The specific evidence for the complexity of mental phenomena is of diverse kinds. If they were as simple as commonsense believes we would surely by now have acquired a good and reasonably complete understanding of them – which is far from being the case. Secondly, the published and unpublished case-histories of psychopathology reveal the incredibly rich structure of patients' thoughts. And, finally, the attempts that have been made to model different kinds of mental performance computationally, have shown spectacularly that even the simplest of them, e.g. that involved in building a tower with toy-bricks, require very complicated programs.

4. Freudian theory

Anyone who has read Freud's classic "Interpretation of Dreams" will know the wealth of evidence and close reasoning that led to his theory of the processes at work in the formation of dreams. It forms a natural starting-point for the study of unconscious processes, although at least two objections might be raised against this view. The first is that dreams are a very special case of the workings of the mind and so will probably be misleading as to its general character. The answer to this is that later works of Freud showed convincingly that the theory could be successfully applied to waking activities like making jokes, or to what he termed parapraxes such as forgetting, or such as mis-reading text. I am inclined to think that it may be applicable too to some of the puzzles of ordinary language use for which linguists seem to invent rather ad hoc theories. Secondly, it might be charged that Freud's evidence came from the study of hysterics, neurotics and other pathological cases, and so his conclusions do not apply to the mental workings of "normal" people. It is true that his interest in and work on dreams started in the context of his clinical practice, but the evidential material in "The Interpretation of Dreams" is by no means confined to that of patients, and in fact many of the most important case-studies in it are of his own dreams. The pathological cases provided the initial clues in his studies, and this is not surprising as – to quote Craik again – "it is only a fault which draws our attention to a mechanism at all". In any case there is plenty of evidence to suggest that the category of "normality" in this context is a highly dubious one: most neurotics were "normal" at one time, and most of us have in our psychic make-up strands of neurosis which can become apparent when circumstances are appropriate for this to occur. There can be little doubt that, incomplete and defective as Freud's theory may be, there is no comparable candidate in the field as a base-line for the investigation of unconscious processes, and in the next section I shall give a brief summary of the processes at work in his theory of the formation of dreams.

5. Dream-work processes

Dreams generally are bizarre and apparently senseless or at least have elements of that character in them. It is a basic assumption of Freud's theory that this appearance is illusory, and that they *always* have a meaning that fits naturally with the dreamer's waking thought, feelings and experiences. Therefore a distinction is drawn between the manifest content of the dream, which is simply the dreamer's account of it, and its latent content which can be inferred from it by techniques, mainly that of free association, which will not be gone into in this paper. The term "dream-work" is applied to the transformation carried out unconsciously from latent to manifest content.

The dream-work is the result of the operation mainly of five activities termed wish-fulfilment, regression, condensation, displacement and secondary revision. The following is a brief account of these process types:

1. Wish-fulfilment: During sleep at night some of the thoughts of the previous day ("the day's residue") that have not been completely dealt with threaten to disturb the subject's sleep, but by being transformed into a dream are made innocuous to sleep. The day's residue constructs a wish. In the case of children the wish left over from waking life is sufficient to call up a dream which is "connected, ingenious, usually short and easily recognised as 'wish-fulfilment'". In adults "it seems to be a generally binding condition" that the wish must be "one that is alien to conscious thinking – a repressed wish – or will possibly at least have reinforcements that are unknown to consciousness".
2. Regression: In this a change is made, in Freud's words, from the optative to the indicative mood, i.e. from "Oh! if only ---" to "It is ...". The latter is given a hallucinatory representation: thought-structures are changed into visual images. Almost all linking relations between the thoughts are lost; only the raw materials of the ideas and not their logical relations are represented – or at any rate the dream-work "reserves the liberty to disregard the latter".
3. Condensation: If a comparison is made of the size (in the sense of number of different ideational items) of the dream itself – its manifest content – and the thoughts behind it – the latent content – it is generally found that the latter is much larger. This is a consequence of the fact that typically a number of dream-thoughts will have converged and found representation in one element of the dream, a so-called "nodal" element. The reader who would like to get a feel for how this is achieved and the richness of reference generated, can study many detailed examples in "The Interpretation of Dreams", one of the most fascinating being Freud's own famous "botanical monograph" dream. The richness of reference is further contributed to by the occurrence also of the opposite activity, namely, individual dream-

thoughts being represented in the dream by several elements. Over-determination is the hall-mark of condensation processes.
4. Displacement: Freud really uses this term for two rather different phenomena, the first one being of absolutely fundamental importance in dream formation. It is responsible for the fact that the elements which appear to be the principal elements of the manifest content are far from playing the same part in the dream-thoughts – in fact, the essence of the dream-thoughts may not be represented in the dream at all. The dream is differently centred from the dream-thoughts. The theory is that in the dream-work a psychical force (what Freud terms the censorship of endopsychic defence) operates, which on the one hand strips the elements which have a high psychical value of their intensity, and on the other hand, by means of the over-determination discussed above, creates from elements of low psychical value new values, which afterwards find their way into the content of the dream. The intensity depends on whether the elements express the wish-fulfilment and on how much condensation has been expended on them.

A second kind of displacement occurs remarkably often in dreams: a verbal one; the usual direction of displacement is from colourless and abstract expressions to pictorial and concrete ones. Perhaps it might have been more appropriate to subsume this process under regression as described above.

5. Secondary revision: This, perhaps not very suitable, name is given by Freud to an activity in dream formation akin to a function of waking thought, namely the function which seeks to establish order in perceptual material, to set up relations in it and to make it conform to our expectations of an intelligible whole. In many dreams there is evidence that in just this way links are introduced and gaps bridged to help remove from the dream its appearance of absurdity and disconnectedness and make it approximate to the character of an intelligible experience. (It is incidentally interesting that this activity appears to be more marked in daydreams than in dreams proper).

6. Computational modelling

What might one expect to gain from developing computational models of unconscious processes in general and Freudian ones in particular? Mainly, I think, greater precision in their formulation, better possibilities for judging the adequacy of particular theories, possible predictive capacity and the prospect of improved rigour in testing the theories, and stimulus for their extension and improvement. Apart from anything else, also, if one accepts the clinical as well as theoretical importance of Freud's discoveries, it surely would be very useful to humanity to have well-systematized, easily available and usable bodies of knowledge in this area, and so not have to rely mainly on the individual insights and intuitions of geniuses like Freud and of others. Once working and well-tested models of this kind were in existence, one would more easily be able to study their applicability and deficiencies in respect of other phenomena than dreams, such as jokes, parapraxes, poems and ordinary language use in conversation.

A good example from the history of science of the benefits that may arise from "formalization" of more or less "intuitive" theories occurred when in the last century Maxwell took over the ideas of another genius, Michael Faraday, about the character of electric and magnetic forces. Faraday had envisaged them as systems of lines and tubes of force filling and interacting with each other in space; Maxwell, by trying to translate this explanatory picture into something more precise and suitable for predictive calculation, ended up with his classical equations of the electromagnetic field, which not only unified electromagnetism with optics and led to much of modern technology (e.g. wireless communication), but also became the paradigm of the "field" theories of today's physical sciences.

Finally, a program of research of the type envisaged would, in my view, be an important development of the discipline of computational modelling as such, since – as discussed below – it would extend in an important new direction the use of the most impressive computational representation of thought yet developed, that of Schank and his collaborators.

7. The modelling of thought

Since the invention of digital electronic computers at the end of World War 2, a great deal of work has been done on programming them to model mental performances of various kinds. For instance, programs of impressive performance have been developed for doing medical diagnosis, for scientific and mathematical reasoning (even of a very creative kind), for visual perception, for playing board games and for understanding natural language. But the profundity, intelligibility and generality of the theories realized or exemplified in such programs are often not equally impressive; not only do ad hoc components sometimes play too large a part in the program designs (though it would be absurd in the present stage of the development of mental science to ban them wholsale), but also there seems to be a tendency for their authors to be too much influenced by the *linguistic forms* in which human thinking gets expressed (whether those of natural, mathematical, logical or computational languages) and so not pay enough attention to the thinking itself. The work of Schank, although aimed specifically only at modelling the understanding of natural language as ordinarily spoken and written, has – I believe – a wider import as providing a basis for the modelling of thought itself, and goes further in that direction than other work in either natural language or other areas of computational modelling.

Only a rather sketchy account can be given here of his approach. It has of course long been recognized that to speak or understand a natural language one has to have knowledge not only of its grammar but also of its semantics. And Schank's starting point is to develop an adequate representation of semantics. For purposes of understanding text or spoken words, the kind of semantics set up by previous language theorists such as the transformational grammarians of the Chomsky school, while of some use in eking out the resources of grammar, is entirely concerned with the relation of words to words in the construction of "correct grammatical" sentences. But, firstly, real language is not tied down by "correct grammar" – in fact, some of the most effective examples of it, in for example conversation or poetry, are quite ungrammatical – and, secondly, as Bar-Hillel pointed out long ago (oddly enough as an argument against the possibility of computational modelling!), knowledge of the ordinary commonsense kind about the way the world is, is essential for understanding utterances or text, as is also their context.

So the representation has to be at a deeper level than that of the "semantics" of the grammarians: it works at the conceptual level. It consists of what Schank terms "conceptualizations" with linking relationships between them. It is interlingual in the sense that for a given subject matter the same representation may be used for understanding or generating text in any language (so that, for example, a program like deJong's FRUMP which skims new stories in American newspapers is able to output summaries in any one of a number of European and Eastern languages).

Conceptualizations are best envisaged as so-called c-diagrams, of which Fig. 1 is an example, somewhat simplified, representing the meaning of "John eats a frog". Here INGEST is the basic action in the conceptualization, associated with three so-called conceptual cases: those of objects (o), directions (D) and instruments (I). In this example, the objective slot is filled by "frog", the

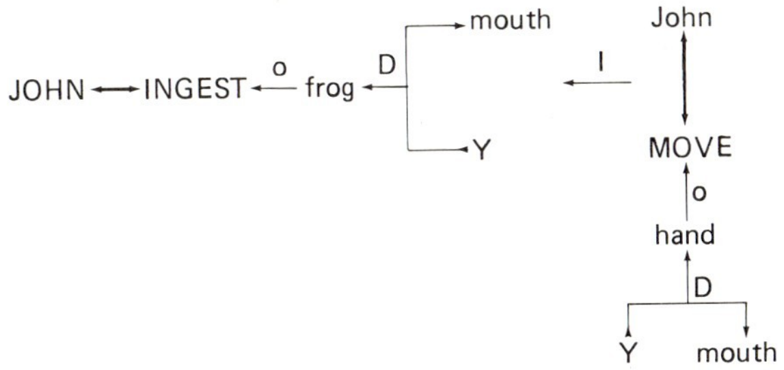

Fig. 1

directional one by an arrow pointing from an unspecified location "Y" to "mouth", while the instrumental one houses another conceptualization: in it the basic action is MOVE, with "John" again the actor, "hand" the object and "Y"-to "mouth" the direction.

This (incomplete) example illustrates one of the two types of conceptualization in the system. In this type the nucleus is a basic ACT like INGEST in Fig. 1 – there are about a dozen of them. Associated with an ACT in a c-diagram there must be slot for an object in the role of the performer of the act. (It is interesting, and probably not fortuitous, that Schank's generic name for objects in his system is PP, standing for picture-producer, when one considers the part played in the theory of the unconscious by regression to visual presentation). Physical ACTS are things that a PP can do to another PP. A mental ACT is an operation that a PP can perform on an idea, i.e. on a conceptualization. An example of a mental ACT is MBUILD – it takes conceptualizations as objects and constructs new conceptualizations from them. Associated also with an ACT are the slots for conceptual cases; besides the ones exemplified in our example – objective, directional and instrumental – there is a fourth, the recipient case (R) which, for example, would be involved in the c-diagrams for the meaning of words like "buy" or "give".

The other type of conceptualization is description of states of PP's (these might be physical or mental). As an example, the c-diagram for "John eats a frog" might be extended on the basis of real-world knowledge to that of Fig. 2, which indicates that as a (plausible) consequence of his action John becomes sick. Here the state HEALTH is followed by its "value" in brackets. (There are about twenty STATES in the system).

Fig. 2 also contains an example of what is possibly the most important type of relationship between two conceptualizations – that of *consequence*; the vertical triple-shafted arrow from the HEALTH to the INGEST conceptualization means that the former is a consequence of the latter; the notion of consequence used is wider than that of cause-and-effect – in fact, four types are distinguished: reason, result, enablement and initiation. It is the network of

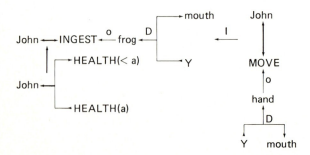

Fig. 2

consequence relationships that makes possible the representation of complex conceptualization like that of a complete episode.

For a fuller account of the theory the reader is referred to Schank's book "Conceptual information processing", where he may also learn how the system handles time, negation, conditionals and conscious mental events. Here it should just be emphasized that the particular choices made for the primitives of the system like the ACTS and STATES are not regarded as sacrosanct – what can be said for them is that they have some psychological plausibility and that they seem to have worked rather well in the various natural language programs that used them; but further research, for example of the kind proposed below, might well lead to their being changed in the pursuit of wider and more accurate psychological modelling.

8. Transformation of c-diagrams

The mere fact that the system is a representation of the *ideational* content of thought, and probably the only reasonably successful one existing today, makes it a promising candidate for the modelling of unconscious processes such as those putatively occurring in dreams, even though it was designed for a different purpose, namely as a component of a system for understanding natural language text and utterances. It is worth examining in broad outline how it is used for the latter.

For that purpose it has to be provided with a parser, which is a program that analyses input text and effectively translates it into a network of c-diagrams; a fascinating account of the problems and design of such parsers is given by Riesbeck in the book referred to above. There has also to be a generator, which is a program that can generate output in the chosen natural language from a c-diagram representation. But the most crucial component of the system, as far as the understanding function is concerned, is the inferencer. For our purpose, it is worth quoting from Schank's book an overall description of what it does by Rieger, its designer (some small changes have been made in his text):

"The program has one central reflex response, conceptual inference, which is activated by incoming c-diagrams. From each, this reflex generates many new, meaning-related diagrams which represent certain or plausible predictions about facets of the larger situation of which the input diagram may have been a part. That is, the program assumes that what it receives is always only a very small part of a much larger diagram, and it is motivated to discover as much of the larger situation as possible, and to relate what it discovers to other c-diagrams it already knows. To determine points at which one diagram joins with another is its single most important goal. To do this the program tries to determine why actions were performed, what an action might have caused, what must have been true for the action to have occurred in the first place. If a person is in state X, what might he desire as a result of being in that state? If a person desires Y, what might he do to achieve Y? The program will make predictions about what is likely to happen next, and can establish when its predictions match subsequent incoming diagrams. It makes assumptions about what other people know, based on what it already knows they know. It can detect when one pattern of meaning conflicts with another one, and it can combine similar patterns which have come from two different sources. By combining them, the program opens new pathways between other information patterns. If there are gaps in the incoming meaning patterns, it tries to fill them in. Based on the larger patterns in which they occur, it can make decisions about whom and what the smaller patterns are referencing. The program can get along with less than perfect data. When it cannot locate information it needs, it can make assumptions about the information, based on patterns of what is normal and expectable, It can guess how long certain states and actions in the world last, and use those guesses in its predictions".

It is clear from this description that c-diagrams and the processes carried out by the inferencer add up to a formidable theory of the understanding of language; but more than that, the depth of the theory is indicated by the fact that at least in fragmentary form the processes involved would account for much other activity of the mind. For instance, the dream-work processes of condensation and secondary revision previously discussed are adumbrated and even an aspect of the mechanism of wish-fulfilment is included. (Remarkably too, although not of immediate interest for our purposes, the operation of the inferencer appears to be a paradigm of the activity of free association, which is used in psychoanalytic practice to gain access to suppressed ideas – and which, in spite of its name, is assumed in Freudian theory to be a strictly deterministic one).

However, whether or not Rieger's particular theory is true, the essential insight is that a powerful theory of the mind seems feasible, based on the notion of *transformations* of c-diagrams (including as a limit case generation of them). Rieger has made a pioneering exploration of this area, but many other types of transformation may need to be studied for fuller theory of the mind.

9. A transformer for dream-work?

Reiger's inferencer then is a particular example of a program that transforms and generates c-diagrams. What would be involved in trying to design a transformer which would operate on a c-diagram containing (besides much else) the representation of the latent content of a dream to generate the c-diagram of the manifest dream itself? The problems would be considerable, and here only a brief discussion of some of them is possible.

The wish-fulfilment component is crucial. There would be no difficulty in the representation of wishes. The problem would be how the input of the "day's residue" would trigger the construction of the nucleus wish. Presumably,the memory of the system would need representations of the more important goals, motivations, drives of the hypothetical dreamer, with various degrees of inaccessibility constituting the Freudian "endopsychic defence" system. If these can be represented as c-diagrams, then the problem is largely reduced to Rieger's central one of determining points at which one diagram joins with another.

Regression: This is an entirely novel type of transformation. The constructed wish will act as a selector of c-diagram components from memory, and regression processes will go to work on them. What form these would take could at this stage only be guessed at. Presumably deletion and substitution of many of the "arrow" (dependency) relations connecting items, resulting in diagrams domited by PP's; similarly various ACTS might be deleted or more concrete ones substituted for more abstract ones. Also certain of what Schank terms "rules of conceptual semantics", which are essentially limitations on what may go into specified slots of c-diagrams, might be relaxed – for instance the rule for the conceptualization of "eat" requires a food in the object slot, so its removal could allow a typically bizarre event in the manifest content of the dream.

As far as condensation is concerned, it appears from Rieger's account that the mechanism of carrying it out may not be too difficult to design, but the more difficult and challenging task is how the "endopsychic defence system" briefly characterised above would determine what mergings were to be effected and how. A typical ploy might be that a highly "sensitive" conceptualization merging with an "insensitive" one would have to result in one much more similar to the latter than the former.

Similarly, displacement – which works hand in hand with condensation – will be determined by the requirements of the defence system. A fundamental problem here is how to characterise computationally Freud's concept of high or low "psychical value".

Secondary revision would probably be the least difficult of the components of the system to design, for many of the essential elements of it, namely those which try to "make sense" of the conceptual situation when there is contradiction, ambiguity or doubt, are already in Rieger's inferencer.

Like all such enterprises, the design of a dream transformer would be a combined theoretical-cum-experimental task, starting with the attempt to build a program which worked successfully on one particular input or limited set of inputs, then modifying it if necessary to deal with a larger set of inputs, under the constraint that it continues to perform adequately on the earlier ones. In the next section an example dream fragment taken from Freud's corpus is presented and briefly discussed as a possible first challenge to the design of a transformer.

10. The "365 Kreuzer dream"

This was part of a dream of one of Freud's patients in Vienna at about the turn of the last century, shortly before her treatment came to an end. She came from abroad and her daughter was at school in Vienna (To understand the dream it is necessary to know that the Austrian currency was based on the florin (= 100 kreuzers) approximately equivalent in value to 40 American cents of the time). The dream fragment is:

"I was going to pay for something. My daughter took 3 florins and 65 kreuzers from my purse. I said to her: 'What are you doing? It only costs 21 kreuzer".

The manifest content of this dream (which, incidentally, would be particularly easy to parse into a c-diagram) shows the characteristic low "psychical value", the apparent pointlessness, of the major part of most dreams. But its rather simple interpretation brings it back in focus. The daughter's school year was due to end in three weeks' time and this also meant the end of the lady's treatment. The day before the dream, the headmistress had asked her whether she would not consider leaving her daughter at school for another year. From this suggestion she had evidently gone on to reflect that in that case she might also continue her treatment. This is what the dream referred to. One year is equal to 365 days. The three weeks which remained both of the school year and of the treatment were equivalent to 21 days. The numbers, which in the dream-thoughts referred to periods of time, were attached in the dream itself to sums of money (not but what, Freud adds, there was a deeper meaning involved, for "time is money"). 365 kreuzer only amounts to 3 florins and 65 kreuzers; and the smallness of the sums that occurred in the dream was obviously the result of wish-fulfilment. The dreamer's wish reduced the cost both of the treatment and the year's school-fees.

So the transformer would have to output the c-diagram of the dream from the c-diagram of something like the following latent content of the dream:

"The headmistress wants my daughter to stay on another year after the present school year ends in three weeks' time. I would very much like this because that would mean I could stay in Vienna another year and so have a further year of treatment from Freud. But both the school and the treatment would be very expensive. I wish they could be much cheaper. And in fact the expense would be so great that really I should not contemplate more than the three weeks remaining".

Again the c-diagrams of this would not be particularly difficult to construct, and the reader should have no difficulty in identifying the various components and processes of the transformation required between the two diagrams: the day's residue, the wish, regression (e.g. the change from intangible, invisible time to solid money), condensation (e.g. the merging of the dreamer's treatment with her daughter's school attendance), endopsychic defence (e.g., neither probable costs or Freud appear in the manifest content), and displacement (all psychically "sensitive" conceptualizations deleted). It should be noted that in this example the displacement is of an extreme character - in other dreams "psychical value" may get transferred to components of the manifest content. In this example too, although the "psychical value" is low, coherence has been achieved by what is presumably a very simple operation of secondary revision.

11. Final remarks

In the earlier section entitled "Computational modelling" reasons were adduced why the attempt to formalize and implement computationally mental activities like those we have just discussed might be useful. A further bonus might be the following. The notions of "psychical value" and "endopsychic defence" would have to be clarified and made more precise in attempts at adequate modelling of these activities, and this could contribute to a better and new understanding of the whole subject of motivations, emotions and even instincts. This is admittedly one of the least well understood areas of mental science. Schank recognizes that the treatment of emotions in this system is quite primitive and deals with only the "tip of the iceberg" of the subject, and – in my view – the treatment of them in psychoanalytic theory is very ad hoc and not much deeper. Recent new ideas of Sloman on a computational approach to emotions may point the way forward.

Chapter 18

AN INTRASYSTEMIC APPROACH TO BELIEF

GABRIELLA AIRENTI and BRUNO G. BARA

Unita' di ricerca di intelligenza artificiale, Universita' di Milano, Italy

MARCO COLOMBETTI

Progetto di intelligenza artificiale, Politecnico di Milano, Italy

Summary

We propose a knowledge representation system consisting of two interacting subsystems, named K-theory and K-model, playing the respective role of conceptual and episodic knowledge. We define belief a model in K-model which is used by thought processes not directly, but through a meta-structure which predicates on it. Therefore, we claim that from an intrasystemic point of view the difference between knowledge and belief is determined by the logical level of representations, rather than by their structure or content.

1. Introduction

The distinction between knowledge and belief has concerned philosophers for a long time. Within artificial intelligence, however, this problem has received little attention, the trend being to consider all representations straightforwardly as knowledge. Quite recently, Abelson (1980) gave a thorough treatment of the differences between knowledge and belief systems. The aim of his work is to establish conditions enabling an external observer to decide to which of the two categories a particular system belongs.

The problem of belief can also be approached from a different point of view, by analyzing a single representation system to attribute the status of knowledge or belief to single representational items (Hintikka, 1962; Miller and Johnson-Laird, 1976). Cohen and Perrault (1979) and Perrault and Allen (1980) deal with this problem in the context of an AI application. To represent the beliefs of a system, they add to a first order predicate language the operator BELIEVE, referring to Hintikka for its definition. The operator BELIEVE is then used to define three different acceptations of the word "know": know that, know whether, and know what. The main point in the definition of "know" is that to know P is reduced to the conjunction of the actual truth of P and the belief that P is true.

While this approach, in the trend of formal logic, provides the neatest treatment of beliefs in an AI system, it is not psychologically adequate. In fact the distinction between knowledge and belief introduced by Allen, Cohen and Perrault relies on the actual truth of a fact. But, as we shall argue in the following, a human system cannot discriminate between external facts and their internal representations. This suggests that beliefs be analyzed from an intrasystemic point of view, that is only on the basis of their internal structure. Here the main question becomes the ability of the human system to subjectively assign to the information it uses the status of knowledge or belief.

As we shall argue in the following, the distinction between knowledge and belief in a human system relies on the differences in the logical level of representations.

2. The structure of knowledge

In Airenti, Bara and Colombetti (1983), we propose a knowledge representation system consisting of two interacting subsystems named K-theory and K-model, playing the respective roles of conceptual and episodic knowledge (Airenti, Bara and Colombetti, 1982). K-theory is essentially a theory of the external world, and can be conceived as a network of conceptual entities describing classes of objects, relations, processes, behaviour strategies, etc. (for example: the concept of a bottle; of x being on y; of x falling from y; of an agent z breaking x; etc.).

In a loose sense, the external world is a model of K-theory. However, the cognitive system does not deal directly with the external world, but with a set of partial internal representations of it, which are models of K-theory and constitute what we call K-model. In fact, there is no way for K-theory to reference entities in the external world: in the cognitive system, representations only can be mentioned and used. K-model contains all episodic knowledge of the cognitive system, i.e. knowledge about particular objects, facts, episodes, etc. (for example: the bottle B I am now perceiving; the fact that B is presently on the table T; the fall of B from T; etc.). These can only be expressed by means of the general conceptual machinery provided by K-theory.

The statement that K-model is a set of models of K-theory cannot be made more rigorous until a complete formal definition of both K-theory and K-model is given and the interpretation function is also formally defined. However, even at the present informal stage, the statement is psychologically significant. In fact, it amounts to the assumption that only those aspects of the external world for which a general conceptual description exists in the cognitive system can be represented and understood. We assume that the essential feature of K-theory is the ability to generate models for insertion and subsequent manipulation in K-model. For example, the concept of "bottle" is a structure in K-theory which constructs models of bottles whenever needed by a thought process. K-model contains the representation of the perceived world, which is continuously changing through time and space. As K-model is intended to capture the cognitive system's subjective experience, it does not only represent the perceived world, but also any possible imagined world. This corresponds to saying that any imagination process must produce data which belong to K-model, and thus satisfy K-theory. So K-theory determines the set of worlds which are possible for the cognitive system, i.e. the spectrum of all its possible subjective experience. This is the reason why K-model has been defined as a set of models of K-theory, each representing a possible external world - presently perceived or remembered or imagined.

Our approach to human knowledge representation can be defined as constructional. That is, the sole reality for the cognitive system is what is constructed by its thought processes using K-theory. Note that in such an approach K-model necessarily satisfies the part of K-theory used to build it. The partition of knowledge into K-theory and K-model is logical rather than functional. This is reflected by the fact that K-model, as noted above, collects data belonging to different thought processes. Actually, all data constituting perception, imagination, illusions, dreams, etc., are introduced through different thought processes, but share the same logical structure.

3. The intrasystemic definition of belief

As an example, let us suppose that Christopher's K-theory contains the assumption that all flying animals have feathers. This implies that in all models built by Christopher on the basis of such information, any flying animal will be represented as feathered. Regardless of the objective truth of this fact, such models will be used as knowledge by Christopher's thought processes.

Now, let us suppose that Christopher happens to see a bat, recognizing it as a flying animal. To represent the bat in his K-model, Christopher must face a problem, which has at least three possible solutions:

(i) since the construction of a model of an unfeathered flying animal would be conflicting with the models which can be derived from K-theory, either the new model is not constructed or the discrepancy is not appreciated;
(ii) the new model is re-interpreted (Christopher may assume that the bat's fur is an odd kind of feather);
(iii) the discrepancy between the models derived from K-theory and the new model is acknowledged.

While in the first two cases Christopher may keep his knowledge unchanged, it is reasonable to assume that ordinary thought processes cannot be carried on in the conflicting situation which arises in the third case. The conflict must therefore be faced by specific thought procedures. These require that the conflict existing in his K-model be represented explicitly.

Ordinary models, that we shall call first level models, refer to entities belonging to the external world, while the representation of the conflict refers to first level models, thus constituting a second level representation. We call belief a first level model, when it is not used directly by ordinary thought processes, but it is accessed through a second level structure, which predicates a relation of conflict of the model itself to other models. Beliefs, as models, are part of the cognitive system's knowledge. Their definition, which is strictly intrasystemic, refers neither to their internal structure nor to their content. Rather, the distinctive feature of beliefs is that they are handled through second level representations by specific thought processes. The first task of such processes is to detect the conflict in K-model and to build the second level structure representing it. Once it has been detected, the conflict has to be handled and possibly solved. To obtain this result, the thought processes can rely on the cognitive system's present knowledge and on any action apt to enlarge it (e.g. acquiring new information by asking somebody, reading a book, looking around, etc.). The goal of these processes is to make the conflict vanish. One possibility is the rejection of the new model with no modifications in K-theory; in this case the conflict will arise again each time the same situation occurs. Another possibility is to reject the old model and to modify K-theory according to the new model. A third solution is the restructuring of K-theory on the basis of both conflicting models. This phenomenon has a crucial role in learning, and has received much attention in psychological research.

4. Interpretations of belief

We have so far introduced a definition of belief applicable to a first level model, when considered in a conflicting relation with other models. Our hypothesis of a treatment through second level representations can be extended to include other usual acceptations of the term 'belief'. Note that we do not analyze this term from a linguistic point of view; instead, we postulate mental structures underlying linguistic expressions.

A relevant case is the attribution of a degree of certainty to a fact. Take for example Christopher's assertion: "I believe that John married Mary in Panama last year". We assume that in this case Christopher's K-model contains a model representing the marriage between John and Mary, and a second level structure which mentions this model and attributes to it a high degree of certainty. If Christopher's assertion were: "I know that John married Mary in Panama last year", only the degree of certainty would be different. The model of the marriage and the second level structure mentioning it would remain the same. Thus, the model of the marriage is treated as a belief also in the context of the expression: "I know that ...".

A further use of the term "belief" is shown by the expression "I used to believe that all flying animals had feathers". In this case the conflict occurred in the past; the old model still exists as an autobiographic memory. We therefore postulate that the cognitive system's self-representation (i.e. the part of knowledge referring to the system itself) contains an episode representing the situation in which the conflict arose and was solved.

Second level structures do not only apply to facts. In particular the assumptions on the existence of the entities represented in K-model can be expressed in a similar way. For example, a second level structure may exist, which mentions a model of Ophelia to predicate her existence in Hamlet's world.

The problem of existence regards not only objects, but also events, actions and episodes. The first level models representing such entities make no assumptions about their existence in the real or in a fictitious world. This allows the cognitive system to deal in the same way with entities which do or do not exist in the real world. As we have stated above, the problem of existence is faced by second level representations.

5. Conclusion

We have discussed the concept of belief, assuming an internal point of view, which we consider to be the most adequate for a psychological explanation. Many researchers commit themselves to the assumption that the distinctive feature of belief with respect to knowledge concerns the actual truth of a fact. From our psychological standpoint we have proposed a different position, focussing on the internal structure of knowledge and belief.

Our thesis is that second level representations allow a cognitive system to deal with a number of situations which fall within usual acceptations of the term "belief". In particular, we analyzed conflicting models, the degree of certainty of facts and the existence assumptions about entities. Our treatment of belief leaves open the problem of specifying the thought processes handling second level representations. In particular, it is not clear so far whether such thought processes structurally differ from the processes manipulating first level models.

Acknowledgments

For this research the Unita' di ricerca di intelligenza artificiale has been supported by a grant of the Consiglio Nazionale delle Ricerche, Comitato di Medicina, Gruppo di Scienze del Comportamento, for the year 1982.

Chapter 19

AN INTELLIGENT SYSTEM CAN AND MUST USE DECLARATIVE KNOWLEDGE EFFICIENTLY

JACQUES PITRAT

*Groupe de Recherche Claude-François Picard du C.N.R.S.
associé à l'Institut de Programmation de l'Université, Paris 6*

Summary

In order to use declarative knowledge efficiently, a program builds a structure representing all the possible solutions of the problem; then it uses the constraints generated from the knowledge for pruning this structure.

1. Introduction

An artificial intelligence program uses a large amount of knowledge. This knowledge is provided by experts, but it has to be formulated and codified in a convenient way. One important characteristic is modularity: knowledge is stored part by part, and any part can be added, erased or modified independently of the others. It is also advisable to favor declarative knowledge and avoid procedural knowledge. In other words, the expert states facts in his field of expertise, but he need not describe how these facts are to be used.

We might think that a program which only uses declarative knowledge is not very efficient. This is not true. For some problems, general programs are more efficient than specific ones. This happens when we use a sophisticated knowledge interpreter. Such an interpreter does not perform a systematic search among many possibilities. It first tries to deduce facts from the given knowledge to constrain the search. In some cases, it finds the solution without backtracking. Let us give a simple example: "John plays tennis with Mike. John defeats Mike 6 games to 3. On five occasions the person who served lost the game. Who served first?" We define the boolean functions:

$JS(I) = 1$ iff John serves the I-th game.
$MS(I) = 1$ iff Mike serves the I-th game.
$JG(I) = 1$ iff John wins the I-th game.
$MG(I) = 1$ iff Mike wins the I-th game.

The problem is given to ALICE [Laurière, 1976,1978] as:

[1] $MS(I) = 1 - JS(I)$.   Only one player serves a game.

[2] $I \neq 1: JS(I) = 1 - JS(I-1)$.   After each game, the player who serves changes.

[3] $MG(I) = 1 - JG(I)$.   Only one player wins a game.

[4] $\sum_{I=1}^{9} JG(I) = 6.$

John wins 6 games and 9 games were played.

[5] $\sum_{I=1}^{9} JS(I) * MG(I) + MS(I) * JG(I) = 5.$

The person who served lost the game on 5 occasions and we must find $JS1 = JS(1)$. The interpreter solved this problem without backtracking. It performed the following manipulations:

Using [1] and [3] in [5], it obtains

$$\sum_{I=1}^{9} JS(I) * [1 - JG(I)] + [1 - JS(I)] * JG(I) = 5$$

or

[6] $\sum_{I=1}^{9} JS(I) + \sum_{I=1}^{9} JG(I) - 2 * \sum_{I=1}^{9} JS(I)JG(I) = 5$

but [4] gives:

$$\sum_{I=1}^{9} JG(I) = 6$$

and using [2] it finds:

$$\sum_{I=1}^{9} JS(I) = 4 - JS1 + 5JS1 = 4 + JS1$$

so [6] becomes:

$$4 + JS1 + 6 - 2 * \sum_{I=1}^{9} JS(I) * JG(I) = 5$$

or

$$5 + JS1 = 2 * \sum_{I=1}^{9} JS(I) * JG(I)$$

JS1 has two possible values: 0 or 1. The second part of the equation is even, so 5 + JS1 is even and JS1 is odd. The only possible odd value is 1. John served first.

For such a problem, an exhaustive search is reasonable. This example has been given in order to show the behavior of the program. For more difficult problems, it can be obliged to perform some backtrack. But it does this when it has reduced the size of the initial problem, and, when it has made a choice, it deduces all the consequences of this choice, reducing the size of the new subproblem.

Two programs based on these ideas have been subject to experiment. First Laurière's program ALICE, which solves combinatorial problems, then my program for understanding natural language (Pitrat, 1981,1982). We will describe the principles of programs which use declarative knowledge efficiently.

2. Using declarative knowledge

As stated above, declarative knowledge is convenient for the experts who have to furnish a large amount of knowledge to an artificial intelligence program. They only state facts and need not indicate in what order the computer has to use them. The program must find a good sequence for their use. Let us for instance take an agreement rule in the grammar of French. In a declarative statement, we can say: "the article agrees with the noun in number and gender". In a procedural statement, we can say: "when we find an article, we look for the noun, then we verify that the gender of the article is the same as the gender of the noun, and finally we verify that the number of the article is the same as the number of the noun". In this last case, several choices have been made: we check the rule when we find an article (it would be possible to check it when we find a noun) and we check the gender before the number.

It is possible to give some indications of order in a declarative form, when this order is a characteristic of the problem, but not when this order indicates the sequence of processes. For instance, we can indicate: "the noun is after the article"; "after" gives an order as to the sequence of words of the input, but we are not forced to process the article before the noun. It is important to distinguish between the sequence of instructions of a program and the various types of orders which may exist in a problem: the order of the words, the order of the moves in a chess game, the chronological order and so on.

A program which receives declarative knowledge is general. If we change the data, it will solve another problem. Paradoxically, this general program may be more efficient than any program which receives procedural information, even programs written specifically for that particular problem class. When we write a procedure, we make choices on the sequence of actions. Usually, the best order is not the same for every set of data. The computer which is obliged to follow the sequence will have poor performances if it receives data for which the choice is wrong. For instance, if the data are a set of constraints, and if the program examines the most restrictive constraint last of all, it wastes a lot of time processing many possiblities which are eliminated by the last constraint. An interpreter of declarative knowledge can choose a sequence of treatment for each set of data. It it is clever, it first considers the most restrictive constraints for each problem, and has to perform a small set of computations. The best order is not always the same, it depends on the data. The intelligent interpreter can choose because it is not obliged to follow an order and its choice depends on the present situation.

We must only give the necessary information for defining the problem; every useless constraint may prevent the program from finding the solution quickly, when we use procedural knowledge.

For this reason, it is interesting to use declarative knowledge, even when the quantity of information given to the program is small. Laurière (1979) has described a problem for which his general program was more efficient than one specially written for that problem. In some cases, it has found in a few seconds of computer time the solution of problems which a specific program could not find in five minutes.

I believe that the approach of an intelligent interpreter of declarative knowledge is similar to the behavior of an intelligent and competent human being. We know how to choose, among the constraints, those which reduce the search. For that reason, people find good solutions in a reasonable time for problems such as the design of school time tables when computers find (only with difficulty) solutions which are not very good. For each school, the drastic constraints are not the same: some have a few special class rooms (for chemistry for example); others have many women teachers who need the extra time in the morning for children and prefer to start their classes one hour later. An interpreter of declarative knowledge will find at each step the constraint which is the most difficult to satisfy and it will adapt itself to all the details of the problem.

The interpreter first reduces the size of the problem, before possibly backtracking. So a problem with a large initial size will be solved without any backtrack if we are lucky, or with a very small number of choices. For instance, Laurière's program has solved the cryptarithmetic addition: DONALD + GERALD = ROBERT. Each letter represents a digit; for different letters, we have a different digit; the initial letters, D, G, R are not zero. The program found the solution and showed that it was unique with only five binary choices. It receives the problem as a set of constraints. Among them, we have:

$$D + D = T + 10 \times C1$$

$$L + L + C1 = R + 10 \times C2 \text{ (C1, C2 are carries)}.$$

It proves first that T is an even number, that E can only be 0 or 9. Its first choice is between $E = 0$ and $E = 9$. If $E = 0$, it deduces that $A = 5$, then $R = 2*L$ or $R = 2*L + 1$. There is a second choice: if $R = 2*L + 1$, we find $L = 3$, $R = 7$ and $D + G = 7$ which is impossible because it knows $D \geq 6$ and $G \geq 2$. So a possibility is eliminated ($E = 0$ and $R = 2*L + 1$) and it considers $E = 0$ and $R = 2*L$...

The program manipulates the constraints and tries to extract as much information as possible in a simpler form. If we have $B = N + R + 1$ and we know $N > 0$ and $R > 0$, we deduce simultaneously:

$$B \geq 4, \quad N \leq 7, \quad R \leq 7.$$

Human beings work in the same way, but are not so efficient. People do not solve this problem with this small number of choices. Computers usually make poor choices, but they counterbalance this weakness with their speed. An intelligent interpreter which makes better choices than we do opens new domains of possible applications.

It is not easy to implement an intelligent interpreter for declarative knowledge. But, as it is general, once the work has been done, it can be used for many problems. I will describe the principles of such an interpreter. I shall take as examples two interpreters which were implemented: the interpreter for the language ALICE (Laurière, 1976, 1978) solves various combinatorial problems. Another interpreter (Pitrat, 1981, 1982) receives syntactic, semantic and pragmatic information in a declarative form for understanding natural language.

3. The interpreter

The interpreter builds a structure concisely representing all the possibilities. It starts with a set of constraints. They are used for eliminating possibilities. If a constraint is always true, this constraint is erased. If a possibility violates some constraint, that possibility is eliminated. In some cases, the program eliminates all the constraints and it directly has the solution (or set of solutions). Otherwise, it backtracks, but in this case:

- the size of the problem is smaller
- it carefully chooses the variable for which it chooses a value
- after this choice, it resumes the main procedure for removing constraints and possibilities.

We will now describe the structure, and then see how the program uses the constraints.

3.1. The structure

The structure represents all the possible solutions. If something is not in the structure, it is not a solution, because it does not satisfy the constraints. At the beginning, the program has only constraints. It translates some types of constraint into the structure and it keeps as statements all the other constraints. The choice of the translated constraints is all important: we choose the types of constraints which are simple to translate and/or frequently occur in the problems. The definition of the structure depends on the choice of these types of constraints. We will consider these points in relation to the two interpreters which have been implemented.

1. The structure for the interpreter solving combinatorial problems (Laurière, 1976, 1978): If the goal is to find a function on the set E into the set F, the program builds:

- the list of the possible images for all i of E
- the list of the possible antecedents for all j of F.

The structure can contain other information:

- cliques of disjunction. Two nodes i and j are in the same clique if their images are different. This is very convenient if we have an injection.
- coefficients and valuations on nodes and arcs.

This information is frequently used in combinatorial problems and it is easy to manipulate it. But there are constraints which are not in the preceding form. For instance $V1 + V2 \leq 10$, where $V1$ and $V2$ are variables. Such a constraint is kept in this form and is not translated in the structure. But the interpreter tries to infer from it simpler constraints which can be put in the structure. So it can use in a weak form in the structure even the constraints which cannot be entirely translated. For instance it has in the structure variables which have integer values and it knows that the variable $V1$ may only have the values 3, 5 or 7 and the variable $V2$ the values 4, 7 or 8. The program deduces from the

Fig. 1

constraint $V1 + V2 \leq 10$ that $V1 \leq 6$ and $V2 \leq 7$. So it removes the possibilities $V1 = 7$ and $V2 = 8$. But it does not eliminate the constraint which is not always true; it is violated by the pair $[V1 = 5; V2 = 7]$. If, later, the program eliminates $V1 = 3$, (so V1 is definitely 5), the constraint will be useful for eliminating $V2 = 7$.

2. The structure for the interpreter understanding natural language (Pitrat, 1981): The program uses the grammar for generating a graph which can represent the ambiguities. In the examples, I will assume the following:

- The nodes of the same subgraph are on the same level.
- We represent the subgraph G1 which is linked to a node N of subgraph G2 as in Fig. 1.
- N is represented by two nodes N1 and N2, N1 being linked to the first node of G1 and N2 to the last one.
- There is also a link between N1 and N2.

It is possible that a node has several sons or several fathers or that a subgraph is linked to several nodes at an upper level.

It is very useful for representing the relatives or the preposition groups. For instance, "le Cavalier de la Dame qui est menacé va en d7" is represented by Fig. 2. There are two paths between "Dame" and "va", but the nodes of "qui est menacé" are represented only once. The interpreter, using the agreement rules, will eliminate later the shorter path between "Dame" and "qui".

The structure contains other information. For instance, the program keeps all the possible elements which can be referred by a pronoun and the pronoun "le" at node N can refer to the pawn d3, the pawn h4 or the bishop h2. At each node, it ties all the meanings which are still possible for the word at this node.

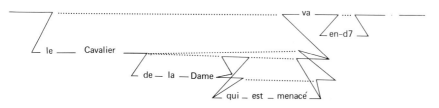

Fig. 2

The meaning representation consists of a set of objects. Each object is described by a list of pairs: attribute-value. The value part of a pair is the list of all the possible values for this attribute. For the attribute "piece that is played" of move Q, we may have two values: the rook d2 or the bishop f4.

The program building the syntactic structure representing all the possible syntactic analysis has been described (Pitrat, 1981).

3.2. Using the constraints

The constraints can be given directly to the program. For instance, in the Mike and John problem, it receives:

$$\sum_{I=1}^{9} JG(I) = 6.$$

But a constraint can also be generated by the program. For instance, in natural language, a rule on the agreement of the article and the noun generates a constraint whenever we have an article and a noun in the same group. A meaning will generate constraints such as: there must be a certain element at a certain node. The conditions which are in the declarative knowledge will also generate constraints. If there is a condition on an arc of the grammar, it will give a constraint whenever this arc is present in the structure.

When the program considers a constraint, it evaluates it, using the structure. For each type of constraint, there is a subroutine which can evaluate it. It is possible that several evaluations can be made, because the structure has many ambiguities: during an evaluation, the program may have to choose between several arcs, several values of an attribute, several meanings .... The number of choices made during the evaluation is important. We have four possible situations:

1. The constraint is always true, the program removes the constraint.
2. The constraint is violated and no choice has been made. The problem is impossible.
3. The constraint is violated and only one choice has been made. This possibility of choice is wrong and must be erased. The program keeps the choices and, in that case, it automatically eliminates the only choice.

Let us consider again the graph given in Figure 2 for "Le Cavalier de la Dame qui est menacé va en d7". A rule indicates that the pronoun "qui" agrees in number, gender and person with the noun which it represents - ("qui" is masculine so there is agreement with "menacé"). There is a choice in the path between "qui" and the noun; two arcs are starting backward from "qui". If "qui" refers to "Dame" which is feminine, the constraint is violated. So we eliminate the only choice which has been made – the shorter path between "qui" and "Dame" – and the ambiguity disappears.

A constraint may have various consequences: removing an arc, a meaning, a morphological possibility, a possible reference for a pronoun ... .
4. The last case happens when the constraint is violated, but the number of choices is greater than one. The program removes nothing, because it may happen that only one choice is wrong, and it cannot find which one.

In natural language understanding, there are many kinds of choices

- a word has several morphological possibilities: "les" may be masculine or feminine.
- a word has several meanings.
- a pronoun may refer to several nodes.
- several arcs start from a node of the syntactic graph.
- several arcs arrive at a node.
- an attribute of an object may have several values.

In all these cases, the interpreter automatically takes the good action if a constraint is violated and only one choice has been made.

An important problem is choosing the constraint to consider. Laurière (1976,1978) describes some metaheuristics for this metachoice. In the natural language interpreter, the idea is to begin with cheap constraints, such as an agreement which is faster to analyse than a verification using pragmatic knowledge. Also it first considers the constraints which will probably be more useful, which are likely to remove parts of the structure.

To sum up, the interpreter automatically finds the consequences of the constraints, removing the constraint or a part of the structure or putting it aside. It also chooses which constraint it will examine.

4. Results

Two programs have been subject to experiment. One (Laurière, 1976,1978) for combinatorial problems, and another (Pitrat, 1981,1982) for understanding natural language. Laurière's program has successfully solved many kinds of puzzles and real problems such as train time tables or a problem given by Pr. Schutzenberger (Laurière, 1979). For this last problem, the program had better results than a specific program written for the same computer in the same language (PL/I) by a good programmer. In a quarter of an hour, the problem was defined in ALICE. In one case, the interpreter found the solution in a few seconds when the specific program had to be stopped after five minutes of CPU!

The understanding natural language interpreter is written in Fortran, with possibilities of list processing. It has successfully treated "1 e2-e4 1 ... d7-d5. Attaquant le Pe4. Bien que pratiquée par des maîtres, cette poussée précoce, en ouvrant immédiatement le jeu, sert la cause des Blancs, qui disposent d'un temps d'avance" ("Attacking the Pe4. Although played by masters, this early move, which immediately opens the game, really helps White who gains a tempo").

The interpreter simultaneously uses syntactic, semantic and pragmatic information for removing ambiguities from the structure. At the end of the process, the structure contains the meaning representation and, as a by-product, the syntactic analysis of the sentence, both without ambiguities.

It is very interesting to use declarative knowledge for a program understanding natural language. It is easy to add, remove or modify the agreement rules, the description of the syntax, the meanings and the pragmatic knowledge. In this case, I use this approach more for giving the knowledge conveniently than for the sake of efficiency, although the computer time is acceptable: 0.6 seconds of Amdahl V/7 is necessary for building the structure for the sentence given above. For Laurière's program, the performance is excellent. This way, two advantages are obtained - problems are easier to define and solutions are found faster.

5. Conclusion

I believe that man is a general interpreter of declarative knowledge, and that we process constraints in ways similar to these interpreters, although not so efficiently. When people communicate, using a natural language, this language usually conveys declarative knowledge; natural language cannot accurately transmit procedural knowledge. Such an interpreter has many qualities:

− it is easy to define the knowledge.
− it is easy to modify the knowledge.
− as there is no a priori choice, it can adapt to the data just received, and it dynamically chooses the knowledge which is most useful. So it may be more efficient than a specific program.
− it infers, from constraints which are difficult to use, weaker constraints which are more manageable.

It is difficult to define an interpreter which has to use a great variety of constraints, but once it has been written it can be used for solving many problems. Naturally, it is always possible to write a specific program as efficient as the general interpreter, but in most cases, this specific program will be a subset of the interpreter from which we remove the subroutines which are used for constraints not present in the definition of this specific problem.

Such general interpreters will have many applications for solving combinatorial problems, especially in Artificial Intelligence. They are interesting because it is more pleasant to give declarative knowledge. But they are also interesting because they may be more efficient.

ARTIFICIAL AND HUMAN INTELLIGENCE (A. Elithorn and R. Banerji, editors)
Elsevier Science Publishers, B.V.
© NATO, 1984

Chapter 20

COMMON AND UNCOMMON ISSUES IN ARTIFICIAL INTELLIGENCE AND PSYCHOLOGY *

ROBERT J. STERNBERG

Yale University, New Haven, CT 06520, USA

Summary

The purpose of this chapter is to compare and contrast the kinds of issues with which scholars deal in the disciplines of artificial intelligence and psychology. In order to make this comparison, I will describe an experiment done in order to understand how people learn the meanings of previously unfamiliar words from the context in which they are embedded. The emphasis in my descriptions will be upon the kinds of issues that psychologists address and the kinds of issues I believe researchers in artificial intelligence address. The goal will be to show similarities and differences in the approaches of the two kinds of scholars to the problems that are relevant to both their concerns. It will be concluded, however, that there is a substantial amount of difference in the level of analysis at which researchers in the two disciplines approach aspects of problems, and in the methodologies they employ to solve these problems.

1. Introduction

When researchers in artificial intelligence and psychology congregate, should they choose to discuss their work, it is quite easy to tell the two kinds of researchers apart. The ease of differentiation of the two positions is not just a matter of the use by one group of researchers of computers and the non-use of computers by the other group of researchers. To the contrary, it is possible and indeed quite plausible for a talk in artificial intelligence not to mention computers at all, at the same time that it is possible and plausible for a talk in psychology to discuss computer implementations at great length. The differences seem to go well beyond mere forms and implementations of theories. My goal in this chapter is to elucidate what some of these differences are, and also to point out some of the similarities in approaches between adherents to the two disciplines. In order to concretize the presentation, I will use as an illustrative example a research project I have conducted in collaboration with Janet Powell, a graduate student at Yale. (This research is described in more

---

* Preparation of this report was supported by Contract N0001478C0025 from the Office of Naval Research to the author.

detail in Sternberg and Powell, 1983 and Sternberg, Powell, and Kaye, 1982.) One should note from the outset that no claim is made that our own psychological approach to the problem of learning new vocabulary from context is fully representative of what psychologist do, either in studying this problem or other problems. Moreover, I make no claim to represent universally the position artificial intelligence researchers would take with respect to the kinds of problems we address. Nevertheless, I believe that our approach is at least somewhat representative of that of the psychologists, and that our characterization of the issues people in artificial intelligence would raise is not totally false.

2. The problem

The psychological problem Jan Powell and I have addressed in our collaborative research is that of how individuals acquire the meanings of new words from context. In particular, we have sought to understand what factors make some words encountered in context harder or easier to learn. Thus, the question we as psychologists address is that of how people learn meanings of new words; from the standpoint of artificial intelligence, the question is one of how an intelligent system can be self-modifying during reading and thereby acquire new knowledge. As psychologists, we have also been interested in accounting for individual differences in people's learning of words from context. The analogue in artificial intelligence is the issue of why it is that some programs, whether they be chess-playing programs, theorem-proving programs, language-comprehension programs, or whatever, perform better or worse than do alternative programs. In summary, the two major questions we addressed are first, what accounts for variation in word difficulty, and second, what accounts for variation in people's levels of performance.

Pursuing for a moment the question of individual differences and their development, we believe that differential levels of expertise in verbal comprehension can be traced to people's differential abilities to acquire meanings of verbal concepts from context. Although we deal with simple verbal concepts (words) in the study I will discuss, we do not believe our theory is limited to word acquisition. An alternative model of verbal comprehension and its development has been proposed by Earl Hunt (1978). On this view, the development of expertise in verbal comprehension and individual differences in verbal comprehension can be seen as deriving from individual differences in speed of access to lexical information in long-term memory. The idea is that high-verbal individuals are more rapid and efficient information processors than are low-verbal individuals. At a general level, it is worth noting that psychologists generally experience a need for comparing their own theories and models to plausible alternatives. If no plausible alternative can be found, the question arises as to whether things could be any other way and as to whether the proposed theory is of any real psychological interest. This perspective seems to contrast with that of artificial intelligence, where the primary goal of researchers often seems to be to build a model that works. The question of alternative models is often not considered at all. But the task of the investigator in artificial intelligence is not therefore an easy one. Consider the present example. We need only account for what makes some words harder to learn than others. The investigator in artificial intelligence must build a system that can figure out how *any* words can be understood. Whereas we take for granted comprehension of words whose meanings are already known, the investigator in artificial intelligence cannot do this because he or she must build a program that understands all of the words with which it is presented. The program needs to read the whole text. In short, we take for granted a lot that the constructor of an expert system cannot.

3. Theory of decontextualization

Our theory of decontextualization consists of two parts. The first specifies the kinds of cues individuals use to infer meanings of words presented in context. The second consists of the variables that affect the usefulness of these cues when they are encountered in the reading of texts. I shall present only the most cursory description of our theory.

In the theory, we specify eight kinds of cues, namely (1) temporal cues (i.e., cues regarding the duration or frequency of X, the unknown word, or regarding when X can occur); (2) spatial cues, (i.e., cues regarding general or specific locations of X, or possible locations in which X can sometimes be found); (3) value cues (i.e., cues regarding the worth or desirability of X, or regarding the kinds of affects X arouses); (4) stative descriptive cues (i.e., cues regarding properties of X such as size, shape, color, odor, feel, etc.); (5) functional descriptive cues (i.e., cues regarding possible purposes of X, actions X can perform, or potential uses of X); (6) casual-enablement cues (i.e., cues regarding possible causes of or enabling conditions for X); (7) class membership cues (i.e., cues regarding one or more classes to which X belongs, or other members of one or more classes of which X is a member); (8) equivalence cues (i.e., cues regarding the meaning of X or contrasts such as antonymy to the meaning of X).

An example of the use of some of these cues in textual analysis might help concretize my descriptive framework. Consider the sentence, "At dawn, *Sol* arose on the horizon and shone brightly." This sentence contains several external contextual cues that could facilitate one's inferring that *Sol* refers to the sun. "At dawn" provides a temporal cue, describing when the arising of Sol occurred; "arose" provides a functional descriptive cue, describing an action that Sol can perform; "on the horizon" provides a spatial cue, describing where the arising of Sol took place; "shone" provides another functional descriptive cue, describing the second action that Sol can do; finally, "brightly" provides a stative descriptive cue, describing a property (brightness) of the shining of Sol. With all these different cues, it is no wonder that most people would find it easy to figure out that *Sol* refers to the sun.

Variables that affect the usefulness of these cues when they are encountered in context include (1) number of occurrences of the unknown word, (2) variability of contexts in which multiple occurrences of the unknown word appear, (3) importance of the unknown word to understanding the context in which it is embedded, (4) helpfulness of surrounding context in understanding the meaning of the unknown word, (5) density of unknown words, (6) concreteness of the unknown word and the surrounding context, and (7) usefulness of previously known information in cue utilization.

For the most part, the cues and variables described above (and discussed in more detail in Sternberg, Powell, and Kaye, 1982) are operationalized by having individuals provide ratings of their frequency or relevance in a given text containing unknown words. Whereas such ratings can be useful in experimental contexts, they are not of much help to the researcher who seeks to construct a program that understands text. In essence, ratings beg the questions of how an intelligent system (1) identifies cues, (2) recognizes the relevance of these cues to the decontextualization of a given word's meaning, and (3) actually uses the cues in figuring out the word's meaning. Thus, again, psychologists are able to gloss over what for investigators in artificial intelligence are crucial and difficult questions. It is not that psychologists are not interested in these questions, but rather that a given experimental investigation usually deals with some questions at the expense of others. In this particular case, our attitude was that there are certain important questions that will be left unanswered, but there are other important questions that we hoped the research would indeed address.

4. Method

The subjects in the experiment we performed to test our theory were 123 high school students. In psychological investigations, it is considered important that the experimenter use a fairly large number of subjects, if possible, and that the subjects be representative of the population to which the experimenter wishes to generalize. Questions of sampling seem to be ignored in most artificial-intelligence research. Indeed, none of the programs discussed in this book have been tested against human data at all. Thus, we have little, if any, idea as to the extent to which the programs model human performance. For psychologists, of course, the question of the degree to which a theory characterizes human data is paramount.

Our materials consisted of 32 textual passages of roughly 125 words in length. Each passage contained from one to four extremely low-frequency words. The subjects' task was to define these unknown words, using contextual information in a given passage to help infer word meanings. Passages were of four types: newspaper passages, literary passages, historical passages, and scientific passages. It was very important to us to obtain representation in the kinds of texts we used, just as it was important to obtain some representation in subjects. Generally, investigators in artificial intelligence seem to be much less concerned with representation of materials. The expert programs discussed in this book, such as CYRUS, MYCIN, and Berliner's chess program, handle only very narrow classes of task. It is quite understandable that artificial intelligence investigators would build programs that are fairly narrow, because as we saw above, they must confront a host of questions that psychologists can gloss over. But the issue remains: many of the expert programs are really quite narrow in the range of materials they can handle.

In our investigation, we also collected data regarding subjects' I.Q.s, standardized reading comprehension scores, and standardized vocabulary scores. The purpose of collecting these data was to relate scores on our task to scores on measures generally considered to assess verbal abilities. It was important to us to demonstrate that our decontexualization task was actually measuring verbal abilities. By correlating the mean rated goodness of subjects' definitions of unknown words (where goodness ratings were supplied by trained outside raters) with test scores, we hoped to show that ours was indeed a verbal comprehension task. I view this validation procedure as roughly comparable to a Turing Test. The question asked in a Turing Test is whether an outside person can converse or otherwise interact with a computer program such that the person cannot tell whether the interactant is a computer or another person. If the program does well what it is supposed to do, then the person testing the program should be unable to tell the difference between the program's behavior and that of an intelligent person performing the same task. In the cases of both psychology and artificial intelligence, the goal is to show by somewhat different methods that one's theory deals and deals well with the phenomena it is supposed to describe or explain.

The basic procedure in our experiment was to have the subjects read each of the 32 passages and define as best they could the unknown word. Fairly elaborate counterbalancing procedures were used to ensure a fair experimental test of the theory. For example, the order in which the passages were presented to the subjects was randomized. These concerns with elegance of experimental design are really quite analogous to programmers' concerns with program elegance.

5. Operationalization of theory

Our psychological theory was tested by mathematical modeling, in particular, linear stepwise multiple regression. In this procedure, a dependent variable is predicted from a set of independent variables. In our case, rated goodnesses of the definitions of each of the unknown words were predicted from rated values on each of the cues and variables in our psychological theory. The details of the quantification are unimportant for our present purposes. What is important is that the mathematical modeling was our analogue to getting a program to run. The mathematical model generates a set of predictions, that is, a pattern of performance, just as does a computer program. In each case, there is a predicted pattern of results that can be compared to human data if one wishes. Thus, mathematical models, like computer models, provide operational implementations of theoretical ideas. In both cases, there can be varying degrees of fit between the conceptual and operational models. In other words, it is the investigator's responsibility to make sure that the operationalization of the theory corresponds as nearly as possible to the theory of which it is supposed to be an operationalization.

6. Results

Our experimental data were quite auspicious for our theory. We performed several tests of the theory. Each of these tests has an analogue to what artificial-intelligence investigators can do to test their theories.

The first test we performed was of the relative strength of the mathematical model in accounting for the data. An analogue test in the case of artificial intelligence is to examine the extent to which program data correspond to human data. We found that the model gave a very strong account of the experimental data. The squared correlations between predicted and observed data ranged from .55 for newspaper passages to .84 for literary passages. The median R^2 was .66 for the four kinds of passages.

Second, we tested whether the predictions of the model differed from the null model. In other words, were we predicting at a level superior to that which would be expected by chance? The analogue in computer implementations is that of whether it is possible to get the program to run. In our experiment, prediction for all four passage types was in fact significantly better than chance.

Third, we tested our theory against plausible alternatives. The analogue in computer implementations is to test the performance of a given computer program against the performance of alternative programs that purport to do the same thing. For example, one might pit alternative chess-playing programs against each other. We found that our theory gave a better account of the data than did the alternatives against which we tested it.

Fourth, we tested whether the predictions of our model differed significantly from the true model. In other words, was there any systematic variation in the data that our model could not account for? A comparable test could be performed in comparing computer-generated data against human data. We found that there was in fact systematic unexplained variance in all four passage types. In other words, our model did not provide a complete account of the variation in our data.

Fifth, we examined whether the parameter estimates provided by the mathematical modeling made sense. In other words, did the regression weights for the various aspects of our theory fit together? In a computer implementation, the analogous question would be that of whether the computer is spending time and finding difficult those aspects of the task that one would in fact expect to involve considerable time or difficulty. One would not want the computer to spend most of its time on trivial aspects of a problem, nor to make errors in easy aspects of a given problem. In our own study, we found that some parameter estimates made sense, but not all of them did.

Sixth, we investigated residuals. The question here is that of where do the failures or misfits predictions occur. The analogue in computer implementations is to examine where, exactly, computer-generated output protocols differ from those of humans. Basically, what we found is that our model was just too simple to account for the many sources of information people used when learning meanings of new words from context.

Finally, we investigated the correlations between task scores and scores on the standardized ability tests. These correlations were .62 with I.Q., .56 with vocabulary, and .65 with reading comprehension. These correlations suggested the task provided a good measure of verbal skill. In sum, then, our account of decontextualization of new vocabulary seemed to be a good one, at least for a first task model.

7. Conclusion

To conclude, I have compared the kinds of thinking and procedures investigators in psychology and artificial intelligence might use in approaching a problem. I have used as a vehicle for this comparison a study Jan Powell and I have done on acquisition of meanings of new words presented in context. Although the procedures of investigators in psychology and artificial intelligence differ in a number of fundamental respects, I believe their concerns are very similar. Each kind of investigator seeks to understand how intelligent information-processing systems operate. Psychologists seek to do this by studying human behavior. Artificial-intelligence investigators seek to do this by building intelligent programs. Obviously, the operational concerns of the two kinds of investigators are quite different. But their substantive concerns seem actually quite alike. Conferences such as the one represented in this book help to elucidate the shared concerns of the two kinds of investigators and to improve communication between them. I would hope that as the years go by, communication will continue to improve, just as it seemed to over the course of this conference, in that eventually, the two kinds of investigators will be able to talk to each other meaningfully and comprehensibly, at the same time that they retain their distinct identities. I believe the maintenance of distinct identities is of some importance, because the converging operations the two kinds of investigators can bring to the study of intelligent systems provide together a more comprehensive understanding of the nature of intelligence than could any single kind of operation taken alone.

Chapter 21

A TAXONOMY FOR THE SOCIAL IMPLICATIONS OF COMPUTER TECHNOLOGY

IRA POHL

Computer and Information Sciences, University of California, Santa Cruz, CA 95064, USA

Summary

Today, because of great progress in machines, software tools, and theories of search efficiency and deductions, we begin to see the introduction of (quasi)intelligent artifacts into general use. Chess programs play at near master level; elaborate medical programs diagnose disease and prescribe treatment; and in limited English, home and office computers can interact, speak to and understand, humans.

Such machines are profoundly affecting the social fabric. This paper will present an analysis of these changes in terms of a three level delineation. This taxonomic hierarchy is novel and is intended to provide a framework to analyze the social and philosophical implications of computer technology.

The first and most minor changes are methodological shifts, such as the change from electric to electronic typing. The second level of change are the dislocating shifts, such as the increasing reliance on automation and robotry. The third and most difficult to grasp are the paradigmatic changes, such as how our self-image is affected by the widespread appearance of intelligent machines.

The paper will trace these developments and will speculate on what will come and what we need to be concerned with as a society.

1. Introduction

To create a machine intelligence is to seek the philosopher's stone of computer technology. Its achievement will lead to a new order of capability in handling intellectual complexity.

Today, partly because of great progress in theories of search efficiency and deduction, society is confronted with the introduction of (quasi)intelligent artifacts into general use. Chess programs play at near master level; elaborate medical programs diagnose disease and prescribe treatment and in limited English home and office computers can interact, speak to and understand humans.

Such machines are profoundly affecting the social fabric. This paper will present an analysis of these changes in terms of a three level delineation. The first and most minor changes are methodological shifts, such as the change from electric to electronic typing. The second level of change are the dislocating shifts, such as the increasing reliance on automation and robotry. The third and most difficult to grasp are the paradigmatic changes, such as how our self-image is affected by the widespread appearance of quasi-intelligent machines.

2. Classifying societal impact

We will use a three level classification of the social impact of computer technology. In increasing order of significance these are:

a) type 1 or methodological shifts;
b) type 2 or dislocating shifts and
c) type 3 or paradigmatic shifts

3. Classification scheme

Type	Examples	Consequence
Methodological	Word processors automated tellers	Improved productivity but essential skills not significantly impacted
dislocating	industrial robotics electronic funcs	large scale shifts in jobs and life styles
paradigmatic	artificial intelligence socialized machines	redefinition of Man's role or essence

4. Social problems of type 1

Type 1 changes are methodological shifts in which the technology changes how we do something but not what we do. In the small, electronic embezzlement of funds is a different method of embezzlement which has no large scale implication for how people will function. Indeed electronic fund transfer and credit use may aid in curtailing certain more violent crime – making them unprofitable.

It may be clever for the embezzler-programmer to remove fractional amounts from each payroll transaction trasferring these minuscule sums to her paycheck. But, we need only devise new methods of electronic auditing or minor emendation to law to accommodate this change in criminal tactics.

Similarly, the change from mechanical, to electric, to electronic typewriters changes some procedures, improves productivity but is a minimal change in procedure and in organized relations. The electronic theft is one to two orders of magnitude larger than conventional theft averaging according to some authorities $500,000. The shift to electronic typing and a displacement of paper technology by a magnetic/electronic technology is indeed a major change. Nevertheless, people will perform the same functions with a higher degree of efficiency.

5. Type 2 shifts: Social problems

Type two effects are those that create dislocating shifts in society and behaviour. One such shift is the beginnings of truly economical robotry with the prospect of totally removing mechanical activity as a form of meaningful human labor.

Currently about 25,000,000 Americans are employed in manufacturing. They chiefly sit on some form of assembly line using tools and machines to manufacture goods. This is on the order of 25% of the total work force. The first industrial revolution was a revolution that replaced human and animal energy by machine-energy by machine-engine power. The second industrial revolution will remove judgment and control of these tools from humans and place this logic within the tools themselves.

Sophisticated PUMA and UNIMATE robots cost between $50,000 and $150,000. Given a three shift day their operating costs are as low as $5 per hour. Human labor in industries that can afford this capitalization frequently cost between $12–20 per hour. Initially these robots are used in the most hazardous of environments such as areas with radioactive and chemical hazard; or as welding machines in auto assembly lines. This is high risk work that most enlightened unions are prepared to give up in return for a share of the overall productivity gain these units bring with them.

Predictions by robotics firms (i.e. optimistic from their viewpoint) are that less than 10,000,000 manufacturing jobs will remain by the year 2000. They expect this form of human labor to not unreasonably follow the employment patterns seen in American farming wherever the last century employment in the direct production of food dropped from over 50% to less than 4% of the labor force.

This furthering of automation will create a society where co-workers will be robots; where goods will not be repaired, as this craft of repair except as a hobby is becoming too labor intensive, but instead goods will be recycled. The dominant trades will be information intensive and include the government and service sectoras main employers. There will be the possibility of working remotely at home so that urban cores will decrease in importance as economic entities. They will increasingly be cultural and social centers. The shift out of an agrarian based labor intensive rural society occurred in the last 100 years. The shift into an information based automated society is seemingly happening within decades.

The principal road maps of this new society will be the telecommunication diagrams of the Bell System. Physical privacy will be far simpler than information privacy (the right to have others not know about you and your activities). We are now moving from an industrial based energy intensive urban socity to a post-industrial society with different living patterns and values.

6. Type 3 shifts: paradigmatic shifts

Type three changes are paradigmatic shifts in that they cause us to view ourselves in fundamentally different terms. For example, one could say that Marx caused a paradigmatic shift in that his theory as developed and practised changed both social relations and people's view of self. Now the prospect of machines which participate in decision making and socially interact requires a review of who we are and what is meant by "sentient being".

Let me propose a mildly ridiculous question:
Will an intelligent trash compactor have rights?

Before answering reflect on the following beliefs:

a) higher animals such as whales are sentient and have rights
b) fetuses have rights
c) aliens of great intelligence exist and would have rights

We use "rights" to mean moral entitlements that are similar to those accorded humans.

While I do not subscribe to all these beliefs many people subscribe to some subset of these beliefs.

Consider that some people will enter a raging fire to save property such as an art treasure; others to save a pet such as a cat; and others to save an infant. Others may become attached to machines as social beings and be prepared to sacrifice for them. We may grow to accept, much as we do in watching R2D2 and C3P0, in STAR WARS, that reasoning machines are socially desirable partners who must be accorded a franchise based on their possession of an identity.

Let us consider a mundane development, the increasing ability of machines to use voice input/output. The prospect of a set of chips having a limited machine English capability in the offing. These chips will speak and more importantly recognize rudimentary English. It will be the universal machine

English vocabulary. Now what can happen:

people will learn machine English
machines will need to know who is addressing them

The command spoken to your radio "turn-on", should not turn on all other appliances within earshot. The command "radio turn-on" should not turn on all radios. Therefore we will give names to appliances, cars, and machines, and they will only respond to voice identification on an ownership or use list.

"George – medium toast", will now turn on the toaster

But if george is told to wash dishes – it will not have that repertoire and will not be able to comply – so George will say "I do not understand – I am George Toaster-".

Just as humans are occupationally named e.g."Hal Ironmonger, Jimmy Smith, Dorris Farmer ..." machines will be to; "Daisy Dishwasher, Tommy Toaster", will be common machine names.

Now how will people be affected if they expect a marginally intelligent response from almost any device. It remains to be seen what can occur if machines are part of a socialized world. Already many children are addicted to playing elaborate electronic games against programs. In early studies autistic children and disturbed adults felt socially comfortable with ELIZA style programs, artificially intelligent dialogue programs able to appear conversational in the unrestricted use of English. Many human characteristics were projected onto the machine.

It is also the case that characteristics such as rationality, sanity, even-temperedness are highly valued. The human deliberative unemotional machine may indeed become a very important role model.

Meanwhile machines will continue to gain intellectual skills. Programs such as MACSYMA can perform marvelously sophisticated mathematics that was once the hallmark of only the most trained theoretical physicists. In its 308 page reference manual it lists such operation as symbolic integration, limits, polynomial simplification, ... operation most of us cannot do well or at all; and also included are mathematics that most of us cannot understand such as tensor functions, and I quote:

"RIEMANN [(i, j, k), (l)] yields the Riemann curvature tensor in terms of the Christoffel symbols of the second kind."

I include the following session where using MACSYMA without more than a naive knowledge of its repertoire I was able to solve a wide variety of calculus problems.

EXAMPLE MACSYMA SESSION solving calculus problems
Script started on Sat Jan 3 16:32:57 1981

1 VAX: vaxima
Vaxima 0.34
Wed Jul 9 17:29:03 1980
(c1) integrate(x**3/(x**4+1)**3 x);

(d1) $\quad -\dfrac{1}{8(x^4+1)^2}$

(c9) integrate (1/sin(x),x);

(d9) $\quad \dfrac{\log(\cos(x)-1)}{2} - \dfrac{\log(\cos(x)+1)}{2}$

(c11) integrate (1/(x*(x+1)**2),x);
  [*list:743(48%); fixnum:32(5%);]

(d11) $\quad -\log(x+1) + \log(x) + \dfrac{1}{x+1}$

Furthermore, work such as my own on search theory have enabled programs to play chess at near master level with the prospect that before the twenty first century machines will outplay all human opponents. Indeed such artificially intelligent search and deductive programs now are consulted in building molecules and selecting treatment for disease. We are of course unaware of the extent they maybe used in selecting national defense and economic strategy – though evidence exists that they are critical to these most important decision making activities.

"The resulting uses of such machines might produce widespread unemployment. They might be used as a centrally-controlled police force. They might produce a cornucopia of goods and a generally affluent egalitarian society. Any number of possibilities, both threatening and beneficial can be imagined. However the possibilities cannot be attributed only to the potential of artificial intelligence. Computer-aided instruction in education, information retrieval systems, and operations research applications all create problems of the same kind. The unique aspect is the realization that an "average" intelligence does not stand as a barrier. The intelligent learning machine will have a nearly "unlimited" eidetic memory and will continue to benefit from faster circuitry and improved programming at a rate unmatched by organic evolutionary refinement.

"The Copernican revolution displaced earth as the center of the universe. The industrial revolution shifted the "burden" of physical labor onto machines. The Darwinian revolution replaced destiny by evolutionary accident. All of these intellectual and societal shifts have acted to reduce "the place of man in the cosmos". They have acted to destroy a presumption of uniqueness. The development of intelligent machines, if it happens, is diminishing a last pillar of human stature. This diminution will occur in proportion to the degree and nature of intelligence created in computers." (The Nature of Computation, by Pohl and Shaw, p. 343, Comp. Sci. Press, 1981.)

It is clear that we are undergoing a paradigmatic shift in our social relations toward our machines and toward our self-conception as productive beings responsible for decision making and economic production. We may end up in a much better place, a place where all this intellectual and productive power increases the richness of our environment. I prefer such an end result to either one which has us parasitic beings in a GARDEN of EDEN or to one which has us servants to the GOLEM. Both of these are longtime myths promoted by those who do not trust to human reason. I prefer to see this instrument as a telescope of the mind, one capable of enabling us to with dignity solve the increasingly complex problems of society.

ARTIFICIAL AND HUMAN INTELLIGENCE (A. Elithorn and R. Banerji, editors)
Elsevier Science Publishers, B.V.
© NATO, 1984

Chapter 22

REASONING IN NATURAL LANGUAGE FOR DESIGNING A DATA BASE *

MARCO COLOMBETTI, GIOVANNI GUIDA, BARBARA PERNICI
and MARCO SOMALVICO

MP-AI PROJECT,
Milan Polytechnic Artificial Intelligence Project, Dipartimento di Elettronica,
Politecnico di Milano, Italy

Summary

The goal of our research is based on the choice of just one knowledge representation framework for both the exigencies of (i) extracting from a natural language sentence the operative information which allows the formalization of data and transactions related to a data base to be constructed, as described by an interested user of such data base, and (ii) setting up the inferential process, by means of a search within the knowledge representation, which allows the definition and incremental improvement of the data base schema upon which the data base will be constructed.

The paper describes both the specifications and the architecture of NLDA (Natural Language Design Aid) system, which is being developed at the Milan Polytechnic Artificial Intelligence Project.

1. Introduction

The role of Computer-Aided Design (CAD) has been, in the last years, increasingly important both for the wide spectrum of application considered and for the increasing effectiveness of computer architecture and software systems. One important performance of any CAD system is related with the man-machine interaction language and with its characteristics of simplicity for the adoption from a casual user (Codd, 1974; Mylopoulos, 1976; Walz, 1977).

One of the most interesting application domains for CAD lies in the field of the design of data bases (Ceri, 1979). An important and difficult task for a CAD system devoted to data bases is the design and construction of a data base schema. In such a CAD system a typical user of the data base to be constructed specifies in natural language to the computer examples of data,

---

* The research reported in this paper has been supported by the Italian National Research Council (CNR), Progetto Finalizzato Informatica, Sottoprogetto P2B, obiettivo DATAID.

transactions, events and constraints which will be performed on the constructed data base. The flow of various interactions of this type, performed by the user, will provide the information utilized to build up, within an incremental process, the data base schema.

What promises to be an interesting standpoint for original research in Artificial Intelligence is the fact that both in natural language (Charniak, 1977: Wilks, 1975) and in problem solving (Hendrix, 1978) there is the need to set up a knowledge representation which contains the information about the semantic domain. The goal of our research is that of choosing just one knowledge representation framework for both the exigencies of (i) extracting, from a natural language sentence, the operative information which allows the formalization of data, transactions and so on and (ii) setting up the inferential process, by means of a search within the knowledge representation which allows the definition and incremental improvement of the data base schema. We will call such union of natural language understanding and problem solving for inferring the data base schema, reasoning in natural language.

Thus, the purpose of this paper is to present a new approach to the development of the role of close interaction between Artificial Intelligence and data bases, namely the application of reasoning in natural language to the development of a CAD system devoted to the inference of a data base system on the basis of user interactions describing the user's requirements in natural language. This research is based on our previous work done in natural language understanding, with the development of the DONAU and NLI systems, both devoted to the query in Italian of relational data bases (Guida, 1978,1979,1980). The new system, which is being developed at the Milan Polytechnic Artificial Intelligence Project, is called NLDA (Natural Language Design Aid) and is part of the Computer Science Program of the Italian National Research Council, Obiettivo DATAID.

In the paper we will present both the specifications of the system together with the description of its architecture. The paper is organized as follows: section 2 will propose the statement and the purpose of the NLDA project; section 3 will present the NLDA functional specification; section 4 will describe the basic architecture for the NLDA system; section 5 will finally illustrate the perspective for future research work together with concluding remarks.

2. Statement and purpose of the project

Our work started with the study of the methodologies of natural language understanding (Courtin, 1977; Weizenbaum, 1977; Winograd, 1973; Woods, 1970).

Extensive bibliographic research on this topic has been done in order to examine the systems already inplemented and their methodologies. The systems already existing that understand natural language for the application to the data base domain are criticizable for a number of reasons: either only queries to a data base are considered or the considered examples are very simple or the application to a data base is only a test for methodologies of natural language understanding (Ershov, 1975: Schank, 1979: Simmons, 1970). Therefore a system has been proposed that formalizes informal specifications of the end users of a data base according to the DATAID methodology that has been chosen for the design of a data base.

The architecture of the interactive system of formalization, building and verifying of the schema is that of Fig. 1. Two things have to be specified in advance:

a) a *dictionary* of the Italian language that understands, besides general type words (articles, prepositions and so on) those words that are related to the particular environment to be examined (for instance a university, a bank);
b) what *kind of texts* can appear in the users' specifications (whole texts, sequences of sentences, kinds of sentences, examples).

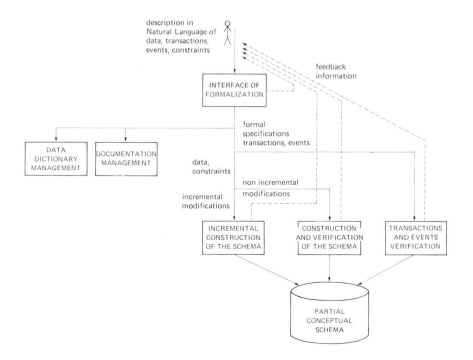

Fig. 1. Architecture of the interactive system of formalization, construction and verification of the schema.

These two elements are necessary to *project* the *interface* between the user and the computer that understands natural language. While the construction of the dictionary is a technical part of the project of the interface, the definition of the kinds of texts that are supplied by the users is already needed in the first steps of the project.

Let us now briefly describe the informal specifications that the user is expected to provide. We assume there are complete texts resulting from already existing files, interviews, specifications of transactions, free texts and so on, already partitioned in sentences. These sentences are examined one by one by the interface that understands natural language. These sentences can be:

- *data sentences*, that describe the environment and the objects to be included in the data base, the relation between them and so on;
- *transaction sequences*, that specify the operations that are to be performed on the data base;
- *event sentences*, composed by a condition part and an operation part. The condition can be a calender condition, something that happens and so on;
- *constraint sentences*, that express that something must happen (or can never happen) in the data base;
- *dialogue sentences*, whose specifications concern both the methodology and the interaction with the user.

We think it is important that the user can write in natural language sentences concerning the requirements of the enterprise that wants to have a data base (the first four types of sentences), while the dialogue with the system can be done in an interactive way following a question-answering procedure. The types of sentences examined by the methodology are those utilised to build the first skeleton of the schema. The sentences used for modifications of the schema are of the same type; only the use that the computer will make of these sentences changes.

First of all, the sentences are to be partitioned in the four types mentioned above. The pieces of information that must be extracted from the sentences are of a different nature:

- information useful for distinguishing between elements of the schema (entities, attributes) and correspondence between these elements;
- information needed by the following steps of the methodology (construction of data glossaries, tables, documentation and so on);
- information for the resolution of conflicts (synonyms, homonyms, understanding of doubtful or inexact words, in this case with the help of the user [feedback]).

3. System specifications

Functional specifications of the system have been largely discussed with possible users and experienced system analysts operating in the area of data base applications. From the hardware point of view the system is conceived as a working station (possibly a portable one) built up of a keyboard, a (graphic) display, and an optional serial (graphic) printer, connected with a host computer, which supports the data base design application. The system accepts as input the users' requirements. Two basic modes of operation are recommended:

- *off-line*: the system is connected with a lower module for collecting, updating, and processing the users' requirements in order to support the development of documentation and data dictionaries;
- *on-line*: in addition to the above specifications, the system is connected with an interactive module for the computer assisted design of the conceptual schema.

The system must operate in an interactive way and the man-machine dialogue must be easy and natural without any overhead for communicating commands, messages and meta-information. Different modes of communication must be allowed: formal query, multiple choice interrogation (hierarchical measures and tables), graphic interaction (diagrams and forms), free text in natural language. The system must operate through stepwise refinements to construct and verify the conceptual model according to the user's requirements. The user must be constantly informed of the design activity performed by the system and must be allowed effectively to interact with it in validating or rejecting the system choice or in proposing different design criteria.

4. A basic architecture

We shall now sketch the architecture chosen for the NLDA system. The interface of formalization (see Fig. 1) is analysed into modules in Fig. 2. The requirements in natural language provided as inputs are analysed by a module having access both to a model description of data, transactions, events and constraints and to a natural language dictionary. Then specifications are generated as output. The process of synthesis will then yield the skeleton schema.

There are two possible design implementation choices for the NLDA system; to illustrate them we shall refer to solutions a) and b) in Fig. 3. In solution a) the only activity of the system is to recognize the types of the sentences and formalize them, using for the Interface a Representation Lan-

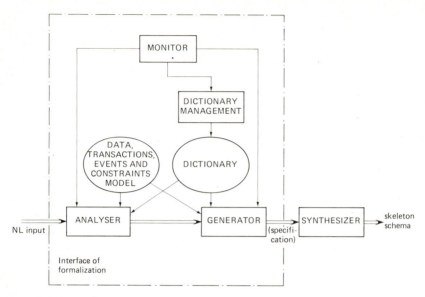

Fig. 2. A basic architecture.

guage RL and formal specifications suited to the four different types of sentences.

However, RL and the specifications are formally equivalent; from this consideration descends solution b) that utilizes the internal complex representation of the sentences in the Interface, not only for the simple formalization of

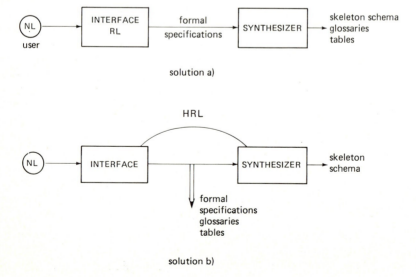

Fig. 3. Two solutions for NLDA.

the sentences, but also for the construction of the skeleton schema, the glossaries and so on. A Homogeneous Representation Language (HRL) is used both by the Interface and by the Synthesizer. While the process of analysis may be reconducted to classical natural language processing techniques, it must be stressed that the generation of schema, glossaries and so on will probably require a large amount of reasoning.

The dictionary and the model of data etc. will constitute the knowledge base allowing the Interface of formalization to carry on generation. We expect the kind of reasoning involved to be mainly about the meaning of natural language words within the context described by the model.

5. Perspective and conclusions

In the paper the specifications and the basic architecture of an interactive system devoted to supporting the use of natural language in the computer assisted design of data bases have been outlined. Particular emphasis has been given to the novel and stimulating research topic of natural language reasoning, which constitutes the case subject of the project proposed, and which involves some of the most basic issues of Artificial Intelligence, such as natural language understanding, common sense reasoning, hypothesis formation, and deduction (Nilsson, 1980).

The research activity on natural language reasoning on which the development of the system proposed is based will involve some basic choices concerning knowledge representation and algorithms. In particular, a frame-like model of knowledge (Minsky, 1975) is being developed to support the definition of the internal representation (HRL) language; a dependency based (Gaifman, 1965) syntactic analysis and a goal-oriented semantic model (Schank, 1979; Guida, 1980) are considered as appropriate for the natural language understanding process; a rule based production system (Nilsson, 1980) will be used to implement reasoning and deduction activities. These topics deserve intensive research effort to be done in the near future both to solve several open problems in the areas of natural language understanding and common sense reasoning and in facing the novel and very stimulating issue of their natural interaction.

The development of this research will involve theoretical and methodological investigation as well as experimental activity on the computer to implement a running version of the system sketched in this paper.

Acknowledgements

We are indebted to the researchers of DATAID project for stimulating discussions and useful suggestions. In particular we are grateful to A. Birga, M. Caldiera, P. Gargiulo, B. Graziado and F. Loiacono of Italsiel s.p.a. for providing useful experience and several case studies of actual interest.

ARTIFICIAL AND HUMAN INTELLIGENCE (A. Elithorn and R. Banerji, editors)
Elsevier Science Publishers, B.V.
© NATO, 1984

Chapter 23

A COMPUTERISED STRUCTURE FOR A GENERALISED INFERENCE-ENGINE

A.G. BURRING

Computer Centre, Plymouth Polytechnic, PL 4 8AA, UK

1. Introduction

This current project is an extension of research undertaken into the structure of existing problem solving methodologies (PSM's). These vary from simple two stage versions to those containing complex 50 + stages/phases. The common background to the greater majority of these PSM's is Systems Analysis/Operations Research. This analysis, together with commentary from authorities on the subject led to the conclusion that the structure of a basic algorithm exists, which is recursive and epistemologically dependent.

Using this algorithm as a bedrock, an "empty" model was adduced which was then fleshed-out to form a generalised problem-solving structure. It must be stressed at the outset that what has been, and is continuing to be, the subject of research is structure and not content.

The objective is to develop and validate the algorithm thence to do the same with the generalised structure.

2. Models

The models to be developed as adduced from prior research are:

BPSA: The Basic Problem Solving Algorithm. Irreducible, recursive and epistemologically determined.
UPSP: The Universal Problem Solving Process. An "empty" model comprising the BPSA together with a "shell" for constraints as declared.

3. BPSA: The basic problem solving algorithm

This logically irreducible model, or algorithm, is isomorphic with e.g. Dewey's (1910) model of Problem; Solution; Selection but has been transformed synonymically in an attempt to reduce ambiguity of terms. The synonyms chosen are Problem; Options; Decision (POD).

This has structure in common with models from other disciplines, e.g. Systems Theory (Input; Process; Output). At a lower level, some form is lost e.g. Stimulus-Response and Black-Box models leave the middle stage inscrutable.

At the lowest and simplest level, the problem and a criterion for decision must be in existence (or at least perceived) and the evaluation is a simple matching of the options against the criterion, i.e. it is deterministic. This leaves only the option stage, which essentially one of knowledge acquisition (or search). The POD structure implies heuristics, yet itself remains an algorithm.

Problem-solving in essence, therefore, is synonymous with knowledge acquisition and knowledge is the province of epistemology.

4. Epistemology

Writers such as Pierce, Hospers and Wallace give taxonomies of epistemology. Hospers' (1956) is the most detailed:

1. Sense experience
2. Reason
3. Authority
4. Intuition
5. Revelation
6. Faith

These 6 elements are used within the "options" stage of the algorithm, and are ranked in the order they are listed. This implies a logical-empiricist Weltanschauung.

The foregoing remarks concern the "statics" of the structure. Problem solving "dynamics" can be argued to be recursive.

5. Recursion

Four of the PSM's analysed use recursive procedures, although the term is not made explicit. Most people would accept that non-trivial problem-solving uses iteration, and some 25% of the PSM's studied refer to the topic.

Recursion is a special case of iteration where the algorithm calls itself, i.e. using multiple incarnations thereof. Humans have trouble with 3 or more levels of recursion as the experiments of Miller and Bard (Miller, 1970) demonstrated. Computers are not subject to such severe limitations.

The dynamics of the model also embrace the facility to broaden or narrow the problem. Easton (1973) uses the terms of "Teleological" and "Instrumental". The terms used in the BPSA are "excursive" and "incursive" respectively.

From the current research project it appears that, even for trivial problem-solving, perhaps as many as 3 or 4 incarnations of a POD are necessary to handle all the constraints present (either explicit or non-explicit).

6. UPSP: The universal problem solving process

The next higher order of model can legitimatley be called a "process". This process is universal as it is considered to be content and environmentally independent, viz. it is an "empty" structure.

It should be remembered that the BPSA is an algorithm which requires entities to process. In computing terms it can be shown as:

$$\text{Symbolic representation} + \text{ALGORITHM} = \text{PROCESS}$$

The first term here is context dependent – i.e. the process is one of computation – and computers deal in symbols. A more context independent formula could be:

$$\text{CONSTRAINTS} + \text{ALGORITHM} = \text{PROCESS}$$

This is declared to be the Universal Problem Solving (UPSP). Similarity between this equation and Michies':

$$\text{Expert System} = \text{Inference Engine} + \text{Knowledge Base}$$

can be seen.

7. Current status of the project

A paper and pencil model has been generated at the UPSP level – i.e. it should be amenable to any class of problem. The rules of excursion and incursion (kinematics) are being created.

The aim is to test and enhance the rules that have been developed to articulate the dynamics of the process. Consultation is maintained with the Polytechnic's department of Psychology, to discuss insights obtained and to ensure progress does not become at variance with models of cognition without there being adequate explanation thereof.

A first-cut computer program (using PROLOG) is expected to be in operation by June 1982. At that stage experimentation can start with the man-machine symbiosis that is anticipated.

Chapter 24

EXPERT EVALUATION IN LOGIC OF ENVIRONMENTAL RESOURCES THROUGH NATURAL LANGUAGE

LUIZ MONIZ PEREIRA, EUGENIO OLIVEIRA and PAUL SABATIER

*Dept. de Informatica, Universidade Nova de Lisboa,
Quinta da Torre, 2825 Monte de Caparica, Portugal*

1. Introduction

Sophisticated artificial intelligence techniques have been increasingly used in knowledge engineering to build useful understandable and highly performant systems called Expert Systems.

There are several formalisms to represent knowledge such as production rules, semantic networks and frames, among others. But for the sake of transparency declarativity and easiness we choose to represent and compute all kinds of knowledge in an unique formalism. This homogeneous formalism is a subset of predicate first order logic named Horn Clause Logic, on which the programming language PROLOG (Warren, Pereira and Pereira, 1977) is based. We use it to represent domain knowledge (inference rules and facts), meta-knowledge (knowledge about that knowledge), natural language syntax and semantics.

Knowledge is expressed not only explicitly (facts encoded by unit clauses) but also by means of axioms which are manipulated deductively in order to answer complex queries by deriving new facts from old ones.

We call this kind of system a Logic Data Base, a query is regarded as a theorem to be proved from the assertions (see Kowalski, 1981, for comparison with work in the Data Base field, namely Relational Data Bases).

2. ORBI

ORBI is an expert system for environmental biophysical resource evaluation, commissioned by the Portuguese Government and developed with the collaboration of the Department of Environment. What makes ORBI of an enormous utility is that it has not only the knowledge of one expert (or a set of them) in a certain restricted domain, but expertise on several disciplines like geology, hydrology, fauna, flora, microclimate and so on, to obtain results about the interdisciplinary domain of biophysical resource evaluation. ORBI makes judgements about the aptitudes of certain regions for industry, agriculture, recreation, and others. Related, observed basic data are digitized into quantified descriptors (e.g. risk of soil erosion). By means of inference rules established with the help of experts, we obtain quantified values for aptitudes which reveal the environmental assets available relative to human needs (e.g. intensive agriculture) The descriptors' values at representative points on a grid over a map are codified as facts in unit clauses. The values range from 0 to 5 and to each is attached a representativeness (from 1 to 5), which measures the extent to which the region represented by the point is homogeneous for that value. ORBI can communicate with the user in two modes: using natural language interface and letting him have the initiative, or by taking the initiative and conducting the user through a menu of fixed questions. The system can be switched from one mode to the other at any time. We want our system to have in the near future more meta-knowledge as well as the ability of acquiring new knowledge directly from the expert, the whole being represented in first order predicate logic.

3. Natural language consultation

In the natural language mode of consultation each question goes through linguistic processors providing for different analysis (morphological, syntactic and semantic). As a result of natural language query the output of the linguistic parsing is a logical sentence (a list of ordered goals) directly executable by Prolog, as in CHAT80 (Warren and Pereira, 1981) and MICROSIAL (Pique and Sabatier, 1981) systems.

The syntactic and semantic analysis is realized by means of grammar containing rules and controls. Rules handle the fundamental structures of Portuguese, in particular:

- yes-no and "why" questions
- affirmative, negative, relative prepositional, coordinate, extraposed and elliptic clauses;
- complex noun complementation and adjunction;
- universal, existential, numeral, definite and indefinite determiners;
- anaphora and pronouns; and nouns, verbs and adjectives specific to the application and to the linguistic terminology.

Controls verify number and gender agreements, designation of complex entities, and noun and verb complementations. unknown words, incorrect queries, grammatical faults, and erroneous designations and complementation are pointed out to the user, inviting him to correct them.

At any time, the user may ask ORBI on how he can formulate his question, calling its structures, vocabulary and examples of queries. The linguistic knowledge necessary for such abilities – which dispense the user from consulting a (complex and difficult) reference manual – is not entirely grouped in a specific database, but also expressed and computable from the different natural language processors' clauses (morphology, dictionary, grammar). Future developments will consider allowing ORBI's grammar to be consulted as a linguistic database for making the accepted structures implicit and for giving examples of queries. Its linguistic abilities might be extended to point out parts of a sentence ORBI cannot understand, to force analysis of incorrect strings, and to allow the user to define new structures and words.

4. Implementation

The PROLOG interpreter, itself a consequent driven production system, has fixed depth-first, right-to-left strategy with backtracking on failure. Nevertheless, we wrote a small interpreter in PROLOG itself embedding a problem-dependent strategy to execute deterministic computations first, and to look at the code to generate explanations. The whole system is implemented on a small 64K DEC LSI 11/23 with associated video terminal, a digitizer and graphic terminal. The programming effort has been of about two man-years.

5. Remark

This paper describes the state of our system in 1981. Subsequent improvements are reported in Pareira, Oliviera and Sabatier (1982), and Pareira and Oliviera (1983).

Chapter 25

A SKETCH ON ACQUISITION BY HIGHER COGNITIVE CONCEPTS *

CHRISTOPHER U. HABEL and CLAUS-RAINER ROLLINGER

Technical University Berlin, Institut für Angewandte Informatik,
Franklinstrasse 28 – 9, D - 1000 Berlin 10, Federal Republic of Germany

It is our view that a (conservative) natural-language question-answering-system is a system with very restricted learning abilities: one has to discover each single inference-rule on one's own as a knowledge engineer, and if the rule-system does not describe the reality in a correct manner, the rule-system has to be changed manually. So there are two problems: the first one is the domain-dependence of the rules and we formulate the question: where do all the inference-rules come from? The other problem arises due to the rule-system to be static: what can we do, if the rule-system is inconsistent with the incoming data or facts, unless it has a possibility to regulate itself?

One of the main classes of inferences in a (human or non-human) natural language system is defined by semantic relations among lexical concepts. By means of the relation "conceptual entailment" (Miller 1978) among sentential concepts the meaning of lexecal concepts can be described (and represented as a bunch of inference rules). We call these "lower" concepts. Furthermore we propose "predicate-attributes" (e.g. "transitivity" operating on two-place predicative concepts, different types of "conversity" (strong and weak converse) operating on pairs of predicative concepts). We believe that they are needed for reasons of cognitive economy. The inferential (procedural) knowledge about "predicate-attributes" is represented by a further theoretical entity, "rule schemata", to generate inferential rules.

The relations among attributes are expressed as meta-rules to generate hypotheses about and for checking the consistency of the rule-system.

By means of the cognitive entity "support set" problems like the transitivity problem and similar ones can be described (and - we believe - be solved). Support sets can be interpreted as the domain of predicate-attributes. Using these "higher" concepts (predicate-attributes and support sets) it is possible to develop limited learning/acquisition-strategies for the meaning of lower con-

---

* This is the abstract of the longer version presented at Lyon (Habel and Rollinger 1981).

cepts and strategies for the detection of inference rules. Presupposing the existence of such concepts in the human mind the notion "characteristic situation for higher concepts" (CS) is defined and explained by the example of transitivity. CSs are the empirical evidences necessary for hypothesizing any correspondence between a pair of a lower and a higher concept. E.g. By finding some CS's for transitivity of a predicative concept (e.g. older-than) the system is able to hypothesize the transitivity of the comparative-relation between "age" and "older-than". By further evidence, for example travelling around the world, the assumption of a global support set of "east-of" is refuted and it is necessary to change the hypothesis to a "local" support set.

In this stage, we do not take into consideration the behaviour of human beings while describing the world. For example people formulate their statements rather in a positive than a negative way. Also we do not profit by the fact, that usually concepts to be learned are offered together - as of now (1981), we have no regard to context.

Further developments of the basic ideas of this article are described in more detail in Emde, Habel and Rollinger (1983).

Chapter 26

SIMULATED COMPUTER SYSTEMS FOR INTELLIGENCE AMPLIFICATION

GERARD DE ZEEUW

Subfaculteit Andragologie, Universiteit van Amsterdam, The Netherlands

Usually intelligence is defined as a property of (the behavior of) an organism, or more formally, a system, its level being dependent both on the internal organization of the system and on the observer who is identifying the system. In attempting to increase intelligence, the most frequent approach is to change the internal structure of the relevant system (e.g. via teaching, change of experience, of memory). The other approach of course is to allow for changes in the observer; i.e. to seek changes of the boundaries of the system, which identify it. When such changes can be imposed on the observer and controlled by the observed system we will speak of collective intelligence amplification (as opposed to the more usual individual intelligence amplification).

This concept of intelligence makes sense especially within the social system. For example if one wants to improve on societal functioning one will have to deal with all kinds of interacting individuals (as systems), with groups of individuals, with organisations – each system supporting maintenance of its own boundary and of its intelligence. General improvement of such functioning will only be possible in terms of collective intelligence amplification for each of the systems involved; individual intelligence amplification can only be locally defined in such cases which introduces (the danger of) negative side-effects for part of the total set of systems.

The boundary changes necessary for this type of improvement can be implemented in various ways. Examples of collective intelligence amplification are: in traffic via the introduction of traffic lights, in organizations via reformulation of tasks, in decision making via changes in the visibility of the environment. Often such changes can be introduced via computer systems, as in important decision support systems. Further improvements may also be realized by simulating such systems in terms of changes of organizations of humans, as actors – i.e. in terms of boundaries.

Several examples of such simulations are provided and the usefulness of this type of work discussed, both in terms of actual implementations and in terms of implications for research methodology.

Chapter 27

NON STANDARD USES OF IF

D.S. BREE and R. SMIT

Graduate School of Management, Delft, The Netherlands

The present study examines the linguistic and computing problems involved in computing the meaning of **if**: is it possible to write a program fragment, a word expert, for interpreting the meaning of **if**?

The simple position that **if** is equivalent to material implication in propositional logic is not tenable. Even the ordinary conditional use of **if** requires the first order predicate calculus together with a distinction between entailment, presupposition and conversational implicature. There are however other uses of **if**, e.g. Austin's stipulative **if**, which fails to contrapose, and his **if** of doubt in which the apodosis is true independent of the truth status of the protasis. The Oxford English Dictionary gives 9 meanings for **if**.

We have taken a sample of **if** sentences from the Brown University Corpus of American English and distinguished 12 different uses of **if**:

1. Lawlike: If people stick to their plans, their behaviour is rigid.
2. Condition: If E had stuck to his plan, we'd meet him tomorrow.
3. Counterfactual: If E had stuck to his plan he'd be famous.
4. Semi factual: If E had stuck to his plan he'd still have been famous.
5. Factual: If R was a liar, he was also a canny gentleman.
6. Speech act: You may come back to Strassbourg, if you wish.
7. Performative: He vowed vengeance on L, if ever the chance came his way.
8. Noun clause: He wondered if the audience would let him finish.
9. Doubt: Perfect entities, if they move at all, don't move towards what they lack.
10. Restriction: Social relations impose courtesy, if not sympathy, toward ...
11. Concession: ... the speedy if temporary rehabilitation of drunkards ...
12. Loose usages: She eyed the chicken with, if she had known it, something of G's look.

We examined each use to see whether it could be accounted for by the standard **if** together with other features in the sentence. One clue for this is that other subordinating conjunctions beside **if** exhibit similar variations and half the uses (1–4,6,7) can be explained on this basis. In these cases the use is accounted for through the interaction of standard **if** with some other feature of the sentence, e.g. a performative main verb or an assumption by the speaker about what the listener knows.

In 3 uses (9,10,11) **if** may occur in a phrase rather than in a full clause. The thesis that such uses are reduced from the standard use with a full clause is explored and rejected. What these 3 uses do have in common is that they indicate an exclusive disjunction between part of the proposition (11) or its negation (9,10).

Aside from loose usages and factuals, what all the uses have in common is that there is doubt about the truth of the protasis proposition. At a minimum **if** provides the possibility of entertaining a proposition whose truth value is in doubt. For the noun clause use nothing further is required. For the variations on the standard **if** and factual use (1–7) there is in addition an inference relationship from the protasis proposition to the apodosis. For use in phrases (9–11) there is a simple exclusive disjunction. It is interesting to note that these 3 catagories are usually translated by different words, e.g. in Dutch the standard uses by *als* or *indien*, noun clause use by *of*, the elliptical use by *zo niet* or *zij het* and the factual use by *al*.

For A.I. programs designed to interpret and understand natural English, a program fragment is required that can handle the variations on the standard uses of **if**, including checks on the presuppositions, conversational implicatures and on the listener's knowledge of the world.

Chapter 28

CONSTRAINTS AND EVENT SEQUENCES

UWE HEIN

Artificial Intelligence Laboratory, Software Systems Research Center, Linkoping Institute of Technology, Linkoping, Sweden

Many of the difficult and unsolved puzzles concerning our understanding of linquistic communication require solutions which have to be sought in the computational architectures of cognitive systems. In order to form and evaluate our hypotheses we have to perform many programming experiments where questions concerning the control structure of the understander system lie at the heart of the research.

Such an endeavor is meaningful only if we can perform these experiments within a computational framework which at least fulfills the following three requirements. For the first, it should be *general* and allow us to experiment with a variety of different models and hypotheses. For the second, it should be *transparent* and allow us to concentrate on the important aspects of the particular models we are interested in. And finally, it should be *flexible* enough so that the task of designing and performing the experiments requires as little work as possible.

In order to generate and test hypotheses or to illustrate consequences of a first design it might be useful to perform a couple of small-scale experiments. These experiments are a source of inspiration rather than a rigorous scientific proof and their success will depend completely on the sophistication of the experimenter whose responsibility it is to find a small set of interesting problems. Given then that we agree on the usefulness of small-scale experiments we also have to find reasonable ways to perform them.

The computational device which I am investigating here for this purpose is constraint systems. Constraint systems have been used sparsely in AI research up to now excepting a few probably well-known examples such as Stallman and Sussman (1977) and Steels (1980). The question I am most interested in here is this: to what extent do constraint systems satisfy the above stated requirements for a computational framework for performing small-scale experiments.

If constraints really deliver what they have been advertised for, then they should be regarded as a strong candidate for our purpose. They are transparent in that the constraining relation has been separated out from the constraint enforcing mechanisms. They are flexible, since they allow the user of the predefined constraint language to build his models with the help of basically two operations: creating networks and defining abstract constraints. Constraints, furthermore, are general, since they allow the user to define and implement a rich variety of control structures. Constraints easily model parallel behavior by propagating information along alternative paths and they contain powerful sychronization mechanisms.

However, some doubts are in order. The degree of flexibility which has been claimed for constraint systems depends to a high degree on the right set of primitive constraints being available to the "application programmer". The design of such a set of primitive constraints is, however, not a trivial task and may vary from domain to domain. It is certainly easier to define a set of primitive constaints for the simulation of switching networks than for natural language understanding.

If a user wants to make more radical changes to his model then he probably will have to make changes to the basic constraints. Typically he will add "pins" or redefine the behavior of the current one. Changes of this kind are tedious and time consuming and in some way or another against the spirit.

Another, more serious limitation of current constraint systems is the lack of any global control mechanism. The strong locality of computations is certainly more of a disadvantage here. Every basic constraint is self-contained in that the values being computed only depend on the terminal values which already are known to this particular constraint and nothing else.

Furthermore, if a constraint has been defined to take care of all combinatorially possible cases, then it must in fact be possible to hook it into any net at any place and get it to operate right. However, it is not easy to define all these local computations without any idea of the context within which this particular constraint should make its contribution. Good examples for these kinds of difficulties are conflict handling strategies which are hard to define locally.

Chapter 29

ARTIFICIAL PSYCHOLOGY VERSUS ARTIFICIAL INTELLIGENCE

JEAN-CLAUDE PAGES

Faculté de Médécine, Broussais-Hotel-Dieu,
Chef de Projet au Centre Scientifique d'IBM France

Research on artificial intelligence has tended to concentrate either on making machines do things that people need to do or analysing intelligent behaviour in terms of information processing. In human beings there is considerable evidence – the work of Freud is one example – to show that the structure of the human central nervous system which determines the character of perception and hence the model of the world which the individual uses is in its fundamental functions illogical.

The present paper seeks to develop a philosophical structure which would integrate both the neurophysiological and the psychoanalytical approaches to this model. The characteristics of PHI and PSY programs which would simulate human rather than artificial intelligence are outlined.

REFERENCES

Abelson, R.P. (1980) Differences between belief and knowledge systems. Cognitive Science Technical report No. 1, Yale University.

Aikens, J.S. (1980) Representation of control knowledge in expert systems. Proc. First National Conf. Artificial Intelligence, Stanford University. August 1980, pp. 121–123.

Airenti, G., Bara, B.G., Colombetti, M. (1982) Semantic network representation of conceptual and episodic knowledge. In "Advances in Cybernetics and System Research" Ed. Trappl, R. *11* Hemisphere, Washington.

Airenti, G., Bara, B.F., Colombetti, M. (1983) Knowledge and thought in a cognitive system, Cybernetica *26* 1.

Allen, J.F. and Perrault, C.R. (1978) Participating in dialogues understanding via plan deduction. AI-MEMO 78-4, Dept. Computer Science, Toronto Univ. July 1978. Also in "Proc. of 2nd National Conf., Canadian Soc. for Computational Studies of Intelligence, Toronto 1978.

Amarel, S. (1966) On machine representations of problems of reasoning about actions - the missionaries and cannibals problem. Technical Report No. PTR-2102, RCA Laboratories.

Amarel, S. (1967) An approach to heuristic problem solving and theorem proving in propositional calculus. In "Systems and Computer Science" Ed. Hart and Takasu. Univ. of Toronto Press.

Amarel, S. (1968) On representation of problem of reasoning about actions. In "Machine Intelligence". Ed. Michie. *3* Edinburgh Univ. Press.

Amarel, S. (1970) On the representation of problems, and goal-directed procedures for computers. In "Formal Systems and Non-Numerical Problem Solving by Computers". Ed. Banerji and Mesarovic. American Elsevier.

Amarel, S. (1971) Representations and modelling in problems of program formation. In "Machine Intelligence" *6* Ed. Meltzer and Mitchie. Univ. Edinburgh Press.

Amarel, S. (1981) Problems of representation in heuristic problem solving: related issues in the development of expert systems. In "Methods of heuristics, Ed. Groner, Groner and Bischof. Lawrence Erlbaum (to appear). Also available as Technical Report CBM-TR-118, Laboratory for Computer Science Research, Rutgers Univ.

Amarel, S., Brown, J.S., Buchanan, B., Hart, P., Kulikowski, C., Martin, W., Pople, H. (1977) Report of Panel on Applications of Artificial Intelligence, in Proc. IJCAI-5 MIT.

Anderson, J.R. (1976). "Language, memory and thought". Hillsdale, N.J.: Erlbaum.

Anderson, J.R. and Greeno, J.G. (1981) Acquisition of problem-solving skill. In "Cognitive Skills and their Acquisition" Ed. Anderson, J.R. Hillsdale, New Jersey 1981.

Anzai, Y. and Simon, H.A. (1979) The theory of learning by doing. Psychological Review *86*.

Arbib, M.A. (1980) Perceptual structures and distributed motor control. In "Handbook of Physiology" Ed. Brooks. V.B., Vol. III: Motor Control" American Physiological Society.

Arbib, M.A. and Manes, E.G. (1976) Machines in a category: an expository introduction. SIAM Reviews *16* 163–191.

Archibald, Y.M. Time as a variable in the performance of hemisphere damaged patients on the Elithorn Perceptual Maze Test. Cortex, XIV *1* 22–31. 1978.

Archibald, Y.M., Wepman, J.M., & L.V. Performance on nonverbal cognitive tests following unilater cortical injury to the right and left hemispheres. J. of Nervous and Mental Diseases *45* 1, 25–36. 1967.

Atkinson, R.L. and Atkinson, R.C. (1980) Mind and behaviour. Readings from Scientific American. Freeman and Co., San Francisco.

References

Averbakh, Y., Maizelis, I. (1974) Pawn endings. Batsford, London.

Beauvois, M.F. and Desrouesne, J. (1979) Phonological alexia: three dissociations. J. Neurology, Neurosurgery and Psychiatry 42 1115–1124.

Banerji, R.B. and Ernst, G.W. (1977) A comparison of three problem solving methods. Proc. of the 5th Int. Joint Conf. on Artificial Intelligence 442. Cambridge.

Beard, R.M. (1965) The structure of perception: a factorial study. Brit. J. Educ. Psychol. Vol XXXV, 210–220.

Bell, R.C. (1960) "Board and Table Games" Oxford University Press.

Berliner, H. (1977) A representation and some mechanisms for a problem-solving chess program. Advances in Computer Chess 1. Ed. M.R.B. Clarke. Edinburgh University Press.

Berliner, H. (1979) The B* tree search algorithm: A best-first proof procedure. Artificial Intelligence 12 No. 1, 23–40.

Berliner, H.J. (1980) Backgammon computer program beats world champion. Artificial Intelligence 14 No 2, 205–200.

Berliner, H. (1984) Search versus knowledge: ana nalysis from the domain of games. Ed. Elithorn and Banerji. North-Holland (This volume).

Berlinger, H.J., (1981) An examination of brute force intelligence. Proc. of the 7th International Joint Conf. on Artificial Intelligence, Vancouver, B.C. Canada, August 1981.

Biederman, I. and Tsao, Y.C. (1979) On processing Chinese ideographs and English words: some implications from Stroop-test results. Cognitive Psychology 11 125–132.

Bien, J.S. (1976a) Multiple environments approach to natural language. American J. of Computational Linguistics, microfiche 54.

Bien, J.S. (1976b) Computational explanation of intensionality. Reprint no. 41 of the Int Conf. on Computational Linguistics, Ottawa.

Bobrow, D.G., Norman, D.A. (1975) Some principles of memory schemata. In "Representation and Understanding" Ed. Bobrow and Collins. Academic Press, NY.

Bramer, M.A. (1977) Representation knowledge for chess endgames: toward a self improving system. Ph.D. Thesis, Open university, U.K.

Bratko, I. (1981) Knowledge-based problem-solving in AL3. Machine Intelligence 10. Ed. Michie and Pao. Ellis, Horwell and Wiley (in press).

Bratko, I. & Michie, D. (1980) A representation of pattern-knowledge in chess edgames. Advances in Computer Chess 2. Ed. M.R.B. Clarke. Edinburgh University Press.

Brown, J.S., Rubinstein, R. and Burton, R. (1976) A reactive learning environment for computer assisted electronics instruction. BBN Report No. 3314.

Butcher, H.J. (1968) "Human Intelligence: Its Nature and Assessment" Methuen.

Carbonell, J.R. (1970) AI in CSL: An artificial intelligence approach to computer assisted instruction. IEEE Transactions on Man-Machine Systems. MMS-11 (4).

Carter-Saltzman, I. (1979) Patterns of cognitive functioning in relation to handedness and sex-related differences. In "Sex-Related Differences in Cognitive Functioning" Ed. Wittig and Peterson. Academic Press, 1979.

Cattell, R.B. (1943) The measurement of adult intelligence. Psychol. Bull. 40 153.

Ceraso, J., Provitera, A. (1971). Sources of error in syllogistic reasoning. Cognitive Psychology, 2, 400–410.

Ceri, S., Pelagatti, G., Bracchi, G. (1979) A structured methodology for designing static and dynamic aspects of data base applications. Politecnico di Milano, Instituto di Elettrotechnica ed Elettronica, Laboratorio di Calcolatori, Interna Report 79–10, Milan.

Charniak, E. (1975) A brief on case. ISSCO working papers No. 22, Geneva.

Charniak, E. (1978) On the useof trained knowledge in language comprehension. Artificial Intelligence 11 225–265.

Charniak, E. (1981) A common representation for problem-solving and language-comprehension information. Artificial Intelligence, 16 3, 225–255.

Charniak, E., Malaprop, M. (1977) A language comprehension program, "Proc. 5th. Joint Conf. Artificial Intelligence". Cambridge, Mass.

Church, A. (1936) A note on the Entscheidungsproblem. JSL *1* 10–41.

Clancey, W.J.L. (1979) Tutoring rules for supporting a case method dialogue. Int. J. Man-Machine Studies *11* 1.

Clark, H.H. (1969). Linguistic processes in deductive reasoning. Psychological Review, *76*, 387–404.

Clark, H. and Marshall, C. (1981) Definite reference and mutual knowledge. In "Elements of Discourse Understanding. Ed. Joshi, A., Sag, I. and Webber, B. Cambridge, 193–213.

Codd, E.F. (1974) Seven steps to rendez-vous with the causal user. In "Data Base Management", Eds. J.W. Klimbie & K.I. Koffeman. North-Holland, Amsterdam.

Cohen, P.R. (1978) On knowing what to say: planning speech acts. technical Report no. 118, Dept of Computer Science, Univ. Toronto.

Cohen, P.R., Perrault, C.R. (1979) Elements of a plant based theory of speech acts. Cognitive Science *3* 3.

Colby, K.M. (1975) "Artificial Paranoia" Pergamon Press, NY.

Coltheart, M., Patterson, K.E. and Marshall, J.C. (Eds) (1980) "Deep Dyslexia" Routledge and Kegan Paul, London.

Condon, J. and Thompson, K. (1981) The BELLE chess hardware. Advances in Computer Chess Conf., London. To appear in Advances in Computer Chess *3* Ed. M.R.B. Clarke. Pergamon Press.

Cook, S. (1971) The complexity of theorem proving procedures. Proc. 3rd ACMS Symp on Theory of Computing 151–158.

Cooper, R. & Elithorn, A. (1973) The organisation of search procedures. In "Artificial and Human Thinking" Elsevier, Amsterdam.

–, Le traitement interactif des langues naturelles. Graduation Thesis, Université Scientifique et Médicale de Grenoble, Institut National Polytechnique de Grenoble, Grenoble, France.

Chrisof, C. (1939) The formulation and elaboration of thought-problems. Amer. J. Psychol. 51: 161.

Davies, A. & Davies, M.G. (1965) Some analytical properties of Elithorn's Perceptual Maze. J. Math. Psychol. *2* 371–380.

Davis, R. and Lenat, D. (1982) AM: Discovery in mathematics as heuristic search. Part 1 of "Knowledge-Based Systems in Artificial Intelligence. McGraw Hill.

Davis, M., Logemann, G. and Loveland, D. (1962) A machine program for theorem proving. CACM 394–397.

De Champeaux, D. and Sint, L. (1977) An improved bi-directional heuristic search algorithm. JACM *24* No. 2 177–191.

De Fries, H.C., Ashton, G.C., Johnson, R.C., Kuse, A.R., McClearn, G.E., Mi, M.P., Rashad, M.N., Vandeburg, S.G., Johnson, R.C. & Rashad, M.N. Parent-Offspring Resemblance for specific cognitive abilities in two ethnic groups. Nature *261* 131–133.

De Groot, A.D. (1965) "Thought and Choice in Chess" The Hague: Mouton.

DeJong, G.F. (1979). Prediction and substantiation: a new approach to natural language processing. Cognitive Science *3* 251–273.

Dewey, J. (1910) "How we think". Heath.

Donders, F.C. 1868–1869). Over de snelheid van psychologische processen. Onderzoekingen gedaan in het Physiologisch Laboratorium der Utrechtsche Hoogeschool. Tweede reeks, *II*, 92–120.

Donnellan, K. (1971) Reference and definite descriptions. In "Semantics" Ed. Steinberg and Jacobvits, 100–114, CUP, Cambridge.

Doran, J.E. and Mitchie, D. (1966) Experiments with the Graph Traverser program. Proc. Roy. Soc. Series A. *294* 235–259.

Duerr, B., Haettich, W., Tropf, H. and Winkler, G. (1980) A combination of statistical and syntactical pattern recognition applied to classification of unconstrained handwritten numerals. Pattern recognition *12* 189–199.

Duncker, K. 91945). On problem-solving, *58* (5) (Whole No. 270).

Easton, A. (1973) "Complex managerial decisions involving multiple objectives". Wiley.

Eisenstadt, M. (1979) A friendly software environment for psychology studnets. AISB Quarterly *34*.

Elithorn, A. (1974) Combining inferences for single sequential trials. Proc. of NATO Conference on Statistical Design and Experimental Field Trials at Rapallo. Ed. Leese, A.L. NATO Ottawa, 1974.

Elithorn, A. & Jagoe, J.R. (1967) The computer analysis of human problem-solving behaviour: the choice of problem. Proc. of 1967 NATO Symposium on the Simulation of Human Behaviour, Paris, 205–217.

Elithorn, A., Jagoe, J.R. & Lee, D.N. (1966) Simulation of perceptual problem solving skill. Nature *211*, 1029–1031.

Elithorn, A. and Telford, A. (1969) Computer analysis of intellectual skills. International Journal of Mann-Machine Studies, *1*, 2, 189–209.

Elithorn, A. & Telford, A. (1970) Game and problem structure in relation to the study of human and artificial intelligence, Nature *227* 1205–1210.

Elithorn, A. & Telford, A. (1973) Design considerations in relation to computer based problems. In "Artificial and Human Thinking", Elsevier, Amsterdam.

Elithorn, A. & Telford, A. (1974) Cain and Abel: Computer games for the study of human and artificial intelligence. In "Advances in Cybernetics Systems" Ed. Rose, J. Gordon and Breach, London, 1974.

Elithorn, A., Cooper, R. & Lennox, R. (1979) Assessment of psychotropic drug effects. In "Drugs and the Elderly", Dundee, 1977. Ed. Crooks, J. and Stevenson, I.H., Macmillan, London 1979.

Elithorn, A., Mornington, S. & Stavrou, A. (1982) Automated psychological testing: some principles and practice. Int. J. Man-Machine Studies. Vol 17.

Emde, W., Habel, Ch. and Rollinger, C.-R. (1983) Learning by higher concepts or the discovery of equator. Proc. of the 8th IJCAI, Karlsruhe.

Engelman, C., Berg, C.H. and Bischoff, M. (1979) KNOBS: An experimental Knowledge Based Aircraft Identification Simulation Facility. Proc. Sixth Inter. Joint Conf. Artificial Intelligence, Tokyo 1979, pp. 247–249.

Engelman, C., Scarl, E.A., and Berg, C.H. (1980) Interactive frame instantiation. Proc. First National Conf. Artificial Intelligence, Stanford University, August 1980. pp 184–186.

Ericson, L.W. (1979) Translation of programs from MACLISP to INTERLISP MTR-3874, The Mitre Corporation, Bedford, MA. November 1979.

Erickson, J.R. (1978). Research on syllogistic reasoning. In "Human Reasoning". Eds. R. Revlin & R.E. Mayer. Wiley: New York.

Ernst G.W. (1969) Sufficient conditions for the success of the GPS. J. of the Association for Computing Machinery. *16* 517.

Ernst, G.W. and Banerji, R.B. (1977) A theory for the complete mechanisation of a GPS-type problem solver. Proc. of the 5th Int. Conf. on Artificial Intelligence, 450 Cambridge.

Ernst, G. and Goldstein, M. (1982) Mechanical discovery of classes of problem-solving strategies. J. ACM. *29* No. 1. Jan. 1982.

Ernst, G.W. and Newell, A. (1969) GPS: a case study in generality and problem solving. Academic Press, NY.

Ershov, A., Mel'chuk, P., Narin'jani, N. (1975). RITA-an experimental man-computer system on a natural language basis. In "Proc. 4th Int. Joint Conf. Artificial Intelligence". Tbilisi, USSR.

Fahlman, S.Z. (1979) NETL: a system for representing and using real-world knowledge. MIT Press, Cambridge, Mass.

Feigenbaum, E.A. (1977) The art of artificial Intelligence. Proc. IJCAI-5. MIT. 1977.
Feldman, L.B. and Turvey, M.T. (1980) Words written in Kana are named faster than the same written in Kanji. Language and Speech 23 141–147.
Fikes, R.E., Hart, P.E. and Nilsson, N.J. (1972) Learning and executing generalised robot plans. In "Artificial Intelligence 3 251–288.
Fikes, R.E. and Nilsson, N.J. (1971) STRIPS: a new application of theorem proving to problem solving. Artificial Intelligence 2 189.
Fischer, M.J. and Rabin M.O. (1974) Super-exponential complexity of Presburger arithmetic. In "Complexity of Computation" STAM-AMS Proc. Ed. Karp, R., 7 27–42.
Fowler, C.A., Wolford, G., Slade, R. and Tassinary, L. (1981) Lexical access with and without awareness. J. of Experimental Psychology: General 110 341–362.
Fraenkel, A.S., Garey, M.R., Johnson, D.S., Schaefer, T. and Yesha, Y. (1978) The complexity of checkers on an N by N board - preliminary report. Proc. 19th IEEE Symp. on Found. of Comp. Sci. 55–64.
Frecon. L. and Lavorel, P.M. (1980) Context sensitive selection models for speech errors. Paris: Klincksieck. TA Informations 1 38–44.
Gaifman, H. (1956) Dependency system and phrase structure system. Info. and Control 8.3.
Gainotti, G., Caltagirone, C., Miceli, G. and Masullo, C. (1981) Selective semantic-lexical impairment of language conprehension in right-brain damaged patients. Brain and Language 13 201–211.
Garey, M.R., Johnson, D.S. (1979) "Computers and Intractability: A Guide to NP-Completeness, W.H. Freeman, San Francisco.
Gelman, R., & Gallistel, C.R. (1978). "The child's understanding of number". Harvard University Press: Cambridge, Mass.
Gillogly, J.J. (1978) Performance analysis of the technology chess program. Ph.D. Dissertation, Computer Science Dept., Carnegie-Mellon University, March 1978.
Goldberg, A. (1979) Average case complexity of the satisfiability problem. Proc. 4th Workshop on Automated Deduction. 1–6.
Goldberg, A. (1981) Using approximation algorithms to limit search in the knapsack problem. Forthcoming UCSC report.
Goldstein, M.M. (1977) The mechanical discovery of problem solving strategies. report No ESCI-77-1, Case Western Reserve Univ..
Goldiamond, I. (1966). Perception, language and conceptualization rules. In "Problem solving: Research, Method and Theory". Wiley: New York.
Greeno, J.G. (1976). Indefinite goals in well-structured problems. Psychological Review, 83, 479–491.
Gruder, C. et al. (1978) Empirical tests of the absolute sleeper effect predicted from the discounting cue hypothesis. J. of Personality and Social Psychology 36 1061–1074.
Guida, G., Somalvico, M. (1980). Interacting in natural language with artificial systems: the DONAU project. Information Systems 5.4.
Guida, G. (1980). goal oriented parsing: improving the efficiency of natural language access to relational data bases. In "Proc. 8th Int. Conf. on Computational Linguistics. Tokyo.
Guida, G. (1978). Natural language interfaces to computer systems: an experimental project. Alta Frequenza XLVII. 9.
Guida, G., Somalvico, M. (1979). A two level modular system for natural language understanding. In "Proc. 6th Int. Joint Conf. Artificial Intelligence", Tokyo.
Guilford, J.P., Kettner, N.M., Christensen, P.R. (1956). The nature of the general reasoning factor. Psychological review, 63, 169–172.
Guyote, M.J., Sternberg, R.J. (1981). A transitive chain theory of sullogistic reasoning. Cognitive Psychology, 13, 461–525.
– and Rollinger, C.-R. (1981) A sketch on acquisition by higher cognitive concepts. Fb 20 Bericht 81/11; Technische Universitaet Berlin.

Hart, P.E., Nilsson, N.J. and Raphael, B. A formal basis for the heuristic determination of minimum cost paths. IEEE Trans. on Sys. Sci. and Cybernetics, SSC-4 100–107.

Hartley, J.R. (1973) The design and evaluation of an adaptive teaching system. Int. J. of Man-Machine Studies 5 2.

Hatta, T. (1978) Recognition of Japanese Kanji and Hirakana in the left and right visual fields. Japanese J. or Experimental Psychology 20 51–59. (In Japanese).

Hayes-Roth, F. and Mostow, D. (1975) An automatically compilable recognition network for structured patterns. In "Fourth International Joint Conf. on Artificial Intelligence" 356–362.

Hayes-Roth, F., Klahr, P., Burge, J. and Mostow, D.J. (1978) Machine methods for acquiring, learning, and applying knowledge. Technical Report R-6241, The RAND Corporation, Santa Monica, CA. 1978.

Hayes-Roth, F. (1982) Proofs, refutations and rectifications: Heuristics for learning from empirical disconfirmations. In "Machine Learning" Ed. Michalski, R.S., Carbonell, J.G. and Mitchell, T.M. Tioga, Palo Alto, 1982.

Hendrix, G. (1977) Human engineering for applied natural language processing. Proc. of the Fifth International Joint Conf. on Artificial Intelligence, Cambridge, MA.

Hendrix, G.G., Sacerdoti, E.D., Sagalowicz, D., Slocum, J. (1978). Developing a natural language interface to complex data. ACM Trans. Data Bases 3.2.

Heron A., Chown, J. & Churchill A. (1967) "Age and Function"

Hintikka, J. (1962) "Knowledge and belief". Cornell University Press, Ithaca, NY.

Hofstadter, D.R. (1981) Metamagical themas. Scientific American, march 1981, p. 20.

Holley-Wilcox, P. and Blank, M.A. (1980) Evidence for multiple access in the processing of isolated words. J. of Experimental Psychology: Human Perception and Performance 6 75–84.

Hospers, J. 91956) "An introduction to philosophical analysis" Routledge.

Huberman, B. (1968) A program to play chess endgames. Technical Report CS 106. Stanford University.

Hunt, E. (1978) Mechanics of verbal ability. Psychological Review, 85, 109–130.

Huttenlocher, J., Higgins, E.T. (1971). Adjectives, comparatives, and syllogisms. Psychological Review, 78, 487–504.

Huyn, N., Dechter, R. and Pearl, J. (1980) Probabilities analysis of the complexity of A*. Artificial Intelligence 15 3, 241–254.

IBaraki, Toshihide (1976) Theoretical comparisons of search strategies in branch and bound algorithms. Int. J. of Comp. and Inf. Sci. 5 No. 4, 315–344.

Ibarra, O.H., Kim, C.E. (1975) Fast approximation for the knapsack and sum of subset problems. J. Assoc. Comp. Mach. 22 463–468.

Jeannerod, M. and Hecaen, H. (1979) Adaptation et restauration des fonctions nerveuses. SIMEP, Lyon.

Johnson-Laird, P.N., Steedman, M. (1978). The psychology of syllogisms. Cognitive Psychology, 10, 64–99.

Kimble, R.B. (1973) Self-optimizing computer-assisted tutoring: theory and practice. Technical Report No. 206 (Psychology and Education Series). Institute for Mathematical Studies in the Social Sciences, Stanford Univ.

Köhler, W. (1925). "The Mentality of Apes". Routledge & Kegan Paul: London.

Kolers, P.A. (1960) Some aspects of problem-solving: 1. method and materials. Wright Air Development Division Technical Report 60-2.

Kolodner, J.L. (1980). Organizing memory and keeping it organized. In Proceedings of the First Annual National Conference on Artificial Intelligence, Stanford, CA.

Kolodner, J.L. (1981). Organization and retrieval in a conceptual memory for events. In Proceedings of the International Joint Conference on Artificial Intelligence, Vancouver, B.C., Canada.

Kolodner, J.L. (1983). Retrieval and organizational strategies in conceptual memory: a computer model. Lawrence Erlbaum Associates, Inc., Hillsdale, NJ.

Korf, R.E. (1980) Toward a model of representation changes. AI Journal *14* No. 1 Aug. 1980.
Kotov, Alexander (1971) "Think like a Grandmaster" Batsford Ltd., London.
Kowalski, R. (1981) "Logic as a Database Language", Imperial College, London.
Langley, P.W., Neches, R., Neves, D. and Anzai, Y. (1980) A domain-independent framework for procedure learning. Journal of Policy Analysis and Information Systems *4(2)* 163–197, June 1980
Larkin, J., McDermott, J., Simon, D.P., Simon, H.A. (1980) Expert and novice performance in solving physics problems. Science *208* 20.
Lassen, N.A., Ingvar, D.H. and Skinhøf, E. (1978) Brain function and blood flow. Scientific American, *239* 62–71.
Laurière, J.L. (1976). Un Langage et un programme pour énoncer et résoudre des problèmes combinatoires. Thèse, Univ. de Paris VI.
Laurière, J.L. (1978). A language and a program for stating and solving combinatorial problems. Artificial Intelligence, *10*, 29–127.
Laurière, J.L. Toward efficiency through generality. IJCAI-*79*, 519–521.
Lavorel, P.M. (1980) Aspects de la performance linguistique. Lyon Univ. II, (Offset)
Lavorel, P.M. (1980) Univers dynamiques et réseaux déformables. Cahiers de Lexologie. *1* 119–132. Klincksieck, Paris.
Lavorel, P.M. (1982) Production strategies. A systems approach to Wernicke's aphasia. In "Neural models of language processes" Ed. Arbib and Caplan D., Academic Press, NY.
Lavorel, P.M. and Arbib M.A. (1981) Towards a theory of language performance. Theoretical Linguistics *1*. Walter de Gruyter, Berlin.
Lawler, F.L. (1977) Fast approximation algorithms for knapsack problems. Proc. 18th IEEE Symp. on Found. of Comp. Sci. 206–213.
Lee, D.N. (1965) A psychological and mathematical study of task complexity in relation to human problem-solving using a perceptual maze test. Ph.D. thesis for the University of London.
Lee, D.N. (1967) Graph-theoretical properties of Elithorn's maze. J. Math. Psychol. *10*, 341.
Lenat, D.B. (1980) The nature of heuristics. Technical Report HPP-80-26, Heuristic Programming Project, Computer Science Dept., Stanford Univ. CA 1980.
Lesser, V. and coll. (1981) A high-level simulation testbed for cooperative distributed problem-solving. Computer and Information Science, Massachusetts Univ. Amherst. Report 81-16.
Lichtenstein, D. and Sipser, M. (1978) Go is Pspace hard. proc. 19th IEEE Symp. on Found. of Comp. Sci. 48–54.
Luria, A.R. and Tsvetkova, L.S. "Les troubles de la résolution de problemes". Gauthier-Villars, Paris.
McCauley, C., Parmelee, C.M., Sperber, R.B. and Carr, T.H. (1980) Early extraction of meaning from pictures and its relation to conscious identification. J. of Experimental Psychology: Human Perception and Performance 6 265–276.
Maier, N.R.F. (1970). What makes a problem difficult? in "Problem solving and creativity in individuals and groups." Ed. Maier, N.R.F.. Brooks/Cole: Belmont, Calif.
Marcel, A.J. (1980) Conscious and preconscious recognition of polysemous words: locating the selective effects of prior verbal context. In "Attention and Performance" Ed. Nickerson, R.S., Lawrence Erlbaum Associates, Hillsdale, N.J.
Michalski, R.S. (1980) Pattern recognition as rule-guided inductive inference. IEEE Transactions on Pattern Analysis and Machine Intelligence PAMI-2(4) 349–361, 1980.
Miller, G.A. (1970) "The Psychology of Communications" Pelican.
Miller, G.A. (1978) Semantic Relations among words. In "Linguistic theory and psychological reality" Ed. Halle, Bresnan and Miller. Cambridge, Mass.
Miller, G.A., Galanter, E., Pribram, K.H. (1960). "Plans and the structure of behavior". Holt, Rinehart, & Winston: New York.
Miller, G., Johnson-Laird, P.N. (1976) "Language and Perception". Cambridge Univ. Press, Cambridge.

Minsky, M., (1975). A framework for representing knowledge. In "The Psychology of Computer Vision". Ed. P.H. Winston. 11–277. McGraw-Hill, New York.

Minsky, M. and Papert, S. (1969) "Perceptrons" MIT Press.

Mitchell, T.M. (1978) Version Spaces: An approach to concept learning. PhD thesis, Stanford Univ. Dec. 1978. also Stanford CS report STAN-CS-78-711, HPP-79-2.

Mitchell, T.M. (1980) The need for biases in learning generalizations. Technical Report CBM-TR-117, Dept. of Computer Science, Rutgers Univ., May 1980.

Mitchell, T.M. (1982) Generalization as search. Artificial Intelligence. To appear.

Mitchell, T.M., Utgoff, P.E., Nudel, B. and Banerji, R. (1981) Learning problem-solving heuristics through practice. In "Proceedings of the Seventh International Joint Conf. on Artificial Intelligence" 127–134. Vancouver, August 1981.

Moore, O.K. (1959) The shortest path through a maze. Proc. of an International Symp. on the Theory of Switching. Harvard University Computational Laboratory Annals. Harvard University Press. 29–30.

Moore, O.K. and Anderson, S.B. (1954) Modern logic and tasks for experiments on problem-solving behaviour. J. Psychol. 38 151.

Moore, R. and Hendrix, G. 91979) Computational models of belief and the semantics of nelief sentences. SRI Technical Note No. 187.

Morikawa, Y. (1981) Stroop phenomena in the Japanese language: the case of ideographic characters (Kanji) and syllabic characters (Kana). Perceptuala nd Motor Skills 53 67–77.

Mostow, D.J. (1981) Mechanical transformation of task heuristics into operational procedures. PhD thesis, Carnegie-Mellon Univ., April, 1981.

Mostow, D.J. (1982) Using the heuristicsearch method. In "Machine Learning" Ed. Michalski, R.S., Carbonell, J.G. and Mitchell, T.M. Tioga, Palo Alto, 1980.

Mulholland, T.M., Pellegrino, J.W., Glaser, R. (1980). Components of geometric analogy solution. Cognitive Psychology 12, 252–284.

Munyer, J. and Phl, I. (1976) Adversary arguments for the analysis of heuristic search in general graphs. UCSC Report 76-1, also in Proc. CSCSI/SCEIO, Vancouver, B.C.

Murrell, G.A. and Morton, J. (1974) Word recognition and morphemic structure. J. of Experimental Psychology 102 963–968.

Murray, H.J., (1952) "A History of Board Games other than Chess". Oxord University Press.

Mylopoulos, J., Borgida, A., Cohen, P., Roussopoulos, N., Tsotsos, J., Wong, H. (1976). TORUS: a step toward bridging the gap between data bases and the casual user. Information Systems 2.

Newborn, M. (1977) PEASANT: An endgame for kings and pawns. In "Chess skill in Man and machine" Ed. Frey, P. Springer-Velag 1977.

Newell, A. (1969) Heuristic programming: ILL structured problems. In "Progress in Operations Research" Ed. Aronofsky. Vol. 3. Wiley, NY.

Newell, A. (1981) Duncker on thinking: An enquiry into progress in cognition. CMU, rept. CMU-CS-80-151.

Newell, A., Shaw, J., Simon, H. (1959) Report on a General Problem Solving Program. Proc. of the Int. Conf. on Information Processing (UNESCO) p. 256. Paris 1959.

Newell, A., Shaw, J., Simon, H. (1960). Report on a general problem-solving program. Proceedings of the International Conference on Information processing. UNESCO: Paris. 256–264.

Newell, A., Simon, H.A. (1956). The logic theory machine. IRE Transactions on Information Theory, IT-2, 3, 61–79.

Newell, A., Simon, H.A. (1972). "Human Problem Solving". Prentice-Hall: Englewood Cliffs, N.J.

Nilsson, N.J. (1965) "Learning machines" McGraw-hill, NY.

Nilsson, N. (1971) "Problem solving methods in artificial intelligence" McGraw Hill, NY.

Nilsson, N.J. (1980). In "Principles of Artificial Intelligence". Tioga Pub. Co, Palo Alto.

Nishikawa, Y. and Niina, S. (1981) Modes of information processing underlying hemispheric functional differences. Japanese J. of Psychology 51 335–342.

Norman, D. and Bobrow, D. (1979) Descriptions: on intermediate stage in memory retrieval. Cog. Psych. *11* 107–123.

Ornstein, R., Herron, J., Johnstone, J. and Swencionis, C. (1979) Differential right hemisphere involvement in two reading tasks. Psychphysiology *16* 398–404.

O'Shea, T. (1979) Self-improving teaching systems. Birkhauser.

Osherson, D.N. (1974). Logical inference: Underlying operations. Logical abilities in children (Vol 2). Erlbaum: Hillside, N.J..

Paige, R. (1981) Formal Differentiation - A program synthesis technique. UMI Research Press 1981; revision of PhD Dissertation, NYU, June 1979.

Pareira, L.M. and Oliviera, E. (1983) Prolog for expert systems – A case study. Proceedings of ISAI. Leningrad.

Pareira, L.M., Oliveira, E. and Sabatier, P. (1982) ORBI: An expert system for environmental resources evaluation through natural language. Proceedings 1st International Logic Programming Conference. Marseille.

Pearl, J. (1981) Heuristic Search Theory: Survey of recent results. UCLA-Enf-CSL-8205.

Perault, C.R., Allen, J.F. (1980) A planbased theory of indirect speech acts. American J. of Computational Linguistics *6* 3–4.

Perdue, C. and Berliner, H.J. (1977) EG - a program that plays pawn endgames. Proc. of the 5th International Joint Conference on Artificial Intelligence. Cambridge, Mass.

Pique, J.F. and Sabatier, P. (1981) "An informative, adaptable and efficient natural language consultable database system" Dept. de Informatica, Universidade Nova de Lisboa, Lisbon.

Pitrat, J. (1977) A chess combinations program which uses plants. Artificial Intelligence *8*, 275–321.

Pitrat, J. (1981). Un interpréteur de contraintes pour la programmation du langage naturel. In "Quelques méthodes en intelligence artificielle". *101–130* Publications du GR 22 du C.N.R.S.

Pitrat, J. (1982). Un langage pour décrire les connaissances pragmatiques. In "Colloque Intelligence Artificielle de Toulouse". *175–205.* Publications du GR 22 du C.N.R.S.

Pohl, I. (1967) A method for finding Hamnilton Paths and Knight's Tours. CACM *10* No. 7 446–449.

Pohl, I. (1969) First results on the effect of error in heuristic search. In "Machine Intelligence" *5* Ed. Meltzer, B. and Michie, D. Edinburgh Univ. Press. 219–236.

Pohl, I. (1970) Heuristic search viewed as path-finding in a graph. Artificial Intelligence 1 193–204.

Pohl, I. (1977a) Practical and theoretical considerations in heuristic search algorithms. In "Machine Intelligence" Vol. 8 Ed. Elcock, E.W. and Michie, D. and Ellis Horwood Ltd. 55–72.

Pohl, I. (1977b) Improvements to the Dinic-Karzanov network flow algorithm. Rept. HP-77-11-001, UCSC, presented SIAM Fall, 1977, Albuquerque, N. Mex.

Pohl, I. (1979) Bi-directional search. UCSC rept., Oct. 1979.

Pribam, K.H. (1969) The neural behavioural analysis of limbic forebrain mechanisms: revision and progress report. In "Advance in the study of behaviour" Ed. Lehrman, D.S., Hind, R.A. and Shawe. Vol. II Academic Press, NY.

Putnam, H. (1975) The meaning of "meaning". In "Mind, Language and Reality" 215–232, Cambridge.

Quinlan, J.R. and Hunt, E.B. (1968) A formal deductive system. J. of the Association for Computing Machinery *15* 625.

Reinfeld, F. "Win at Chess" Dover Books, 1958.

Rendell, L.A. (1981) An adaptive plan for state-space problems. PhD Thesis. Univ. of Waterloo.

Revlis, R. (1975). Two models of syllogistic reasoning: Feature selection and conversion. Journal of Verbal Learning and Verbal Behavior, *14,* 180–195.

Roberts, R.B. and Goldstein, I.P. "The FRL Manual", MIT AI Lab., Memo 409, September 1970.

Robinson, J.A. and Sibert, E.E., "The LOGLISP User's Manual" School of Computer Science, Syracuse University. Dec. 1981.

Rosenbloom, P.S. (1981) A world-championship level othello program. Computer Science Dept., Carnegie-Mellon Univ., Technical Report, August 1981.

Ross, R. (1973) Adaptive aspects of heuristic search. PhD Thesis, Edinburgh Univ.

Ross, R. (1978) An improved characterization of a class of heuristic search algorithms. Dept. of Inf. and Comp. Sci., Osaka Univ., Toyonaka, Japan.

Sacerdoti, E.D. (1974) Planning in a hierarchy of abstraction spaces. Artificial Intelligence *5* 115.

Sacerdoti, E.D. (1975) The non-linear nature of plans. Proc. of the 4th Int. Joint Conf. on Artificial Intelligence 206. Tbilisi, 1975.

Sacerdoti, E.D. (1975) A structure for plans and behaviour. PhD. Thesis, Stanford Univ. 1975. also published be Elsevier, NY. 1977.

Samuel, A. (1967) Some studies in machine learning using the game of checkers II. Recent progress. IBM J. of Research and Development Vol II, No. 6 Nov. 1967.

Sasanuma, S. (1975) Kana and Kanji processing in Japanese aphasics. Brain and Language *2* 369–383.

Sasanuma, S., Itoh, M., Mori, K. and Kobayashi, Y. (1977) Tachistoscopic recognition of Kana and Kanji words. Neuropsychologia *15* 547–553.

Schaefer, T.J. (1978) On the complexity of some two-person perfect information games. JCSS *14* 146–167.

Schank R.C. (1980). Language and memory. *Cognitive Science*, Vol 4, No. 3.

Schank, R.C., De Jong, G. (1979). Purpositive understanding. In "Machine Intelligence". Eds. J.E. Hayes, D. Michie & L.I. Mikulich. Ellis Horwood.

Schank, R.C. (1975). In "Conceptual information processing". Ed. R.C. Schank. North Holland: Amsterdam.

Schvaneveldt, R.W., Meyer, D.E. and Becker, C.A. (1976) Lexical ambiguity, semantic context and visual word recognition. J. of Experimental Psychology: Human Perception and Performance *2* 243–256.

Searle, J. (1969) "Speech Acts" CUP, Cambridge.

Shortliffe, E.H. (1976) Computer-Based Medical Consultations: MYCIN, American Elsevier, New York.

Sidtis, J.J., Volpe, B.T., Holtzman, J.D., Wilson, D.H. and Gazzaniga, M.S. (1981) Cognitive interaction after staged callossal section: evidence for transfer of semantic activation. Science *212* 344–346.

Siegler, R.S. (1978). The origin of scientific reasoning. In "Children's thinking: What develops?". Ed. R.S. Siegler. Erlbaum: Hillsdale, N.J..

Siegler, R.S. (1981). Developmental sequences within and between concepts. In Monograph of the Society for Research in Child Development *46*, no. 189.

Simmons, R.F. (1970). Natural language question-answering systems: 1969. Comm. ACM. *13.1.*

Simon, H.A. and Hayes, J.R. (1976) The understanding process: problem isomorphs. In Cognitive Psychology *8*.

Simon, H.A., Kotovsky, K. (1963). Human acquisition of concepts for sequential patterns. Psychological Review *70*, 534–546.

Skinner, B.F. (1966). An operant analysis of problem solving. In "Problem solving: Research, method, and theory". Ed. B. Kleinmuntz. Wiley: New York.

Slate, D.J. and Atkin, L.R. (1977) The North-Western University Chess Program. In "Chess skill in man and machine, Ed. Frey, P. Springer-Verlag.

Sleeman, D.H. (1974) A problem solving monitor for a deductive reasoning task. Int. J. of Man-Machine Studies 7 2.

Smith, J., Jones, D. and Elithorn, A. (1978) The Perceptual Maze Test. Pub. Medical Research Council, Reprinted with addendum, 1978.

Smith, D.E. and Clayton, J.E. (1980) A frame-based production system architecture. Proc. First Annual National Conf. Artificial Intelligence, Stanford University, August 1980. pp. 154–156.

Smith, E.E., Adams, N., and Schorr, D. (1978). Fact Retrieval and the Paradox of Interference, Cognitive Psychology, *10* 438–464.

Smith, M.C. and Magee, L.E. (1980) Tracing the time course of picture-word processing. J. of Experimental Psychology: General *109* 373–392.

Spearman, C. (1923). "The nature of 'intelligence' and the principles of cognition". Macmillan: New York.

Spearman C. (1927). "The abilities of man". Macmillan: New York.

Stallman, R.M. and Sussman, G.J. (1977) Forward reasoning and dependency directed backtracking in a system for computer-aided circuit analysis. Artificial Intelligence *9* 135–196.

Staudenmayer, H., Bourne, L.E., Jr. (1977). Learning to interpret conditional setences: A developmental study. Developmental Psychology *13*, 616–623.

Steels, L. (1980) The constraint machine. Schlumberger-Doll Research AI memo 1.

Sternberg, R.J. (1977). "Intelligence, information processing, and analogical reasoning: The componential analysis of human abilities." Erlbaum: Hillsdale, N.J..

Sternberg, R.J. (1979). Developmental patterns in the encoding and combination of logical connectives. Journal of Experimental Child Psychology, *28*, 469–498.

Sternberg, R.J. (1980a). Representation and process in linear syllogistic reasoning. Journal of Experimental Psychology: General, *109*, 119–159. (a)

Sternberg, R.J. (1980b). In "Sketch of a componential subtheory of human intelligence. Behavioral and Brain Sciences, *3*, 573–584. (b)

Sternberg, R.J. (1981). Toward a componential theory of human intelligence: I. Fluid ability. In "Intelligence and learning". Eds. M. friedman, J. Das, N. O'Connor. Plenum: New York.

Sternberg, R.J. (1982). Reasoning, problem solving, and intelligence. In "Handbook of human intelligence". Ed. R.J. Sternberg. Cambridge University Press: New York.

Sternberg, R.J. & Lasaga, M.I. (1984) Approaches to human reasoning: an analytic framework. In "Artificial and Human Intelligence" (This volume) Ed. Elithorn, A. & Banerji R. North-Holland, Amsterdam.

Sternberg, R.J. and Powell, J.S. (1983). Comprehending verbal comprehension. American Psychologist *38*, 878–893.

Sternberg, R.J., Powell, J.S., and Kaye, D.B. (1982) The nature of verbal comprehension. Poetics *11*, 155–187.

Sternberg, R.J., Powell, J.S., and Kaye, D.B. Teaching vocabulary-building skills: A contextual approach. In "Communicating with computers in classrooms: Prospects for applied cognitive science." Ed. Wilkinson, A.C. New York. Academic Press, In press.

Sternberg, S. (1969). The discovery of processing stages: Extensions of Donders' method. Acta Psychologica, *30*, 276–315.

Szentágothai, J. and Arbib, M.A. (1974) Conceptual Models of Neural organization. neurosciences *12* 3. (Republished MIT Press, 1975)

Taft, M. and Forster, K.I. (1975) Lexical storage and retrieval of prefixed words. J. of Verbal Learning and Verbal Behaviour *14* 638–647.

Tan, S.T. (1977) Describing pawn structures. Advances in Computer Chess *1* Ed. M.R.B. Clarke. Edinburgh University Press.

Tappel, S. (1980) Some algorithm design methods. Proc. AAAI 1980 Conf. Stanford Univ. Aug. 1980.

Taylor, I.K. and Taylor, M.M. "Psychology of Reading" Academic Press, New York. (In press).

Taylor, G. and Whitehill (1981) A belief representation for understanding deception. Proc. of the 7th IJCAI, Vancouver, 388–393.

Thurstone, L.L. (1983). "Primary mental abilities". University of Chicago Press: Chicago.

Townsend, J.T. (1971). A note on the identifiability of parallel and serial processes. Perception and Psychophysics, *10*, 161–163.

Tsao, Y-C. and Wu, M-F. (1981) Stroop interference: Hemispheric differences in Chinese speakers. Brain and Language *13* 372–378.

Turing, A.M. (1936) On computable numbers with an application to the Entscheidungsproblem. Proc. London Math. Soc. *42* 230–265.

Tzeng, O.J.L., Hung, D.L., Cotton, B. and Wang, W.S.Y. (1979) Visual lateralization effects in reading Chinese characters. Nature *282* 499–501.

Underwood, G. (1981) Lexical recognition of embedded unattended words: some implications for reading processes. Acta Psychologica *47* 267–283.

Vere, S.A. (1975) Induction of concepts in the predicate calculus. In "Fourth International Joint Conf. on Artificial Intelligence" 281–287. Tbilisi, USSR, 1975.

Walz, D.L. 91977). Natural language interfaces. ACM SIGART Newsletter *61.2.*

Wapner, W., Hamby, S. and Gardner, H. (1981) The role of the right hemisphere in the apprehension of complex linguistic materials. Brain and Language *14*15–33.

Warren, D., Pereira L.M. and Pereira F. (1977) PROLOG - The language and its implementation compared with Lisp. Sisart Newsletter, *64*

Warren, D. and Pereira, F. (1981) "An efficient easily adaptable system for interpreting natural language queries" Dept. of Artificial Intelligence, University of Edinburgh.

Warrington, E.K. (1975) The selective impairment of semantic memory. Quarterly J. of Experimental Psychology *27* 635–657.

Wason, P.C., Johnson-Laird, P.N. (1972). "Psychology of reasoning: Structure and content". B.T. Batsford: London.

Waterman, D.A., Hayes-Roth, F. (1978) "Pattern-directed inference systems". Academic Press, New York.

Weisberg, R.W., Alba, J.W. (1981). An examination of the alleged role of "fixation" in the solution of several "insight" problems. Journal of Experimental Psychology: general, *110*, 169–192.

White, S.H. (1970). The learning theory tradition and child psychology. In "Carmichael's manual of child psychology" (Vol. 1), 3rd ed. Ed. P.A. Mussen. Wiley: New York.

Whitely, S. (1977). Information-processing on intelligence test items. Some response components. Applied Psychological Measurement, *1*, 465–476.

Wiezenbaum, J. 91977). ELIZA - a computer program fo th study of natural language communication between man and machine. Comm. ACM. *91.*

Wilkins, D.E. (1979) Using patterns and plans to solve problems and control search. Report STAN-CS-79-747. Ph.D. Thesis, Stanford University, Computer Sc. Dept.

Wilks, Y. (1975a). An intelligent analyzer and understander of English. Comm. ACM. *18* 5.

Wilks, Y. (1975b). Natural language systems with the AI paradigm. Artificial Intelligence Lab. *Memo 337,* Stanford University, Stanford, California.

Wilks, Y. (1975c) A preferential, Pattern-seeking, semantics for natural language inference. Artificial Intelligence *6* 53–74.

Wilks, Y. (1977) Making preferences more active. Artificial Intelligence *11* 197–223.

Wilks, Y. and Bien, J.S. (1979) Speech acts and multiple environments. Proc. of 6th IJCAI, Tokyo, 968–970.

Williams, D.S. (1972). Computer program organization induced from problem examples. In "Representation and meaning: Experiments with information processing systems". Eds. H.A. Simon & L. Siklossy. Prentice-Hall: Englewood Cliffs, N.J..

Wilson, J.R., De Fries, J.C. McClearn, G.E., Vandenburg, S.G., Johnson, R.C. & Rashad, M.N. Cognitive Abilities: Use of family data as a control to assess sex and age differences in two ethnic groups. Int. J. of Ageing and Human Development. *6* (3) 1975.

Winston, P.H. (1975) The Psychology of Computer Vision. Mcgraw Hill, New York, 1975.

Winograd, T.A. (1973). procedural Model of language understanding. In "Computer Models of Thought and Language". Eds. R. Schank & K. Colby. freeman: San Francisco.

Woods, W.A. (1970). Transition network grammars for natural language analysis. Comm. ACM. *13. 10.*

SUBJECT INDEX

Adversary analysis, 47
Advice languages, 119–130
Algebra, boolean, 271
Algorithms,
  A, 18–19, 47, 50
  alpha-beta, 120
  B, 114–115, 117
  basic problem solving (BPSA), 305
  Davis Puttnam, 53
  general problem solving (GPS), 47, 50
  polynomial time, 45
  probabilistic, 53
Artificial intelligence, and
  belief systems, 265
  brain theory, 234
  complexity theory, 43–55
  computer aided instruction, 181
  constraint systems, 319
  data bases, 297–303
  expert systems, *see* expert systems
  human reading, 239
  knowledge based systems, 120, 265
  natural language understanding, 147, 151, 298, 318
  intelligent computer tutors, 181
  real world applications, 132
  solution of combinatorial problems, 280
  comparison with human problem solving, 2–5, 41, 221
  research compared with psychology research, 281–288
Attitudes, 164
Automated
  psychological tests, 209
  robotics, 219

Belief, definition and formulation of, 147–149, 153, 171, 235–236, 267
  algorithm, 149
  and knowledge, 265
  mechanisms, 235

Brain, *see also* left and right hemisphere and information processing
  and intelligent systems, 230
  frontal lobe lessions, 232
  language centers, 232
  left and right hemisphere, 232, 240
  neural control of movement, 233
  parietal lobe lesions, 231, 232
  parietal-occipital lesions, 232
  prefrontal lesions, 237
  split brain, 240
Brain scan, 242
Brain theory, 229, 234

Calculus
  lambda, 234
  solving program, 294
C-diagrams, 259
  transformations of, 260
  for dreams, 260–262
Chess, 105–109, 111–116
  ability, 48, 55
  as problem solving, 120–124
  as complex calculus, 205
  comparison between human and machine play, 203
  end game, 119–130
  in AI research, 203
  middle game, 120
Chess programs, 48–49, 286, 289
  knowledge based, 119, 120
  knowledge vs. search, 105, 119–120
  search based, 119, 120
  programs
    BELLE, 111, 112, 119
    BLITZ, 111
    CHAOS, 105, 106
    CHESSxx, 109, 111
    TECH, 109
Cognition, 215, 218, 251
Cognitive concepts, 313
Cognitive images, 231

Cognitive psychology, 229, 251
Cognitive science, 171, 229, 235
Cognitive systems, 266, 268, 319
Cognitive theory, 55
Complexity theory, 43–55
  and AI, 43–55
    average case time complexity, 44, 53
    worst case time complexity, 44, 46, 53
Comparative psychology, 202
Computability theory, 43–44
Computational modelling, 252, 255–256, 263
  architectures, 319
  framework, 319
Computer aided design, 297
Computer technology
  and social implications, 289–295
Computer tutors, 181–199
Consciousness, contents of, 251
Constraints,
  language, 320
  abstract, 320
Control knowledge, 12–14, 17
Control structures, 320
Cooperative computation, 230, 233
Copernican revolution, 294
Cybernetics, 229

Darwinian revolution, 294
Data base, 309
  schema, 297–298
Decision procedure, 2, 44
Decontextualization theory, 283, 287
  task, 285
Deduction systems, 46
Difference tables, 67, 69–79
Domain expert system, 185
Dreams, 267
  formation of, 253–255
  latent content, 254
  manifest content, 254
  transformer, 260–261
Dyslexia, 245–246

EEG, 202, 240
Episodic memory organisation packets, 59–66
Epistemology, taxonomies, 306
Experimental
  design and program elegance, 285
  domain, 120
  methods, 202
  sub-domain, 120
  tasks, 203
Expert behaviour, 1–41
Expert systems, 120, 132, 140, 283, 307, 309
Expertise acquisition, 2–4, 38

Eye-movements, during reading, 232

Factor analysis, 214–215
Forgetting, 254
Frame theory, 132–133, 141–146
Fuzzy automata theory, 234

Games
  advice, 210
  backgammon, 105–106, 110, 202
  backgammon, program BKG9, 9, 105–106, 110
  bridge, 203
  checkers, 46–47, 105, 206
  chess, *see* Chess
  go, 46, 204
  halma, 206
  mancala, 202
  o-pat-ko-no, 205
  othello, 105, 110, 202
  othello, program IAGO, 110
  of strategy, 203, 204
  of race, 203
Game calculus, 205
Game tree, 120
Generalization
  problem, 81, 85, 92
  process, 63–66, 81–103, 134–135
  language, 82, 89, 91, 93, 99
  strategy, 87
General Problem Solver, 47, 50, 55, 67–79
Gestalt
  approach to reasoning, 203, 207, 217, 222
  approach to problem soving, 217
Global control, 320
Graph traverser, 47

Heuristics
  cost-to-date information, 47
  cultural, 202
  divide and conquer, 51–53
  partially learned, 87–89
  power, 48
  search, 46–55
Hierarchical tree, 134
Human thinking, 209

Indexing, 58–66
Industrial relations, 291, 294
Individual differences, 214
  in verbal comprehension, 282
Inference, 81–103
Inference engine, 305, 307
Inference rules, 309, 313

Information processing, 55, 207, 222, 321
  approach to reasoning, 203, 218–221
Types of
  computer based, 221
  response-time based, 218–219
  rule-based, 291
Information processors, 282
Information system, 133
Inheritance relations, 142, 153
Intellectual complexity, 289
Intellectual skill, 55, 201, 202, 293
Intelligence (human) *see also* problem solving
  and reasoning
  collective, 315
  compared to biological and mechanical systems, 202
  crystalized, 201
  definition of, 315
  fluid, 201
  general (g), 201, 214–215
  tests of, 202
Intelligent automation, 201
Intelligent interpreter, 274, 275
Intelligent performance, 233
IQ, 285, 287
Intelligent system, 201, 202, 234, 238, 271, 282, 284

K-model, 266
K-theory, 266
Knowledge, 1, 2, 13, 306
  and belief, 265
  and search, 105–117, 119–120
  based programs, 119, 120, 141
  conceptual, 266
  control, 12–14, 17
  declarative, 125, 132, 271, 273, 274, 280
  episodic, 266
  -meta, 125, 132, 309
  representation, 120, 151, 266, 298
  root, 109
Knowledge engineering, 2, 313

Language (natural)
  Chomskian school, 234, 257
  learning, 177
  machine translation, 178–179
  study of, 252
  translation, 173–180
Learning, 229
  abilities, 313
  trial and error, 217
Left hemisphere
  and reading, 240–250
  and speech, 240
  lesions, 231–232
Lexical information, 282
Linguistics, 229
  knowledge, 311
  processors, 310
Logic
  analyst, 202
  based language, 70
  first order (FOL), 44, 309
  formal, 265
  Horn Clause, 309
  intentional, 151
  predicate, 309
  quantified propositional, 46

Machine intelligence, 201, 289
Macro-moves, 25, 67–68, 74–79
Man-machine interaction, 297
Mathematical modelling, 286
Memory, 55–57
  episodic, 59–66, 150
  organisation of, 55–66
  long-term, 282
  retrieval, 55–66
  semantic, 150
Mental abilities, 214
Mental processes, 218
  complexity of, 252
Models
  mathematical, 286
  computer, 286
  conceptual, 286
Multiple environments, 147
Multiple regression, 286

Networks, 320
Neurophysiology, 229, 234, 321
Neuropsychology, 237
Neurosis, 253
NP completeness theory, 45–46, 49

Objects
  related through, 131
  structure of, 132, 133
Object-oriented programming, 133, 134

Pattern directed, 120, 125
Pattern knowledge, 129
Pattern recognition, 239
Perception, 217, 251, 267, 321

Perceptual field, 217
Perceptual test, 202
Personality, 238
Plans, ingredients of, 122
Presburger arithmetic, 44, 46
"Predicate attributes", 313
Post-industrial society, 292
Problems, *see also* Puzzles
    analogies, 221
    blocks world, 6
    combinatorial problems, 273, 276
    knight's tour, 49–50
    missionaries and cannibals, 6
    monkey and bananas, 47
    Piagetian type, 219
    PSPACE class, 46
    Rubik's cube, 68, 71–72, 74–76
    subset-sum, 48
    Tower of Hanoi, 1, 4–41, 71
    transportation scheduling type, 5
    travelling salesman, 6, 47, 209
Problem formulation, 2, 4, 5, 11
Problem domain language, 6–10
Problom domain specification, 6–10
Problem solver, 14, 55
Problem solving, 2, 47, 67, 124, 202, 217, 237, 306
    heuristics, 213
    human and computer, 221
    schemas, 2, 4
    skills, 3
    strategies, 223
    monitor, 185, 188
Problem representation, 1–41, 71
Problem state, 69, 83, 101
Programs, *see also* chess programs
    ABSTRIPS, 78
    AL3, 119–130
    ALICE, 273, 279
    BKG 9, 9, 105–106
    CHAT80, 310
    CAPS2, 120
    CYRUS, 57–66, 285
    E-MOP, 59, 66
    ELIZA, 293
    FRUMP, 65, 285
    GPS, 47, 50, 55, 67–79
    IAGO, 110
    INERLISP, 142
    KNOBS, 141–144
    LEX, 81–103
    MACSYMA, 293
    MYCIN, 143, 285
    MICROKNOBS, 43
    MICROSIAL, 130
    NLDA, 298, 301
    ORBI, 309–311
    ORBIT, 131–140
    SOLO, 181
    SOPHIE, 185–186, 188
Programming
    action orientated, 133
    object orientated, 133
Programming languages
    FORTRAN, 136, 279
    FRL (frame representation language), 142–144
    LISP, 131, 136–137
    PROLOG, 129, 309, 311
Protocol analysis, 55
Psychological tests
    computer based, 208
    perceptual maze test, 207–210
Psychometric, approach to reasoning, 203, 214–215
Psychopathology, 253
Puzzles, 204
    fifteen block puzzle, 50, 76–78
    fool's disc, 50, 73–74, 76
    instant insanity, 78
    Rubik's cube, 50, 68, 71–72, 74–76

Reading (human)
    the bilateral cooperative model, 239–250
Reasoning (human)
    approaches to, 203, 213, 221
    criteria for comparison, 223–226
    framework of, 220, 222
    general, 215
Retrieval, 58
Right hemisphere, 209, 240
    lesions, 204, 209
    holistic, 232
    reading, 240–250
Robotics, and human labor, 291

Satisfiability, 45–46, 122
Schema
    procedural, 12
    production, 12
    reduction, 12, 20
Search
    and complexity, 46
    and knowledge, 105–117, 119–120, 298
    and intelligence, 55
    errors, 48–49

Search strategies, 115
Search tree, 14, 48
Search, types
　B, 114–115, 117
　bidirectional, 50–53
　brute-force, 105–117
　heuristic, 46–55
　knowledge directed, 105
　sequential, 58
　unidirectional, 51
Semantics, 232, 257
Semantic analysis, 310
Semantic networks, 309
Semantic systems, 234
Semantic relationships, 248, 313
Semi-decision procedures, 44
Sentence structure, 174, 177
Simulation, of
　human problem solving, 208, 221
　pathological speech, 229
　war-games, 237
Situation
　description of, 8
　space, 9, 10
　trajectory, 9
Solution
　aggregates, 13
　construction process, 12
　candidate, 12
　grammar, 13
　schemas, 13
　tree, 95, 96, 101
Stimulus-response, 306
　approach to reasoning, 203, 215–216, 222
　operant, 216

Strategy
　forcing tree, 123
　insertional, 152
　presentation, 152
Systems, *see also* Expert systems
　design philosophy, 196–197
　knowledge-based, 141
Systems theory, 306
Subtraction method, 218–219

Teaching, 181–199
　computer based model, 182–183
　courseware design templates (CDTs), 183–198
　drill and practice, 184
　examples of, 186–195
Turing
　criticism of, 201
　machine, 45
　test, 285

Unconscious processes, 251, 252, 259
Undecidability, 43–46, 49
Universal problem solving process (UPSP), 305, 307
User-friendly, 195

Verbal abilities, 285
Verbal comprehension, 282, 285
Verbal concepts, 282
Voice input/output, 292

Word
　acquisition, 282
　difficulty, 282
　expert program, 317
　meaning, 249, 282

AUTHOR INDEX

Abelson, R.P., 265
Adams, N., 57
Airenti, G., 265, 266
Alba, J.W., 217
Allen, J.F., 147, 170
Amarel, S., 1, 4, 6, 12, 68
Anderson, J.R., 81, 218, 219, 226
Anzai, Y., 3, 20, 29
Arbib, M.A., 229, 232, 234
Archibald, Y.M., 209
Atkin, L.R., 105, 109
Averbakh, Y., 120

Banerji, R.B., 65, 68
Bara, B., 265, 266
Beard, R.M., 209
Beauvois, M.F., 246
Becker, C.A., 247
Bell, R.C., 205
Berliner, H.J., 105, 112, 119, 120
Biederman, I., 244
Bien, J., 147
Blank, J.A., 247
Bobrow, D.G., 151
Bornat, R., 181
Bourne, L.E., 219
Bratko, I., 119, 120, 122, 129
Bree, D.S., 317
Brown, J.S., 181, 185
Burring, A.G., 305

Carbonell, J.R., 185
Carter-Saltzman, I., 209
Cattell, R.B., 202
Ceraso, J., 219
Ceri, S., 297
Charniak, E., 150, 162, 298
Chown, J., 210
Christensen, P.R., 215
Church, A., 44
Clancey, W.J., 181, 185
Clark, H.H., 218, 219
Codd, E.F., 297

Cohen, P.R., 147, 170, 265
Colby, K.M., 237
Colombetti, M., 265, 266, 297
Coltheart, M., 245
Condon, J., 111
Cook, S., 45
Cooper, R., 201
Cotton, B., 244
Crisof, C., 203

Davies, A., 209
Davies, M.G., 209
Davis, M., 53
Davis, R., 40

De Champeaux, D., 53
De Fries, H.C., 209
De Zeeuw, G., 315
De Groot, A.D., 48
DeJong, G.F., 65
Desrouesne, J., 246
Dewey, J., 305
Donders, F.C., 203, 218
Doran, J.E., 47
Du Boulay, B., 181
Duncker, K., 217

Easton, A., 307
Eisenstadt, M., 181
Elithorn, A., 201, 203, 206
Emde, W., 314
Engelman, C., 141
Erickson, J.R., 219
Ernst, G.W., 40, 65, 68, 70
Ershov, A., 299

Faraday, M., 256
Fehlman, S.Z., 236
Feigenbaum, E.A., 2
Feldman, L.B., 244
Fikes, R.E., 70, 86
Fischer, M.J., 45
Forster, K.I., 246

Fowler, C.A., 247
Fraenkel, A.S., 46
Frecon, L., 237
Freud, S., 251, 252, 253

Gaifman, H., 303
Galanter, E., 218
Gallistel, C.R., 219, 224
Garey, M.R., 45
Gazzaniga, M.S., 240
Gelman, R., 219, 224
Gillogly, J.J., 105, 109
Glasser, R., 218, 219
Goldberg, A., 43, 48, 53
Goldiamond, I., 216
Goldstein, M.M., 40, 71, 73
Greeno, J.G., 221
Gruder, C., 164
Guida, G., 297, 298, 303
Guilford, J.P., 215
Guyote, M.J., 218, 219, 226

Habel, C.U., 313, 314
Hartley, J.R., 181
Hatta, T., 244
Hayes, J.R., 7
Hayes-Roth, F., 1, 85, 86, 92
Hecaen, H., 230
Hein, U., 319
Hendrix, G.G., 171, 298
Heron, A., 210
Herron, J., 240
Higgins, E.T., 218, 219
Hintikka, J., 265
Hofstadter, D.R., 71
Holley-Wilcox, P., 247
Holtzman, J.D., 240
Huberman, B., 120
Hung, D.L., 244
Hunt, E.B., 70, 282
Huttenlocher, J., 218, 219
Huyn, N., 48

Ibaraki, T., 47
Ibarra, O.H., 48
Ingvar, D.H., 241

Jagoe, J.R., 206
Jeannerod, M., 230
Johnson, D.S., 45
Johnson, R.C., 209
Johnson-Laird, P.N., 213, 219, 265

Johnstone, J., 240
Jones, D., 209

Kaye, D.B., 282
Kettner, N.M., 215
Kim, C.E., 48
Kimball, R.B., 185
Kohler, W., 217
Kolers, P.A., 203
Kolodner, J.L., 57, 58
Korf, R.E., 1, 2
Kotov, A., 55
Kotovsky, K., 221
Kowalski, R., 309

Larkin, J., 1, 2, 35
Lasaga, M.I., 203, 213
Lassen, N.A., 241
Laurière, J.L., 68, 272, 274, 275, 279
Lavorel, P.M., 229, 237
Lawler, F.L., 48
Lee, D.N., 209
Lenat, D.B., 40, 81
Lesser, V., 34
Lichtenstein, D., 46
Luria, A.R., 237

Magee, L.E., 245
Maier, N.R.F., 217
Maizelis, I., 120
Marcel, A.J., 247
Marshall, J.C., 245
McCauley, C., 247
Meltzer, B., 251
Meyer, D.E., 247
Michalski, R.S., 85
Michie, D., 120, 122
Michlski, A.S., 81
Miller, G.A., 218, 265, 306, 313
Minsky, M., 150, 303
Mitchell, T.M., 40, 81, 83, 85, 87
Mitchie, D., 47
Moore, R., 171
Morikawa, Y., 244
Morton, J., 246
Mostow, D.J., 40, 81, 85, 86, 92
Mulholland, T.M., 218, 219
Munyer, J., 48
Murray, H.J. 204
Murrell, G.A., 246
Mylopoulos, J., 297

Nagao, M., 173
Newborn, M., 116
Newell, A., 1, 2, 55, 65, 70, 218, 221
Niina, S., 244
Nilsson, N.J., 12, 18, 47, 65, 70, 303
Nishikawa, Y., 244
Norman, D.A., 151

O'Shea, T., 181
Oliveira, E., 309
Ornstein, R., 240
Osherson, D.N., 219

Page, I., 181
Pagès, J.C., 321
Paige, R., 40
Patterson, K.E., 245
Pearl, J., 47
Pellegrino, J.W., 218, 219
Perdue, C., 113
Pereira, L.M., 309
Pernici, B., 297
Perrault, C.R., 147, 170, 265
Pique, J.F., 309
Pitrat, J., 120, 271, 273, 279
Pohl, I., 43, 47, 48, 49, 51, 289
Powell, J.S., 282
Pribram, K.H., 218, 238
Provitera, A., 219

Quinlan, J.R., 70

Rabin, M.O., 45
Rashad, M.N., 209
Reinfeld, F., 112
Rendell, L.A., 20
Revlis, R., 219
Rollinger, C., 313, 314
Rosenbloom, P.S., 110
Ross, R., 54

Sabatier, P., 309
Sacerdoti, E.D., 12, 21, 65
Samuel, A., 20
Sasanuma, S., 244, 246
Schaefer, T.J., 46
Schank, R.C., 62, 221, 252, 257, 299, 303
Schorr, D., 57
Schvaneveldt, D.W., 247
Searle, J., 171
Shaw, J., 65, 218, 221
Sidtis, J.J., 240

Siegler, R.S., 218, 219
Simmons, R.F., 299
Simon, H.A., 3, 7, 20, 29, 65, 218, 221
Sint, L., 53
Sipser, M., 46
Skinhof, E., 241
Skinner, B.F., 216
Slate, D.J., 105, 109
Sleeman, D.H., 185
Smit, R., 317
Smith, E.E., 57
Smith, J., 209
Smith, M.C., 245
Somalvico, M., 297
Spearman, C., 215
Stallman, R.M., 319
Stanton, W.M., 141
Staudenmayer, H., 219
Stavrou, A., 210
Steedman, M., 219
Steels, L., 131
Sternberg, R.J., 203, 213, 281, 282
Sussman, G.J., 319
Swencionis, C., 240
Szentagothai, J., 234

Taft, M., 246
Tappel, S., 40
Taylor, G., 152
Taylor, M.M., 239
Telford, A., 201
Thompson, K., 111, 119
Thurstone, L.L., 224
Townsend, J.T., 218, 219
Tsao, C.C., 244
Tsvetkova, L.S., 237
Turing, A.M., 44, 201
Turvey, M.T., 244
Tzeng, O.J., 244

Underwood, G., 247

Vandenburg, S.G., 209
Vere, S.A., 81, 85
Volpe, B.T., 20

Walz, D.L., 297
Wang, W.S., 244
Warren, D., 309
Warrington, E.K., 246
Wason, P.C., 213
Waterman, D.A., 120

Weisberg, R.W., 217
White, S.H., 216
Whitehall, A., 152
Wiezenbaum, J., 298
Wilks, Y., 147, 149, 152, 298
Williams, D.S., 221

Wilson, D.H., 240
Wilson, J.R., 209
Winograd, T.A., 298
Winston, P.H., 85
Woods, W.A., 298